THE FOOD LABORATORY

A NERD IN THE KITCHEN

LIANG WAN SU

THE FOOD LABORATORY

A NERD IN THE KITCHEN

The Food Laboratory

A Nerd in the Kitchen

Greenery Press

ISBN: 9798447966034

I am a nerd,
and I'm
proud of it.

Celebrating food maker, analyst and individual legend Harold McGee around twenty years earlier, offered an essential articulation: contrary to predominant reasoning, separating meat before cooking it doesn't "secure the juices.†" Now, saying this to a cook resembled let a physicist know that stones fall up or an Italian that pizza was concocted in Iceland. Since the time the mid-nineteenth century, when German food researcher Justus von Liebig had first advanced the hypothesis that burning meat at exceptionally high temperatures basically sears its surface and makes a moistureproof boundary, it had been acknowledged as culinary reality. Furthermore, for the following century and a large portion of, this extraordinary disclosure was embraced by undeniably popular culinary specialists (counting Auguste Escoffier, the dad of French food) and gave from guide to disciple and from cookbook author to home cook.

You'd feel that with all that neutralizing him, McGee probably utilized the world's most remarkable PC, or in any event an examining electron magnifying lens, to demonstrate his declaration, correct? Probably not. His verification was all around as straightforward as checking out at a piece of meat. He saw that when you burn a steak on one side, then, at that point, flip it over and cook it on the subsequent side, juices from the inside of the steak are extracted from the top-the exceptionally side that was evidently now impermeable to dampness misfortune!

It was a perception that anybody who's always cooked a steak might have made, and one that has since driven cafés to totally update their cooking strategies. For sure, some top of the line cafés nowadays cook their steaks first, fixed in plastic, in low-temperature water showers, burning them just toward the end to add flavor. The outcome is steaks that are juicier, moister, and more delicate than anything the world was eating before von Liebig's mistaken affirmation was at last refuted.

The inquiry is, if exposing von Liebig's hypothesis was a particularly straightforward assignment, for what reason did it require almost hundred and fifty years to make it happen? The response lies in the way that cooking has generally been viewed as a specialty, not a science. Café cooks go about as disciples, learning, however not addressing, their gourmet specialists' methods. Home cooks follow the notes and plans of their moms and grandmas or cookbooks-maybe tweaking them to a great extent to suit present day preferences, however never testing the basics.

Just lately cooks have at last started to break out of this shell. Eateries that revel in utilizing the study of cookery to think of new strategies that outcome in satisfying and frequently astonishing results are multiplying as well as are reliably positioned as the most incredible on the planet (Chicago's Alinea or Spain's currently shut El Bulli, for instance). It's a sign that as a populace, we're at last starting to perceive the truth about cooking: a logical designing issue where the sources of info are crude fixings and procedure and the results are delightfully palatable outcomes.

Presently, don't entirely misunderstand me. I'm not out to attempt to demonstrate to you that froths are the method of things to come or that your eggs should be cooked in a steam-infused, pressure-controlled broiler to come out right. I'm not here to push some kind of modern, fancified, plated-with-tweezers, deconstructed/reproduced cooking. A remarkable inverse, truth be told.

My occupation is straightforward: to demonstrate to you that even the least difficult of food sources burgers, pureed potatoes, simmered Brussels sprouts, chicken soup, even a g&#amn salad-are just as intriguing, fascinating, celebrated, and flavorful as what the culinary specialists wearing the fanciest jeans these days are creating. At the end of the day, have you at any point halted to wonder about the exact thing happens inside a burger when you cook it? The concurrent intricacy and effortlessness of a patty shaped from the hacked bulk of chosen pieces of a strikingly complex creature, prepared with salt and pepper, burned on a hot piece of metal, and afterward slipped into a delicate toasted bun? You haven't? All things considered, let me give you a fast once-over to show you what I'm referring to.

ON HAMBURGERS

Burgers start as patties of meat . . . , no, let me hold back a little. Burgers really start as ground hamburger that is then framed into . . . , no, sorry, considerably further back. Burgers start with entire cuts of hamburger that are then ground into . . . Stand by a moment, how about we get all Inception on this and go one level further: burgers start with cows-creatures that carry on with extremely convoluted lives, that can vary in breed and feed, yet additionally as far as exercise, territory they're presented to, how and when they're butchered, and whether they live on grass their entire lives or are enhanced with grain. From these creatures come many cuts of meat that differ in flavor as per fat substance, their capacity during the creature's life, and its particular eating routine. Mixing uncommonly chosen slices will prompt ground meat with the ideal flavor and fat profile.

From that point, it's a straightforward matter of crushing, shaping patties, and cooking, correct?

Not all that quick. How you grind your meat can significantly affect the surface of the completed burgers. Think everything ground meat is made equivalent? Reconsider. Also, shouldn't something be said about salting? Do you salt the meat and mix it in, or do you salt the outside of the patties? How would you shape those patties? Squeezing the meat into a ball and leveling it works, yet is that actually the most effective way? Also, what makes those burgers puff up into softball-molded round masses when you cook them in any case? When you begin opening your brain to the miracles of the kitchen, when you begin asking what's truly happening inside your food while you cook it, you'll observe that the inquiries keep endlessly coming, and that the responses will turn out to be increasingly interesting.

Not in the least does responding to inquiries concerning burgers assist you with cooking your burgers better, however it likewise uncovers applications to a wide range of different circumstances. We get gigantic burgers going on the cooler side of the barbecue and finish them with a singe to get a pleasant, completely even medium-uncommon shading all through, alongside a solid, hard burn. Think about what the most ideal way to cook a huge steak is? It made perfect sense to you: precisely the same technique applies, in light of the fact that the proteins and fat in a steak are like those in a burger.

Still not excessively certain what I mean? Simply relax, we'll respond to these inquiries and more in due time.

LEARNING HOW NOT TO FAIL IS THE FIRST STEP TO WINNING

Have you made similar formula multiple times with incredible outcomes, just to observe that on the seventh time, it totally comes up short? The meat portion comes out extreme, maybe, or the pizza batter simply doesn't rise. Generally it's challenging to highlight the very thing turned out badly. Assuming you're a hobbyist in the kitchen, you like to alter plans a piece to a great extent to suit your own taste or mind-set. That is fine and dandy, and fortunately, the initial multiple times, your adjustments didn't influence the result of the formula. What changed on that seventh time? Would it be able to be the additional salt you added? Maybe the temperature of the room? Or then again perhaps it's that you ran out of olive oil and utilized canola all things considered. Maybe your stand blender was acting up, so you mixed everything manually.

The fact of the matter is, there are numerous ways you can wander from a composed formula, however just a portion of those invasions will make the formula fall flat. Having the option to recognize precisely what portions of a formula are crucial for the nature of the completed item and what parts are simply enhancement is a commonsense ability that will open up your chances in the kitchen as at no other time. When you comprehend the fundamental study of how and why a formula functions, you unexpectedly observe that you've liberated yourself from the shackles of plans. You can alter as you see fit, completely certain that the result will be a triumph.

Take a formula for Italian hotdog, for example. The formula in this book has you consolidate pork shoulder with salt and some aromatics, let the meat rest for the time being, and afterward grind it and manipulate it the following day. Presently, you've tasted my Italian wiener, and all good, you believe it has an excessive amount of fennel. Alright, so you utilize not so much fennel but rather more marjoram the following time all things being equal. Since you've perused the hotdog part and comprehend that the keys to an extraordinary finished wiener are the association between the salt and meat and the strategy by which the ground meat is blended, you're sure that changing the flavoring will in any case permit you to deliver an incredible tasting join. Simultaneously, you realize that salt breaks down muscle proteins and permits them to cross-connect, giving your hotdog that smart, delicious surface, so you can't scale back the salt the same way you can with the fennel. Similarly, you realize that you can make your wiener out of turkey or sheep assuming you'd like, yet you can't change the fat substance in the event that you need it to stay delicious.

Truth: Cooking through repetition in any event, when your tutors are probably the best gourmet specialists on the planet is deadening. Exclusively by understanding the basic standards associated with cookery would you be able to liberate yourself from the two plans and indiscriminately acknowledged customary way of thinking.

Beginning to find out about what I'm referring to? Opportunity. That is what.

WHY THIS BOOK?

In numerous ways, the blog design is great for the sort of work I do. I get to expound on things in a really casual manner and consequently, my perusers let me know their thought process, pose shrewd inquiries, and let me in on what they might want to see me tackle straightaway. It's public, and I owe my prosperity as a blogger as much to my perusers and my consistently steady, generally fun, extraordinary colleagues and individual bloggers as I do to myself.

All things considered, there are cutoff points to what the writing for a blog stage can uphold. It's incredible for short articles, it does pictures OK, yet great diagrams? Great diagrams? Great, straightforward design? Long-structure content? Just drop it. This book comes into picture in this place. It addresses the climax of not simply 10 years and a portion of cooking and concentrating on the study of regular food sources, yet of long periods of figuring out how to apply this science in manners that can assist with homing prepares cook ordinary food in better, more delectable ways.

What you won't find in this book are extravagant jeans plans calling for fascinating fixings or troublesome strategies or synthetic substances or even a lot of extraordinary hardware past, say, a food processor or a lager cooler. You likewise won't track down any treats. They simply aren't my thing, and as opposed to counterfeit a couple of them, I figured I'd quite recently take ownership of the way that they don't show me the manner in which appetizing food does. (Recollect that entire thing about not doing anything that I don't cherish doing?)

What you will find here is a careful assessment of exemplary plans. You'll figure out why your seared chicken skin gets fresh, what's happening inside a potato as you squash it, how baking powder assists your hotcakes with rising. That, however you'll find that in some (most?) cases, the most conventional strategies for cooking are as a matter of fact not the best method for arriving at the ideal final products and you'll track down a lot of plans and directions that let you know how to obtain better outcomes. (Did you had any idea about that you can parcook pasta in room-temperature regular water? Or then again that the way to consummate French fries is vinegar?)

You'll presumably observe that I talk about my significant other and my canines altogether too much, and that I seriously love both the Beatles and the joke, that least type of mind. I may legitimately be blamed for making complex references to any or the accompanying points in general: The Simpsons. Kid's shows and films from the 1980s. Star Wars. English humorists. The Big Lebowski. MacGyver. To these wrongdoings, I confess, yet I won't atone.

Incidentally you will go over an examination intended for you to do yourself at home. These analyses are party-accommodating, and a large portion of them are kid-accommodating as well, so ensure you have organization around in the event that you will endeavor them!

Some of you might utilize this book exclusively for the plans, and that checks out. I'll in any case like you. I've put forth a valiant effort to think of them as plainly and briefly as could be expected, and I ensure all of them will function as publicized (gave you adhere to the guidelines). In the event that they don't work for you, I need to find out about it! Others might peruse the whole book while never cooking anything from it. I could even like you folks more than I like the formula just folks, for it's what's happening in the background, or under that very much cooked covering, that truly interests me.

Assuming you're the rocker cook type, bless your lucky stars. This book was composed to work from front to back. Plans in later parts expand on essential logical standards talked about in before sections. Then again, on the off chance that you like skipping around-say, potato salad doesn't intrigue you however cook meat sure progresses admirably, you will not have a difficult situation all things considered. I've given my all to make every example independent, cross-referring to prior parts when essential.

One thing I need to clarify here: This book is not even close to thorough. How could I put myself down that way? Indeed, this is on the grounds that the general purpose of science is that it's an endless mission for information. Regardless of the amount we are familiar our general surroundings, the world inside a square of cheddar, or the world contained in an eggshell, the sum that we don't realize will generally be a lot more noteworthy than what we do. The second we think we realize every one of the responses is the second we quit learning, and I genuinely trust that opportunity never arrives for me. In the expressions of Socrates Johnson: "All we know is that we don't know anything."

Assuming there are three standards that I think would make the world a superior spot assuming that everybody followed them, it'd be these: challenge everything constantly, taste everything no less than once, and unwind, it's just pizza.

SO WHY TRUST ME?

When I ring in on web-based message sheets, when I compose blog entries that make a few pretty striking cases (like, say, that singing in more sweltering oil really causes food to assimilate more oil, not less-see here), I frequently have similar inquiries chance back at me: Says who? For what reason would it be a good idea for me to trust you? I've been preparing my food [X] way since before you were conceived, why should you say that there's a superior way?

Indeed, there are various responses I could provide for this inquiry: It's my responsibility to concentrate on food, test it, and answer inquiries concerning it. I have a degree from one of the top designing schools in the country. I endured a decent eight years cooking behind the ovens of probably the best eateries in the country. I've altered plans and articles in food magazines and on sites for just about 10 years. These are altogether very valid justifications to place your confidence in what the future held, reality of the situation is this: you shouldn't confide in me.

"Simply trust me" was the method of the old cooks. The MO of the expert understudy relationship. Do what I say and do it now, since I say as much. What's more, that is by and large the attitude we're attempting to battle here. I need you to have one or two doubts. Science is based on incredulity. Galileo didn't arrive at the resolution that the Earth rotates around the sun, not the opposite way around, by indiscriminately tolerating everything every other person was saying to him. He tested customary way of thinking, concocted new theories to portray his general surroundings, tried those speculations, and afterward and really at that time did he request that individuals have faith in the franticness that he was rambling from behind that amazing facial hair of his. He did, obviously, pass on detained at home subsequent to being attempted by the Roman Inquisition for his inconveniences as a whole. (Hopefully that doesn't occur to any of you sprouting kitchen researchers.) And that was for something as unimportant as portraying the state of the nearby planet group. In the mean time, we're here handling the large issues. Hotcakes and meat portion merit essentially as much investigation!

The fact of the matter is this: if whenever while perusing this book you run over something I've composed that simply is apparently less than ideal, something that appears as though it hasn't been adequately tried, something that isn't thoroughly made sense of, then I completely anticipate that you should call me out on it. Test it for yourself. Make your own theories and plan your own trials. Hell, just email me and let me know how you think I veered off-track. I'll see the value in it. Truly.

The principal decide of science is that while we can constantly draw nearer to reality, there will never be a last response. There are new disclosures made and explores played out each day that can turn the tried and true way of thinking on its head. On the off chance that a long time from now someone hasn't found that no less than one truth in this book is extremely off-base, it implies that individuals aren't thinking fundamentally enough.

Yet, some of you may be pondering now, what precisely is science? It's a great inquiry, and a theme that is regularly misconstrued. We should discuss it a piece.

{ The keys to great kitchen science }

Science isn't about large words. There's actually no need to focus on sterile jackets and wellbeing goggles, and it's certainly not tied in with attempting to make yourself sound extravagant. Science isn't an end all by itself, however a way. It's a technique to assist you with finding the fundamental request of your general surroundings and to utilize those revelations to assist you with foreseeing how things will act from now on. The logical technique depends on mentioning observable facts, monitoring those perceptions, thinking of theories to make sense of those perceptions, and afterward performing tests intended to invalidate those speculations. In the event that, notwithstanding your hardest, most genuine endeavors, you can't figure out how to invalidate the theories, then you can say with a very decent arrangement of sureness that your speculations are valid. That is the thing science is, and it tends to be just about as straightforward as seeing that of the initial three brews you had, the coldest one was the most delicious, and accordingly it's likely really smart to chill down the fourth before you air out it, or as mind boggling as deciding the quality that concludes whether the eye of your child is brown or blue.

The vast majority of us practice science each and every day, frequently without knowing it. For example, when I originally got hitched, I saw that there appeared to be an immediate relationship between's a portion of my better half's terrible temperaments and my inclination to leave the latrine seat up. (Perception.) I then pondered internally, maybe on the off chance that I put the latrine seat down more regularly, my better half's temperament and in this way my own bliss would get to the next level. (Theory.) I had a go at putting down the latrine seat a couple of times and holding back to perceive how my better half responded. (Testing.) Noticing an improvement in her mind-sets, I began investing the seat down pretty much every effort, just sometimes surrendering it to test the proceeded with legitimacy of my theory. A few people would call this simply being a decent flat mate/spouse. I call it science.

In all honesty, the kitchen is maybe the most straightforward spot for a normal individual to rehearse science consistently. You've surely played out your own logical trials before. Here is a model: You purchase another toaster oven with a haziness handle that goes from one to eleven (in the event you need it one shade more obscure than ten) and afterward notice your toast is coming out excessively dim on level six, so you turn it down to even out four. Presently your toast is excessively light. Working from these two perceptions, you speculate that maybe five is the right level for your bread. Lo and see, your next cut of toast and each cut of toast after that come out perfectly.

Presently, that may not be the most earth shattering perception throughout the entire existence of science, and it is in fact extremely restricted in its application (I mean, you couldn't ensure that the following toaster oven you own will have a similar scale), yet it's science by and by, and in that sense, it's the same as what proficient researchers do consistently.

Researchers realize that inclination can be a strong power in tests. Regularly researchers just see what they need to see and observe the responses they need to find, regardless of whether they understand it. Have you heard the narrative of Clever Hans the counting horse? From the get-go in the 20th century, Hans made truly a name for himself by clearly being smart to the point of getting German, do math, perceive the times of the week, separate between melodic tones, and, surprisingly, read and spell. His coach would ask him inquiries and Hans would answer by tapping his foot. When inquired, for example, "What is twelve in addition to eight?" he would stamp his foot multiple times. The pony was a sensation, visiting around Germany and astonishing groups with his extraordinary capacities.

After an escalated study did by the German leading body of instruction, the spectators arrived at a stunning resolution: the entire thing was a trick. Turns out that Hans couldn't do any math whatsoever. What he was very great at was deciphering the looks and perspectives of his mentor. As he gradually stepped his foot against the ground, he'd notice the pressure in the mentor's face; when he arrived at the right number, the coach would unwind, Hans would realize that he was done, and he'd quit tapping. It's an ability to be respected, without a doubt. Hell, the greater part of my conjugal issues would be tackled if I would tell when my better half was tense versus loose. However, would the pony be able to do math? Not a chance.

However stop and think for a minute: the mentor didn't understand what he was doing. He thought he had an incredibly keen pony. Truth be told, the pony was so great at perusing faces that in any event, when a total outsider was posing him the inquiries, he would answer similarly well. How did the individuals from the board at long last demonstrate that Hans' alleged capacities were phony? They planned a progression of logical examinations. The least complex included blindfolding the pony or having the mentor pose his inquiries out of Hans' view. True to form, abruptly his astounding mind vanished. The most intriguing trial of all included having the mentor ask the pony inquiries the coach himself didn't have a clue about the solutions to. Prepare to have your mind blown. In the event that the mentor didn't have a clue about the response, neither did Hans.

THE POINT here, obviously, is that planning a fruitful examination whether it includes a numerical pony or happens in your own kitchen-is tied in with killing the predisposition of the experimenter (for this situation, you). This is generally difficult to do, yet all the same it's quite often conceivable.

Allow me to educate you concerning an investigation I completed a short time back to outline the seven vital stages to a decent tasting in the kitchen: kill inclination, present a control, detach factors, remain coordinated, address sense of taste exhaustion, taste, and examine.

PIZZA IN NEW YORK, IS IT TRULY ALL ABOUT THE WATER?

Similarly as muscle heads like to stay together and geeks travel in packs, obsessives verging on the crazy (like me) search out the associate of others such as themselves, in a way that some say verges on the, indeed, the fanatical. Whenever I first heard that the mineral substance of water could affect the properties of bread batter was around a decade prior, when I read Jeffrey Steingarten's superbly over the top piece about Roman breads in the part named "Absolutely" in his book It Must Have Been Something I Ate:

In the shower, the cleanser will not foam. This implies that Roman water is high in minerals, which can be great for the shading and surface of bread, yet eases back aging and fixes the mixture. I go after my scuba jumper's submerged composing record, as seen on Baywatch, irreplaceable for recording those glimmers of knowledge that so regularly strike one in the shower. We should try things out of Rome.

Tragically, regardless of the gallant endeavors he went through to bring genuine pizza bianca and sheet Genzano to the home cook, the water issue was rarely acceptably settled.

Indeed, after eight years, I chose to attempt to determine it for myself, alongside the assistance of another over the top: Mathieu Palombino, gourmet expert proprietor of New York City's Motorino, who benevolently elected to help me in my little trial. The thought is basic: the minerals broke up in water (generally magnesium and calcium) can assist proteins in the flour with holding together more firmly, framing a more grounded gluten structure, the organization of interconnected proteins that gives mixture its solidarity and flexibility. In this way, the higher the mineral substance of water (estimated in parts per million, or ppm), the more grounded and chewier the batter. In principle, it seems OK, and it is effectively provable in a lab. The seriously fascinating inquiry to me was, are the impacts of the minerals in the water (alluded to as Total Dissolved Solids, or TDS) adequately critical to be identified by an ordinary eater in a true circumstance?

To respond to the inquiry, I accused Mathieu of making Neapolitan pizzas utilizing waters with various TDS substance and got a board of pizza specialists to taste the completed pies. The issue is that this present reality is, indeed, genuine, and accordingly, truly challenging to control. In any logical undertaking, there are various key rules that should be complied with to guarantee that your outcomes are precise and repeatable-the sign of any sound investigation.

Anyway pause and think briefly: the tutor failed to see what he was doing. He thought he had an extraordinarily sharp horse. In all honesty, the horse was so incredible at examining faces that regardless, when an all out outcast was presenting him the requests, he would answer correspondingly well. How did the people from the board finally show that Hans' supposed limits were fake? They arranged a movement of coherent assessments. The most un-complex included blindfolding the horse or having the coach represent his requests out of Hans' view. Exactly as expected, suddenly his bewildering mind evaporated. The most captivating preliminary of all included having the tutor ask the horse requests the mentor himself hadn't the foggiest about the answers for. Get ready to have your psyche blown. If the guide hadn't the faintest idea about the reaction, neither did Hans.

THE POINT here, clearly, is that arranging a productive assessment whether it incorporates a mathematical horse or occurs in your own kitchen-is connected to killing the inclination of the experimenter (for the present circumstance, you). This is by and large challenging to do, yet generally a similar it's frequently possible.

Permit me to instruct you concerning an examination I finished a brief time frame back to frame the seven essential stages to a respectable tasting in the kitchen: kill tendency, present a control, separate variables, stay facilitated, address feeling of taste depletion, taste, and analyze.

PIZZA IN NEW YORK, IS IT REALLY ABOUT THE WATER?

Also as health nuts like to remain together and nerds travel in packs, obsessives coming close to the insane (like me) search out the partner of others like themselves, such that some say comes close to the, without a doubt, the over the top. At the point when I initially heard that the mineral substance of water could influence the properties of bread player was around 10 years earlier, when I read Jeffrey Steingarten's amazingly ludicrous piece about Roman breads in the part named "Totally" in his book It Probably Been Something I Ate:

In the shower, the chemical won't froth. This suggests that Roman water is high in minerals, which can be extraordinary for the overshadowing and surface of bread, yet moves back maturing and fixes the blend. I pursue my scuba jumper's lowered forming record, as seen on Baywatch, indispensable for recording those flashes of information that so consistently strike one in the shower. We should give things a shot of Rome.

Lamentably, no matter what the chivalrous undertakings he went through to bring certifiable pizza bianca and sheet Genzano to the home cook, the water issue was seldom acceptably settled.

Without a doubt, following eight years, I decided to endeavor to decide it for myself, close by the help of one more preposterous: Mathieu Palombino, connoisseur master owner of New York City's Motorino, who kindly chosen to help me in my little preliminary. The thinking is fundamental: the minerals separated in water (for the most part magnesium and calcium) can help proteins in the flour with keeping intact all the more immovably, outlining a more grounded gluten structure, the association of interconnected proteins that gives blend its fortitude and adaptability. Thusly, the higher the mineral substance of water (assessed in parts per million, or ppm), the more grounded and chewier the player. On a fundamental level, it appears to be alright, and it is successfully provable in a lab. The truly entrancing request to me was, are the effects of the minerals in the water (insinuated as Complete Broke down Solids, or TDS) sufficiently basic to be recognized by a conventional eater in a genuine situation?

To answer the request, I blamed Mathieu for making Neapolitan pizzas using waters with different TDS substance and got a leading body of pizza experts to taste the finished pies. The issue is that this current the truth is, without a doubt, veritable, and appropriately, really testing to control. In any legitimate endeavor, there are different key principles that ought to be agreed with to ensure that your results are exact and repeatable-the indication of any sound examination.

Key to a Decent Tasting #3: Know What You Are Asking (Disengage Factors)

In Douglas Adams' Drifter's Manual for the System, a group of researchers constructs a supercomputer that is at last ready to respond to the Unavoidable issue: the Solution to Life, the Universe, and Everything. A definitive incongruity is that when they're at long last offered the response 42 they understand that they never truly knew the very thing they were asking in any case.

Presently, these were extremely unfortunate researchers. Rule Numero Uno with regards to science is this: Be exceptionally exact about the thing question you are attempting to reply. The more restricted the extent of your inquiry, the simpler it will be to plan a test to respond to it. There are around a gajillion factors with regards to pizza, every single one of them fascinating in its own particular manner. In any case, here, I was keen on only one: how does the water's mineral substance influence the batter? What that implied was that to disengage that solitary variable, I'd need to guarantee that each and every other variable out of those gajillion remained precisely something very similar from one example to another. Easy to talk about, not so easy to do.

In reality especially with cooking-there are a crazy measure of factors to attempt to control for. Maybe that sign in the wood-consuming broiler will consume somewhat more blazing for pizza #2 than for pizza #1, raising the temperature by two or three degrees. Or on the other hand perhaps Mathieu should hang tight for a server with a heap of dishes to pass by prior to embedding pizza #5 into the stove, adding a couple of moments to its outing. This is an inescapable, unavoidable reality with regards to science. What we can trust, notwithstanding, is that these small changes in technique from one example to another will have an insignificant effect contrasted with the variable we are really trying for. We can likewise give our all to ensure each example is dealt with something similar.

I requested that Mathieu gauge the elements for each clump of batter unequivocally and to guarantee that each bunch was massaged for a similar time allotment and permitted to age at a similar temperature. While typically the pizzaioli at the café alternate forming, saucing, and baking the pizzas, this time Mathieu himself made every one beginning to end, guaranteeing that the technique utilized was basically as reliable as could be expected.

On top of those actions, I likewise chose to introduce each example in two structures: as a finished Margherita pizza and as a straightforward plate of batter heated all alone, to kill any fluctuation that distinctions in fixing circulation could add.

Key to a Decent Tasting #4: Remain Coordinated

Who preferred to taste pizzas over New York's chief pizza cognoscenti, Ed Levine and Adam Kuban? Furthermore, Alaina Browne of the Genuine Eats group went along with us, alongside my significant other (as an award for her solid counsel), and-through a marvelously game changing demonstration of good systems administration Jeffrey Steingarten himself, the very man who had unconsciously begun me down the way of pizza (and, to be sure, of food composing, period). Prior to showing up at the eatery, I drew up tasting sheets for my board to finish up. Every pizza was to be assessed in four classes, and every classification was appraised on a scale from one to ten:

- Mixture Durability: Is it delicate like cake or as chewy as cowhide?

- Batter Freshness: Does it snap, or is it flabby?

- Broiler Spring: Did it structure enormous, vaporous air pockets, or is it minimized and thick?

- Generally speaking Quality: How would you like it?

The initial five testers (counting myself) showed up expeditiously at 4 p.m., with cook Mathieu hanging tight for us. Jeffrey, in any case, was no place to be seen, however he had cautioned me that he may be a piece late because of a significant gathering. Ed called up his collaborator. Clearly, his significant gathering was in his bed with Sky Lord, his canine, yet not to stress his coat was on, and he was working diligently on his shoestrings.

In the interim, Mathieu educated us that he'd dropped half regarding the primary example on the floor, truly intending that for that bunch, we'd taste one pie, as opposed to two. No significant reason to stress. Indeed, even Tesla more likely than not dropped a couple of loops in his day, isn't that so? My impeccably coordinated plans were starting to slip, yet a glass of Brachetto and a little plate of fingerling potatoes threw with anchovies and olives assisted me with pulling my faculties back into center.

Key to a Decent Tasting #5: Watch Out for Sense of taste Exhaustion

When Mr Steingarten showed up, straight from his rest, I went to Mathieu and gave him the approval. In somewhere around three minutes, the principal panther spotted, delicate fresh excellence was on the table. Eight pizzas among six individuals is a ton to eat in a solitary sitting, in any event, for epic eaters like our modest tasting board, and it was basically impossible that the pizzas in the last 50% of the tasting planned to get a decent deal. Preferably, we'd have every tester taste tests in an alternate request. Like that, one would be beginning with number one, one more with number six, one more with number three, etc, ideally evening out the battleground. In any case, considering that the pizzas must be prepared each in turn, this was essentially unrealistic. So we did the following best thing: one pie out of each clump of two was eaten straight out of the stove and the subsequent one was saved until every one of the eight were on the table. Like that, we could return and retaste to guarantee that our unique considerations were sound, and we could taste every one of the eight one next to the other.

Shimmering water and wine were given (the last option after much pondering) to wash our mouths between chomps.

Key to a Decent Tasting #6: Taste

Tasting is unique in relation to eating. I regularly get inquired, "How might you audit a café reasonably or how might you say one item is better compared to another? Doesn't it rely upon how hungry you are at that point?" And, without a doubt, mind-set and craving can powerfully affect the amount you appreciate eating a specific food at any one time. Be that as it may, the objective of scientific tasting is to evaluate characteristics of the food past your stomach response of whether it's fortunate or unfortunate. With pizza, for instance, I start by taking a cut from every pie with an across-pie-normal of scorching, air pockets, sauce, and cheddar. I then, at that point, nibble simply the tip, taking note of the strain of the hull on my lower teeth to measure its level of freshness. As I pull the cut away from my mouth, applying only an exposed soupçon of force, I judge the work it takes for the batter to tear. (For this situation, Pizza #5 was plainly harder than the rest, I thought victoriously one should never converse with his kindred testers during a visually impaired tasting in case your viewpoint impact those of others-so it should unquestionably be one of those high-mineral examples.)

After cautiously moving gradually up the side of each cut, I assess the cornicione (the raised edge of the pizza). It's elusive shortcoming with any of them, however does #3 look simply a shade paler than the rest, showing a lower-mineral-content water? Could be. In any case, assuming this is the case, for what reason isn't it additionally more delicate? It's just plain obvious, these are perceptions you can make moderately experimentally that is, liberated from inclination. Without a doubt, eating a similar pizza while starving versus when stuffed will evoke two distinct responses, yet by lessening every one to essential components that are all the more effectively evaluated freshness, chewiness, level of burning you can get a more precise image of the pizza generally speaking, separating from it from the psychological predisposition of your present status of brain.

With the pizzas tasted, we expressed gratitude toward Mathieu for his extraordinary pizza (the best in the city, for my cash), and courageously made our different routes as the night progressed, a few degrees more happy and a few pounds heavier.

Key to a Decent Tasting #7: Examine

When all the tasting has been done and every one of the information gathered, you must examine it to create the most sensible evaluation you can about the thing factors are influencing your variable. On account of the pizzas, that implied graphing the information and posting it all together from least mineral substance (which ought to probably convey all the more delicate, milder, less-sprung, paler batter) to most noteworthy. In the event that everything went by hypothesis, the lines for freshness, durability, and breeziness should all show unmistakable patterns, going up or down as the mineral substance of the water increments.

For reasons unknown, no such patterns existed. Valid, the two groups made with Evian-the most noteworthy mineral substance of all the water we attempted conveyed the crispest outside layers, however generally, there was not a sufficient pattern in the information to offer an authoritative expression. Furthermore, guess what? Once in a while generally an analysis, regardless of how firmly controlled, doesn't create the outcomes you were searching for. Which isn't to say that we came by no outcomes by any means. Truth be told, requiring another once-over at the information, I saw that the rankings for freshness continue in sync very intimately with the rankings for by and large pleasure inferring that our satisfaction in pizza is straightforwardly connected with how fresh it is. We as a whole need a fresh outside, not a spongy one.

Historic, I know.

Then again, we can now lovely authoritatively say that the little distinctions that emerge normally over making a decent pizza by hand far offset any distinction the mineral substance of the water could make. In other words, extraordinary New York pizza is unquestionably not reliant upon utilizing New York City regular water, which is uplifting news for every other person on the planet.

<h1 align="center">{ What's cooking? }</h1>

I know you're anxious to hop right in and begin cooking, however first response this inquiry: What is cooking?

Assuming you're my significant other, your response will be, "It's that thing you do when that insane look comes at you." An extraordinary culinary expert could perceive you that cooking is life. My mother would likely say that it's a task, while my significant other's auntie would let you know that cooking is culture, family, custom, and love. Also, indeed, cooking is those things, however here's a more specialized method for mulling over everything: Cooking is tied in with moving energy. It's tied in with applying hotness to change the construction of particles. It's tied in with empowering synthetic responses to modify flavors and surfaces. It's tied in with getting flavorful things going with science. Furthermore, before we could start to get what happens when we barbecue a cheeseburger, or even what hardware we should stock our kitchen with, we need to get one vital idea into our heads first, as it'll influence all that we do in the kitchen, beginning with which pots and container we use. It's this: Heat and temperature are not exactly the same thing.

At its generally fundamental, cooking is the exchange of energy from a hotness source to your food. That energy causes actual changes looking like proteins, fats, and carbs, as well as rushes the rate at which synthetic responses occur. Intriguing that more often than not, these physical and synthetic changes are super durable. When a protein's shape has been changed by adding energy to it, you can't transform it back by accordingly eliminating that energy. At the end of the day, you can't uncook a steak.

The differentiation among hotness and temperature can be one of the most befuddling things in the kitchen, yet understanding the idea is crucial for assisting you with turning into a more judicious cook. Through experience, we realize that temperature is an odd measure. At the end of the day, essentially we all have strolled around serenely in shorts in 60-degree weather conditions yet have felt the crazy chill of bouncing into a 60-degree lake, correct? For what reason does one yet not the other make us chilly, despite the fact that the temperature is something very similar? Give me the opportunity to do something reasonable.

Heat is energy. 3rd grade material science lets us know that everything from the air around us to the metal on the sides of a stove is made out of particles: small things that are quickly vibrating or, on account of fluids and gases, quickly bobbing around in an irregular way. The more energy is added to a specific arrangement of atoms, the more quickly they vibrate or bob, and the more rapidly they move this development to anything they are contacting whether it's the vibrating particles in a metal skillet moving energy to a succulent rib-eye steak sizzling endlessly or the skipping particles of air inside a stove moving energy to the hard portion of bread that is baking.

Hotness can be moved starting with one framework then onto the next, for the most part from the more vivacious (more smoking) framework to the less enthusiastic (cooler). So when you place a steak in a hot skillet to cook it, what you are truly doing is moving energy from the container burner framework to the steak framework. A portion of this additional energy goes to raising the temperature of the steak, however quite a bit of it gets utilized for different responses: it takes more time to make dampness dissipate, the compound responses that occur that cause sautéing require energy, etc.

Temperature is an arrangement of estimation that permits us to measure how much energy is in a particular framework. The temperature of the framework is reliant not just on the aggregate sum of energy in that body, yet in addition on a few different attributes: thickness and explicit hotness limit.

Thickness is a proportion of the number of particles of stuff there are in a given measure of room. Medium of a denser, it has more energy at a given temperature. Generally speaking, metals are denser than liquids,‡ which, thusly, are denser than air. So metals at, say, 60°F will contain more energy than fluids at 60°F, which will contain more energy than air at 60°F.

Explicit hotness limit is how much energy it takes to raise a given measure of a material to a specific temperature. For example, it takes precisely one calorie of energy (indeed, calories are energy!) to raise one gram of water by one degree Celsius. Since the particular hotness limit of water is higher than that of say, iron, and lower than that of air, a similar measure of energy will raise the temperature of a gram of iron by very nearly ten fold the amount and a gram of air by just half so much. The higher the particular hotness limit of a given material, the more energy it takes to raise the temperature of that material by similar number of degrees.

Alternately, this implies that given a similar mass and temperature, water will contain around 10 fold the amount of energy as iron and about half as much as air. That, however recollect that air is undeniably less thick than water, and that implies that how much hotness energy contained in a given volume of air at a given temperature will be just a little part of how much energy contained in a similar volume of water at a similar temperature. That is the justification for what reason you'll get a terrible consume by staying your hand into a pot of 212°F bubbling water however you can stick your arm into a 212°F broiler without even batting an eye (see "Analysis: Temperature Versus Energy in real life," here).

Befuddled? How about we attempt a similarity.

Envision the article being warmed as a chicken coop lodging twelve possibly wild chickens. The temperature of this framework can be checked by observing how quick every individual chicken is running. On an ordinary day, the chickens may be nonchalantly strolling near, pecking, scratching, crapping, and for the most part doing anything that chickens do. Presently we should add a touch of energy to the situation by several jars of Red Bull in with their feed. Appropriately energized, the chickens start to go around two times as quick. Since every individual chicken is going around at a quicker pace, the temperature of the framework has gone up, as has the aggregate sum of energy in it.

Presently suppose we have one more coop of a similar size however with twofold the quantity of chickens, along these lines giving it twofold the thickness. Since there are two times as numerous chickens, it will take twofold how much Red Bull to get them generally running at a sped up pace. Nonetheless, despite the fact that the last temperature will be something similar (every individual chicken is running at similar last rate as the initial ones), the aggregate sum of energy inside the subsequent coop is twofold that of the first. In this way, energy and temperature are not exactly the same thing.

Presently imagine a scenario where we set up a third coop, this time with twelve turkeys rather than chickens. Turkeys are a lot bigger than chickens, and it would accept two times as much Red Bull to motivate one to go around at a similar speed as a chicken. So the particular hotness limit of the turkey coop is two times as incredible as the particular hotness limit of the principal chicken coop. This means given twelve chickens going around at a specific speed and twelve turkeys going around at a similar speed, the turkeys will have two times as much energy in them as the chickens.

To summarize:

• At a given temperature, denser materials by and large contain more energy, thus heavier skillet will prepare food quicker. (Alternately, it takes more energy to raise denser materials to a specific temperature.)

• At a given temperature, materials with a higher explicit hotness limit will contain more energy. (Alternately, the higher the particular hotness limit of a material, the more energy it takes to carry it to a specific temperature.)

In this book, most plans call for cooking food varieties to explicit temperatures. That is on the grounds that for most food, the temperature it's raised to is the essential element deciding its last construction and surface. A few key temperatures that show up over and over include:

• 32°F (0°C): The edge of freezing over of water (or the dissolving point of ice).

• 130°F (52°C): Medium-uncommon steak. Additionally the temperature at which most microbes start to bite the dust, however it can take up of 2 hours to securely clean food at this temperature.

• 150°F (64°C): Medium-well steak. Egg yolks start to solidify, egg whites are murky yet at the same time jam like. Fish proteins will fix to the point that white egg whites will be constrained out, giving fish like salmon an unappealing layer of coagulated proteins. After around 3 minutes at this temperature, microbes experience a 7 log decrease which implies that main 1 microorganisms will stay for each million that were at first there).

• 160° to 180° F (71° to 82° C): Well-done steak. Egg proteins coagulate completely (this is the temperature to which most egg-based hitters or custard are cooked to set them completely). Microscopic organisms experience a 7 log decrease in 1 second or less.

• 212°F (100°C): The limit of water (or the buildup point of steam).

• 300°F (153°C) or more: The temperature at which the Maillard cooking responses the responses that produce profound brown, flavorful outsides on steaks or portions of bread-start to happen at an extremely quick speed. The more sizzling the temperature, the quicker these responses occur. Since these reaches are well over the edge of boiling over of water, the coverings will be fresh and got dried out.

WELLSPRINGS OF ENERGY AND HEAT TRANSFER

Now that we know the very thing energy is, there's a second layer of data to consider: the means by which that energy gets moved to your food.

Conduction is the immediate exchange of energy starting with one strong body then onto the next. It happens when you consume your hand by getting a hot skillet (answer: don't do that). Vibrating particles from one surface will strike the generally still atoms on another surface, in this manner moving their energy. This is by a long shot the most effective technique for heat move. Here are a few instances of hotness move through conduction:

- Burning a steak

- Crisping the lower part of a pizza

- Cooking fried eggs

- Making barbecue blemishes on a burger

- Sautéing onions

Steaks burning hotness through conduction.

Convection is the exchange of one strong body to one more through the go-between of a liquid that is, a fluid or a gas. This is a tolerably productive technique for heat move, however in cooking its effectiveness relies enormously upon the way the liquid streams around the food. The movement of the liquid is alluded to as convection designs.

When in doubt, the quicker air goes over a given surface, the more energy it can move. Still air will quickly surrender its energy, however with moving air, the energy supply is continually being recharged by new air being cycled over a substance like food. Convection stoves, for example, have fans that are intended to keep the air inside moving around at a decent clasp to advance quicker, more in any event, cooking. Essentially, fomenting the oil while profound fricasseeing can prompt food sources that fresh and earthy colored all the more proficiently.

Here are a few instances of hotness move through convection:

- Steaming asparagus stalks

- Bubbling dumplings in stock

- Profound browning onion rings

- Grilling a pork shoulder

- The highest point of a pizza baking in a stove

Dumplings bubbling hotness through convection.

Radiation is move of energy through space by means of electromagnetic waves. Sit back and relax, that is not so frightening as it sounds. It requires no medium to move it. It is the hotness you're feeling when you sit near a fire or hold your hand over a preheated dish. The sun's energy goes to the earth through the vacuum of room. Without radiation, our planet (and to be sure, the universe) would be in a difficult situation!

A significant truth to recollect about brilliant energy is that it rots (that is, gets more vulnerable) by the backwards square regulation the energy that arrives at an article from a brilliant energy source is corresponding to the reverse of the square of its distance. For instance, have a go at holding your hand 1 foot away from a fire, then, at that point, move it 2 feet away. Despite the fact that you've just multiplied the distance, the fire will have a main outlook on one-quarter as hot.

Here are a few instances of brilliant hotness move:

- Simmering a pig on a spit close to hot coals

- Toasting garlic bread under the grill

- Getting a tan from the sun

- Cooking some marinated salmon

The highest point of a pizza cooks by means of radiation.

More often than not, in cooking, every one of the three strategies for heat move are accustomed to differing degrees. Take a burger on the barbecue, for instance. The barbecue grind warms the patty straightforwardly where it is in touch with it through conduction, quickly searing it at those spots. The remainder of underside of the patty is cooked by means of radiation from the coals under. Put a piece of cheddar on the burger and pop the just a little, and convection flows will shape, conveying the hot air from straight over the coals over-top the highest point of the burger, softening the cheddar.

Barbecued burgers cook through every one of the three types of energy move.

You could see that these three kinds of hotness move heat just onto the outer layer of food sources. For food to prepare through to the middle, the external layer should move its hotness to the following layer, etc, until the actual focal point of the food starts to heat up. Thus, the outside of most cooked food sources will quite often be more all around good than the middle (there are stunts to limiting the inclination, which we'll get to on schedule).

Microwaves are the main other standard strategy for energy move we regularly use in the kitchen, and they have the remarkable capacity to infiltrate through the outside of food while warming it. Very much like light or hotness, microwaves are a type of electromagnetic radiation. Whenever microwaves are focused on an article with attractively charged particles (like, say, the water in a piece of food), those particles quickly flip to and fro, making grating, which, thusly, makes heat. Microwaves can go through most strong items to a profundity of at minimum a couple of centimeters or thereabouts. Therefore microwaves are an especially quick method for warming up food sources you don't have to sit tight for the generally sluggish exchange of energy from the outside to the middle.

EXPERIMENT:
Temperature Versus Energy in Action

The difference between the definition of *temperature* and the definition of *energy* is subtle but extraordinarily important. This experiment will demonstrate how understanding the difference can help shape your cooking.

Materials

- 1 properly calibrated oven
- 1 able-bodied subject with external sensory apparatus in full working order
- One 3-quart saucier or saucepan filled with water
- 1 accurate instant-read thermometer

Procedure

Turn your oven on to 200°F and let it preheat. Now open the oven door, stick your hand inside, and keep your hand in the oven until it gets too hot to withstand. A tough guy like you could probably leave it in there for at least 15 seconds, right? 30 seconds? Indefinitely?

Now place a pan of cold water on the stovetop and stick your hand in it. Turn the burner to medium-high heat and let the water start to heat up. Stir it around with your hand as it heats, but be careful not to touch the bottom of the pan (the bottom of the pan will heat much faster than the water). Keep your hand in there until it becomes too hot to withstand, remove your hand, and take the temperature.

Results

Most people can hold their hand in a 200°F oven for at least 30 seconds or so before it becomes uncomfortably hot. But let it go much above 135°F, and a pan of water is painful to touch. Water at 180°F is hot enough to scald you, and 212°F (boiling) water will blister and scar you if you submerge your hand in it. Why is this?

Water is much denser than air—there are many times more molecules in a cup of water than there are in a cup of air. So, despite the fact that the water is at a lower temperature than the air in the oven, the hot water contains far more energy than the hot air and consequently heats up your hand much more rapidly. In fact, boiling water has more energy than the air in an oven at a normal roasting temperature, say 350° to 400°F. In practice, this means that boiled foods cook faster than foods that are baked or roasted. Similarly, foods baked in a moist environment cook faster than those in a dry environment, since moist air is denser than dry air.

There's a great deal of babble to swim all through there while attempting to stock your kitchen. Do you truly require that $300 blade? How frequently would you say you will take out that salad spinner? Furthermore, precisely which something they sell on TV is truly going to replace each and every piece of gear in my kitchen? (Here's a clue: not a solitary one of them.) The issue with the vast majority of individuals advising you to purchase things is that they're typically the ones selling it. Who would you be able to trust? Indeed, this section is a straightforward, no horse crap manual for guide you to what you truly need in the kitchen and what is simply commotion.

Any Eddie Izzard fans in the crowd? "Human kills human, as per him, firearms don't kill human. The National Rifle Association says that . Be that as it may, I think the firearm helps." Funny joke. Be that as it may, what's it have to do with cooking?

I recollect a period back when I initially began working in cafés. One of my positions was to two or three quarts of weighty cream down to a few pints. I'd get a major weighty pot with an aluminum base, empty the cream into it, and cook it over the most minimal conceivable hotness so that it'd lessen without percolating. I'd do this each day, and it would two or three hours, however not a problem; I had a lot of different errands to keep me involved stripping potatoes, stripping salsify, stripping carrots (ah, the existence of a green cook). Then, at that point, one morning, the pot I generally diminished the cream in was being utilized. As opposed to hang tight for it to free up, I just snatched one of the more slender stockpots off the rack, poured in my cream, and warmed it not surprisingly.

What I wound up with was a pot loaded with oily, broken cream, with a wrecked self image to coordinate (the inner self has since been fixed, however the cream was an act of futility). Tipping it out into the sink uncovered a ½-inch-thick hull of earthy colored muck on the base. The issue? My pot was too slim and its conductivity was excessively low. Instead of circulating the hotness equally over the lower part of the whole pot, the hotness was packed in the areas straight over the flares. Those regions got overheated, influencing the proteins in the cream straight above them to coagulate, adhere to one another (and to the pot), and in the end consume. Without the emulsifying impact of the proteins, the fat in the cream isolated out into a particular, oily yellow layer. Yuck.

Clearly, it was the pot's issue, correct? All things considered, not by and large. You regularly hear the articulation "An awful cook faults his devices," and it's valid: terrible food is seldom awful in light of the fact that the pot was too dainty or the blender was broken. However, I think this is frequently confused. No one is saying that a decent cook ought to have the option to cook any dish no matter what the nature of their hardware. Decreasing cream without a weighty, sufficiently conductive pot or a satisfactorily low fire is almost unthinkable, regardless of how great a cook you are. Meager pots don't consume cream-individuals consume cream. In any case, I think the flimsy pot makes a difference.

In actuality, awful food is frequently awful in light of the fact that the cook decided to attempt to cook something that he didn't have the legitimate devices for. This is, obviously, simply a more muddled approach to saying, "Don't be moronic." And that is a word of wisdom for varying backgrounds, regardless of whether they include homogenized emulsions of milk proteins, water, butterfat, and phospholipids.

All of this is only an indirect approach to saying that the actual equipment you stock your kitchen with is similarly all around as significant as the fixings you pick or the procedures you use when you cook. Great gear is the third side of the Triforce of cooking: great fixings + great hardware + great method = great food.

POTS AND PANS

Since it is now so obvious about heat move, we should discuss the devices we use to move heat from a hotness source (your burner or your stove) to your food. I'm talking pots and dish. There's a shocking cluster of sizes and types accessible planned for an assortment of purposes, some of them exceptionally specific (think long, restricted fish poachers or tall, thin asparagus pots), and others considerably more flexible. Except if you're the sort who poaches fish and bubbles asparagus for each and every dinner, the last option are the sort you ought to go for.

Materials

With regards to the presentation of the given material in a skillet, there are truly two things that matter: its capacity to disperse heat uniformly across its whole surface (its conductivity) and its capacity to hold hotness and move it productively to food (its particular hotness limit and thickness).

Here are a few normal metals, alongside their properties:

Treated steel is extremely simple to keep up with as its name suggests, it won't rust or pit, regardless of the amount you abuse it. In any case, it additionally is an incredibly unfortunate hotness guide. This means hotness won't travel quickly through it. Tempered steel dish will generally foster unmistakable hot and cold spots that match the hotness example of your burners. This can prompt lopsided cooking, coming about in, for instance, an omelet that is singed in certain spots despite everything crude in others.

How would you measure the hotness dissemination execution of a skillet? The simplest way is to extended a far layer of sugar equitably over the base, then heat it over a burner. The example wherein the sugar melts will show the container's hot and cold spots. An extraordinary skillet will dissolve sugar equally.

Aluminum is a much better guide of hotness truly outstanding, as a matter of fact. It's additionally an exceptionally cheap material. For what reason aren't all skillet made of aluminum, you could inquire? All things considered, there are two issues. It's not extremely thick, and that intends that notwithstanding its high-heat limit, you'd require a container that is a ludicrously cumbersome thickness for it to hold a sensible measure of hotness. Besides, it stains and pits whenever presented to acidic fixings: wine, lemon juice, tomatoes, and so forth

Anodized aluminum has been blessed to receive give it a fired like completion that is sensibly nonstick, as well as impervious to corrosive. This is the ideal metal for cooking food varieties that don't need an uncommonly elevated degree of hotness. You would have no desire to singe a steak in an anodized aluminum skillet, yet nothing is better for cooking an omelet.

Copper is significantly more conductive than aluminum. It's likewise very thick, with an incredible hotness limit. In any case, copper dish are extravagant. I'd very much want to have an extraordinary arrangement of copper pots. I'd likewise very much want to have a lifetime supply of Stilton and a yacht with a locally available petting zoo. It won't work out. On the off chance that you can bear the cost of a bunch of copper pots, you are a lot more extravagant individual than I. For most of us, how about we continue on.

Covered, or tri-utilize, container offer the smartest possible solution. By and large, they are developed with a layer of aluminum sandwiched between two layers of treated steel. They have the high thickness of a hardened steel skillet, with the incredible conductivity of aluminum, settling on them the dish of decision for most home cooks (counting me!).

Time was that nonstick dish were really hard to suggest. Coatings that chip off or emit poisonous exhaust when warmed a lot of are not something you need to cook with. Nowadays, nonstick coatings are more sturdy and far more secure. You'll need to possess something like one great nonstick prospect cookery.

The subject of solid metal cookware is troublesome to such an extent that I want to delve into somewhat more insight regarding it. Being a glad proprietor of both a doggy named Hambone and some truly decent cast-iron cookware, I've observed that they are surprisingly comparable in many regards. The two of them require a little work, a little tolerance, and a ton of faithfulness. The principle distinction is that as a trade-off for my venture, my cast-iron skillet give me brilliant brown singed chicken, sizzling bacon, johnnycake, fruity desserts, very much scorched hash, impeccably burned steaks, effervescent pizzas, and fresh dumplings. Hambone, then again, gives me generally licks, bites, and a ton of crap. You figure it out.

To the extent that holding heat goes, nothing beats a decent solid metal skillet. Its particular hotness limit is lower than of aluminum, but since it is so thick, for a similar thickness of container, you get about double the hotness maintenance ability. This is significant: the skillet doesn't chill off when you add food to it. While the temperature in a flimsy aluminum skillet might come around however much 300 degrees when you add a half-pound rib-eye steak to it, a cast-iron dish will remain nearby its unique temperature, conveying a thicker, crisper, all the more uniformly cooked covering. Additionally, you can pull off utilizing somewhat less oil while browning chicken, since the hotness held by the cast iron will quickly warm the oil when the chicken you add chills it off.

The way that cast iron is broiler safe implies that you can braise and heat in it similarly too as you can broil or burn. Chile cake emerges with an excellent brilliant earthy colored hull, and pies, even with clammy fillings, come out magnificently fresh on the base. Its hotness maintenance capacities imply that in any event, when your stove's temperature varies (as most indoor regulator driven broilers do), the dish's hotness will remain genuinely consistent.

What's more, talk about strength! Project iron cookware is one of a handful of the things in your kitchen that really gets better as it progresses in years. A portion of the absolute best container have been gone down through various ages, their very much utilized surfaces worn as smooth and nonstick as a Teflon-covered dish without the harmful synthetic compounds. Furthermore, on the grounds that cast-iron dish are given from a form a role as a solitary piece of metal, there are no welded joints or even bolts to break down.

There are, obviously, a couple of disadvantages to project iron:

• Until a decent layer of preparing has developed, food will adhere to it. This goes for even the "preseasoned" skillets available now, which have an average degree of preparing, best case scenario. With regular use, a cast-iron skillet will be impeccably prepared (I characterize this as sufficiently nonstick to cook eggs in) inside half a month. With less continuous use, you can anticipate that the interaction should require a few months. It's a long stretch, yet consider how glad you'll be (very much like housebreaking a doggy) when that first egg slides mysteriously off the base.

• It warms unevenly. As opposed to mainstream thinking, iron is an unfortunate guide of hotness, and that implies that the hotness doesn't go a long way from its source. Attempting to utilize a 12-inch cast-iron skillet on a 3-inch burner ring is a waste of time: the edges of the dish won't ever get hot. To warm a cast-iron container actually, you really want a burner equivalent in size to the dish, and a lot of time for even hotness circulation. Then again, a cast-iron container can be preheated in a hot broiler prior to moving it to the oven. (Remember to utilize a kitchen towel or pot holder!)

• It can rust. While a decent layer of preparing will forestall this, indiscretion (like cleaning the dish or not permitting it to dry completely prior to putting away it) can prompt rust spots.

• You can't cook excessively acidic food varieties in it. Acidic food sources will get flavor and shading from the iron, turning them soiled and metallic-tasting. This really intends that until a generally excellent layer of preparing has grown, even speedy wine-based skillet sauces are impossible, as are acidic plans like pureed tomatoes.

• It's weighty. There's no way to avoid this one. The thickness of the material makes cast iron so great at holding a lot of hotness energy in a limited quantity of volume. Developments like aide handles help, yet more modest cooks will presumably battle with assignments like flipping food or pouring a sauce from a cast-iron skillet.

• It requires unique cleaning. Since the cooking characteristics of solid metal cookware are subject to how very much prepared it is, care should be taken while cleaning to forestall unintentionally eliminating the layer of preparing, or you must beginning without any preparation.

Everything that expressed, there's truly not much to it with regards to preparing, keeping up with, and putting away your cast-iron cookware.

THE MOST EFFECTIVE METHOD TO SEASON AND MAINTAIN CAST-IRON COOKWARE

Starting Seasoning

At the point when you initially get a solid metal dish, it will have either a shot dim dull completion (assuming it's an unseasoned container) or a smooth looking dark surface (a preseasoned skillet). Except if you purchased a 75 year-old skillet at a carport deal, it will likewise have a pebbly-looking surface, similar to this:

Current cast iron is rough similar to that since it isn't cleaned the manner in which old cast iron was and holds some surface from the form. I've analyzed my gleaming, absolutely smooth 1930s Griswold dish (gained at a swap meet) to my kid Lodge skillet (which I purchased new and prepared myself) and tracked down slight benefits with the old container, however the upgraded one really does fine and dandy.

So the key is all in preparing it appropriately. How can it function?

Indeed, in the event that you take a gander at the outer layer of a cast-iron skillet under a magnifying lens, you'll see a wide range of little pores, breaks, and abnormalities. Whenever you cook food in the container, it can saturate these breaks, making it stick. That, however proteins can really frame substance bonds with the metal surprisingly contact with it. At any point have a piece of fish tear in half as you attempt to turn this is on the grounds that it appears as though it's really reinforced with the skillet? That is on the grounds that it has.

To keep both of these things from occurring, you want to fill in the little pores, as well as make a defensive layer in the lower part of the dish to keep proteins from coming into contact with it. Enter fat.

At the point when fat is warmed within the sight of metal and oxygen, it polymerizes. Or on the other hand, to lay it more out plainly, it shapes a strong, plastic-like substance that covers the skillet. The more times oil is warmed in a dish, the thicker this covering gets, and the better the nonstick properties of the skillet.

This is the way to develop the underlying layer of preparing in your container:

• Clean the skillet by add ½ cup genuine salt into it and scouring it with a paper towel. This will scour out any residue and pollutants that have gathered in it. Then, at that point, wash it completely with hot, foamy water and dry completely. Assuming that your stove has a self-cleaning cycle, one outing through with the dish left inside will crush even the hardest cooked-on muck and give you an uncovered container to begin with.

• Oil your dish by scouring each surface-including the handle and the base with a paper towel absorbed a profoundly unsaturated fat like corn, vegetable, or canola oil. Unsaturated fats are more responsive than immersed fats (like shortening, fat, or other creature based fats), and subsequently polymerize better. It's an old legend that bacon fat or fat makes the best flavoring specialist, most likely borne of the way that those fats were exceptionally modest back in solid metal's prime.

• Heat your dish in a 450°F broiler for 30 minutes (it will smoke), or until its surface is particularly darker than when you began. A stove will warm the container more uniformly than a burner will, prompting a superior introductory layer of preparing.

• Rehash the oiling and warming stages three to multiple times, until the dish is almost completely dark. Haul it out of the broiler and put it on the burner to cool. Your container is currently prepared and all set.

Until you have a decent layer of preparing developed, abstain from utilizing a lot of cleanser or cooking acidic sauces, as both can make the flavoring system take more time.

Maintenance

Many people ar without reasoning terrified of caring for forged iron. the reality is, once you've got a decent layer of seasoning, forged iron is pretty powerful. You can't scratch it with metal utensils. You can't destroy it by exploitation soap (modern dish soaps ar terribly mild on everything aside from grease). to keep up the seasoning and build upon it, simply bear in mind some key points:

• Use the pan usually. a decent layer of polymers ought to build up slowly {in a|during a|in an exceedingly|in a terribly} succession of very skinny layers. this implies exploitation your pan the maximum amount as possible—particularly for oil-based preparation like cookery or searing.

Avoid creating liquid-based dishes within the pan till it's nonheritable a fairly sensible layer of seasoning.

• Clean the pan at once once use. Removing food dust is way easier with a hot pan than one that has cooled. If you clean your iron cooking pan whereas it's still hot, likelihood is all you'll would like may be a small little bit of soap and a sponge.

• Avoid powerful abrasives. These embrace metal scouring pads and cleaners like extraterrestrial object or Bar Keepers Friend. The scrubby aspect of a sponge ought to be lots for many tasks. I'm significantly cautious regarding this at dinner parties, once a well-meant guest might plan to kick in once the meal and acquire a touch too generous with the effort, scrub out a number of my seasoning.

• Dry the pan completely and oil it before storing. once remotion the pan, set it on a burner and warmth it till it dries and simply starts to smoke, then rub the whole within surface with a towel lordotic gently in oil. Take it off the warmth and let it cool to temperature. The oil can kind a protecting barrier, preventing it from coming back into contact with wetness till its next use.

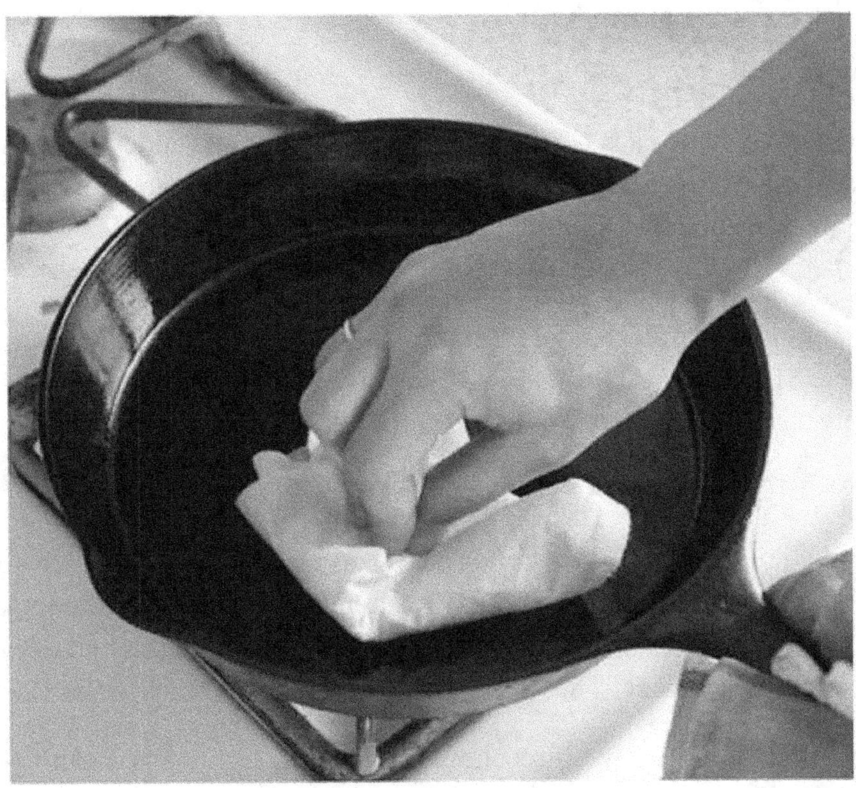

A good rub-down with oil prevents erosion.

Worst-Case eventualities

There ar primarily solely 2 very dangerous things that may happen to your iron cooking utensil, scaling and rust—and neither of them is that dangerous.

Scaling happens after you heat the pan too usually while not adding additional oil to that. instead of coming back off in microscopic bits, because the seasoning commonly can, the layer of polymers sloughs off in giant flakes. For the pan to achieve this state, I hold on it within the kitchen appliance for a month's value of heating cycles, while not ever oiling the surface. It's straightforward to avoid the matter by oiling the pan once every use and not warming it (if you're storing it within the kitchen appliance, don't leave it there throughout the cleanup cycle, for instance), however once it happens, there's no turning back—you'll ought to reseason it from the beginning.

Rust will seem on a iron pan that's not seasoned to a tolerable degree and is left to dry. Unless the whole pan has rusted (in that case, you'll ought to reseason the entire thing), a rust spot isn't abundant to fret regarding. Rinse out the pan, heat it till it dries and smokes, and rub it with oil. once some uses, the rusted spot ought to be absolutely seasoned once more.

Which Pan ought to I Buy?

If you're lucky enough to come back across a fairly priced iron pan (under $50 or so) from the first twentieth century at a sales event or marketplace, scoop it up at once. you'll be able to conjointly often notice sensible deals on eBay and sites am fond of it.

I in person notice it ridiculous to pay the $150-plus that some sellers ar inquiring for previous forged iron once a brand new iron pan, just like the 10¼-inch Seasoned iron cooking pan from Lodge prices a mere $16.98 and can provide you with associate degree equally lustrous slippy surface with simply a small amount of your time and care.

THE CORE: THE EIGHT POTS AND PANS EACH ROOM DESIRES

I'm a saver naturally. i purchase pleasure out of getting as large associate degree array of pots and pans as doable, continuously telling myself that I'm attending to use them often, that they very aren't a waste of cash. But, altogether honesty, the sole real use i purchase out of ninety p.c of my pans may be a strictly aesthetic one. They're sort of a tie for my pot rack—and I ne'er wear a tie.

The majority of the time, I notice myself reaching for constant eight pans. I can't consider one dish that can't be created exploitation one in every of these, or a mixture, and they're all you'll have to be compelled to cook the recipes during this book. Here they're, the cornerstones of any well-stocked room.

1. A 12-Inch (Laminated) Tri-Ply Straight-Sided Lidded Sauté Pan

A large cooking pan is that the true workhorse of the room. It's good for apace browning giant quantities of vegetables or meat. Pan-roasting an entire chicken? this is often the pan of selection.

have to be compelled to brown a undercut or a 3-rib beef roast? No downside. It's conjointly glorious for preparation and for reducing sauces. it's a tightly fitting lid and is oven-safe, which suggests you'll be able to brown your cut of beef, add the liquid, cover, and cook within the kitchen appliance, then scale back the sauce on the stovetop and serve all out constant pan.

All-Clad is that the benchmark for excellent tri-ply cooking utensil, however it will be prohibitively valuable. In side-by-side tests, I've found that Tramontina-brand All-Clad knockoffs perform nearly additionally for each task, at a few third of the value. the selection may be a task.

2. A 10-Inch iron cooking pan

Nothing beats forged iron for searing a cut or a pleasant skin-on, bone-in pigeon breast. I truly keep a group of iron cooking pans altogether sizes in order that I will do everything from cookery one egg and serving it directly from its small skillet to baking pies, however the one i exploit most is my 10-inch pan. It's simply the proper size to sear {a couple|a few|one or 2|a handful|some} of steaks on behalf of me and therefore the better half (I'll sear in batches or use 2 pans and two burners if I've got a lot of individuals to cook for, to maximise heat transfer to the steaks), it's simply the proper size for corn bread, it's a fine looking serving vessel. the chances are very limitless.

3. A 10-Inch Tri-Ply Nonstick Skillet or Anodized Aluminum

Individuals will let you know that a very much prepared cast-iron skillet that is appropriately prepared will be basically as smooth as a genuine nonstick skillet. Hell, I've presumably said exactly the same thing myself. Perhaps here in this book. Indeed, here's the miserable information: that ain't exactly evident. Indeed, even the absolute best solid metal skillets won't ever be essentially as smooth as a nonstick skillet. Any materials-science specialist can let you know that. That, however dissimilar to a cast-iron skillet, a nonstick container can be light to the point of moving effectively while, say, moving an omelet or flipping two or three radiant side-ups.

What's more, that is the reason a medium nonstick skillet is an unquestionable requirement in your armory. It's the best vessel for a wide range of egg cookery, from ideal brilliant omelets to cushioned scrambles to fresh edged seared eggs. Informal breakfasts would be a lot more chaotic, more rushed, and out and out less pleasurable undertaking in my loft without one.

The main disadvantage to nonstick? You can't warm it past 500°F or something like that, as the covering will disintegrate, sending harmful exhaust into the room. More current materials are far more secure, yet even with them, you're in a difficult spot: it's hard to shape a decent, substantial outside layer on food prepared on a nonstick surface, and you're restricted by the kinds of utensils you can utilize. Metal will scratch off the covering. Stay with wood, nylon, or silicone utensils made explicitly for working with nonstick skillet.

Here is the thing with nonstick: in contrast to different skillet, these won't last you your entire life, and that implies that burning through a boatload of cash on one is definitely not an insightful move. You need a midrange container: something with enough heave that it holds heat genuinely well, however not one that you'll be so terrified of scratching that it winds up sitting toward the side of kitchen cupboard. I as of now have a Cuisinart treated steel nonstick skillet, however I'm not intensely dedicated to it. You ought to never become focused on a nonstick container.

4. A 2½-to 3-Quart Saucier

The contrast between a pan and a saucier is inconspicuous however significant. Pots have straight sides; sauciers are expected to keep their substance actually whiskable and stirrable, so they have carefully skewed sides. This is a huge advantage while cooking. It suggests that you don't have to endeavor to drive a round spoon or race into a square corner. This is a significant benefit while cooking. It implies that you don't need to attempt to push a round spoon or race into a square corner.

I utilize a saucier for little clumps of soup or stew, for cooking short pasta shapes (you needn't bother with a major pot for this-see here), for warming extras, for making cheddar sauces or wiener sauce, for stewing pureed tomatoes or perspiring a couple of vegetables, and in any event, for one-chicken-sized clusters of stock.

Likewise with a nonstick skillet, any brand will do as long as it's thick, weighty, broiler safe, and, ideally, tri-utilize. I utilize the Farberware Millennium Clad Stainless Steel Saucier. It has an incredible lip for pouring and a pleasant profound shape. I've been in a profound relationship with it for around eight years, with not a solitary protest from one or the other party. That is beyond what I can say about some other relationship I've been in.

5. A 12-to 14-Inch Carbon Steel Wok

You're excused for not claiming a wok in the event that you grew up with a Western kitchen. However, I'm here to attempt to persuade you that everyone, in addition to the individuals who like to sauté, can profit from a decent huge wok. There could be no more excellent vessel for profound browning, steaming, or smoking. For more data on purchasing and really focusing on a wok, see here.

6. A 6-to 8-Quart Enameled Cast-Iron Dutch Oven

My plated Dutch broiler is the principal pot I claimed that made me ponder internally, Wow, you've truly got something particularly amazing here. It's a blue oval Le Creuset number, it's as yet perfectly healthy today, working in some measure as well as it did the day my mother got it for me fifteen years prior. A decent plated Dutch broiler will keep close by forever. On account of its weight and haul, it's the best vessel for slow braises, in or out of the broiler. It's just plain obvious, all that weighty material consumes a large chunk of the day to warm up or chill off. This implies that regardless of whether your stove is cycling here and there with its temperature causing sine ripple effects that stretch a decent 25 degrees more sweltering and cooler than the number on the dial, the inside of your pot will show scarcely any changes whatsoever. This is something beneficial for steadfastness and consistency in plans.

Le Creuset sets the norm for quality with regards to plated cast iron, but on the other hand it's incredibly expensive. Assuming you get one, you'll esteem it everlastingly, and just mostly in light of the fact that you've burned through such a lot of cash on it (they're somewhat similar to kids in like that). Stop makes an entirely functional adaptation for about 33% of the cost, however purchaser be careful: I've seen a couple chip and break in my day.

7. A 3-to 4-Gallon Stockpot

The enormous daddy of pots: this is the person you take out when you need to make pasta for twenty, when you have about six lobsters to bubble, or when you have a few cadavers of chicken bones sitting in the cooler simply ready to be transformed into magnificent stock. Until you own a major stockpot, you won't ever acknowledge the amount you really wanted one. The uplifting news here is that with regards to stockpots, irrefutably the least expensive will do. You won't ever be doing anything in here beside bubbling or stewing tremendous measures of fluid, so all you want is something that will hold water and remain level. You shouldn't need to spend more than $40 or so on one.

8. Something to Roast In

Nice simmering dish are costly; there's no doubt. Very much like with skillets, the best simmering container are made with layered metals-treated steel sandwiched with an aluminum center. While picking a broiling container, I search for one that I can utilize straightforwardly on a burner on the burner as well as in the stove, something with agreeable handles, and something thick enough that it won't twist under the hotness of the broiler or the heaviness of a turkey. My Calphalon container is enormous and tough, and it has a decent U-molded rack for holding huge meals. It's about $140, and I use it about double a year, when I cook enormous meals on vacations.

Need to know the fair truth? I could undoubtedly live without it. What I was unable to live without is a substantial aluminum rimmed baking sheet with a wire cooling rack set on it. It's lighter and less expensive, stores directly in the stove, and enjoys the additional benefit that it's shallow, making it a lot simpler for hot air to circle around the food that is cooking. It's what I use for broiling the other 363 days of the year. Mine has seen innumerable dish chickens, and it is twisted and bowed to excess, however it actually takes care of its business similarly as well as it could possibly do. I got it for about $10 at a cooking supply store, alongside a rack that cost another $5 or $6. (You can get these dish online also they're called half sheet container. Nordic Ware makes a fine one for about $15.)

INSTRUCTIONS TO BUY AND CARE FOR A WOK

A decent wok is one of the most flexible skillet in the kitchen. There are the people who contend that on a Western oven, with its level, generally low-yield burners, a normal nonstick skillet is a predominant vessel for sautéing; they might have even showed you a few extravagant graphs demonstrating that a skillet gets to a higher temperature and keeps up with its hotness better. This is utter and finish babble. Every one of the graphs on the planet won't tell you as much as your mouth, and the truth of the matter is, sautés improve when made in a wok, in light of the fact that a decent pan fried food isn't just about the temperature the metal ranges. It's about right throwing and aerosolization of fats and squeezes as they jump up past the edges of the wok and are moved by the fire of the burner. It's about the capacity to quickly hotness and cool a piece of food as you flip it again and again through the different hotness zones made by the dish as (much as flipping a burger oftentimes will further develop its cooking-see here). It's about wok hei, the marginally smoky, scorched, metallic flavor that main comes from a carefully prepared cast-iron or carbon steel skillet warmed to tearing hot temperatures.

I diverge. Clearly, woks are the most ideal decision for sautéing, but on the other hand they're the best vessel for profound searing, steaming, and indoor smoking. My wok is by a long shot the most normally involved skillet in my kitchen.

Likewise with most things, nonetheless, not all woks are made equivalent. They arrive in a confounding exhibit of sizes, shapes, metals, and handle plans. Luckily for us, the best woks additionally end up being on the economical finish of the scale. Here are an interesting points while buying one.

Materials

• Hardened steel woks are a misuse of cash. Not exclusively are they incredibly weighty and hard to move, they additionally consume most of the day to warm up and chill off a horrendous defect for something that requires quick, on-the-fly hotness changes like a pan fried food. Also, food-especially protein-tends to adhere to steel.

• Project iron is a superior decision, however it actually consumes most of the day to warm up and chill off. It offers a superior nonstick surface. The primary issue with cast iron is that assuming it's meager, it is very delicate I've seen solid metal woks break in half when put down excessively hard. Furthermore, when made thick to the point of being sturdy, they are incredibly unwieldy to lift, which is fundamental for legitimate flipping during a pan fried food.

• Carbon steel is your smartest option. It warms rapidly and uniformly, is profoundly receptive to burner input, is both tough and cheap, and, if appropriately focused on, will wind up with a basically nonstick surface. Search for carbon steel woks that are no less than 14-measure (around 2 mm thick). They shouldn't give when you push on the sides.

Manufacture

Woks are made in three ways:

• Conventional hand-pounded woks (like the ones they used to sell in those infomercials during the 1980s) are a superb decision. The slight spaces left by the pounding design permit you to push prepared food to the sides of the container while adding fixings to the middle without them slipping back. Furthermore, hand-pounded woks are modest. The main issue is that it very well may be troublesome (incomprehensible?) to find one with a level base and a handle (to a greater degree toward that later).

• Stepped woks are made by removing a round piece of meager carbon steel and squeezing it by machine into a shape. They are very modest, yet they are totally smooth, making it hard to pan sear appropriately. What's more, they are, as a general rule, produced using low-check steel and inclined to creating hot and cold spots, as well as appearing to be wobbly.

• Turned woks are created on a machine, providing them with a particular example of concentric circles. This example offers similar benefits as a hand-pounded wok, permitting you to handily keep food set up against the sides of the dish. Turned woks can be found in weighty measures, with level bottoms, and with flip-accommodating handles. They are reasonable.

Shape and Handles

Customary woks have a profound bowl shape, intended to squeeze into a roundabout opening straight over the hearth. Except if you have a custom wok embed in your reach (and assuming you do, you presumably aren't understanding this), you need to stay away from round-lined woks. They won't work, period, on an electric reach and are difficult to use on a gas range even with one of those wok rings. Then again, woks with bottoms that are too level invalidate the point of the dish, making it intense to flip food appropriately and to move it all through the high-heat zone.

Your smartest choice is a wok with a 4-to 5-inch-wide leveled region at the base and tenderly inclining sides that flare out to somewhere in the range of 12 and 14 inches. This will give you a lot of high-heat space for singing meats and vegetables at the base, with adequate volume and space to move while flipping. Concerning handles, you have two options: Cantonese-style woks have two little handles on one or the other side, while northern-style woks have one long handle and normally a more modest aide handle on the contrary side. This is the sort of wok you need. The long handle works with flipping and pan-searing, while the short handle makes it simple to lift.

At last, keep away from nonstick woks at all costs. Most nonstick coatings can't deal with the high hotness fundamental for an appropriate sautéed food. They begin disintegrating, delivering poisonous vapor, well before they arrive at the essential temperature. They make searing troublesome, and it's difficult to get food to stick set up against the sides of the wok when you need to clear a surface to cook in the center.

Care and Maintenance

Very much like a decent solid metal dish, a carbon steel wok's exhibition will further develop the more you use it. Generally accompany a defensive film of oil to keep them from rusting or discoloring in the store. It's vital to eliminate this layer prior to utilizing it the initial time. Clean the wok out with hot lathery water, dry it cautiously, and place it over a burner at the most elevated heat conceivable until it begins to smoke. Cautiously turn the dish so every area of it-including the edges-is presented to this super-high hotness. Then rub it down with oil, utilizing a paper towel held in a couple of utensils, and you're all set. After use, try not to scour the wok except if totally vital. Normally a flush and a rubdown with a delicate wipe is too's essential. Perfectionists might tell you not to utilize cleanser. Yet, I do, and my wok is still very much prepared and totally nonstick. In the wake of washing it, dry the wok with a kitchen towel or paper towels and rub a vegetable oil into the surface to give it a vaporproof covering that will keep it from rusting.

With rehashed use, the oil you heat in your wok separates into polymers that fill the minuscule pores in the metal's surface, delivering the material totally nonstick. As you break in your wok, the material will step by step change from silver to caramel and, at long last, to a profound dark. This is the thing you are searching for.

With appropriate consideration, your wok won't just endure forever yet additionally really age gracefully.

ESSENTIAL WOK SKILLS

Sautéing is the quintessential wok strategy; nonetheless, we're not actually going to invest any energy on that here, as there is anything but a solitary pan fried food formula in this book (perhaps you can keep in touch with my distributer and persuade them you might want to see a Food Lab: Chinese Classics eventually). But on the other hand it's the best device for profound fricasseeing, steaming, and smoking food inside. This is the way to do everything:

• Profound browning in a wok is incomprehensibly better than doing it in a Dutch broiler. The wide sides intends that there's less wreck any splattering oil hits the sides and falls down to the middle. The shape likewise makes it a lot simpler to move food, prompting crisper, all the more uniformly cooked outcomes. Once more bubble overs become a relic of days gone by, because of the wide, inclining shape, which takes into account a lot of air pocket development before the oil takes steps to gush out over the edges. At last, it's a lot simpler to sift through pieces of garbage and debris from the skewed sides of a wok than from the sharp corners of a Dutch broiler.

• Steaming in a wok is likewise a lot simpler than in another vessel. You can utilize a standard liner embed for an enormous pot. Essentially lay it straightforwardly on the lower part of the wok over stewing water, and utilize the vault molded top to cover the skillet. The benefit, obviously, is that in a wide wok, you have undeniably more surface region for steaming. This benefit can be extended considerably further assuming you get yourself a few bamboo liners. Bamboo liners are intended to fit straightforwardly into a wok and are stackable, implying that you can have a few levels of food all steaming in a similar wok simultaneously. Have a go at doing that in a Dutch broiler!

• Smoking is additionally simple in a wok. All you must do is line the base with a piece of foil that stretches out over the edges by something like 3/4 the absolute width of the wok, then place your smoking medium (wood chips, tea leaves, sugar, rice, flavors, whatever) straightforwardly on the base and set your food on a rack or a liner on top of it. Place the wok over high hotness until the smoking material on the base starts to seethe, then overlay over the edges of the aluminum foil and pleat them to make a pocket, catching the smoke inside.

CUTTING BOARDS, KNIVES, SCISSORS, AND OTHER NECCESSARY CUTTING TOOLS

Assuming wedded life has shown me anything, it's that you're rarely generally right, in any event, when you are. A valid example: picking the best kitchen gear. At the point when I initially began dating my better half, the main blade she possessed was a minuscule plastic-dealt with, lopsided, dull blade from IKEA that seemed as though it'd be more at home sitting close to an Easy Bake broiler. To be sure, I spent a decent lump of 2007 attempting to clandestinely persuade her to changing to the unbelievably provocative, hand-pounded Japanese Damascus steel santoku blade that I'd purchased explicitly to dazzle any future spouses with my great taste.

She wound up picking the IKEA blade without fail, asserting that the huge size and unequivocally hand-engraved creator's mark on the grip of the santoku sharp edge threatened her (you can definitely relax, she was still reasonably intrigued by my crude manly energy at whatever point I employed it). I've since inspired her to move up to a decently nonintimidating Wüsthof 5-inch granton-edged santoku, however the point continues as before: when you restricted your decisions to those inside a specific quality level, the best blade for you is the one that you are most open to utilizing. Any individual who tells you different is selling something. Most likely blades.

While purchasing a blade, there are three fundamental attributes to consider: material, shape, and ergonomics.

The material a blade is made from decides a few elements, including how sharp it tends to be, the manner by which long it holds its edge, that it is so natural to resharpen once it's dull, and the way in which it responds with acidic food sources. By and large, you have three choices: carbon steel, clay, or treated steel.

• Carbon steel is a milder metal that is not difficult to hone, and it tends to be ground down into a phenomenally sharp edge. Its impediments are that it dulls generally rapidly, expecting you to resharpen it at regular intervals or so to keep a decent front line; it can rust in the event that not really focused on appropriately; and it will stain assuming it comes into delayed contact with acidic natural products or vegetables. You need to painstakingly spotless, dry, and oil it after each utilization to save its shine. Carbon steel is the material of decision for blade nerds who enjoy extraordinary the most common way of honing a cutting edge down to a slice through-anything-without-even-seeing edge. Very much like a canine, it requires a lot of difficult work to keep it all around focused and sound, however it'll remunerate you with a long period of steadfast, dedicated help. Furthermore, not at all like a canine, your blade won't ever pee on the floor covering. That is something to be thankful for.

• Ceramic cutting edges are for the most part an unfortunate decision. The facts confirm that they can be ground to a dangerously sharp edge, and that that edge doesn't dull even with delayed use, however their significant disadvantage is a whopper: they chip effectively and are unrepairable. A metal blade is adaptable, and that intends that on a tiny level, the sharp edge of its edge is continually bowing and twisting as indicated by the fluctuating tensions being applied along its length. In view of its glasslike structure, an artistic edge, then again, is uncommonly fragile. Indeed, even the smallest shearing movement with the edge can make it chip or break along the edge, consigning it to the "totally pointless however I'll keep it in any case since I'm actually holding out trust" cabinet. These blades are additionally extremely light, which, for certain, individuals (like me), can be a hindrance.

• Tempered steel used to be the material for suckers: hard, pretty, and simple to keep up with however totally unfit to shape an appropriately sharp edge. Nowadays, as materials science keeps on propelling, hardened steel blades are turning out to be increasingly alluring, since they consolidate the simple honing qualities of carbon steel with the simple cleanup and rust-and stain free nature of treated steel. I actually love my carbon steel blades, yet frankly, I have more impeccable blades in the kitchen now.

Blades and Cutting Boards

Whenever you are buying new blades, the value reach and fluctuation in quality level can genuinely falter. At the end of the day, you can hit the neighborhood megastore and observe a 24 piece set valued to try you cuts a few bucks out, or you can burn through hundreds or even a large number of dollars on a solitary blade. What gives?

Here is reality: Once you get to a specific degree of value, blades are generally an issue of individual taste. Do you have to burn through $300 to get a respectable blade? In no way, shape or form. Is it safe to say that you are probably going to track down a decent blade under $35 or somewhere in the vicinity? Most likely not. In any case, regardless blade you pick, these are the characteristics to look out for:

• An end to end length. The tang is the expansion of the sharp edge into the handle. In a decent blade, the tang ought to stretch out the whole way to the furthest limit of the handle. This gives greatest strength and equilibrium.

• A fashioned, not stepped, sharp edge. Fashioned cutting edges are made by emptying metal into a form, beating it, managing it, honing it, and cleaning it manually. This makes an extremely impressive, exceptionally adaptable edge from edge to heel. A stepped edge is removed of a solitary sheet of metal and honed on one edge. Stepped sharp edges generally bear an indication of equal stripes (brought about by the rollers used to smooth the metal) when you mirror light off it at you. Stepped sharp edges are for the most part lopsided and wobbly. The lower-end blades of most significant producers are stepped.

• A reasonable handle and an agreeable hold. At the point when you hold a blade, it should feel adjusted in your grasp, neither weighty nor light on the cutting edge end. It should likewise fit easily in your grasp. Keep in mind a blade should be an expansion of your hand. All things considered, it should feel totally regular.

THE CORE: THE KNIVES EVERY KITCHEN NEEDS IS A 6½ KNIVES

Gathering blades is fun, yet assuming I needed to pick, there are 6½ blades (I figure that between them, a peeler and a steel represent 1½ blades) that I'd never need to be without. Here they are.

THE ANATOMY OF A KNIFE

A blade comprises of two principle parts: the sharp edge and the handle. In an all around made blade, the metal that the edge is made of will broaden the whole way through the handle. Various pieces of this single piece of metal fill various needs. Here are the fundamental highlights of most blades:

• The Cutting Edge is the honed, sharpened edge of the edge. It ought to be dangerously sharp a very much honed blade can in a real sense take the hairs off your arm (don't attempt it). Cook's blade cutting edges come in shifting levels of ebb and flow, intended for different undertakings, for example, cutting or rock-hacking.

• The Back, or Spine, is the long side inverse the sharp cutting edge. This is the place where you hold your non-blade hand while shaking the blade to and fro for quick mincing. It can likewise be utilized as a shoddy seat scrubber for moving bits of food around on your cutting board (you ought to never do this with the bleeding edge it'll dull it).

• The Tip is the sharp point toward the finish of the cutting edge. It's utilized principally for accuracy work.

• The Heel is at the lower part of the edge. In numerous Western-style cuts, the metal thickens altogether at the heel. This is to make it simpler to grasp the blade utilizing the sharp edge hold.

• The Bolster is the piece of the cutting edge that meets the handle. It is thick and weighty, giving a decent adjusting point to the sharp edge and the handle. In an even blade, the focal point of mass ought to be some place close to the support, so you can shake the blade this way and that with negligible exertion.

• The Tang is the expansion of the sharp edge that goes through the handle. It gives balance as well as solidness. A blade with an end to end length (that is, metal that stretches out to the butt of the handle) is probably not going to at any point lose its handle.

• The Handle is the place where your entire hand rests assuming that utilizing the handle grasp, or where your three more modest fingers rest on the off chance that utilizing the edge hold (which I suggest). Handles can be made of wood, polycarbonate, metal, or different intriguing materials. I like the vibe and grasp of a genuine wood handle, yet there is no set in stone here.

• The Butt is the swelled area at the actual lower part of the handle.

THE TWO GRIPS

The initial step to consummate blade abilities is figuring out how to hold a blade. There are two fundamental grasps: the handle hold and the cutting edge hold.

• The Handle Grip: With the handle hold, your hand is totally behind the impact point of the blade, with every one of your fingers tucked behind the support. It is by and large utilized by starting cooks or cooks with outstandingly little hands. It's agreeable, yet it offers possibly restricted control while accomplishing accuracy blade work.

• The Blade Grip: The cutting edge grasp is the favored hold for more experienced cooks. Your thumb and index finger should rest before the reinforce, straightforwardly on the edge. This hold is somewhat scary, however it offers much better control and equilibrium. It very well might be troublesome and additionally awkward with less expensive stepped blades that don't have a support.

Whenever I initially began cooking, I utilized the handle grasp. All in all, it just sounded good to me. It's known as the handle for an explanation, correct? However, when I moved into proficient kitchens and was quickly taunted for my beginner grasp (proficient kitchens are perseveringly macho), I did the switch and saw a prompt and emotional improvement in my blade abilities. I'm not one to pass judgment on somebody in light of how they hold their blade (or on the other hand on the off chance that I judged, I'd do it quietly), yet here's how things are: If you've just at any point utilized the handle grasp, check the sharp edge grasp out you might observe your cuts improving significantly. Consequently, I vow to pass judgment on you just somewhat assuming you return to utilizing the handle hold.

What might be said about your non-blade hand? As a general rule, there are two positions you'll track down that hand in. The most widely recognized is known as "the hook," and when individuals cut themselves with a blade, it's generally probable since they weren't utilizing the paw. Utilize this grasp while dicing and cutting. Safeguard the fingertips of your non-blade hand by twisting them internal, utilizing your knuckles to direct your blade. While cutting food, consistently place it in a steady position, ideally with a cut surface level against the cutting board. Then, at that point, guide the blade sharp edge against the food with your paw hand.

For mincing, an alternate methodology is required. Put the tip of your blade on the cutting board and hold it set up with your free hand. Rock the edge all over to decrease spices (or whatever else) to a fine mince.

EAST VERSUS WEST:

Which Knife Style Is Superior?

The distinction among Japanese-and Western-style blades used to be night and day. Western blades had tenderly inclined, bended edges that came to a point, with a somewhat thick spine contrasted with their length, and could shake on a cutting board. Japanese-style blades had level edges made for cutting and hacking, not shaking, with a slim profile and a somewhat light weight.

Nowadays, the gap isn't all that unmistakable. Western blade creators presently offer santoku-style blades, alluding to the staple blade of the Japanese home cook. Indeed, even blades with a Western shape have been thinned down and made lighter because of a developing business sector of people used to the simpler to-move Japanese-style edges. Japanese blade creators, then again, have started applying their abilities to gyutou, Western-style blades delivered with Japanese producing strategies to make what can frequently be the smartest possible solution.

So which style is awesome? There is no right solution to that. I initially figured out how to cook with the Western-style cuts that everybody was utilizing at that point, so my initial blade assortment for the most part comprised of weighty German blades like Wüsthofs and Henckels. However, as I started trying different things with Japanese-style blades, I observed that I very much wanted the accuracy they offered, and that their powerlessness to perform shaking undertakings like mincing merited the compromise for me. Nowadays, I utilize a blend of Western-and Japanese-style blades.

A Western-style cook's blade has a bended, tightened sharp edge.

A Japanese-style santoku blade has a straighter bleeding edge and a blockier tip.

The critical contrast in how the two sorts of blades are utilized is that with a Western-style blade, shaking, establishing the tip of the blade on the cutting board and lifting just the heel end as you feed food under, is an exceptionally normal movement. With a Japanese-style blade, this is unimaginable the state of the blade doesn't consider shaking. Cutting and hacking are the more normal developments, and mincing spices turns into a question of continued cutting as opposed to shaking.

The best way to tell which blades you incline toward is to go into a store and give them a shot.

1. A 8-or 10-Inch Chef's Knife or a 6-to 8-Inch Santoku Knife

This is my blade. There are numerous others like it, however this one is mine.

Your culinary specialist's blade should be an augmentation of your hand thus should feel totally normal. While I'm feeling down and I want a touch of actual help, I don't request that my significant other hold my hand. I don't rub my canine on his midsection. No, I go to my blade and simply hold it. We've really gotten to know each other. I know all her bends (I recently now started to understand that my blade is female) and precisely the way in which she squeezes into my hand and likes to be held, and consequently, she is steady, steadfast, and evil sharp.

The gourmet expert's blade is the one you will use for 95% of your cutting undertakings, so you would do well to ensure that you're OK with it, and here's the key: neglect each audit you've at any point perused. When you move beyond a specific quality level, no single blade is better compared to another. All things considered, there are sure qualities you can search for, contingent upon your cooking style, size, and solace level in the kitchen. The following are a couple of my essential proposals, however let me rehash: no one but you can conclude which blade is best for you. Go to a store, give approximately a shot, and reflect on it over for a little while. You and your gourmet specialist's blade will have a long, delightful, and commonly advantageous relationship. Pick admirably.

Western-Style Chef's Knives

• For the normal cook: The 8-or 10-inch Wüsthof Classic Cook's Knife (about $140). This was the principal respectable blade I possessed, I actually have it right up 'til the present time.

• Experts: It has a thick spine with a lot of haul, which assists it with doing a great deal of the cutting work for you. It has a bended cutting edge that permits you to shake to and fro for fast mincing. What's more, there's a lot of room under the handle for your knuckles while cleaving.

• Cons: Some cooks might think that it is excessively weighty, and little gave cooks might track down the handle awkwardly enormous.

• For the little given cook: The Global G-2 8-inch Chef's Knife (about $120). Snappy and practical.

• Masters: It's manufactured from a solitary piece of metal, implying that it's fundamentally indestructible. It has a very sharp, exact edge and an even handle (it's loaded up with sand) to assist it with remaining adjusted even while moving.

• Cons: There's no support or heel, so utilizing the edge hold for quite a while on this one might disturb your pointer where it rubs against the spine. Furthermore, there's not a lot of room under the handle when the edge is against your cutting load up, so you could wind up sending a clear message a couple of times. The everything metal handle can get tricky assuming it gets untidy (however no one ought to cook in a chaotic kitchen at any rate!). Ideal for vegans who need exact veg work and don't manage muddled meats.

• The best purchase choice: The 8-inch Victorinox Fibrox Chef's Knife (about $25). This is a number one among starting cooks who aren't yet certain they need to set down more than $100 for a culinary specialist's blade.

• Masters: It's exceptionally sharp right out of the container, and it's actual light, which a few clients might like. Grippable handle, and a lot of knuckle space.

Japanese-Style Chef's Knives

• For the normal cook: The 7-inch Misono UX10 Santoku (about $180). This is my undisputed top choice. It's not the very first blade I felt connection to, yet it's the first I at any point became hopelessly enamored with. Would that we never be separated.

- Aces: It's impeccably adjusted, with an entirely agreeable support that makes the sharp edge hold a fantasy. The cutting edge is Swedish steel, which is incredibly sharpenable and will hold an edge for a significant length of time. In spite of the fact that it is intended for cutting and hacking, the edge has a sufficient bend that you could actually do some Western-style shaking with it, providing you with the smartest possible solution. Solid, tough development, and a lot of heave a genuine marvel to view.

- Cons: Just one: cost. It's anything but a modest blade, yet taking into account that it will last you a lifetime, $180 appears to be fair.

- For the little given cook: The 7-inch Wüsthof Classic Hollow Ground Santoku (about $100). I utilized this blade widely in eateries, where accuracy vegetable cutting was required-to such an extent that it lost a decent centimeter of its width with rehashed sharpenings. I became very partial to it simultaneously.

- Experts: Like all first in class Wüsthof items, it's flawlessly developed. It has a substantially more thin edge than Western-style Wüsthofs, so it's simpler to make little, exact cuts and more agreeable for certain cooks. The empty ground granton edge (with dimples along the two sides of the edge) implies that food varieties like potato cuts won't adhere to it.

- Cons: It's not large enough for most truly substantial undertakings say, parting a butternut squash or hacking through a chicken. Fortunately, your knife will deal with that (see here).

- The best purchase choice: The MAC Superior 6½-inch Santoku (about $75). A #1 among masters and home cooks the same.

- Experts: An extremely sharp cutting edge, agreeable handle, and simple mobility.

- Cons: The cutting edge is difficult to hone, and at 6½ inches, it's excessively little for some, kitchen undertakings. It has neither the weight of the Misono nor the granton edge and strong feel of the Wüsthof, however it's an extraordinary blade by most guidelines.

2. A 3-to 4-Inch Sheep's Foot Paring Knife

For a long time, I utilized an exemplary bended 3-inch paring blade from Wüsthof, and right away, the state of the exemplary paring blade appears to seem OK. A major bended gourmet expert's blade is for cutting, hacking, and slashing huge things, so to cut, hack, and cleave little things, you'd need to utilize a little form of a cook's blade, isn't that so? Thing is, there's a key distinction between how you utilize a paring blade and how you utilize a culinary expert's blade so how could you need them both to be a similar shape? The genuine issue with the normal paring blade is the arch of the sharp edge. With a culinary expert's blade, this bend is intended to permit you to shake the blade for mincing. However, for a paring blade, it has neither rhyme nor reason: no one is shaking a paring blade.

The way in to a decent paring blade is accuracy, and that implies having a superthin sharp edge and the capacity to make cuts with negligible hand movement (the more you need to move your hand, the more lopsided the cut becomes). A level sheep's foot-molded blade is great for this undertaking. With a sheep's foot blade, it's feasible to connect with the cutting board with almost the whole length of the edge while the tip is solidly embedded into the food: the straightness of the cut is characterized by the straightness of the sharp edge. Speedier, more exact, and less opportunity for client mistake are all pluses in my book.

A similar thinking applies significantly more firmly assuming you are utilizing the blade to strip little things, similar to little potatoes or grapes. While utilizing a bended paring blade, the bend of the sharp edge and the bend of the article you are stripping run in inverse headings, so practically none of the food really interacts with the edge, expecting you to dig further and eliminate more tissue than is needed. Those of you who are accustomed to utilizing santoku blades instead of gourmet specialist's blades will quickly perceive these benefits.

The 3-inch Kudamono Hollow-Edge Paring Knife from Henckels ($50) is one of the least expensive fair blades of this sort you can get, with the additional benefit of having an empty ground granton edge. You can get the 3-inch Sheep's Foot Paring Knife from Wüsthof at a similar cost. It comes up short on granton edge, yet it is somewhat heavier, sturdier, and feels much improved in the hand. In the event that you need what I view as a definitive paring blade, attach another $5 to get yourself a similar Wüsthof yet with a granton edge. That is the one my blade unit packs.

3. A 10-to 12-Inch Serrated Bread Knife

I'm definitely less fastidious about bread blades than I am about culinary specialist's blades. For a certain something, I don't utilize them frequently. For cutting delicate breads like burger buns or sandwich bread, my culinary specialist's blade is more delicate than a bread blade. As a matter of fact, pretty much the main thing I utilize my bread blade for is cutting dry bread, similar to a roll or a natural Italian portion. Assuming you never eat these, you have no requirement for a bread blade. That is the reason I don't want to ensure my bread blade suits my hand perfectly. Furthermore, since serrated cutting edges are troublesome, in the event that certainly feasible, to hone at home, a bread blade won't keep going you as long as your gourmet expert's blade will.

You'll track down bread blades with pointed teeth, scalloped teeth, and microserrations. I observe that the best blades have wide sharp teeth, a fashioned (not stepped) edge for better sharpness and weight, and a decent length. My first bread blade was the Zwilling J. A. Henckels Twin Pro S 8-inch Bread Knife (about $85), and it served me well for about 10 years. My present bread blade is the F. Dick Forged 8-inch Bread Knife (about $65). It works similarly as well as the Henckels. In the event that you're on a more tight financial plan, you could do more terrible than the Victorinox Fibrox bread blade (around $25).

4. A 6-Inch Boning Knife

Of course, you don't believe you will do a ton of boning in your kitchen. . . . Stand by, that came out off-base. How about we begin once again: you may not be eliminating the bones from numerous chickens or pig's legs at this moment, yet I trust I'll have the option to persuade you that those are the two merchandise abilities to have added to your repertoire. It sets aside you cash (heaps of it), however it likewise expands the scrumptiousness you can create in your kitchen (we'll get to why later on).

A boning blade ought to be flimsy and modestly adaptable, with an extremely sharp tip. The thought is that you need to have the option to get that blade in the middle of all the meat and the bones, working your direction in, out, and around structures that aren't really straight. A flimsy, adaptable cutting edge helps with this cycle. A decent boning blade ought to likewise be made with a foot-an additional piece of metal sticking out of the impact point which you can use to scratch meat and connective tissue off the unresolved issues them. I've yet to find a more able boning blade than the Wüsthof Classic 6-inch Flexible Boning Knife (about $85).

5. A Good Heavy Cleaver

Priorities straight: keep away from costly Japanese or German knifes, period. Assuming they sell it at Williams-Sonoma, you don't need it. A knife is intended to be for hands down the hardest of the difficult tasks, and it will get beat up. It doesn't need the well honed edge-keeping up with capacities of costly German or Japanese steel, so there's no sense in addressing a greater expense for one when less expensive models are comparably functional.

My most loved is a rock solid 2-pound, end to end length, 8-inch-bladed behemoth of a knife that I got for $15 at an eatery supply store in Boston's Chinatown. I use it almost everyday for dismantling chickens, hacking through creature bones, mincing hamburger or pork for hand-slashed burgers or dumplings, separating generous vegetables, and attempting to look truly boss in the mirror (it's not great at that specific capacity). Assuming you live close to an eatery supply store, look at it for comparable arrangements. Similarly as with all blades, you're searching for strong development and an end to end length. A knife ought to be bounty weighty also.

Then again, you can get the more mass-market 7-inch wood-took care of knife from Dexter-Russell (about $40). It's a touch more costly you're paying for the name yet it does the very thing it should do: hack the poop out of things.

6. A Y-Shaped Vegetable Peeler

A normal vegetable peeler has an edge lined up with the handle, expecting you to hold both vegetable and peeler at an off-kilter point, restricting your accuracy. With a Y-peeler, you hold the peeler as though you're getting an iPod, giving you far more prominent precision. The outcome is prettier vegetables, quicker prep (when you become accustomed to utilizing it), and less waste. The Kuhn Rikon Original Swiss Peeler ($10.95 for 3) comes in grouped colors, has an inherent potato-eye remover, and is modest, tough, and exceptionally sharp. I purchased a bunch of about six out of 2002 despite everything have four of them in wonderful working request. (To make things abundantly clear, the other two were lost, not broken or broken down.)

7. A 10-Inch Honing Steel

Sharpening prepares (in some cases inaccurately alluded to as honing prepares) are the long, weighty, finished metal bars that butchers and chronic executioners run their blades over prior to going at their meat.

Many individuals mistake sharpening for honing, yet there is an unmistakable distinction. At the point when you hone a blade, you're effectively eliminating material from the edge, making a fresh out of the box new well honed angled edge. At the point when you sharpen a blade, everything you're doing is ensuring that edge is straight. The thing about metal is, it's pliant. That intends that with normal kitchen use, that flimsy honed edge can get infinitesimal scratches in it that toss the cutting edge askew. Regardless of whether the cutting edge is still sharp, it can feel dull on the grounds that the sharp edge has been pushed out of the way. That is the place where a sharpening steel comes in. When utilized appropriately, a steel will realign the edge of the cutting edge so the honed piece is all looking in the correct heading. You ought to steel your blade with each cooking meeting to guarantee that you're getting the most ideal edge.

While buying a steel, search for a weighty model somewhere around 10 inches long. I utilize the Wüsthof 10-inch steel, which costs about $20. Very much like a decent blade, a great steel will endure forever. The edges might wear out over the long haul, yet don't stress it's actually taking care of its business.

Precious stone prepares are acquiring notoriety nowadays. These are sharpening prepares that have fine precious stone powder inserted in them. This permits them to shave off a tiny measure of edge material each time you run your blade across one of them. In this sense, they really are honing prepares. The benefit of utilizing them is that you'll have the option to marginally expand the time between evident stone sharpenings. Excellent models will quite often run somewhat more than two times however much customary sharpening prepares.

CUTTING BOARDS

A decent cutting board is pretty much as significant as great blades. The ideal slicing load up is adequately huge to give you adequate space to deal with (no less than 1 foot by 2 feet, ideally a lot bigger); weighty enough that it doesn't slip, slide, or break under the strain of a weighty bang from a knife; and made of a material that is delicate enough that it won't dull your edge.

Of the sorts of sheets available, plastic (polyethylene) and wood are the only ones you ought to consider. A glass slicing board is like passing to your sharp edge: slow, difficult, anguishing demise as, many strokes, the ideal edge that you endeavored to accomplish is persistently eroded. A couple of years back, assuming you'd asked a wellbeing master which type to utilize, they would have said plastic, not wood. Plastic is dormant and unwelcoming to microbes, they'd say, though wood can house hazardous microscopic organisms and move them to your food.

Turns out those wellbeing specialists weren't right. Various ongoing impenetrable examinations have shown that wood is less inclined to be a method for moving microscopic organisms, because of its normal antimicrobial properties. A wooden cutting board can be a demise snare for microscopic organisms. Insofar as you give it a scour and a careful drying after each utilization (which, obviously, you ought to do with plastic sheets also), it's a completely protected material.

Concerning its genuine capacity as a cutting surface, wood likewise brings back home the gold, for certain advanced plastic sheets coming in a nearby second. Wood is exceptionally delicate, implying that your blade can connect with each stroke, yet it likewise has a few self-recuperating properties-stroke imprints will quit for the day disappear (however with rehashed use, your board will become more slender and more slender).

I'm sufficiently fortunate to have a couple of enormous, weighty, butcher-block-style sheets, which I got as a gift from an old culinary expert of mine, that precisely accommodated my prep region. The best business models I've seen are the ones made by Ironwood Gourmet. They have a 20-by-14-inch rendition for about $50 that will last you in some measure a unimaginable length of time. Try not to have the mixture to spend? A plastic one isn't great, however it will in all actuality do fine and dandy. The OXO Good Grips 15-by-21-inch adaptation is a fourth of the expense and an extraordinary worth.

With a wooden board, you'll need a little jug of mineral oil to rub into the surface with a delicate material or paper towel after each utilization to forestall finishing and upgrade its life.

FEELING SHARP

There isn't anything more disappointing than a dull blade. In addition to the fact that it makes prep work a task and your completed item less appealing, it's additionally tremendously risky. A dull edge requires more strain to cut into a food, and it can undoubtedly sneak off a hard onion skin, for instance, and into your finger. Oof. Most home cooks ought to hone their blades somewhere around double a year, substantially more regularly assuming they utilize their blades consistently. There are three approaches.

Technique 1: Use an Electric Sharpener. A decent quality electric sharpener is a choice, however I unequivocally beat their utilization down. For one thing, they eliminate a huge measure of material from your edge. Hone your blade multiple times, and you'll have lost a decent ½ centimeter of width, startling it and delivering any edge with a reinforce (i.e., most top notch fashioned edges) futile. Second, even the best models give just a sufficient edge. On the off chance that you wouldn't fret supplanting your blades at regular intervals and are content with the edge an electric sharpener gives you, this is a choice. Yet, there are vastly improved decisions.

Technique 2: Take It to a Professional. Given you have a decent blade sharpener close by and will pay to have the help played out, this is a decent choice. However, on the off chance that you hone your edges twelve or so times each year, as I do, this can get very costly. And everything except the best masters utilize a crushing stone, which will remove considerably more material than is needed from your cutting edge, diminishing its life expectancy. Need to fashion a more grounded relationship with your edge? Pick the following choice.

Technique 3: Use a Sharpening Stone. The best technique by a wide margin. Not exclusively will it give you the best edge, however it will likewise eliminate minimal measure of material. Moreover and I'm completely serious about the significance of this one-the demonstration of honing your own blade will assist you with making a lot more grounded bond with your edge, and a blade that is dealt with deferentially will act much better. You will have a hard time believing the distinction a sharp blade can makes in your cooking.

Stones are intended to either be greased up with oil or with water. I incline toward water stones.

Shopping and Maintenance

While purchasing a water stone, search for an enormous one, somewhere around 2½ inches wide and 8 inches long and an inch thick. Stones come in different coarseness sizes, going from around 100 up to 10,000+. The lower the number, the coarser the coarseness, and the more material it will remove your blade. The higher the coarseness, the more keen the edge you will get, however the more strokes it will take to get you there.

I suggest keeping two stones in your unit: one with a medium coarseness (around 800 or somewhere in the vicinity) to perform major honing position and one with a fine coarseness (no less than 2,000) to tune the edge to an extremely sharp completion. For genuine professionals, a stone with a ultrafine coarseness (8,000 or more) will leave a mirror-like completion on your sharp edge, however most cooks won't see the distinction regarding cutting capacity. Assuming you just have the spending plan or space for a solitary stone, I'd suggest one with a coarseness somewhere in the range of 1,000 and 1,200. Two-sided stones are additionally accessible (coarse and fine coarseness), however these are as a rule of substandard quality. You will likewise require a stone fixer to fix any lopsidedness in the outer layer of your honing stones. I've yet to go farther down the dark hole to buy a stone fixer. The two stones and fixers are accessible through Amazon.com.

Cautiously dry your stone after each utilization, and store it enveloped by a kitchen towel in a dry, oil free climate. Oil can douse into the permeable material, demolishing its honing capacity (and your opportunities to at any point cut your onions dainty enough for that soup). Also, once more, make sure to sharpen your blade on a steel each time you use it. While this cycle will not really take any material off the cutting edge (see here), it will assist with keeping the sharp edge adjusted, making cutting and dicing a lot simpler.

Bit by bit: How to Sharpen a Knife

Stage 1: Work in Batches. Despite the fact that it merits the work, blade honing can require a touch of exertion and time. Assuming you will set up a station to hone a blade, think ahead and hone each blade that might require honing to finish the entire cycle in one meeting rather than a few.

Stage 2: Soak Your Stone(s). While working with water stones, it's fundamental to lower them in water for somewhere around 45 minutes prior to utilizing. On the off chance that the permeable stone isn't completely soaked, it will dry out during honing, making the blade edge catch and giving your edge scratches and dings. On the off chance that you have two, douse both your stones, as well as your stone fixer.

Stage 3: Set Up Your Station. Put your stone on a towel laid on a cutting board. Keep a holder of water close by to keep your stone dampened during the honing system. The stone ought to be arranged with a short end corresponding to the edge of the counter.

Step 4a: Begin the First Stroke. Hold your blade with the sharp edge pointing away from you. Put the impact point of your blade on the furthest edge of the stone and, holding the sharp edge delicately however immovably with two hands at a 15-to 20-degree point and utilizing even tension, gradually drag the blade over the stone toward you down its length while at the same time moving the blade so the contact guide moves to the tip of the cutting edge.

Step 4b: Maintain the Angle. Be mindful so as to keep up with the 15-to 20-degree point as you threaten to use the blade across the stone. Tension ought to be firm yet delicate, and the cutting edge ought to coast flawlessly across the stone.

Stage 5: Repeat. Each stroke ought to wrap up with the tip of the blade contacting the base edge of the stone. Lift the blade, reset the heel at the top edge of the stone, and rehash.

Stage 6: Look for Silty Water. As you rehash the cycle, a slight film of silty-looking water should gather on top of the stone and on the sharp edge. This grating fluid will steadily take material off the edge of your blade, honing it.

Stage 7: Check for Burr. As you keep on rehashing strokes on the main side, a little burr will ultimately frame on the opposite side of the cutting edge. To check for it, put the sharp edge on your thumb and pull it in reverse. Assuming burr has framed, it ought to get marginally on your thumb (with truly fine-coarseness stones, however say, 2,000 or above, you won't feel it). It might take more time to 30 or 40 strokes before a burr structures, and that is the sign that you ought to switch and begin honing the opposite side.

Stage 8: Start Sharpening the Second Side. Turn the blade over so the edge is highlighting you. Place the impact point of the cutting edge close to the foundation of the stone, again keeping a 15-to 20-degree point, then, at that point, tenderly push the edge away from you while at the same time hauling it across the stone toward the tip.

Stage 9: Repeat. Your stroke ought to end with the tip of the edge against the top edge of the stone, actually keeping a 15-to 20-degree point. Dampen your stone between strokes assuming that it starts to dry out. Rehash for however many strokes as it took more time to shape the burr on the primary side. Flip the blade back finished and rehash stages 4 through 8, utilizing increasingly few strokes for each side, until you are down to one. (The cutting edge won't frame a burr during this stage.)

Stage 10: Fix the Stone. After rehashed use, your stone will start to foster notches in it, which can decrease its honing power. To fix it, utilize a low-coarseness stone fixer. Place the fixer level against the stone and push it this way and that to crush down the stone and make another level surface.

Stage 11: Clean Up. You ought to have a committed towel for this reason, as the coarseness from the stone won't ever come out. After completely drying the stone (permit to dry on a rack for at minimum daily), store it enclosed by its towel.

Stage 12: Hone and Test Your Blade. In the wake of honing, sharpen your cutting edge on a sharpening steel to get the edge in arrangement, then test it for sharpness. Certain individuals prescribe attempting to cut a piece of paper in half by holding it up and slicing through it. I observe that even a generally dull blade will breeze through that assessment yet fall flat at other kitchen assignments. The best test is to just utilize the blade to prepare a vegetable. Do you see any opposition, or does it fly through that onion? Would you be able to cut a ready tomato thin to the point of perusing it? Indeed? Then, at that point, you're finished!

MY KNIFE KIT

Need to find out about the basics for good cooking? This is my blade unit, the apparatuses I take with me at whatever point I branch out into an unfamiliar kitchen. These are the things I need to ensure I have available constantly.

Top line: sharpening steel; center column: little offset spatula, Y-formed vegetable peeler; base line, from left: Western-style gourmet expert's blade, serrated bread blade, santoku blade, sheep's foot paring blade and wine key, boning blade, adaptable fish spatula, wooden spoon, elastic spatula, microplane grater.

FUNDAMENTAL SMALL ELECTRIC TOOLS

The fact that you totally need makes there no lack of fun devices for the kitchen, yet there a not many. Here is your fundamental starter unit, in plunging request of significance. Notice that the three most significant things on this rundown are instruments utilized for estimating. That isn't a mishap.

1. Moment Read Thermometer

This is all there is to it, parents: the one thing that beyond what some other buy you can cause will to truly reform your cooking (particularly assuming you frequently cook, or have at any point been anxious about cooking, proteins). A decent moment read thermometer is the best way to guarantee that your dishes, steaks, chops, and burgers come out that ideal medium-intriguing without fail. Disregard jabbing meat with your finger, depending on mistaken planning guides, or the scratch and-look strategy. Purchase a top notch computerized moment read thermometer, and never serve a piece of over-or half-cooked meat again.

The Splash-Proof Super-Fast Thermapen by ThermoWorks has a powerful sticker price ($86), yet it's cash very much spent. It's far superior to the opposition, with a shocking scope of - 58° to 572°F (- 50° to 300°C), one-10th of a degree accuracy, unrivaled exactness, and a read season of under three seconds. As a result of its wide reach, you won't require separate meat, candy, and profound fry thermometers-a solitary instrument does each of the three undertakings, and how.

Beside my blades, it's my number one piece of unit. For the best economical model, which is increasingly slow challenging to utilize yet completely functional, look at the CDN Pro Accurate Quick-Read Thermometer ($16.95).

2. Advanced Kitchen Scale

On the off chance that you're wavering about regardless of whether you want a kitchen scale, leap to here, "Weight Versus Volume," and read that segment. Alright? See the reason why you have any actual desire for a computerized scale? When I got one, I've utilized it pretty much each and every day. A decent advanced scale will make mistakes and irregularities a relic of past times. Furthermore, assuming you're the fanatical kind, a scale can likewise assist you with sorting out how much dampness your chicken lost during cooking, or precisely how far you've decreased that stock. Yahoo!

Things to search for in a decent scale: something like 1-gram (⅛-ounce) precision; a limit of no less than 7 pounds; a tare (zero) work; estimations in both measurement and majestic units; an enormous, simple to-understand show; and an overlap level plan for capacity.

The OXO Good Grips Food Scale with Pull-out Display ($45.95) has got all of that, in addition to a slick take out show that permits you to peruse estimations easily, in any event, while weighing huge, massive things that would somehow or another dark the screen. The main issue? Irritating parts in the presentation rather than decimal spots. Who in the world needs to gauge ⅜ ounce? The Aquatronic Kitchen Scale by Salter ($49.95) misses the mark on pull-out-show highlight, yet it utilizes simple to-understand decimals, which makes both math and looking cool before Europeans a lot more straightforward.

In the event that you wouldn't fret portions or plan to go all measurement, then stay with the OXO (that is the thing I use). In any case, the Salter Aquatronic wins.

3. Computerized Timer/Stopwatch

Did you had at least some idea that in eatery kitchens, bread garnishes are the main thing generally copied by line cooks?§ I can't see you the times I've popped a plate of cut bread in the broiler for crostini just to haul it out thirty minutes after the fact after it sets off the smoke caution.

Basically I used to.

Nowadays, I keep a Polder 3 of every 1 Timer, Clock, and Stopwatch ($13.95) around my neck consistently. It has a simple to-understand show, a subtle size, instinctive buttons, a boisterous alert, a magnet for taking advantage of the ice chest, and a nylon cord for keeping it around your neck, so it's basically impossible that you can disregard your broiling peppers, regardless of whether you leave the kitchen. With both count-up and count-down capacities, what more would you be able to need in a kitchen clock?

4. Submersion Blender

Truly? some of you may say. You'd truly say that your inundation blender is a higher priority than your food processor or blender? Indeed, in the event that you rate significance by recurrence of purpose, totally. I utilize my submersion blender so much of the time that I have it mounted on a holster on the divider right close to my oven and cutting load up, prepared immediately to emulsify a sauce, prepare a cluster of mayonnaise, generally puree a few entire canned tomatoes straightforwardly in the pot, mix a cheddar sauce, puree soup, whip cream in a matter of moments . . . you understand everything. It's an adaptable apparatus, and you needn't bother with a senseless infomercial from the 1980s to let you know that.

Need a pitcherful of margaritas? The standard blender's your companion. Need to make two quarts of pesto? Alright, take out the food processor. Be that as it may, for more modest, regular mixing assignments, a submersion blender is the device for the gig. At any point get irritated at those ropy bits of egg white you go over while breading food? Mix the eggs for a couple of moments, and they'll be entirely uniform and smooth. You like foam on your hot cocoa? Heat it up in the pot and buzz it to make a lavish froth. Bumps in your béchamel? All gone. What about if you have any desire to make only a couple of ounces of entirely smooth cauliflower puree or a half-cup of mayonnaise? That's right, you can do that with a drenching blender as well.

The Braun PowerMax, which is just about $30, has been performing splendidly no less than three times each week in my kitchen for the beyond eleven years now. It's the most dependable companion I know. Sadly, it's not generally accessible nowadays, as I figured out while loading the kitchen at the Serious Eats World Headquarters. So there we utilize the KitchenAid Immersion Blender (about $50), which works similarly as well. You can get it as a feature of a bundle that incorporates a whisk connection and a small scale food processor, however accept me, those are dust authorities and you don't require them.

5. Food Processor

At an absolute minimum, a decent food processor ought to have the option to:

- Finely slash dry fixings like nuts and bread scraps. To do this, a processor should have a simple to-utilize beating activity and an engine that stops and starts on a turn.

- Generally puree vegetables for things like marinades, plunges, and rural soups (for all out perfection, utilize a standard blender). Bowl shape, power, and edge configuration all influence how well a processor can achieve this. It should likewise not spill.

- Grind meat. Shy of a committed meat processor or a connection for a stand blender, the food processor is the most ideal way to crush new meat. Meat can be difficult to hack, so an extremely sharp cutting edge and strong engine are essential.

- Effectively structure emulsions while making sauces like mayonnaise or a light vinaigrette. Bowl configuration can influence the manner in which the sharp edge connects with fluids.

- Massage bread batter rapidly and productively. This is the most-substantial kitchen assignment of all, and the processor's adequacy depends for the most part on the force of the engine.

I additionally prefer to have essentially a 11-to 12-cup-limit processor, which makes crushing meat and making mixture a lot more straightforward. A few models accompany a smaller than usual prep bowl that can be embedded into the fundamental bowl for little errands. These are adorable yet basically futile. Anything the minuscule bowl can do, I can do with a blade. That might take somewhat longer, yet assuming you consider the time it takes to wash the edge, bowl supplement, and cover, it's no challenge.

There's additionally no utilization for a processor that will get gummed up or stuck each time it hits a hard nut or tacky batter. Especially inclined to disappointment are models with a side-mounted engine that drives the cutting edge by means of a belt. Fizzling at even the most straightforward of undertakings, those processors do not merit the container they come in. All things being equal, search for models with a strong state engine connected straightforwardly to the cutting edge shaft, with no mediator belt or chain. These occupy some additional room with regards to tallness, on the grounds that the engine should be set under the processor bowl, however that is a simple compromise.

The two best processors that fit this rules at a sensible cost are the KitchenAid 12-cup Food Processor ($199.95) and the Cuisinart Prep 11 Plus 11-cup Food Processor (about $165). Also, at such comparative costs (in fact significantly more costly than numerous pointless models), everything comes down to bowl plan, and in this classification, the Cuisinart wins: it has a bigger feed tube, as well as straight sides that guarantee that all your food falls down into the edge. For reasons unknown, the KitchenAid has inclining sides. Fixings can ride up the sides all the more effectively and may not be cleaved or emulsified appropriately.

6. Stand Mixer, with Meat Grinder Attachment

A decent stand blender is a genuine workhorse for any individual who heats more than sporadically. While choosing one, there are a couple of models that I search for:

- It ought to have a batter snare connection and an engine sufficiently strong to blend something like 2 pounds of bread mixture without stressing, shaking, or wearing out.

- It ought to have a whisk connection to whip cream and to whip egg whites rapidly and proficiently into foamy meringues and froths.

- It ought to have an oar connection to cream spread and sugar easily, as well as quickly take care of pureed potatoes and frankfurter blends.

- It ought to highlight planetary movement, meaning the whisk connection twirls around its pivot in one course and circles around the work bowl the other way, to expand contact and blending power.

- It ought to have a port for connections like a meat processor or pasta creator.

Yet again similarly likewise with food processors, the incredible fight for kitchen prevalence (essentially for the home purchaser) comes down to KitchenAid and Cuisinart. Notwithstanding the way that numerous makers gloat their engine wattages in their publicizing (for example, Cuisinart does a one next to the other examination of their 800-watt SM-55 blender versus the 325 watts of the KitchenAid Artisan), these numbers mean very little. Inside a given maker's item setup, it is a sign of how strong the engine will be, however the wattage is really the power consumed by the blender, not the power delivered by the engine. It's an advertising contrivance, straightforward as can be. Given a decision between two engines that perform similarly well (say the 325-watt engine of the KitchenAid Pro 500 versus the 800-watt engine of the Cuisinart SM-55), it's smarter to pick the one with lower wattage and save money on power.

Both the KitchenAid and the Cuisinart have a meat processor connection accessible, an outright should in my kitchen. It sets aside cash and creates boundlessly better outcomes for burgers, wieners, meatballs, and meat portions. Here, the Cuisinart's all-metal Large Meat Grinder Attachment ($128.95) enjoys an upper hand over KitchenAid's plastic-and-metal Food Grinder Attachment ($49.95). However, at the cost of the Cuisinart connection, you could purchase an all out devoted meat processor. The KitchenAid processor has served me fine for a really long time.

While either brand will do you competently, the KitchenAid Pro 500 ($299.95) gets my decision in favor of wedding-vault need numero uno. Ideal for both hard core dough punchers make bread several times each week and need a genuine force to be reckoned with and for the people who will be generally blending players, whipping cream, or in any event, crushing meat.

7. Strong Blender

There are a huge load of respectable blenders available undeniably more than great stand blenders or food processors. On the other hand, there are additionally a huge load of unfortunate blenders out there. You need a blender that is adequately strong to puree soup to a totally smooth, smooth surface, with enough vortex activity to completely blend a thick blue cheddar dressing or squash a pitcherful of ice for frozen drinks. You likewise need a blender with straightforward, straightforward controls; the capacity to beat; and the ability to gradually and equally develop from a sluggish speed to a quick one, to keep the cover from brushing off when you mix hot food varieties excessively quick. (Lift your hand on the off chance that you've done this. That's right, thought so.)

The best of the best with regards to blenders, the one that will transform your shoes into soup or terrify the fat child in The Goonies, the one that will turn all your cheffy foodie companions spinach-green with envy, is one from the Vitamix Pro Series. This is the very thing each expert kitchen I've at any point worked in has utilized, and not surprisingly. It's incredibly strong, has an exceptionally enormous limit, and is fabricated like a stone. They get started at around $450 and up, putting them immovably out of the scope of most home cooks. Almost as great and way cooler looking is the BlendTec, which, for around $400, will divert everything from a carrot to a standard Alpine ski into dust. (Try not to trust me? Simply Google it. Truly, it's an extraordinary video.)

For a blender that won't burn through every last cent, I'd go with the KitchenAid Vortex 5-Speed Blender (around $150). It has a simple to clean wide polycarbonate pitcher and a sharp edge that makes a sufficiently large vortex that I can mix a full clump of cheddar sauce for Cheesy Broccoli Casserole (here) in one do without it gumming up.

8. Rice Cooker

There could be no more straightforward, more idiot proof method for cooking rice and different grains than in a rice cooker. Without a doubt, you can cook rice in a pot, cautiously checking the fire, trusting that you've added the perfect proportion of water and that your rice isn't consuming on the base, and taking it off the hotness at the perfect second, however assuming you're in any way similar to me, you've consumed one an excessive number of bunches to object with that technique any longer. With a rice cooker, you simply add your rice and water, shut the cover, flip the switch, and go, with the additional benefit that it'll keep the cooked rice (or other grain) hot for a really long time.

Indeed, even the least expensive rice cooker will do-I had a $25 model I got in Chinatown that endured me all through school and a decent five years thereafter. Whenever I got hitched, I moved up to an extravagant jeans model with a fluffy rationale processor¶ and a clever hooking top that keeps the dampness level inside at the specific right level. I love my rice cooker nearly however much I love my moment read thermometer, which is only a hair more than I love my significant other (simply joking, honey).

FUNDAMENTAL KITCHEN HAND TOOLS AND GADGETS

An all around supplied summer home most likely has a few drawers worth of devices, of which just half are even recognizable and maybe three or four are at any point utilized. Coming up next is a rundown of devices that you'll utilize constantly. Get them.

1. Utensil Holder

Priorities straight: assuming your apparatuses are at the rear of a cabinet, you presumably won't utilize them. Furthermore, on the off chance that you don't utilize them, you likely won't cook as regularly. Also, in the event that you don't cook, why bother living, truly? An utensil holder with a limit of something like 2 quarts assists keeps your devices convenient right where you with requiring them. Assuming that style is the thing you're later, Le Creuset makes attractive fired models in an assortment of tones for around $25. On the off chance that, then again, unadulterated usefulness is your objective, any old little can will do. I utilize a $5 metal form from IKEA.

2. Seat Scraper

A seat scrubber is one of those apparatuses whose benefits aren't clear until you begin utilizing it consistently. I keep one on my cutting board while I'm accomplishing prep work. It rapidly moves hacked mirepoix to my pot or carrot strips to the junk. I use it to separate batter while making pizzas, or ground meat while making burgers. For cleanup, a seat scrubber takes care of batter scraps that have dried onto the work surface, and it productively gets smidgens of slashed spices and other garbage. (Incidentally, you ought to never utilize the edge of your blade to lift this stuff up off your board. It's risky, and it will quickly dull the edge of your blade.) A seat scrubber likewise makes eliminating stickers from glass jugs or names from plastic holders a snap.

With its agreeable handle, tough development, advantageous inherent 6-inch ruler, and an edge adequately sharp to unpleasant cleave vegetables, the OXO Good Grips Pastry Scraper ($8.99) is the best option for home kitchens. In my blade unit, in any case, I keep a lightweight plastic C. R. Producing scrubber (50 pennies), which performs the greater part of those capacities for a portion of the expense, in a significantly more minimal bundle.

3. Saltcellar and Pepper Mill

How could anybody require a saltcellar? Underseasoning food is the most well-known culinary bumble. Ask me for what reason your food tastes blander than you'd like it to, and 90 percent of the time, all it needs is a little touch of salt. Having a holder of a salt in a conspicuous spot by your prep station or oven fills in as a steady suggestion to prepare, taste, season, and taste again until you get it spot on. I ensure that on the off chance that you don't as of now make them put, a saltcellar on your counter will make you a superior cook. Any wide-mouthed covered compartment with a simple open top will do, yet a committed saltcellar does it with style. Mine is a wooden occupation with a flip-top cover to forestall residue, water, or oil from getting in.

Also, pepper? Assuming that you've been utilizing preground pepper, help yourself out and purchase an economical container of pepper with an underlying factory. Then taste the new ground stuff next to each other with the preground. Which could you rather be putting on your food? In the event that that doesn't persuade you to go out and get yourself a pepper factory, I can accept that you are dead from the tongue up.

You'll need to put resources into a factory that has a strong metal crushing component. Modest ones are typically made of plastic and will quit crushing following a year or less of standard use. In spite of the fact that $35 to $60 could appear to be a major load of cash, a genuine pepper plant will further develop basically every appetizing food thing you cook. Peugeot is the Rolls-Royce of pepper plants. Impeccably created, sumptuously styled, and magnificently proficient, these plants look great and drudgery like a fantasy. They additionally run vertical of $55. More reasonable and similarly great assuming that absolutely utilitarian is the Unicorn Magnum Pepper Mill ($36.90). It has an intense nickel-plated crushing system, a simple to-stack plan, and a fast toil size change screw.

4. Prep Bowls, everything being equal,

Here is a mantra for yearning culinary specialists: A methodical kitchen is a decent kitchen.

Isn't it irritating attempting to hack carrots on your cutting board when that little heap of parsley in the corner is hindering you? For sure about wildly attempting to gather up the hacked ginger to get it into that pan fried food in the works before your bok choy withers? I utilize a few prep bowls with a little limit (we're talking 1-cup or less) basically every time I cook to keep slashed aromatics, estimated flavors, ground cheddar, whatever, off my load up, inside simple reach, and coordinated. This is the very thing extravagant cooks call their mise en place. In the cupboard straight over my cutting board, I two or three dozen quarter dollar ceramic topping and cereal dishes from IKEA for this very reason. (If you have any desire to go extravagant, you can get sets of Pyrex clear glass prep bowls.)

Enormous blending bowls are similarly significant. While the all-glass ones gaze pleasant upward on the rack, they're an all out pain to work with. I recollect numerous days at Cook's Illustrated magazine when we'd need to look through endlessly heaps of glass bowls while dealing with a photograph shoot to observe the a couple of that weren't chipped on their edges. Where do these glass chips end up? On the floor? In the food? In my own kitchen, I'd prefer not to find out. Plastic dishes appear as though a sensible arrangement until you understand that plastic retains the two stains and scents from sleek and different food sources. Pour a clump of olive-oil-and-margarine based marinara sauce (here) into a white plastic bowl, and you'll track down that you're presently the glad proprietor of an orange plastic bowl.

All things considered, I utilize modest hardened steel bowls that I got from a café supply store (in the event that you don't have a decent one close to you, attempt the ABC Valueline brand from amazon.com). I have about six in sizes going from a few quarts up to 5 quarts. They're lightweight and simple to deal with, shatterproof, stainproof, breakproof, odorproof, and microwavable.# Add to that their shallow plan, which makes whisking and throwing a snap, and you've done made yourself another dearest companion.

5. Wooden Spoons

Shy of being conceived a lady in Italy and trusting that your girl will have a kid, nothing causes you to feel more like an Italian grandma than gradually and intentionally mixing a lethargically stewing pot of ragù with a wooden spoon. Blood runs profound between a decent spoon and his cook. I almost cried the day I broke the idea about the spoon that had endured me through nine years and thirteen unique kitchens-a level headed beechwood model that I think I took from my mom's secret optional utensil cabinet. It was so very much utilized that the handle had adjusted to the state of my hand, and the head had been worn into a point that impeccably fit the edges of my Dutch broiler.

Whether mixing sauces, tasting soups, or tenderly whacking saucy companions who upset you in the kitchen, a wooden spoon is the instrument you'll need 90% of while you're cooking on the burner. I have about six of different shapes and sizes that I utilize pretty much every time I cook. In any case, assuming I needed to pick a solitary spoon to play out each errand, I'd pick one with a measured segment for tasting and a head that comes to a point, as opposed to being totally round, making it more straightforward to get into the sides of pots and dish.

Whether you need a spoon with a totally level segment on the head or a more three-sided profile is absolutely dependent upon you. Like my number one Beatles collection, my #1 wooden spoon will in general waffle to and fro among the various spoons in my set.

6. Opened Flexible Metal Spatula

Adequately adaptable to flip delicate bits of sensitive fish without breaking them yet solid enough to triumph ultimately every single piece of a crushed burger off the lower part of your skillet, an opened metal fish spatula is a flat out fundamental in your tool stash. It's great for smudging abundance oil off cooked steaks and hacks. Simply get the meat from the skillet and put it on a paper towel, still on the spatula, then move to the serving plate-the wide spaces permit the oil to deplete off without any problem. The spatula is lightweight and flexibility enough to flip delicate eggplant cuts in a skillet of oil, however it will likewise deal with entire barbecued pork slashes easily. Its slight adaptability loans it readiness and control, in contrast to stiffer spatulas (which have their spot in the kitchen-we'll get to that).

Furthermore, here's some uplifting news: the greater part of the costly models are very solid to do the occupation admirably. I keep a $25 Lamsonsharp model in my unit, and the much less expensive Peltex (around $15) is the norm in most café kitchens.

7. Utensils

A tough sets of utensils is like a heatproof expansion of your fingers. Powerful development, slip-confirmation holds (at any point attempt to get a couple of treated steel utensils with oily fingers?), a spring-stacked class-3 switch design,** and scalloped edges ideal for getting everything from delicate stalks of spring asparagus to the greatest bone-in pork cook are the characteristics to search for in a decent arrangement of utensils. The OXO Good Grips 9-inch Stainless Steel Locking Tongs ($11.95) set the bar for quality.

8. Microplane Zester Grater

While you're talking fine-toothed graters, essentially only one brand rings a bell: the Microplane Zester Grater ($14.95). It is something beyond a valuable contraption it's the main one to get.

My #1 thing to do with a zester is to get down to business with it on an orange and watch as the little pile of zing easily develops on my cutting board. Stand by my #1 thing to do is grind fragile wisps of Parmigiano-Reggiano over my Bolognese. No, I take that back. My #1 thing is to grind new nutmeg on top of my gin flip. Or on the other hand is it to sprinkle chocolate shavings over my soufflé? Gracious, yet I in all actuality do beyond a doubt cherish the exquisite little hill of ginger that smells quite beautiful as it tumbles off the zester into my bowl. No, I have it, and this time I'm certain: it's having the option to toss out my bewildered single-entrusting garlic press and utilizing my Microplane to grind garlic into small, even mince.

Such countless things to grind, so brief period!

9. Whisks

They're fundamental for blending fast bread hitters or emulsifying hollandaise. Utilize one in an enormous pot of soup to consolidate preparing considerably more rapidly than a wooden spoon can. What's more, a whisk is the best device to whip cream or froth egg whites into foamy meringue. Models with firm wires require substantially more development and difficult work from your wrist. The OXO Good Grips 9-inch Whisk ($8.95) has slender, adaptable wires, which make getting vinaigrettes ready an easily pleasant undertaking.

10. Salad Spinner

Indeed, it will get your greens dry, and we as a whole realize that dry greens are better at holding dressing (right?), yet the plate of mixed greens spinner is really one of the genuinely extraordinary multitaskers in the kitchen. I fill mine with water and pick spice leaves straightforwardly into the bowl. Whenever they're picked, I wash them around, lift them up in the crate, dump the sandy water, and twist dry.

You can wash sensitive things like berries and afterward dry them in a serving of mixed greens spinner fixed with a couple of layers of paper towels to expand their timeframe of realistic usability by a couple of days. Or then again take cleaved tomatoes for a twist for simple cultivating (the seeds fall through the container while the tissue waits). Washed mushrooms, cut peppers, broccoli florets-whatever you might consider pan-searing or sautéing-will cook better after an exhaustive drying in the spinner. Utilize the force of divergent power to whip away overabundance marinade from shrimp, chicken, or kebab meat. Also, assuming you have a solid one with little spaces, similar to the OXO's Good Grips Salad Spinner (about $30), there's compelling reason need to claim a colander-simply channel beans, pasta, and vegetables in the spinner crate.

11. Solid Spatula

My Due Buoi Wide Spatula (about $35) is extremely hot, in that for the most part non-romantic lifeless metallic article sort of way. It has a business end that is 5 inches long, a liberal size of 3.9 creeps at the front, and a heavy weight of 7.76 ounces. A size can't be bested sufficiently enormous to crush a bundle of hamburger into a 4-inch patty or several parts of cooking home fries, without being huge to the point that it doesn't squeeze into a little skillet. I've gotten an entire pizza off a hot stone with this thing. I might want to see your weak plastic spatula do that!

The edge and tang are framed out of a solitary piece of cast tempered steel, which times in at a thickness of 0.04 inch (1 mm, or around 18 measure). This is significant: it permits you to lift an entire turkey or rib cook with total surrender. Assuming you flip the spatula over, its sharp and strong front edge substitutes helpfully for a paint scrubber, permitting you to guarantee that every single piece of tasty, fresh outside stays immovably connected to your burger or steak, rather than staying in the skillet. The handle is produced using extreme, strong polycarbonate and highlights an end to end length, for ideal strength and equilibrium. This child will endure forever.

Also, there's a melodic reward: When struck gently against the cutting board, the spatula vibrates at unequivocally 587.33 hertz (truly!), with an exceptional hint series. Indeed, even Stradivarius would be pleased to apply his well known stain to it. It's the very thing during that all-too-normal circumstance when I frantically need to tune the fourth line of my guitar while applying cheddar to my burgers.

You'd be unable to track down a superior firm spatula.

12. Japanese-Style Mandoline

Of course, you can prepare for quite a long time and go through hours daily honing and sharpening your blades to reach the place where you can whip out fennel wisps so slim you can peruse them or cut through your prep work at 100 onions each hour. Furthermore, I'll be the first to let you know that you're ridiculously cool. In any case, for most of us, a mandoline deals with monotonous cutting and julienning errands. At a certain point in my life, I claimed an extravagant jeans $150 French model. Yet, guess what? It was weighty, cumbersome, and an undeniable irritation to clean. Furthermore, with its straight sharp edge, it didn't actually work effectively. The Benriner Mandoline Plus ($49.95), then again, highlights a sharp calculated edge that cuts significantly more proficiently than those abnormal straight edges or cumbersome V-formed cutters. Stroll into the kitchen of any four-star café in the city, and I ensure you'll find several Bennies (as they are warmly called by line cooks) involving a conspicuous spot.

Irregular random data: "Benriner" signifies "Gracious, how convenient!" in Japanese (regardless of the way that the Japanglish on the container front declares "Dry cut radishes additionally OK.")

13. Insect

An insect/skimmer achieves nearly all that an opened spoon does, and better, for a portion of the expense. It dominates at fishing dumplings, vegetables, or ravioli out of a pot of bubbling water.

Furthermore, its wire development and somewhat open lattice makes less disturbance in the fluid than a standard opened spoon, making it a lot more straightforward to fish out food.

Concerning the undertaking it was intended for-dunking and mixing food varieties for profound searing the main thing that even comes close as far as nimbleness and control is a long sets of chopsticks, and even Mr. Miyagi would experience difficulty getting peas from a pot of bubbling water with a couple of chopsticks. Wire-network insects with bamboo handles are accessible at most Chinese food merchants and café supply stores for a couple of bucks a pop, yet assuming you need something that will keep going quite a while, go with an all-metal bug like the Typhoon Professional Cook's Wire Skimmer, accessible for about $10 on the web.

14. Little Offset Spatula

However these modest 4½-inch-long spatulas are expected for applying icing to little cakes like cupcakes, you'll observe that they have a large number of different purposes in both the sweet and flavorful kitchen. At any point wind up attempting to unstick a delicate piece of food from a skillet with a spatula multiple times too huge? The dainty, adaptable sharp edge of a little balanced spatula can sneak by food things that even a fish spatula is excessively thick for. Skillet loaded with thin breakfast hotdogs to flip each in turn? This is your apparatus. It's additionally irreplaceable for plating and show. A lightweight vibe, agreeable handle, and ultrathin sharp edge make the Ateco Small Offset Spatula (about $2) the business standard, offering accuracy, control, and artfulness. More control implies less wreck and better-tasting food. Gracious, and it's really great for cupcakes also, assuming that is your pack.

15. Fine-Mesh Strainer

A regular colander is extraordinary assuming that you have a full pot of pasta to deplete, yet it seldom gets utilized in any case (and, surprisingly, then, I simply utilize the bushel of my plate of mixed greens spinner). For more modest regular errands like depleting a jar of tomatoes or beans, or guaranteeing that your crepe player is entirely smooth, a little hand sifter is what you want. I keep one holding tight a snare close by my pots and searches for gold access. Substandard models comprise of only a round network container connected to a handle, however the 8-inch Stainless Steel Strainer from OXO ($24.95) additionally has a circle of metal staying on the contrary side of the bin. This permits you to set the sifter over a bowl for no-gave activity. It might appear to be somewhat expensive for a basic sifter, however its substantial development implies it will endlessly endure.

16. Chopsticks

I just own it: this one is somewhat questionable. Possibly you grew up utilizing chopsticks and couldn't be gotten dead almost a pot of stewing water or a wokful of hot oil without them or you didn't-and, provided that this is true, you will presumably ponder, "Do I truly require them?"

Regardless, precise tips and a fragile touch will treat nearly nothing, delicate pieces of scorched or grilled food (say, a tempura of squash blossoms or thin stalks of asparagus on the grill) most certainly more softly than a by and large off-kilter sets of utensils, which are more qualified to enormous things like seared chicken or a rack of ribs. I go through chopsticks for picking pieces of food from a sautéed food in the works to taste for doneness. They are likewise great for choosing a couple of elusive noodles from a pot of bubbling water to ensure that they are impeccably still somewhat firm prior to depleting.

While standard chopsticks will do much of the time, high-heat applications require extra-long sticks made explicitly for cooking. Assuming you are sufficiently fortunate to have an East Asian kitchen supply store close by, you can pick these up several bucks a couple. Any other way, you can track down OK models on the web, similar to the Extra-Long Chopsticks from Hong Kong Imports Ltd. ($2).

17. Wine Key

Customary wine tools and $100 hare formed models will get your plug out, and quick. Be that as it may, with a little practice, a server's wine key will open wine containers (and brews) similarly as quick, and make you look limitlessly cooler. The key is to involve it as a switch. Assuming you are pulling on it hard, you're treating it terribly! I keep a couple in my cutlery cabinet (like pens and razors, they will generally stray into the world all alone now and again), as well as one in my blade unit.

18. Citrus Juicer

Each expert kitchen has its own initiation ceremonies, and as a youthful cook in-preparing, I got through a timeframe a decent eight months or somewhere in the vicinity when my first obligation each and every morning was to ream 24 limes, 24 lemons, and twelve oranges for new squeeze to use on the line during administration. Furthermore, the main device I was permitted to use to do the work (in case I risk being known as a weakling accept me, a weakling is the last thing you need to be in the macho universe of expert kitchens) was a wood lemon reamer from Scandicrafts, Inc. ($4). It was fourteen days before I could get done with the responsibility beginning to end without enjoying some time off to nurture my horrendously enlarged hands, and I went through four of the reamers over those eight months, gradually wearing them out until the scored edges on the business end were just about as smooth and delicate as waterway stones.

It is not necessarily the case that it's a terrible item I'd unequivocally suggest it for an intermittent juicer-however assuming you go through a great deal of citrus squeeze (certain individuals accept that lemon juice is all around as significant as salt, simply ask the Greeks!), there are various different choices available. I utilize the Two-in-One Juicer from Amco ($19.95). You place the citrus cut side down in the punctured cup-molded holder, then crush the handles together to remove the juice. It's quick, effective, and a lot simpler on the hands than an ordinary reamer. The main issue is that it some of the time abandons a touch of juice, driving you to physically crush the unfilled citrus shells for most extreme extraction. What's more, however it comes in little (green), medium (yellow), and enormous (orange) sizes, expected for limes, lemons, and oranges, the yellow one turns out great for the two limes and lemons, making it the one of a kind to get.

19. Cake Tester

I know numerous culinary experts and cooks who keep a cake analyzer got into the pen pocket of their whites and none who use them to test cakes. Not that you can't test a cake's doneness with them, it's exactly how could you, when there are so many really fascinating helped jabbing undertakings at which it dominates? Basically a weighty check wire with a handle, it's similarly basic as an instrument can get. The thought is that you stick it into the focal point of a cake and haul it out. In the event that it confesses all, the cake is finished. Along these lines, it's similar to a celebrated toothpick, yet the way that it's long and made of metal implies that it's valuable for a wide range of different things.

The clearest is trying the doneness of vegetables. Have you at any point been told to stick a paring cut into a bubbling potato to check assuming it's delicate the entire way through? The issue is that even the most slender of paring blades makes an enormous cut injury in the potato, delivering starch and immeasurably expanding the possibilities that it'll fall to pieces, especially assuming you've kicked up for those small, delectable fingerlings. A cake analyzer perfectly deals with that issue. Need to know whether those stewing carrots are sufficiently delicate to puree? What about assuming those child radishes are cooked through? With a cake analyzer, you can find out without leaving behind any implicating proof. My #1 method for cooking beets is in a firmly fixed foil pocket a technique that totally keeps you from jabbing them with a paring blade. A blade makes an opening in the foil too huge to even consider recuperating from. Not so a cake analyzer.

I utilize my cake analyzer rather than a fork to conclude regardless of whether my braising brisket or short ribs are "fork delicate." If the cake analyzer slides in and out easily, the meat is prepared. Loads of fish have layers between layers of tissue that just mellow at around 135°F or thereabouts (an ideal medium-uncommon). Stick your cake analyzer into that poaching salmon filet, and it if meets opposition (i.e., assuming it seems like punching through bits of paper), it's half-cooked. Grilling a pork shoulder low and slow? You can check assuming it's managed without losing any juices through the barbecue grates. At last, in the event that you ever (god prohibit!) wind up without your dependable thermometer close by, a cake analyzer is the following best thing. Stick it into the focal point of your meat and leave it there for around 5 seconds, then haul it out and hold it under your lower lip (a region especially touchy to warm). You'll know right away whether your steak is cool, warm, or hot in the middle. As precise as a thermometer? No. Great when there's no other option? Of course.

You can go full scale and pay the $5 for a cake analyzer from OXO, which has a grippy dark handle, yet you might risk being ridiculed for being too extravagant jeans. The cake analyzer from Fox Run ($1.29) is the least expensive I've viewed as on the web.

20. Heaps of Squeeze Bottles

I'm speculating a decent 80 percent of you have perused Anthony Bourdain's declaration of adoration to his crush bottles in Kitchen Confidential:

The key article in many gourmet specialists' shtick is the straightforward plastic crush bottle, . . . basically similar items you see at sausage stands, stacked with mustard and ketchup. Veil a lower part of a plate with, say, an emulsified spread sauce, then, at that point, run several concentric rings of more obscure sauce-demi-glace, or broil pepper puree-around the plate, and . . . drag a toothpick across the lines or rings.

Certainly, it's a decent instrument to have if obsolete, weary plating is your thing. Be that as it may, there are better motivations to possess a crush bottle than style. To be specific, they'll make you a superior cook and a superior eater.

Before crush bottles showed up in my kitchen, I'd eat servings of mixed greens maybe on more than one occasion per month, and just when I was facilitating a supper get-together. The problem of making a new cluster of vinaigrette only for me as well as my significant other was essentially excessively (disregard utilizing packaged dressing). Nowadays, I keep a few unique vinaigrettes all set in 12-ounce crush bottles in the refrigerator. Stick your finger over the top, give it a decent shake, spurt it onto your greens in a blending bowl, and blast: lunch is served. (To ensure that thick things like shallots or squashed nuts will not get found out in the tip, here and there you must clip off the tip of the container with a paring blade or a decent sets of kitchen shears.)

To the extent that fixings go, crush bottles are another lifeline. Indeed, you can fill them with the norms: mustard, ketchup, and mayo, and, obviously, you set aside cash by purchasing those things in mass rather than in individual squeezy compartments. They are additionally incredible for getting a good deal on a wide range of sauces and oils: I purchase olive oil, sesame oil, soy sauce, hoisin sauce, clam sauce, tonkatsu sauce, and Chinkiang vinegar (to give some examples) in large jars. Then, at that point, I simply store the jars far removed under the sink or in the wardrobe and top off my crush bottles on a case by case basis. It'll make within your fridge look all cool, coordinated, and cheffy also.

Need to set up an extravagant mixed drink party? Press bottles are your companion. Fill a major one with straightforward syrup, more modest ones with new pressed citrus squeezes or enhanced syrups. You'll be cleaner, neater, and more proficient, slicing the time it takes to make every mixed drink by a not-immaterial degree, and your visitors will wonder about how genius you look.

To the extent that getting them goes, don't bother getting extravagant. I two or three dozen at a Chinese eatery supply store. Amazon sells them for a couple of bucks each. Purchase about six and check whether they don't transform yourself to improve things.

Furthermore, better believe it, as Tony says, you can utilize them to make your plates all frou-frou on the off chance that you want.

{ The fundamental storage space }

The storage space is the foundation of your kitchen. Many starting cooks are scared by plans in light of the sheer number of fixings that should be bought whenever they first cook something. In any case, hotcakes are an advantageous food exactly on the grounds that they are produced using fixings you essentially consistently have close by. Envision purchasing flour, spread, eggs, buttermilk, baking powder, sugar, oil, and vanilla concentrate each and every time you needed to make hotcakes!

I like to keep an all around loaded kitchen, and, accordingly, my storeroom is an enormous one. I as of late totally purged my kitchen racks and fridge and revamped them, in the process inventoriing each storeroom thing I had into a solitary record that lives on the web, where I can get to it whenever to see the exact thing I need to work with. (What? Doesn't everyone do that?) I thought of 357 unique food things, including 8 sorts of salt and 63 distinct flavors (yowser!).

There's no requirement for you to keep a storage space that enormous, yet every kitchen ought to be supplied for certain rudiments. Here you'll discover a few hints on the best way to best utilize your fridge, as well as a rundown of fixings that will assist you with traversing the greater part of the plans in this book with just the need to buy transitory fixings new. I isolated it into refrigerated merchandise, baking supplies, grains, canned products, flavors, and what I call wet storage room things.

Refrigerated Goods

Like cells and clean clothing, a fridge is a unique little something that you never truly consider the significance of until it quits taking care of its business (like mine did last week)††. Arranging your cooler for greatest productivity concerning food time span of usability, sanitation, and simple admittance to the things you go after most-ought to be a main concern. It'll make all of your cooking projects speed up and all the more effectively, and having some good times in the kitchen unavoidably prompts seriously cooking. That is whats needed to say thank you in this book.

An ice chest is fundamentally only a major virus enclose with a couple racks it, isn't that so? Indeed, that is valid, however where you store food in the cooler can an affect its time span of usability. Most coolers have cold and problem areas, with temperatures that reach from 33° to 38°F or somewhere in the vicinity. By and large, the rear of the base rack, where cooler, heavier air tumbles to, and the rear of the first rate, nearest to the fan and condenser, are the coldest spots, while the center of the entryway is the hottest. How you coordinate your food in the ice chest ought to be founded on how cool it should be kept.

To begin with, a few fundamental tips on taking advantage of your cooler space consistently:

• Get an ice chest thermometer. There are various things that can make your refrigerator separate or lose power: electrical shorts or floods, stopped up ventilation, and so forth So conceivable even with your temperature dial acclimated to the right position, your ice chest may be far hotter than it ought to be. A basic dial thermometer assists you with observing things to guarantee that you're rarely trapped in obscurity.

• Move food to more modest holders. I keep a heap of half-16 ounces, half quart, and quart plastic shop holders to store practically all food whenever it's emerged from the first bundling. Air is the foe of most food sources and can expand their pace of decay. By moving them to more modest holders, you limit air contact, however you likewise assist with keeping your cooler coordinated and simple to explore.

• Name everything. When you move food into a more modest stockpiling compartment, name the holder, utilizing indelible marker on covering tape with the date of capacity, as well as what's inside. However much I advance great science, there are a few things that essentially do not merit trying different things with: making life inside your cooler is one of them.

• Forestall drippage. To keep away from wrecks and hazardous cross-pollution, consistently store crude meat-regardless of how very much wrapped-on a plate or a plate to get any dribbles.

• Keep fish extremely cold. It's ideal to utilize new fish right away, yet assuming you should store it, envelop it by plastic and sandwich it between two ice packs on a plate to guarantee that it stays at 32°F or colder until prepared to utilize. (Try not to stress on account of disintegrated solids in its cell structure, it won't freeze until well underneath 32°F.)

Where to Store Food in the Refrigerator

There are three superseding elements to think about while choosing what to store where in the cooler.

• Food handling is of most extreme significance. Ice chests keep food new for longer, however that doesn't imply that unsafe microscopic organisms can't duplicate to risky levels given sufficient opportunity. To limit risk, here's a guideline: the more probable the chance a food could make you wiped out and the higher the last temperature you plan to cook it to, the lower in the fridge it ought to be put away, both to keep it cooler and to forestall cross-tainting. For example, don't store crude chicken above extras from the prior night. Juices from the bird can trickle down inconspicuous, sullying your food.

• Temperature changes all through your cooler, with, as referenced prior, either the exceptionally back of the base rack or the rear of the best in class, close to the vent, being the coldest spot, contingent upon the model. For most extreme stockpiling life, your fridge ought to be set to hold a base temperature of 34°F in these spots. No piece of your cooler ought to transcend 39°F.

• Moistness assumes a part in the newness of vegetables. The crisper drawers in the lower part of your fridge are intended to keep new virus air from circling into them. Vegetables normally produce a touch of energy as they approach their ordinary energy cycles, warming up the space in the cabinet, consequently empowering it to hold more dampness. Wet air can assist with keeping vegetables from wilting or drying out. Most crisper drawers have a slider that controls the ventilation so you can change the dampness level inside the cabinet. The key is to boost it, up to simply beneath the point that dampness would fire beading up on the vegetables' surfaces.

To provide you with a thought of good cooler stockpiling association, permit me to take you on a little visit through my ice chest. This is what you'll typically track down there:

The Main Compartment

The Top Shelf

• Prepared to-eat arranged food varieties. Simmered red peppers, jolted tomatoes, a jar of white asparagus, sun-dried tomatoes.

• Prepared to-eat toppings that I don't utilize time and again. An assortment of Chinese bean and chile glues, curry glue, a half container of coconut milk, jars or containers of tahini, harissa, tomato glue, chipotles in adobo, olive tapenade, anchovies.

• Cured items. Dill lances and chips, bread-and-butter pickles, inclines, jalapeños, tricks, olives.

• Cooler amicable natural products like apples, oranges, berries, melons, and grapes.

The Middle Shelf

• Extras in fixed compartments. Extra macintosh and cheddar, a couple of bits of cooked chicken, my canine's food, braised asparagus, pizza sauce, salsa.

• Cheddar (in its unique bundling or enclosed by material and put away in a fixed baggie). A half hunk of goat's-milk Gouda, disintegrated Cotija, custom made American cheddar cuts, sharp cheddar, a major hunk of Parmesan, Gorgonzola.

• Eggs in their container. In the event that it requires you in excess of two or three weeks to go through a container of eggs, store them on the rear of this rack, where it's somewhat cooler to expand timeframe of realistic usability. If not, you can keep them in the entryway (regardless of everything anybody says to you). They'll save for at minimum half a month, even in this somewhat hotter climate.

• Cold cuts and sandwich bread. Martin's potato rolls, Arnold multigrain bread. Cut sandwich bread will keep fine in the refrigerator. Notwithstanding, lean breads like rolls or Italian-style breads ought to be put away at room temperature or in the cooler the fridge will advance staling.

The Bottom Shelf

• Crude meat and poultry, wrapped cautiously and on a plate. Ground meat, skirt steak, new pork midsection, Italian wiener.

• Crude fish, in its covering and put on a plate. I purchase my fish the day it will be consumed, and you ought to as well however see the tip here assuming you should store it short-term.

• Milk and other dairy items. Weighty cream, acrid cream, curds, cream cheddar, natively constructed crème fraîche, buttermilk.

The Vegetable Crisper

• Vegetables, put away in breathable plastic packs or plastic sacks with the tops left marginally open. Radishes, Broccoli, scallions, carrots, celery, cucumbers, asparagus, turnips

• Spices. Parsley, cilantro, chives, thyme, rosemary, basil (in the late spring). I wash and pick my spices when they return home, then store them moved up in soggy paper towels in plastic zipper-lock sacks.

The Fridge Door

The cooler entryway is the best spot to store every now and again utilized things and those that don't need the coldest temperature.

The Top Shelf

• Eggs-assuming you go through a container inside half a month.

• Margarine and habitually utilized cheeses. Cabot 83 unsalted margarine, modest Danish blue (love it on toast), Brie and other delicate cheeses. Margarine remains marginally gentler in the cooler entryway, which makes it more straightforward to spread on toast. Assuming you eat a great deal of cheddar, you should store it here also, so that it's not exactly as chilly when you snatch it.

The Middle Shelf

• Toppings in their unique bundling or in press bottles if hand crafted. Ketchup, stew sauce, a few sorts of mustard, hand crafted mayo, Japanese grill sauce.

• Premixed vinaigrettes in press bottles. Straightforward red wine vinaigrette, soy-balsamic vinaigrette.

The Bottom Shelf

• Drinks. Entire milk, newly pressed pineapple juice, pitchers of chilled faucet water, a periodic Cheerwine or Mexican Coke. Milk ought to go on a rack in the fundamental refrigerator compartment in the event that you don't utilize a lot, however for day to day consumers, the entryway is a fine spot for it, all things considered for juices, soft drinks, and so on

The Freezer

Everybody, obviously, keeps frozen meats and vegetables in the cooler, but at the same time it's a superb spot to store any hotness or light-touchy things that could go rank. In my cooler, beside meat and veg, you'll view as nuts (which can be toasted or squashed straight out of the cooler); relieved meats like salt pork, bacon, and guanciale; dried narrows leaves (I get them in mass); chicken stock frozen in 1-cup segments; bread morsels; additional margarine; yeast; hotdog housings; entire grain flours (they contain fats that can turn rotten at room temp); and new pasta, in addition to other things.

Here are a few hints for better cooler stockpiling:

• Keep your vents clear. Ensure you don't stack food against the air vents, or you'll strain the cooler, extraordinarily decreasing its effectiveness and viability.

• Move meat from its unique bundling. To forestall cooler consume as well as to freeze the meat as fast as could really be expected (the quicker it freezes, the less harm it will bring about simultaneously), move it to level impenetrable bundling. Best of everything is to utilize a vacuum-sealer like a FoodSaver, which will totally wipe out the chance of cooler consume. Next best is to wrap the meat firmly in foil, trailed by a few layers of cling wrap (cling wrap on its own will be air-penetrable), or to utilize a cooler pack intended for long haul stockpiling.

• Freeze level. Wide, level shapes freeze quicker and can be stacked more effectively than cumbersome bundles. Freeze meats in a solitary layer in vacuum-fixed bundles or cooler sacks. Not exclusively will this assist you with getting sorted out your cooler space, it'll likewise enormously eliminate thawing out time.

• Mark everything! All bundles ought to have the substance and date composed on them. No one gets a kick out of the chance to play the frozen-secret speculating game.

• Thaw out securely. The most effective way to securely thaw out meat is on a plate or a rimmed baking sheet in the fridge. Know that it'll presumably take more time than you suspect: permit for the time being for meager things like steaks, burgers, chicken bosoms, and such; as long as 2 days for meat and pork dishes or entire chickens; and up to 3 or even 4 days for enormous turkeys. In crises, more slender food varieties can be quickly thawed out by setting them in a bowl of cold water under a gradually running tap or, even better, put on an aluminum plate or container, which will rapidly send energy from the space to the food. Steaks will thaw out around 50% quicker on an aluminum plate than on a wooden or plastic cutting board. Turn them over each half hour or so as they defrost. Try not to attempt to thaw out enormous things quickly the gamble of hazardous microscopic organisms becoming on the outside before the inside thaws out is excessively incredible.

FUNDAMENTAL PANTRY INGREDIENTS

Cold Pantry

Here are the refrigerated things I have close by consistently:

• Bacon, section (will most recent a little while in the refrigerator, can be frozen for longer capacity)

• Margarine, unsalted (will most recent half a month in the cooler; I keep a couple of additional pounds in the cooler, where it will keep endlessly)

• Buttermilk

• Cheddar, Parmigiano-Reggiano

• Eggs, enormous

• Ketchup

• Maple Syrup, Grade A dim golden

• Mayonnaise

• Milk, entire or 2% (or then again, on the off chance that you should, skim)

• Mustard, Dijon

• Mustard, brown

Baking Pantry

Certain individuals are bread cooks, some are not. I wasn't conceived a cook, yet I've found that subsequent to getting sorted out my baking storeroom, making bread and baked good has become undeniably more pleasurable for me. I used to store my flours and such in their unique sacks in a bureau. To prepare something, I'd need to haul everything out, attempt and measure out of a paper sack with a restricted opening, lastly wind up collapsing the pack down, driving it to deliver a puff of flour that'd get all around my garments and kitchen. Baking was a task.

Then I chose to put resources into a few huge, sealable, wide-mouthed plastic tubs to store essential baking storeroom things like flours and sugar. This permits me to rapidly and effectively gather up as the need might arise without making a wreck. Nowadays, I make a lot a greater number of pizzas than I used to.

Every one of the things in the graph here ought to be put away in a cool, dry spot, first moved to a fixed holder if proper.

ENTIRE WHEAT VERSUS REFINED WHITE FLOUR

A bit of wheat is a really confounded thing, however, all things considered, it tends to be isolated into three essential parts: the endosperm, the frame, and the microorganism. Entire wheat flour is by and large the thing it seems like-the whole grain from the wheat plant, ground up. Refined white flour contains just the dull, proteinaceous segments from the endosperm, with the entirety of the frame and microbe eliminated. How could anybody need to do that? Everything unquestionably revolves around gluten development. We'll talk a considerable amount about gluten in this book, however for the present, all you want to know is that gluten is the stretchy grid of proteins that gives batters their adaptability. It's shaped when the proteins gliadin and glutenin, found in the endosperm, are combined as one within the sight of water.

White flour is brilliant at creating gluten, conveying breads that are cushy, chewy, and very much risen. Entire wheat breads, then again, will more often than not be thick and generally dry. This is on the grounds that ground-up segments of the body and microorganism act similar to small extremely sharp edges, cutting through the creating gluten and keeping individual strands from becoming excessively lengthy. You can substitute entire wheat flours in plans assuming you'd like, yet don't anticipate getting similar light, very much risen breads you'd accomplish with white flour.

ITEM	HOW LONG WILL IT KEEP?
Baking Powder	6 months to a year, depending on humidity; to test for activity, place a teaspoon in a bowl and add a teaspoon of water: it should bubble and fizz vigorously.
Baking Soda	8 months to a year
Cornstarch	Indefinitely
Dutch-Process Cocoa	1 to 2 years
Flour, all-purpose	Transferred to a sealed container up to a year
Flour, bread	Transferred to a sealed container up to a year
Gelatin, powdered	Indefinitely
Sugar, brown	In an airtight plastic bag, 3 to 4 months optimally—after that, it may harden; hard brown sugar can be restored by briefly microwaving.
Sugar, granulated	Transferred to a sealed container, indefinitely
Vanilla Extract	1 to 2 years
Yeast, instant (rapid-rise)	If possible, purchase in bulk and transfer to a sealed container; individual packets are harder to use and far more expensive. Keeps indefinitely in the freezer; if stored at room temperature or in the fridge, it will need to be proofed occasionally: add 2 tablespoons warm water and 1 teaspoon sugar to ½ teaspoon yeast and let sit for 10 minutes—it should produce foam. If not, replace.

Grains and Legumes

Grains and vegetables ought to be put away in a cool, dry spot. Beans will keep from a half year to a year, while normal pasta and white rice will endure endlessly. Entire wheat pasta and earthy colored rice will go malodorous after broadened capacity (typically 6 to 8 months): smell them prior to utilizing. On the off chance that there is any smidgen of an off-putting smell, dispose of.

- Beans, dried dark

- Beans, dried cannellini

- Beans, dried kidney

- Pasta, lasagna

- Pasta, short and holey (like elbows or penne)

- Pasta, long (like linguine or spaghetti)

- Rice, white or brown

Canned Goods

Canned products will endure endlessly, yet it's better not to open them to serious temperature changes.

- Anchovies, oil-stuffed: after the compartment has been opened, anchovies can be put away in a fixed holder under a layer of olive oil in the cooler for as long as a month; for longer capacity, roll up individual filets, move to a zipper-lock cooler pack, and store in the cooler. I use Ortiz or Agostino Recca brand.

- Chipotle chiles, stuffed in adobo sauce

- Dissipated milk

- Tomato glue: I purchase my tomato glue in tubes rather than jars so I can utilize just what is required for a formula, without figuring out how to store the overabundance.

- Tomatoes, entire canned. I use Cento brand.

Flavors and Salts

Do you have a jar of paprika or oregano in your kitchen that has been around since He-Man and MacGyver were as yet on TV? Help yourself out: toss it out. Flavors lose their flavor over the long run, in any event, when put away in fixed compartments out of direct daylight (as they ought to be). Entire flavors might save for as long as a year or so without critical flavor misfortune, however preground flavors will turn out to be perceptibly less tasty very quickly.

For the best flavor, you have two choices. The first is to purchase your flavors entire and in little clumps, supplanting them at regular intervals to a year or something like that. The option is to purchase entire flavors in mass, keeping limited quantities of them in containers in your zest rack and putting away the rest of vacuum-fixed pockets (like those for a FoodSaver-type vacuum-sealer) in a cool, dim spot or, ideally, in the cooler. Salt will keep going always, inasmuch as it's kept dry.

- Narrows leaves, entire (store in the cooler)

- Dark peppercorns

- Bean stew powder

- Cinnamon, ground

- Coriander seeds

- Cumin seeds

- Fennel seeds

- Nutmeg, entirety

- Paprika

- Red pepper, squashed

- Oregano, dried

- Wise, dried

- Salt, legitimate

- Salt, Maldon

Oils, Vinegars, and Other Liquids

Oils are the most delicate wet storage room thing in your kitchen. Put away severely, they can go malodorous inside a range of weeks. The adversaries of oil are hotness and light, and that implies that the manner in which a great many people store them-in clear containers near the oven is just about the most obviously terrible thing you can do. I store my cooking oil and ordinary extra-virgin olive oil in dim green wine bottles that I've washed and dried, fitted with modest pour spouts for the reason. They stay on my counter, far away from the window and the oven. The oils keep going for about a month in those compartments before I top off them.

I keep costly extra-virgin olive oils in their unique holders in a dim bureau, where they will keep going for around 2 months. Keep in mind, it's an exercise in futility to have incredible olive oil on the off chance that you don't utilize it before it begins to lose flavor or go rank. I've realized this the most difficult way possible. Olive oil's for eating, regardless of how costly it is. Eat it.

- Honey, clover

- Marmite, Vegemite, or Maggi Seasoning

- Molasses, customary

- Oil, canola (for sautéing)

- Oil, extra-virgin olive (for enhancing)

- Oil, nut (for profound browning)

- Soy sauce (on the off chance that you won't go through a container in somewhere around 2 months, store it in the cooler). I use Kikkoman brand.

- Vinegar, juice

- Vinegar, balsamic (grocery store)

- Vinegar, refined white

- Vinegar, white wine

WHICH SALT SHOULD I USE?

Nowadays you see a bigger number of sorts of salt on general store racks than there are apparatuses under Inspector Gadget's overcoat. However, there's one in particular that you totally need in your kitchen: genuine salt. I use Diamond Crystal brand since I like the size of its grains. In case it wasn't already obvious, fit salt isn't called legitimate in light of the fact that it's OK to eat under Jewish dietary regulation all salt is genuine in that sense. Legitimate salt ought to be called koshering salt, in light of the fact that its huge grains proficiently draw blood out from tissue during the koshering system (which, coincidentally, makes it a very productive salt for dry-tenderizing inclining further toward that later).

Why utilize fit salt over customary table salt? Single word: sprinkling. Table salt is fine assuming you use it out of a saltshaker, yet you find out about how much salt you're really placing into or on your food assuming you add the salt with your fingers, and genuine salt is just more straightforward to get and apply that way. To apply an even layer of salt to your food, get a spot of fit salt, then, at that point, hold your hand high over the food prior to sprinkling it. Due to disturbance in the air, your salt will pour downward on your food in an example that shows a typical (ringer bend) dispersion from where you drop it. The higher you drop it from, the more even the appropriation.

Every one of the plans in this book were tried with Diamond Crystal genuine salt. In the event that you should utilize table salt, you ought to involve just 66% as much as is called for, as table salt packs all the more firmly into an estimating spoon (more often than not it's called for in sums excessively little to successfully gauge with a scale). In most exquisite plans, you'll have the option to taste the salt level as you cook, changing it to suit your own sense of taste. At whatever point suitable (for baking ventures, brackish waters, and so on), I've given salt estimations in weight.

Furthermore, what might be said about all the extravagant "architect" salts? The pink or dark ones? The grayish ocean salt from Guérande in France that comes in huge, damp bunches or the white pyramid-molded Maldon ocean salt from England? I have a negative behavior pattern of gathering them, somewhat on the grounds that they're pretty and I like the manner in which they look on my food, however generally to contend with my significant other's shoe assortment. (One new salt for every sets of shoes appears to keep her shopping propensity under control.)

Be that as it may, what are they really great for? These are on the whole completing salts, salts that are intended to be applied not long prior to serving or even at the table. In spite of cases in actuality, you'll find that flavorwise, there is practically no contrast between these salts and customary or fit salt. Disintegrate similar loads of the stuff into glasses of water, and they generally become basically indistinguishable. Their shape makes them fascinating the crunch and extraordinary eruption of, indeed, pungency that they give. Figure you could see the distinction? Go out and get yourself a container of Maldon ocean salt (the completing salt that I utilize most frequently), a case of fit salt, and a crate of customary table salt, then, at that point, place three indistinguishable cuts of ready tomato on a plate (or on the other hand assuming you like, three indistinguishable cuts of steak). Sprinkle a touch of table salt on the first and eat it. Then, sprinkle some fit salt on the second and eat it. Notice the distinction? Perceive what amount all the more effectively you can sprinkle the salt uniformly across the outer layer of the food? At last, sprinkle a couple of shards of Maldon salt on the last and eat it. Notice the snap of salt precious stones under your teeth and the going with eruption of flavor? That is the reason I keep genuine salt close to my oven and cutting board and an enormous gem ocean salt on my lounge area table

EGGS, DAIRY, AND
THE
SCIENCE
of
BREAKFAST
1

SOUPS, STEWS, AND
THE
SCIENCE
of
STOCK
2

STEAKS, CHOPS,
CHICKEN, FISH, AND
THE
SCIENCE
of
FAST-COOKING
FOODS
3

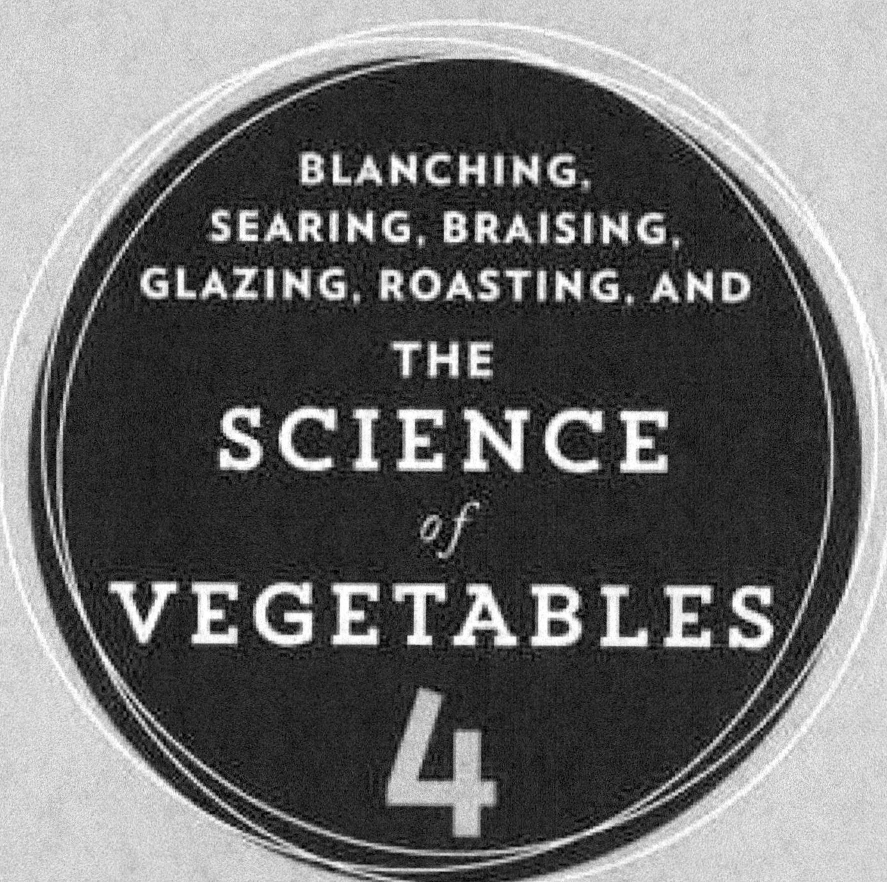
BLANCHING,
SEARING, BRAISING,
GLAZING, ROASTING, AND
THE
SCIENCE
of
VEGETABLES
4

BALLS, LOAVES,
LINKS, BURGERS, AND

THE
SCIENCE
of
GROUND
MEAT

5

CHICKENS, TURKEYS,
PRIME RIB, AND
THE
SCIENCE
of
ROASTS
6

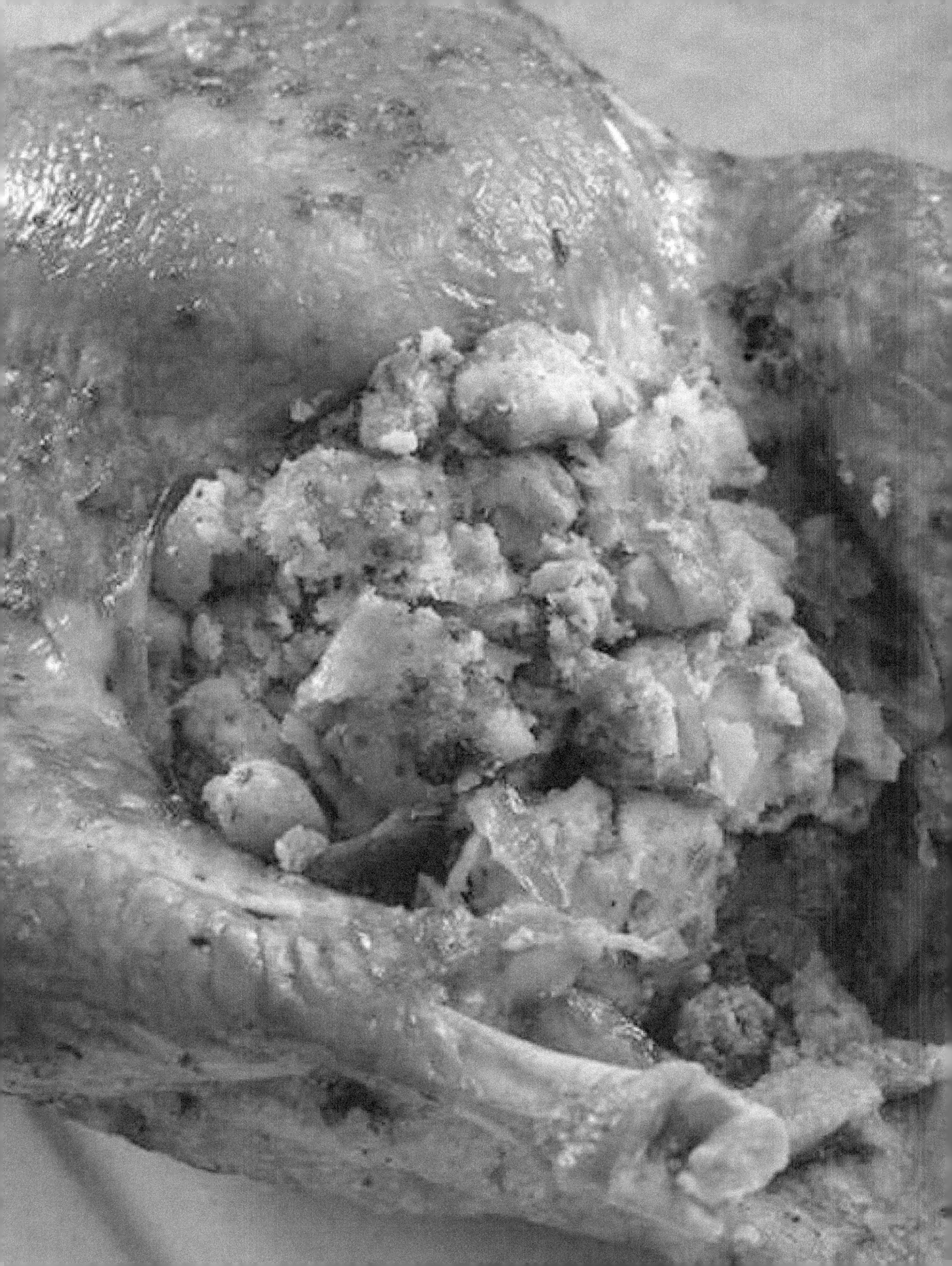

TOMATO SAUCE,
MACARONI, AND

THE
SCIENCE
of
PASTA

7

"Everything about is science. The best feeling is when you taste or eat it." – Alton Brown

GREENS,
EMULSIONS, AND
THE
SCIENCE
of
SALADS
8

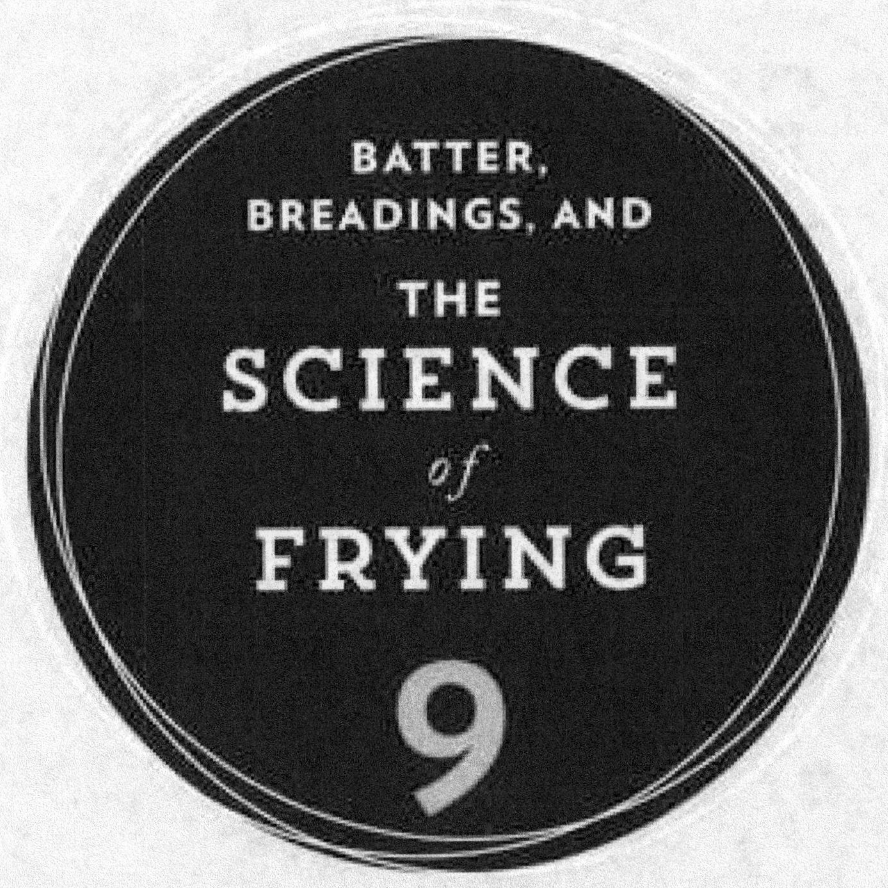
BATTER,
BREADINGS, AND
THE
SCIENCE
of
FRYING
9

"I couldn't care less assuming you're broiling canine s*&$. Assuming it emerges from the fryer, put some salt on it."- Ken Oringer

To Adri, who loves me notwithstanding the burgers;

To Ed, Vicky, and the entire Serious Eats group, for assisting me with doing my thing;

To my dad, the researcher;

To my granddad, the nutty teacher;

To the one sister I like better compared to the next;

To my mom, who might have favored a specialist;

To the next sister also;

To Dumpling, Hambone, and Yuba, the best taste-analyzers a man might at any point expect;

Also, to my grandma, who might have favored a Tostitos container.

My granddad was a natural physicist, my dad was a microbiologist, and I was a little nerdling.

I was never intended to be a cook. Simply ask my mother, she'll tell you. Specialist? Sure. Attorney? That's right I can contend with the best of them. Researcher? Most certainly. In 4th grade, we were given a task: compose a book about ourselves later on. I unmistakably recall my future life as indicated by my ten-year-old self. I'd be hitched at 24. I'd have my first child at 26. I'd get my PhD by 29 (how I'd figure out how to get my PhD while attempting to bring up a child was an inquiry I never posed to myself). By thirty, I'd find a solution for malignant growth, winning a Nobel prize. Having left behind a legacy, I'd go through the following forty years satisfying my obligations as the President of LEGOLAND before at last resigning and leaving the world a superior spot at the age of 87.

Grandiose dreams for sure, yet things appeared to be going on target all through secondary school. I did well in math and sciences (and especially ineffectively in English, to make things abundantly clear), spending my summers playing music (ambiance music camp, not band camp, much thanks!) or working in science labs. Did I at any point show a tendency to cook? Not actually. I took an after-school cooking class in 3rd grade, where I figured out how to simplify syrup and stone soup. My father prepared me in the craft of making open-confronted fish softens on Saturdays. He additionally showed me a significant illustration in how not to cut a square of frozen meat directly from the cooler into steaks-an important evening that incorporated the line, "Kenji, go get me the sledge," and closed with shards of blade all around the kitchen floor hamburger still as blocky as it at any point was.

My claims to fame all through secondary school were shabby guacamole and impeccably warmed frozen chicken potpies. The one time I endeavored in the kitchen, I delivered a group of my thought process were some really magnificent almond tuiles covered in chocolate and loaded up with raspberry jam. Being the hopeless heartfelt that I am, I'd sweat over them for my secondary school sweetheart for Valentine's Day, see? Transforms out she wasn't as into heartfelt geeks as I naturally suspected she was. I got unloaded on Valentine's Day, her father ate the tuiles, and my juvenile cooking profession was placed on rest.

The ideal opportunity for me to move up and ahead with my advanced degree at long last came, and I entered the Massachusetts Institute of Technology-that sanctuary of science where nerdfolk gather altogether to talk hertz and bytes and the normal understudy wears just 66% of a couple of shoes during winter (I cut down the normal).

For some time I fit right in, at long last at home among my kindred nerds, delighting in the interesting subculture and learning more than I'd at any point learned (for the most part about such logical riddles as unequivocally the number of bourbon and-Cokes it takes before the following morning's headache will keep you from going to a 11 a.m address). Yet, gradually a terrible reality occurred to me: I cherished science and science, however I abhorred working in science labs. It was the gradualness, all things considered, the many long stretches of testing that could at last uncover results that showed you were off-base from the start and would you be able to kindly recurrent those tests? I got fretful. I got irritated, and I did what all legends ought to do in a period of emergency: I took off.

Truth be told.

That late spring, I settled on the cognizant choice not to take one more occupation in a science lab. Here I was, in the prime of my childhood, pissing it away playing with pipettes and DNA sequencers. I put forth out fully intent on taking as nonacademic a task as I could. Waitering appeared to be a decent gig. Meet charming young ladies, eat great food, spend time with cooks, party consistently on the grounds that I don't need to appear for work until 3 p.m. Fundamentally, a quelled school child's fantasy. As it worked out, the main eatery I strolled into-an appalling Mongolian barbecue style joint in Harvard Square-wasn't needing servers, however it was frantically needing cooks.*

Without delaying, I endorsed on. Also, that was the start of the end for me. Like a head-injury patient who abruptly fosters a pristine character, something snapped the second my hand contacted a blade in an expert kitchen. I was at this point not in charge of my own predetermination. Since that day, since whenever I first wore that senseless baseball cap and the T-shirt that recognized me beyond all doubt as a Knight of the Round Grill (truly), I was a cook. It didn't make any difference to me that I didn't know anything about cooking and that my occupation for the most part comprised of flipping asparagus lances with my twofold fisted spatulas. I realized at that moment that I'd found how I planned to manage the remainder of my life.

I was covetous. I tore through each cookbook I could lay my hands on. Going to the ocean side? Disregard the Frisbee-I'm bringing Pépin. Companions making a beeline for a film? I'll be in the kitchen with my canine eared Chinese cookbook. I worked in eateries however much my class timetable would permit, compensating for absence of involvement in beast force and sheer resolve. Tragically, what with attempting to achieve a degree and a concluded absence of a cooking guide (the nearest I had was our organization gourmet expert, who was better at grunting coke off the piano than tourné-ing a potato), cooking for me was loaded up with a perpetual series of unanswered inquiries.

For what reason do I need to cook pasta in an immense volume of water? For what reason does it take such a ton longer to heat a potato than to bubble it? Why my hotcakes generally suck? What's more, what's truly in baking powder in any case? I made an agreement with myself without even a second's pause that when I was done with school, I'd at no point in the future do anything that I didn't appreciate doing. I'd go through my time on earth attempting to respond to these inquiries that so intrigued me. The way that cooks bring in almost no cash and work insane timetables I probably won't see my loved ones on siestas at any point in the future didn't dissuade me. I'd tracked down my energy, and regardless of whether it made me a homeless person, I'd be doomed on the off chance that I didn't follow it.

My mom didn't take the news well.

Certainly, I wrapped up my tutoring (in the long run graduating with a degree in engineering) while at the same time working parttime in eateries, and I gained some significant knowledge about great science en route (not even once did I lose my advantage in science itself-simply in the act of science), and subsequent to graduating, I began working for probably the best culinary specialists in Boston, yet to my mother, a cook was a cook was a cook. Cautiously plating an impeccably sautéed filet of striped bass with a caviar beurre blanc and adorable little tournéed radishes was the same as flipping burgers to her. (Incidentally, she was somewhat correct nowadays I find flipping burgers more intriguing than extravagant café food.)

At any rate, I pondered internally, working in these incredible eateries, I'll at long last have the responses I've been looking for.

Not really quick.

First day on the line, I was given an illustration in the customary twofold fry procedure for French fries: a dunk in low-temperature oil for a couple of moments, trailed by a second fry in high-temperature oil. My first inquiry would one say one was that I believed was clear to any independent person: assuming the motivation behind the principal fry is only to cook the potatoes the entire way through, as many individuals had told me, shouldn't it be imaginable rather to heat up the potatoes first until cooked through, trailed by a solitary fry?

The culinary specialist de cooking's reaction: "Em . . ., it very well may be conceivable, yet you simply don't make it happen. Try not to ask such countless inquiries, I lack opportunity and willpower to answer them all." Right as his response was, it was not really the zenith of academic feeling or logical request that I had expected. In all honesty, as an expert cook, and with the hours that went with the job, I had even less chance to seek after the solutions to the cooking questions I had, which were currently starting to mount like request tickets on a bustling Saturday night.

In this way, following eight years of working in cafés, I chose to move tracks: maybe formula advancement and distributing were the place where the responses lay. It wasn't long after I made this shift that my interest at last started to be satiated. As a test cook and supervisor at Cook's Illustrated magazine, I not just had the potential chance to begin addressing my inquiries, I was additionally paid to get it done! Here was a task that at last consolidated the main three of my four biggest loves: tasting extraordinary food, the logical quest for information, and the actual demonstration of cooking (my better half would be the fourth), and it was a really freeing experience. I found that by and large even in the best eateries on the planet the techniques that customary cooking information shows us are obsolete as well as once in a while absolutely off-base.

Then I moved back to New York City with my significant other and found some work far and away superior to the one I had at Cook's Illustrated. As boss innovative official at Serious Eats (www.seriouseats.com) and the creator of its well known "The Food Lab" section, I was at long last 100% allowed to do the exact thing I needed to do, investigate the inquiries I needed to investigate, test the things I needed to test, and cook the food I needed to cook. What's more, the most amazing aspect? Doing it for a local area of food sweethearts just as energetic and insightful about what they put in their mouths as I am.

Certainly, I procure my keep in various ways, and testing and composing plans is just a little piece of it. I push commas, I stick words together, I babble about pizza this or cheeseburger that on the web, I counterfeit my direction through a periodic irritating conference or socialize fest foodie occasion; hell, incidentally, I even compose a book occasionally. In any case, eventually, I'm a cook, and that is all I actually at any point needed to be.

Eggs and Beacon: Two perfect food

IS THERE ANY FOOD

SO PERFECT, SO COMPLETE, SO PROFOUNDLY SIMPLE YET STAGGERINGLY COMPLEX AS THE

EGG?

It's effectively the most flexible and valuable fixing in the storage space. Simply consider how you can manage eggs: You can eat them singed, mixed, delicate bubbled, hard-bubbled, poached, prepared, or transformed into an omelet. They make the breading adhere to your chicken parm. Their proteins can be set into a thick grid that thickens custards or whipped into a breezy froth that raises hitters. They can unite your meat portion without overloading it, or go about as culinary representatives, helping transform oil and water into a steady, velvety mayonnaise. This, and they come in their own helpful, simple to-quantify, simple to-store bundling for sure. They basically sell themselves.

Eggs are genuinely a wonder, and it's no big surprise that their culinary purposes are so changed. Simply think: given treatment and sufficient opportunity, a whole no nonsense animal can be framed from the substance of an eggshell. The beginning of life, the beginning of numerous plans. I can't imagine a superior subject with which to begin this book.

THE FOOD LAB'S COMPLETE GUIDE

TO BUYING AND STORING EGGS

At the point when I say eggs, I'm basically continuously alluding to chicken eggs, by a wide margin the most predominant sort of avian egg on the planet. In any case, are altogether chicken eggs made equivalent? Show improvement over others? What elements influence how they work in plans, and how might I make a point to get the best out of them? Here are the responses to that large number of inquiries from there, the sky is the limit.

ID

Q: What precisely is an egg?

An egg is a vessel for the creating incipient organism of a creature that recreates through sexual proliferation. In the culinary sense, we're normally alluding to eggs from avian creatures that are removed from the body, similar to chicken eggs.

Q: What's inside the egg that makes it so culinarily helpful?

There are two fundamental parts to an egg: yolk and white.

The yolk is the nutritive hotspot for the creating incipient organism, and it represents around 75% of the calories in an egg. Yolks might seem rich and greasy, however, as a matter of fact, they are basically sacks of water that contain broke down proteins, alongside bigger masses of protein and fat connected along with lecithin, an emulsifying atom that permits fat and water particles get along together agreeably. We'll return to that in a second.

The white is additionally for the most part water, alongside a couple of proteins-the most significant being ovalbumin, ovomucin, and ovotransferrin, which enable it to both set when cooked and be whipped into firm, shaving cream-like pinnacles.

Since the proteins in eggs are as of now broken down and fan out in a fluid, it is extremely simple to fuse them into different food sources significantly more than, say, meat proteins, which are moderately solidly set up according to each other. (Have you at any point took a stab at whipping a steak? I have. It doesn't work.) Additionally, the way that eggs contain such a wide assortment of proteins, every one of which acts in a marginally unique manner when heat or mechanical activity is applied, intends that as a cook, you have extraordinary command over the last surface of your completed dish. Eggs cooked to 140°F, for instance, will be delicate and custard-like, while those cooked to 180°F will be fun and firm.

Naming: Size and Quality

Q: Eggs arrive in perhaps a couple sizes at the grocery store. Which ones would it be advisable for me to go after?

Any container of eggs that shows the United States Department of Agriculture (USDA) safeguard on it was stuffed by USDA weight norms, which characterize six distinct classes, as displayed in the graph underneath.

WEIGHT CLASS	MINIMUM WEIGHT PER EGG
Jumbo	2.5 ounces
Extra large	2.25 ounces
Large	2 ounces
Medium	1.75 ounces
Small	1.5 ounces
Peewee	1.25 ounces

Truly, you're probably not going to see little or peewee eggs at the grocery store chickens these days are reproduced to create eggs medium-size and up. Huge eggs are the norm in many plans, remembering the ones for this book. I in all actuality do jump at the chance to have gigantic eggs close by in my ice chest, however, for those post-night-out mornings when I can truly utilize that additional half ounce of singed egg to top me off. You're additionally bound to find one of the desired twofold yolks in a bigger egg.

Q: What about those letter grades on the container? Are Grade An eggs better compared to Grade B?

Like estimating, reviewing of eggs is a willful activity that most producers decide to follow to get the USDA blessing on their crates. USDA evaluating specialists look at test eggs from each bunch to decide the grade in light of the nature of the whites, yolks, and shells. Eggs with the firmest whites, tallest-standing yolks, and cleanest shells will get an AA stamp, while eggs with watery whites, level yolks, and stained shells get a B. Grade A lies in the center and most retail locations convey for buyers. To the extent that cooking quality goes, a firm white and yolk are significant for things like poached eggs and seared eggs where a pleasant, tight appearance is wanted, yet in most cooking or baking application, any grade'll do-it's a restorative distinction alone.

Egg Freshness

Q: You referenced that lower-reviewed eggs have watery whites thus will more often than not spread out more than higher-evaluated ones. Be that as it may, doesn't newness assume a part in this as well?

For sure it does. Exceptionally new eggs have more tight yolks and whites that will hold their shape much better during poaching or fricasseeing, as well as yolks that will stay better focused when bubbled. In view of the manner in which their proteins separate, eggs become increasingly loose as they age. There's another significant change as well: as eggs age, they become increasingly basic. This is especially significant in meringue-based dishes, as the pH of egg whites can enormously influence their frothing power. Egg whites froth best in somewhat acidic conditions, and that implies that old eggs will create looser, wetter froths. To neutralize this, a touch of acidic cream of tartar will help your meringues stay solid and sob free.

Loses its white color in old age

Q: I've heard that more established eggs are better for bubbling in light of the fact that they are simpler to strip. Is this valid? Is there any culinary benefit to utilizing more seasoned eggs?

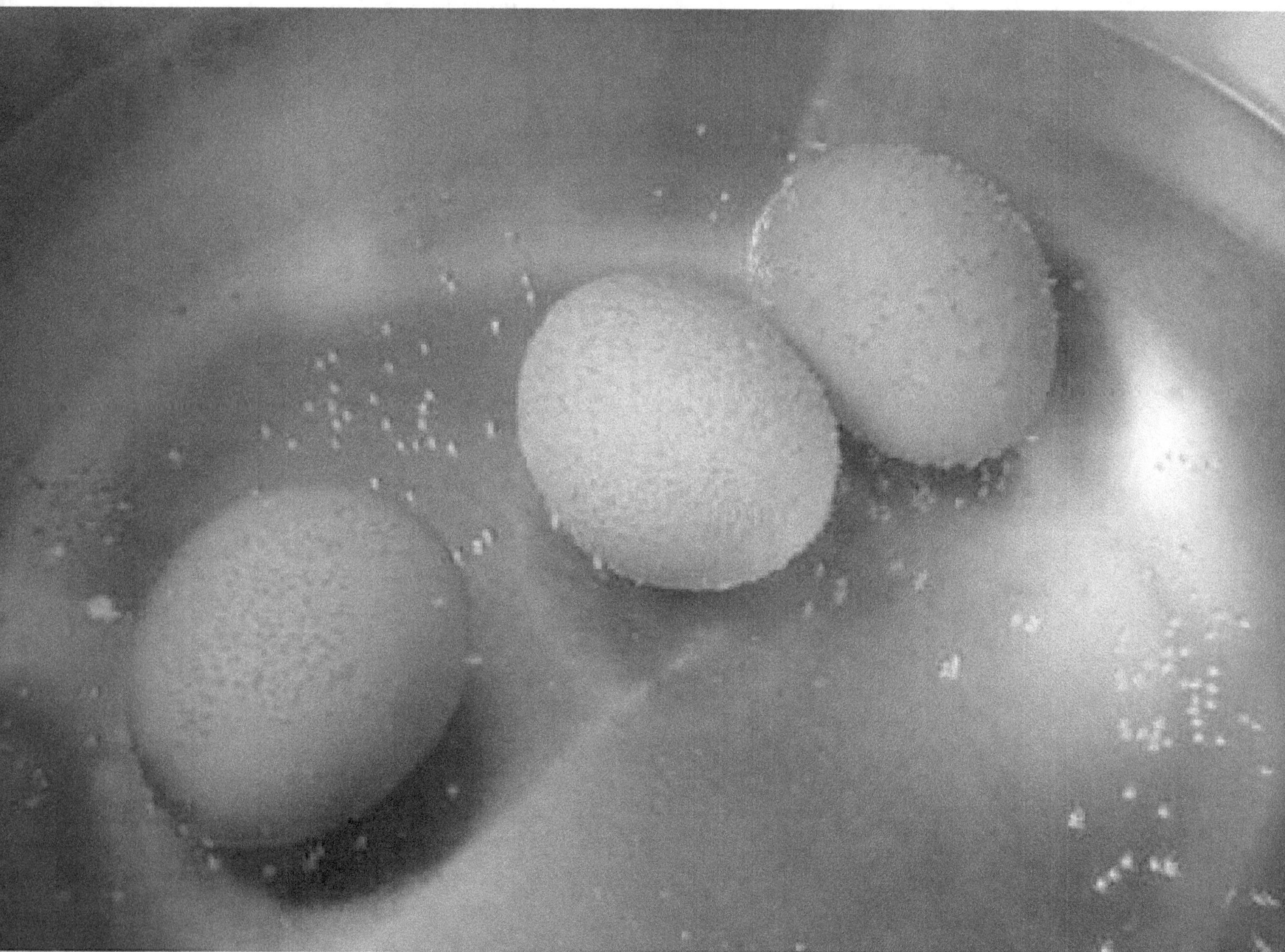

I trusted this for a very long time-until I really tried it with a couple of containers of eggs from various sources, contrasting them and a few eggs I got from my neighbor in Brooklyn's lawn that were under seven days old. Learn to expect the unexpected. Whether the eggs were seven days old or over two months old, they were similarly prone to have shells that adhered to them while stripping. In addition, with more established eggs, the yolks become uncentered, inclining toward the egg divider, making for ugly cuts. Regardless of how you anticipate cooking them, new eggs are superior to old ones.

Q: Is there a stunt to getting the shell off a hard-bubbled egg without ruining the white?

I've attempted each strategy known to man, ticking them off each in turn. Stunning the eggs in ice water? It has no effect. Punching a hole in the shells prior to cooking them? No, apologies. Steaming or pressure-cooking them? Nuh-uh. Adding vinegar to the water? Everything that does is disintegrate the peripheral layer of shell.

Eggs brought down into bubbling water or hot steam have the most obvious opportunity with regards to stripping without any problem.

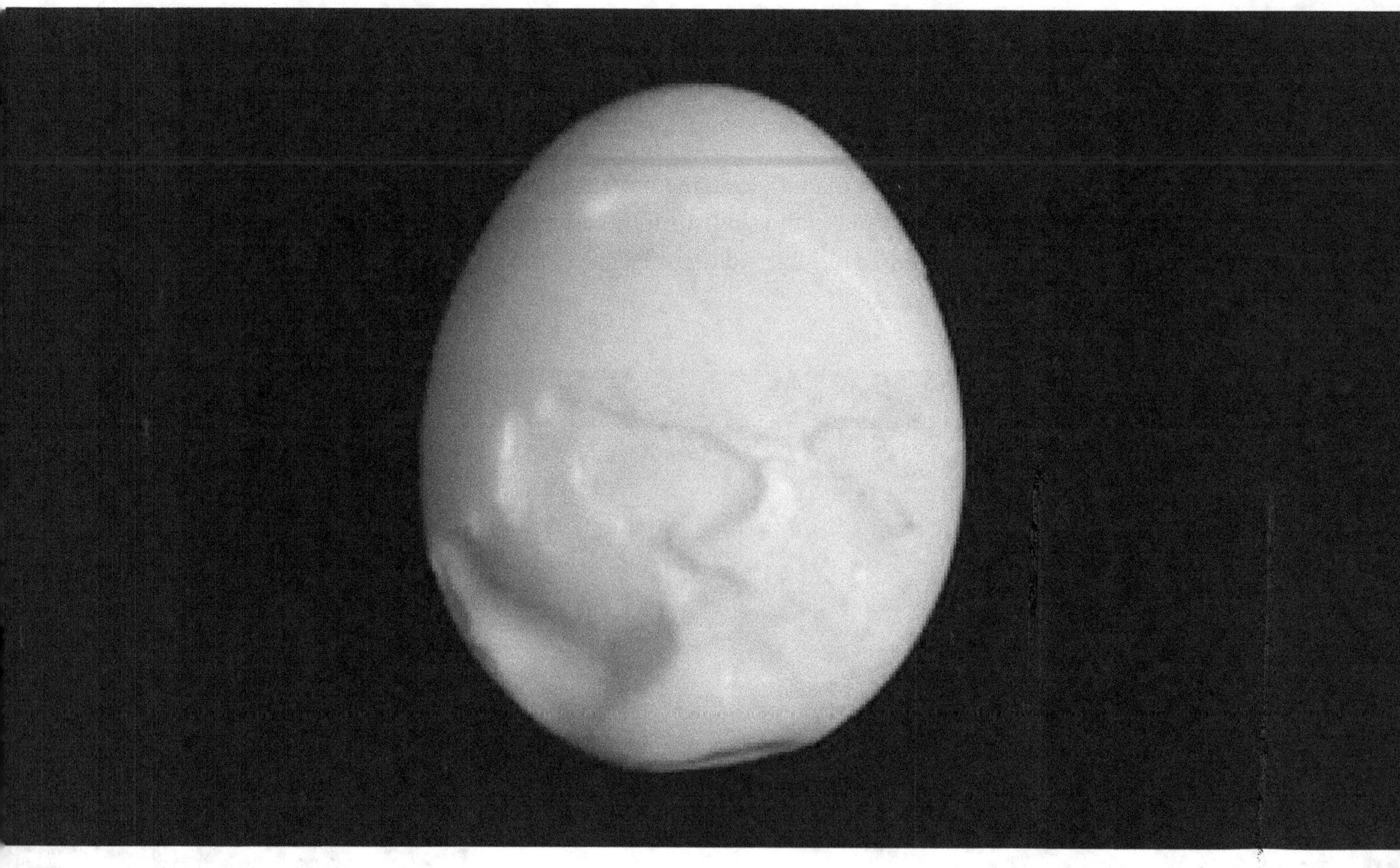

Eggs gradually warmed in chilly water will adhere to their shells.

Truth be told, I found that the main thing that truly appears to have an effect is the underlying cooking stage. Drop the eggs into boiling water, and they'll strip quite effectively (however even this doesn't work 100% of the time). Heat them up leisurely, beginning with cold water, and the egg proteins will wind up intertwined to within the shell.

To the extent that the genuine stripping process, the simplest way is to strip the still-hot eggs under cool running water, beginning from the fat end, where the air pocket is found. Whenever the eggs are hot, the association between the film and egg white is more vulnerable, making it simpler to eliminate the shell. The cool water not just aides delicately oust difficult pieces of shell, it likewise keeps your fingers from getting singed. I put a fine-network sifter or colander in the sink to get the shells, for simple cleanup.

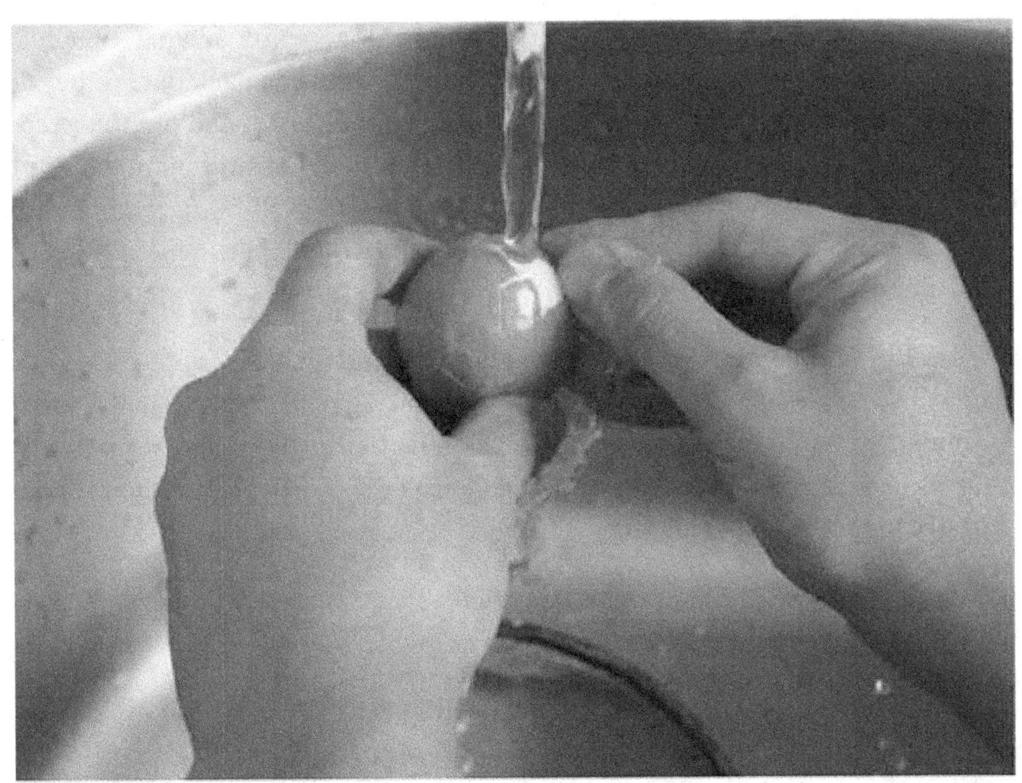

Stripping under running water relaxes the strip.

Q: How do I have any idea about how old an egg is?

You can have a go at checking the container mark, which will give you a harsh thought. On essentially every bundle of eggs, you'll see a sell-by date, as well as a pack date (otherwise called the Julian date), the date on which the eggs were investigated, cleaned, and put in the container. The pack date is the three-digit number quickly over the sell-by date, beginning with 001 for January 1 and finishing at 365 for December 31. Legitimately, the sell-by date can be something like 45 days after the pack date, yet when appropriately refrigerated, eggs will stay healthy for well past this 45-day time frame 60 to 70 days is sensible.

While it's conceivable that the eggs you're purchasing were laid inside a couple of days of their pack date, makers have as long as 30 days to clean and pack eggs, and that actually intends that, in principle, assuming you purchase a container of eggs on its termination date, it might currently be 75 days old! Obviously, checking the termination date isn't the most solid method for ensuring new eggs. You're vastly improved checking the pack date.

Q: What assuming I purchase eggs without a pack date or I've moved the eggs to the egg compartment in my fridge entryway and never again know the date?

For one thing, everybody lets you know that if you need to expand timeframe of realistic usability, you ought to get those eggs out of the ice chest entryway and into the coldest piece of your refrigerator. Valid. Yet, everything they neglect to say to you is that even on a rack in the entryway, eggs will keep going for quite some time past their pack date. So except if you eat or cook with eggs just on extremely interesting events, feel free to keep them in the entryway. You'll go through them some time before they turn sour.

All things considered, there's a fast and simple test to check the newness of an egg: drop it into a bowl of water. Eggshells are permeable: they can lose around 4 microliters of water a day to vanishing while at the same time bringing air into the space between the shell and the inward layer close to the fat end. In exceptionally new eggs, the air space is small and the egg will sink to the lower part of the bowl and lie on its side. As eggs progress in years, the air space will develop, so old eggs will sink and afterward stand on their focuses as the air in the bigger end attempts to rise. Assuming you have an egg that floats, it's presumably over the hill and ought to be disposed of.

Old eggs stand up when lowered in water.

Q: My neighborhood ranchers' market sells unrefrigerated eggs, and I've seen a few general stores in Europe where the eggs simply sit out on racks. Is it true that they are insane, or is it me?

In all probability it's you. Whenever eggs are first laid, they are shrouded in a flimsy wax-like covering called the fingernail skin. This fingernail skin is the egg's first obstruction against bacterial disease and inordinate dampness misfortune. In the United States, USDA-stepped eggs are completely washed preceding bundling, a stage that eliminates the fingernail skin. It might imply that our bundled eggs are cleaner regardless, however it implies that they have less security against future bacterial disease as they sit in the store refrigeration is important to assist with forestalling this. Be that as it may, many eggs sold at ranchers' business sectors or in European grocery stores have not been washed before pressing. The fingernail skin stays in one piece, so refrigeration is pointless, however the eggs will generally have a more limited timeframe of realistic usability than refrigerated eggs.

Q: What about the "purified eggs" I'm seeing available nowadays?

Purified eggs are a moderately new item. They are sanitized by lowering the eggs in a water shower at around 130°F, a temperature that, given sufficient opportunity, is adequately hot to dispense with any unsafe microscopic organisms on or inside the egg yet cool sufficient that the egg won't cook. Sanitized eggs are valuable for individuals who like to eat their eggs runny or in crude arrangements like mayonnaise however don't have any desire to run the (exceptionally insignificant) hazard of becoming ill from them. For most cooking purposes, sanitized eggs will turn out great, however you'll see that the whites are runnier (making them challenging to poach or broil), and that they accept about two times as lengthy to whip into tops. The yolks work similarly as well as those from customary eggs in mayonnaise or Caesar salad dressing.

Q: Is it genuine that earthy colored eggs are more grounded than white?

By no means. The shade of the eggshell has to do with the variety of chicken, and it is generally constrained by market requests. In a large portion of New England, earthy colored eggs are the standard, while most of the remainder of the nation inclines toward white eggs. They are totally tradable.

Egg Labeling

Q: I miss the days of yore, when I could stroll into the general store and get a container of eggs without feeling like I was settling on a significant choice. Nowadays, there are many assortments to look over. What do every one of the marks mean?

It is befuddling, and it generally has to do with developing buyer mindfulness about the circumstances in which egg-laying chickens are kept. Most spend their lives as minimal more than egg-creating machines, housed in batteries of individual enclosures, unfit to spread their wings or even move, with practically no admittance to a space where a chicken could play out its normal ways of behaving. The mark on the container can be a sign of better government assistance preposterous.

• Regular shows that the eggs are negligibly handled, however since all eggs are sold insignificantly handled, the name actually amounts to nothing. Essentially, the term Farm-Fresh conveys with it no certifications, in light of the fact that apparently no one is selling spoiled eggs that don't come from a homestead.

• Free roaming, Free-Roaming, and Cage-Free eggs come from chickens that are not kept in battery confines, however rather in enormous open outbuildings or stockrooms. That is a significant improvement in personal satisfaction for the chickens, permitting them to participate in normal ways of behaving like pecking, dust-washing, and spreading their wings. Unfenced and Free-Roaming chickens for the most part additionally approach outside regions, yet the naming regulations have no necessities to the extent that the size or nature of the area goes, nor for how lengthy the chickens should be permitted out. Truth is, a large portion of these chickens never walked external the animal dwellingplace. These marks are not examined you're going on the expression of the maker alone.

• Affirmed Organic eggs come from chickens kept in open horse shelters or stockrooms with an undefined level of outside access (once more, all things considered, likely none). They should be taken care of a natural, all-vegan diet liberated from animal results, anti-microbials, and pesticides, and ranches are checked for consistency by the USDA.

• Ensured Humane eggs have been confirmed by outsider evaluators, and this mark requires stricter controls on loading densities, enabling the chickens to take part in regular ways of behaving like settling and roosting. Makers are not permitted to take part in constrained shedding, the act of inciting hens into a laying cycle by starving them (this training is considered any remaining kinds of eggs).

• Omega-3-Enriched eggs come from chickens that have been taken care of enhancements produced using flaxseed or fish oil to expand the degrees of omega-3 unsaturated fat a fundamental unsaturated fat promoted with a few medical advantages in their yolks. While certain individuals guarantee eggs high in omega-3s have a "off-putting" fragrance, in blind tastings, I've observed no tremendous contrasts in the manner in which these eggs taste.

Assuming creature government assistance is a worry, you are making a decent positive development by buying just Certified Organic or Certified Humane eggs. On the off chance that you have a neighborhood ranchers' market where you can really converse with the rancher delivering the eggs you're buying, you're settling on a stunningly better choice. Obviously, everything thing you can manage is to construct your own coop (or, even better, persuade your neighbor to do as such) and several chickens. It won't set aside you much cash over the long haul, except if you keep an enormous herd and eat a great deal of eggs, yet you'll have the freshest-potential eggs and most likely make a lot of companions simultaneously.

Q: That's just fine for the chickens, however do Certified Organic or nearby eggs taste better, similar to the folks at the ranchers' market could like you to think?

That is a decent inquiry, and one that I've pondered frequently. It appears to be regular that a more joyful, better chicken wandering around a terrace jabbing, scratching, eating bugs and worms, clacking, and doing every one of the beguiling and amusing things chickens in all actuality do ought to create more delicious eggs, correct? When it's all said and done, I realize that the absolute best-tasting eggs I've at any point eaten have come just out of the coops or lawns of companions who keep their own groups. The yolks were more extravagant, the whites more tight and more tasty, and it was only an overall better encounter. Or then again was it? Consider the possibility that all their significance was essentially in my mind.

To test this, I coordinated a visually impaired tasting in which I had testers taste customary grocery store eggs, plain natural eggs, natural eggs with differing levels of omega-3, and eggs straight from 100% free-wandering, field raised chickens. Each of the eggs were served mixed. The outcomes? Without a doubt the fed eggs and omega-3-enhanced eggs fared better compared to the standard general store eggs. In any case, I additionally saw another connection: the shade of the eggs shifted a lot, with the fed eggs on the more strongly orange finish of the range. Also, the more omega-3s the eggs contained, the more profound orange the yolk. The plain natural eggs and standard production line eggs were the palest of the part. This distinction in pigmentation can be credited to the differing diets of the chickens. Fed hens eat bugs and blossoms, the two of which contribute shading to yolks. Chickens reared for eggs with high omega-3 acids are taken care of with an eating routine improved with flaxseeds and ocean kelp, which contribute shading. Chickens that lay these more costly eggs are additionally here and there took care of pigmented supplements, similar to marigold leaves, that make their yolks overall quite splendid. Would it be able to be that the flavor distinctions testers were revealing had more to do with their response to the shading than to the real kind of the egg?

These eggs were colored green to sort out exactly the way in which enormous a job shading plays in our view of flavor. This is the clue: That was a great deal.

To dispose of shading as a variable, I concocted similar sorts of eggs, this time biting the dust them green with some food shading. Whenever I re-directed the tasting with green eggs, there was positively no connection among's flavor and provenance. Individuals loved the standard store eggs similarly as much as the eggs that had come directly from the field.

Need to see a similar impact for yourself? Investigate these two (indistinguishable put something aside for some, Photoshop tone dabbling) container of eggs and let me know which one you'd prefer eat:

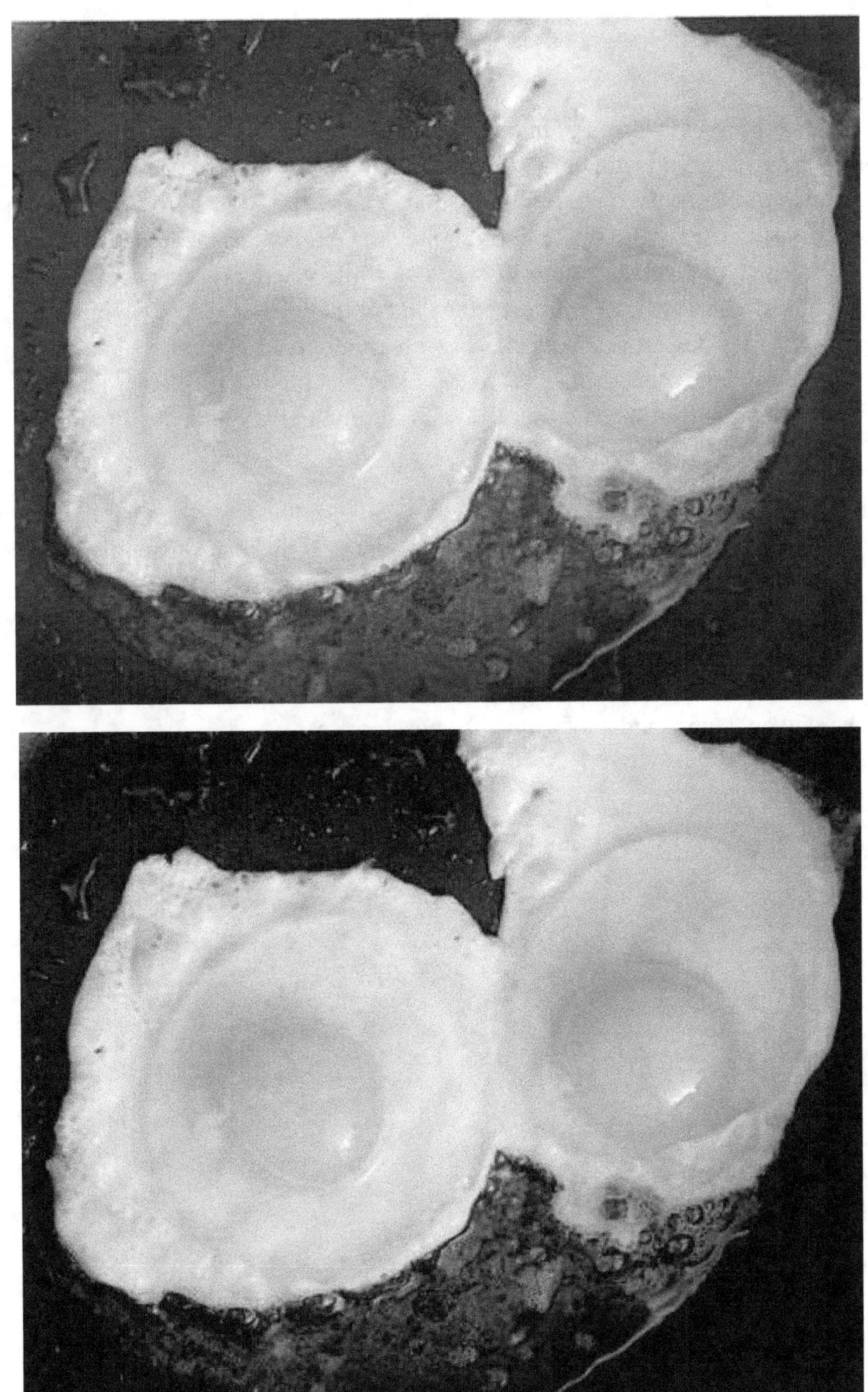

The familiar axiom that you eat with your eyes? It's valid.

Q: So you're letting me know that it doesn't make any difference whatsoever where I get my eggs from?

No, I'm not saying that by any means. Our psyches are uncommonly strong, and our taste inclinations have as a lot to do with our psychological predispositions and childhoods as they do with genuine quantifiable actual qualities in the food. You've likely seen it yourself. Doesn't a super cold brew taste better while you're drinking it with companions on an open air porch on a warm summer evening than on those forlorn evenings while you're drinking solo? Doesn't the climate and administration in a café influence the kind of the food to you? Do you truly imagine that your mother's fruity dessert is superior to any other individual's? Chances are, the explanation you like it so a lot is on the grounds that it's your mother making it. The blend of actual appearance, climate, organization, environment, and, surprisingly, your state of mind can influence the kind of food.

I prefer to consider it such: I will keep eating the freshest eggs I can view as created by the most sympathetically raised chickens since I care a piece about the chickens' prosperity. The way that my psyche fools me into thinking these eggs really taste better is simply good to beat all. You mean I get to make the best choice and my eggs will taste better? Most definitely! Another benefit: eggs purchased straightforwardly from the rancher at a ranchers' market are for the most part a lot fresher (I've figured out how to purchase eggs that had been laid the day they were offered), improving them to cook with and a lot simpler to poach or sear.

BOILED EGGS

Bubbled eggs are about the easiest formula in any cook's collection, isn't that so?

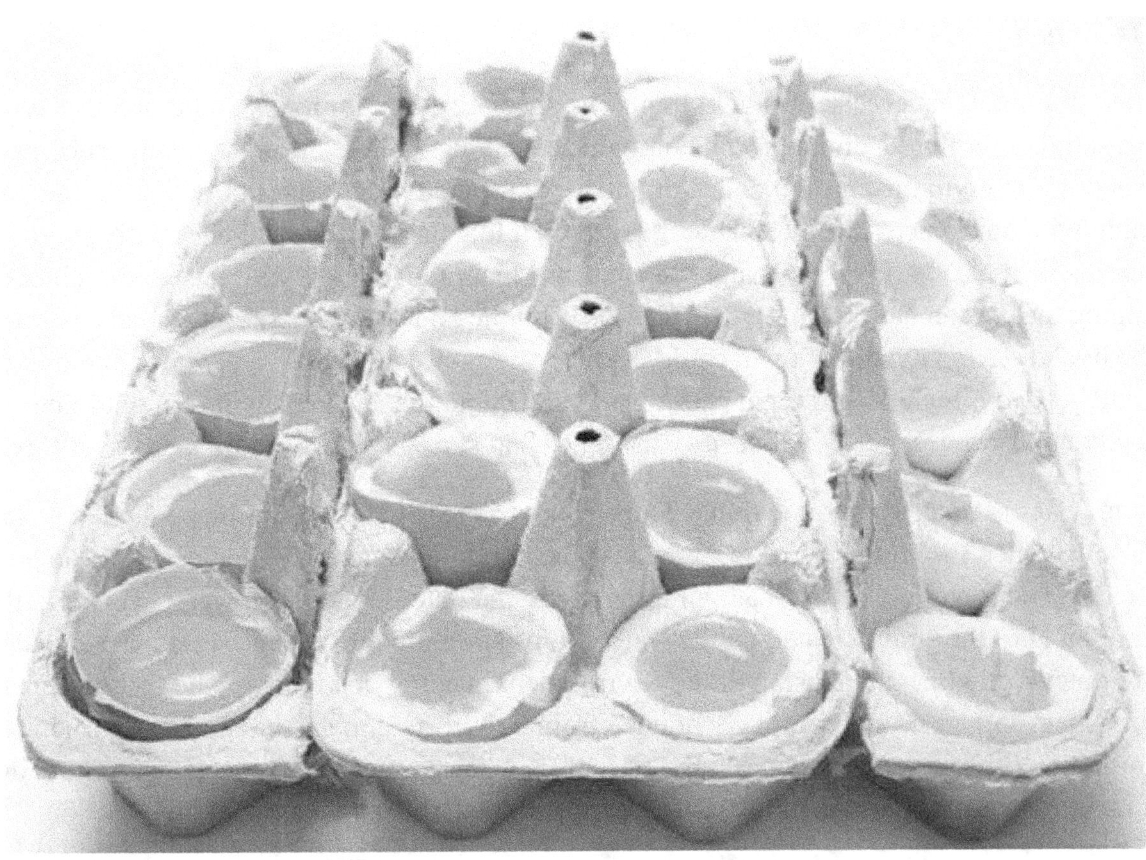

Eggs boiled for 30-second spans from 0 to 12 minutes.

In any case, how regularly do you get really wonderful bubbled eggs? Hard-bubbled eggs ought to have completely set, however not rubbery, whites encompassing yolks that are cooked through yet at the same time dazzling yellow and rich, without really any sprinkle of pastiness or disintegrating, and surely no part of that feared sulfurous green hint at the yolk-white connection point that overcooked eggs procure. Delicate bubbled eggs, then again, ought to have completely set whites with fluid yolks that slime out like a delicate custard, washing your toast in their brilliant stream and improving your fresh bacon. There's something else to heating up an egg besides what might be expected. Substantially more.

Essentially every fundamental cookbook offers an alternate procedure for how it ought to be finished: begin the egg in chilly water, or tenderly lower it into bubbling water; add vinegar to the water to bring down its pH, or add baking soft drink to the water to raise it; cover the pot, or don't cover it; utilize old eggs, or utilize new eggs; unendingly. However, not many proposition proof concerning why any of these methods ought to work any better compared to another. Evidently, bubbling eggs isn't . . . ahem . . . an eggsact science. We should attempt to change that.

Priorities straight: what precisely is bubbling? The specialized definition is that it happens when the fume strain of a fluid is more prominent than or equivalent to the air pressure that encompasses it. We should return to the chicken coop similarity we utilized here. Your pot of water is a coop brimming with chickens. The chickens will quite often like one another and cheerfully stay together inside the coop. Presently, suppose we begin including energy with the existing blend by exchanging their water supply out with espresso. With the additional energy, the chickens start to become hyperactive-a couple of them could even be so vigorous as to have the option to hop the fence and getaway. Include sufficient energy, and in the end the chickens will turn out to be hyperactive to the point that they'll destroy the fence and start getting away quickly to be sure.

Bubbling water is exactly the same thing. The water particles are caught in the pot and kept set up by their own fence-the strain of the air in the air pushing down on them. Add energy to the pot as hotness, and water particles start to get jumping going the outer layer of the water. This is called vanishing. At last the strain created by the water atoms attempting to escape becomes equivalent to or more noteworthy than the tension of the environment pushing down on it. The fence breaks, the conduits open, and water atoms quickly bounce from a fluid state to gas, rising brutally. This transformation of fluid water to water fume (steam) is what you see when you take a gander at a pot of bubbling water; with unadulterated water adrift level, this happens at 212°F (100°C).

Here is a fast overview of what happens while you heat a pot of water to the point of boiling:

• Shuddering: At somewhere in the range of 130° and 170°F, little air pockets of water fume start framing at nucleation destinations (inclining further toward those later) along the base and sides of the pot. They won't be sufficiently huge to really bounce and ascend to the outer layer of the water, however their development will make the top surface quiver a little.

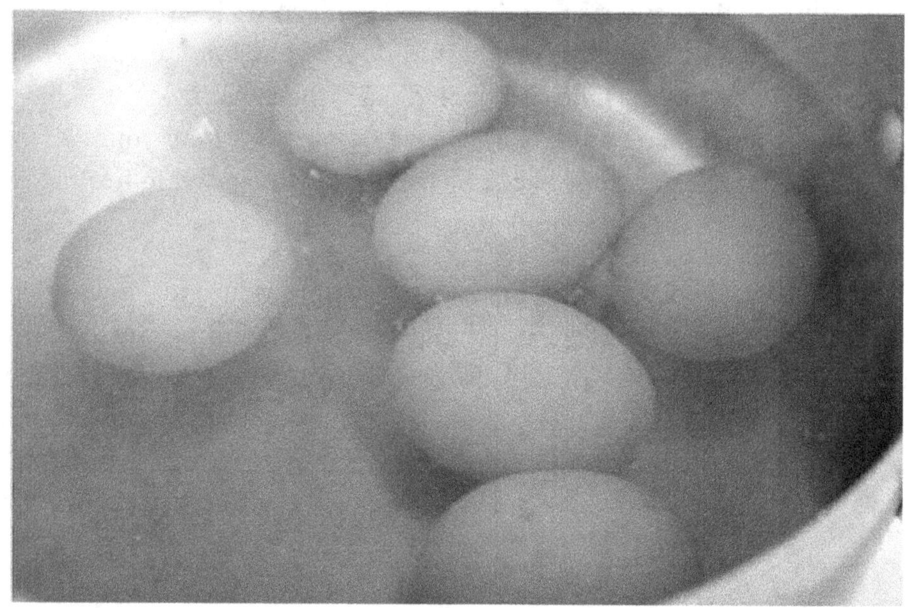

Shuddering water beneath 170°F.

A subsimmer just underneath 195°F.

• Subsimmer: At somewhere in the range of 170° and 195°F, the air pockets from the sides and lower part of the pot start to ascend to the surface. Normally you'll see several surges of minuscule, champagne-like air pockets ascending from the lower part of the pot. Generally, nonetheless, the fluid is still moderately still.

• Stew: At somewhere in the range of 195° and 212°F, bubbles break the outer layer of the water consistently, and from all focuses not only a couple of individual streams, as in a subsimmer.

• Full bubble: At 212°F, air pockets of water fume escape very quickly. This is the most sultry that water can get adrift level without the guide of a tension cooker.

HOTNESS AND EGGS

However certain individuals guarantee that adding salt, vinegar, or baking soft drink to the water when you heat up an egg can influence its last surface, in my testing, I tracked down that the possibly factors that matter while heating up an egg in its shell are time and temperature.

To figure out precisely the way that quick an egg cooks in bubbling water, I cooked twelve and a half eggs, eliminating them from the pot at 30-second stretches prior to dividing them open.

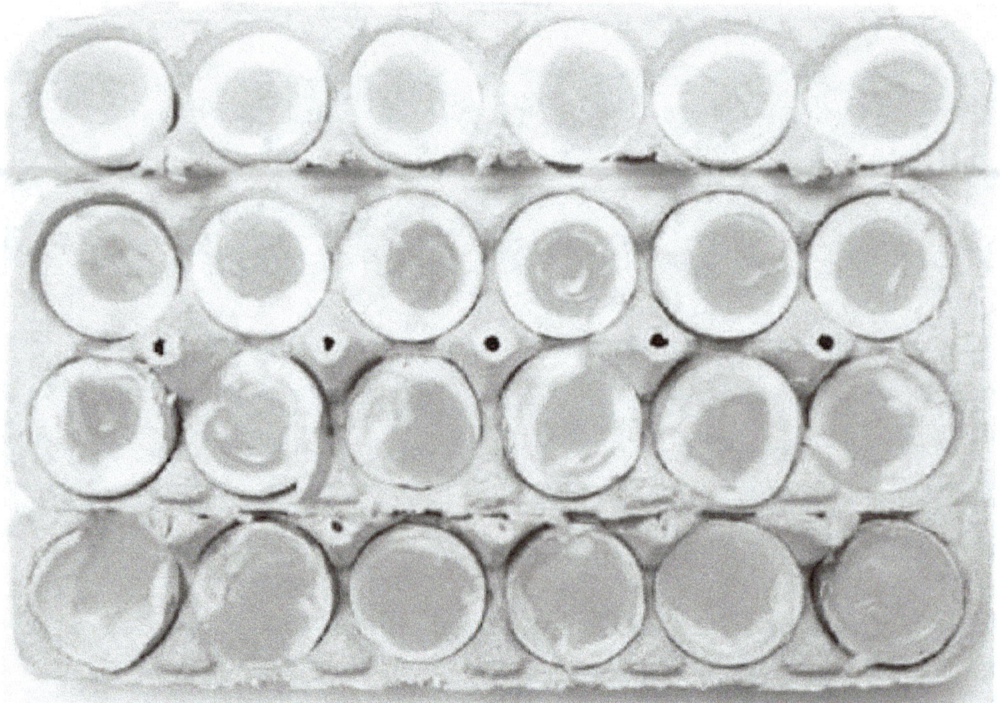

Presently, there are a couple of things you'll see right away. First and most clear is that the more you keep an egg in bubbling water, the more smoking it gets. In any case, here's something more significant, which might appear to be inconsequential right away, yet, as we'll see, is instrumental in an impeccably cooked egg: food sources in a hot climate cook from an external perspective in, and the greater the temperature differential between the food and the climate, the more lopsided the cooking will be.

This means assuming you bring down an egg into bubbling water, it's feasible to accomplish an outcome with a white that is intense, rubbery, and overcooked while the yolk is still scarcely cooked in the middle, similar to this one:

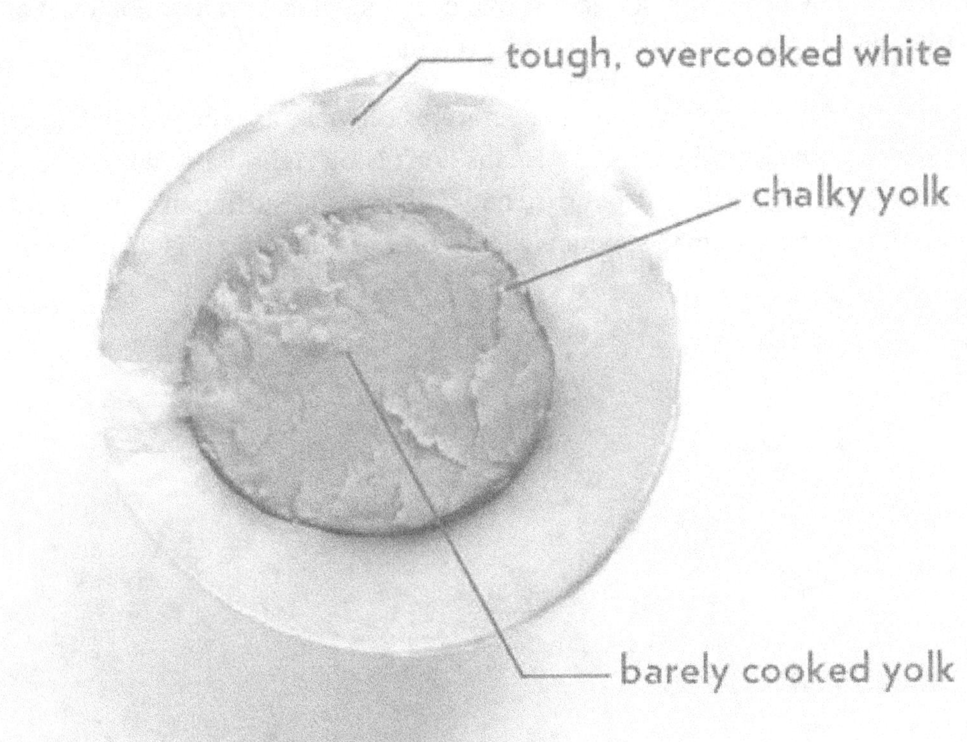

All in all, what's the best temperature to cook an egg to? This is what happens to an egg white as it warms up:

• From 30° to 140°F: As the white gets hot, its proteins, which look like looped wads of yarn, gradually begin to uncoil.

• At 140°F: One of these uncoiled proteins, ovotransferrin, starts to bond with itself, making a semisolid grid that turns the egg white smooth and jam like.

• At 155°F: The ovotransferrin has framed a murky strong, however it is still very delicate and soggy.

• At 180°F: The principle protein in the egg white, ovalbumin, will cross-connect and cement, giving you a thoroughly firm yet at the same time delicate white.

• Past 180°F: The more blazing you get the egg, the more firmly the egg proteins bond, and the firmer, drier, and more rubbery the egg white becomes. At last, hydrogen sulfide, or that "spoiled egg" smell, starts to create. Congrats: your egg is overcooked.

ALTITUDE AND BOILING

On account of gravity, the higher you go, the less air atoms there are in a given space-so the air is less thick. Lower thickness implies lower air strain, and lower air pressure implies that water atoms in a pot need less energy to escape high up. In Bogotá, Colombia, where my significant other is from, for instance, you're a decent 8,000 feet above ocean level and water bubbles at a temperature around 14 to 15 degrees lower than it does adrift even out.

The diagram beneath outlines the bubbling temperatures of water as you go into higher elevations. The height impact can unleash ruin on plans. Beans don't cook right. Pasta won't ever relax. Stews take more time to braise. Hotcakes can overrise and collapse. Go sufficiently high, and you will not have the option to cook vegetables, which should be warmed to no less than 183°F to separate.

For a portion of these issues, most strikingly including stews, dried beans, and root vegetables, a strain cooker can be a lifeline. It works by making a vaportight seal around the food. As the water inside it warms up and converts to steam, the tension inside the pot increments, since steam occupies more room than water. This expanded tension holds the water back from bubbling, permitting you to carry it to a lot higher temperature than you would in the outside. Most strain cookers permit you to cook at temperatures somewhere in the range of 240° and 250°F, regardless the height. To this end pressure cookers are so famous all through the Andes-no self-regarding Colombian home is without one.

WATER-BOILING MYTHS

Fantasies about bubbling water flourish. The following are four Water-Boiling myths most well-known:

• Cold water reaches boiling point quicker than heated water. Bogus. It's totally false, yet there is a valid justification to utilize cold water rather than hot for cooking: heated water will contain additional broke down minerals from your lines, which can give your food an off flavor.

• Water that has been frozen or recently bubbled will reach boiling point quicker. Bogus, however there is somewhat logical thinking behind this one. Bubbling or freezing water eliminates disintegrated gases (for the most part oxygen), which can marginally influence the bubbling temperature-so somewhat, truth be told, that neither my clock nor my thermometer could recognize any distinction.

• Salt raises the edge of boiling over of water. Valid . . . kind of. Broken up solids like salt and sugar will truth be told increment the edge of boiling over of water, making it reach boiling point all the more leisurely, however the impact is negligible (the sums regularly utilized in cooking impact under a 1-degree change). For it to have any huge effect, you'd have to add it in truly huge amounts. So generally, you can disregard this one.

• A watched pot won't ever bubble. Most certainly evident. Turn away your eyes.

On Salt and Nucleation

Anyway, in the event that salt doesn't bring down the limit of water, why tossing a modest bunch of salt into a stewing pot will cause an unexpected emission of air pockets? This is a result of little things called nucleation destinations, which are, basically, the origin of air pockets. For air pockets of steam to shape, there must be some kind of inconsistency inside the volume of water-infinitesimal scratches within surface of the pot will do, as will smidgens of residue or the pores of a wooden spoon. A small bunch of salt quickly presents large number of nucleation destinations, making it exceptionally simple for air pockets to shape and get away. A similar standard is utilized to "seed" mists. Letting dusty particles out of a plane causes a great many nucleation locales to be made in the damp environment so water fume beads can mix and shape mists.

An egg yolk follows an alternate arrangement of temperatures:

• At 145°F: The yolk proteins start to denature, thickening the fluid yolk.

• At 158°F: The egg yolk is firm, ready to hold its shape and to be cut with a fork or blade. Its appearance is as yet dull and clear, with a nearly fudge-like surface.

• Somewhere in the range of 158° and 170°F: The yolk turns out to be increasingly firm until ultimately it abruptly moves from clear and fudge-like to light yellow and brittle as minuscule circular chambers imperceptible to the unaided eye separate from one another.

• Above 170°F: The yolk turns out to be progressively brittle as the temperature goes up. The sulfur in the white rapidly answers with the iron in the yolk, making ferrous sulfide, tingeing the outside of the yolk a monstrous green.

Bubbling eggs is tied in with adjusting the distinctions between the manner in which the whites and the yolks cook.

SOFT BOILED EGGS

For my purposes, the ideal delicate bubbled egg has a white that is totally obscure, yet not to the mark of rubberiness (some place in the scope of 155° to 180°F), and a yolk that is essentially 100% fluid (no more sultry than 158°F). Thusly, with every spoonful, you get delicate chomps of delicate, smooth white washed in a sauce of magnificent, radiant brilliant, rich, delightful yolk.

Along these lines, recollecting that food sources cook from an external perspective in and that the more smoking your cooking climate, the more prominent the temperature slope that structures in your egg, you understand that for delicate bubbled eggs, you need to begin with chilly eggs and lower them in steaming hot water, so the whites cook and set while the yolks remain liquidy. I had a go at diving the eggs straightforwardly into bubbling water to cook until the whites were recently set, however I ran into an issue: the peripheral layers of the whites end up marginally overcooking. A vastly improved method for doing it is to heat a pot of water to the point of boiling, shut off the hotness, drop the eggs into it, cover the pot to assist it with holding some hotness, and afterward start the clock. Since the water in the pot gets cooler as it sits, the eggs stand significantly less of a possibility overcooking and turning rubbery.

The other significant thing to consider is the proportion of water to eggs-add such a large number of eggs, and they'll chill the water off such a lot of that they won't cook as expected. Thus, 3 quarts is sufficient water to concoct to 6 eggs. Anything else than that, and you'll need to cook in bunches, or in a bigger pot.

FOOLPROOF SOFT-BOILED EGGS

NOTE: Depending on how hot your kitchen is and your cookware's hotness maintenance capacities, cooking times might fluctuate somewhat. It's smart to do a training run with a solitary egg and change the time as required. Cooking times ought to be expanded on the off chance that you inhabit a respectably high height. At extremely high heights, you ought to keep a bubble for the initial couple of moments of cooking.

1 quart water for each 2 eggs

1 to 12 huge eggs

Pick a lidded pot (or pot) little enough that the eggs will be completely lowered when you add them to the water. Heat the water to the point of boiling over high hotness. Add the eggs, cover the container, and eliminate from the hotness. Cook the eggs as indicated by the times given in the diagram, then, at that point, eliminate with an opened spoon and serve right away.

COOK TIME	DESCRIPTION	BEST USES
1 to 3 minutes	Outer white set just enough to allow egg to retain its shape when carefully peeled	I use 1- or 2-minute eggs when I'm tossing the eggs with salad or pasta where the uncooked egg will emulsify with other ingredients; they're not pleasant to eat on their own.
4 minutes	White is opaque nearly all the way through but retains a bit of translucency next to the yolk; yolk is barely warm and completely raw	Serve as a topping to vegetables or grains; place on top of blanched asparagus or green beans or in a bowl of noodle soup.
5 minutes	White is opaque but still quivering and barely set toward the yolk; yolk is warm but completely raw	Breakfast
6 minutes	White is opaque, firm all the way through; yolk is warm and starting to firm up at the edges	Breakfast
7 minutes	White is fully cooked and as hard as that of a hard-boiled egg; yolk is golden and liquid in the center but beginning to set around the edges	Breakfast

Hard-bubbled eggs are somewhat more confounded. The objective is to have both the white and yolk where they are obscure however not rubbery. The really fanatical kitchen geek's method for doing it is to keep up with the water at unequivocally 170°F so the yolk comes out impeccably cooked and the white is as yet delicate. What's more, this strategy works. It's likewise a significant pain. Fortunately, there's a more straightforward way.

We definitely know that assuming we drop the eggs straightforwardly into bubbling water, the outside warms up a lot quicker than the inside, so that when the actual focus of the yolk arrives at 170°F, the white and external layers of yolk are terribly overcooked. You may be leaned to place the eggs in chilly water and heat them to the point of boiling steadily. This strategy works, however there's an issue: it makes the eggs circuit to the shells.

In this way, cooking them tenderly gives you even outcomes, yet cooking them quick makes it more straightforward to eliminate the shell. What I really wanted was a procedure that spanned both of these. Imagine a scenario where I were to begin the eggs in an exact volume of bubbling water and let them cook sufficiently lengthy so the whites set however stay isolated from the shells, then bring down the temperature of the water quickly by adding a couple of ice shapes and complete the process of cooking them.

It took a couple dozen attempts to get the specific planning and ice estimations down accurately, yet prepare to have your mind blown. It works. By utilizing a quick beginning and a gradual cook as far as possible, you reliably get eggs that are both impeccably cooked completely and simple to strip.

FOOLPROOF HARD-BOILED EGGS

NOTE: Depending on how hot your kitchen is and your cookware's hotness maintenance capacities, cooking times might fluctuate somewhat. it's really smart to do a training run with a solitary egg and change the times as the need might arise. Assuming that you inhabit a high height, a thermometer is fundamental.

2 quarts water

1 to 6 large eggs

12 ice cubes

Turn the water into a 3-quart lidded saucepan and boil over high heat. Carefully lower the egg(s) and cook for 30 seconds into the water. Add an ice cubes and allow the water to boil, at about 190°F, reduce to a subsimmer. Cook for 11 minutes. Drain and peel the egg(s) in cool water running.

POACHED EGGS

What might eggs Benedict be without wonderful delicate poached eggs, their cold whites rested in a robe of radiantly thick, rich genuine hollandaise and fluid, brilliant yolks prepared to overflow out over your ham and into the little hiding spots of your buttered and toasted English biscuit?

All things considered, we definitely have a ton of experience with delicate bubbled eggs, and a poached egg is basically a delicate bubbled egg cooked naked (that is the egg, not the cook). This does, obviously, present a wide range of cerebral pains. How can one hold the white back from spreading in the pot of water? How would you keep the yolk from breaking? How would you get the entire darn thing to keep its shape? Some suggest enveloping eggs by cling wrap prior to bringing down them into the water, to assist them with holding their shape. The eggs end up with terrible, wrinkled surfaces. Other innovative strategies require hours-long showers in impeccably temperature-controlled water to somewhat set the eggs, to assist them with keeping their shape while poaching. I'm not ready to awaken an additional an hour ahead of schedule just to poach my eggs.

In any case, investigate your poached egg issues, then, at that point, pose yourself several inquiries. When do your poached eggs work? That answer is simple: when the eggs are new. The more established an egg gets, the more vulnerable the film that encompasses the white becomes, and the almost certain it is that your egg will spread when it hits the water. This drives us to our first rule of poached eggs: utilize extremely new eggs.

What compounds the chance of the white self-destructing? Disturbance. The more the egg shakes and shimmies, the more probable it is it'll isolate. It's standard practice to poach eggs in stewing water, however we definitely realize that eggs will coagulate even at a subsimmer, so there's not an obvious explanation to keep the water remotely close to a bubble. Heat it up to the point of boiling, then switch the hotness off when you add the eggs.

In any case, imagine a scenario where you have new eggs and a subsimmering pot of water, your eggs actually discrete and get shady. The truth is that regardless of whether you are taking your egg directly from the chicken and into the dish, you will get some spreadage. With a grocery store egg that might have been laid as long as 60 days sooner, that is a much greater gamble.

How would you dispose of the egg white that is as of now isolated? The arrangement is a clever strategy that I previously saw exhibited by Heston Blumenthal of The Fat Duck, an eatery in England. Assuming that you break an egg and move it to a fine-network sifter, every one of the free pieces of white will deplete through while the tight white and yolk ensnared by their layer will remain totally in salvageable shape. You can then just lower the sifter into the water (the boiling water quickly encompasses the egg and starts the cooking system), and delicately slide the egg out into the container. The outcome is an impeccably formed poached egg like clockwork, without any "floaters."

Move eggs to individual little dishes.

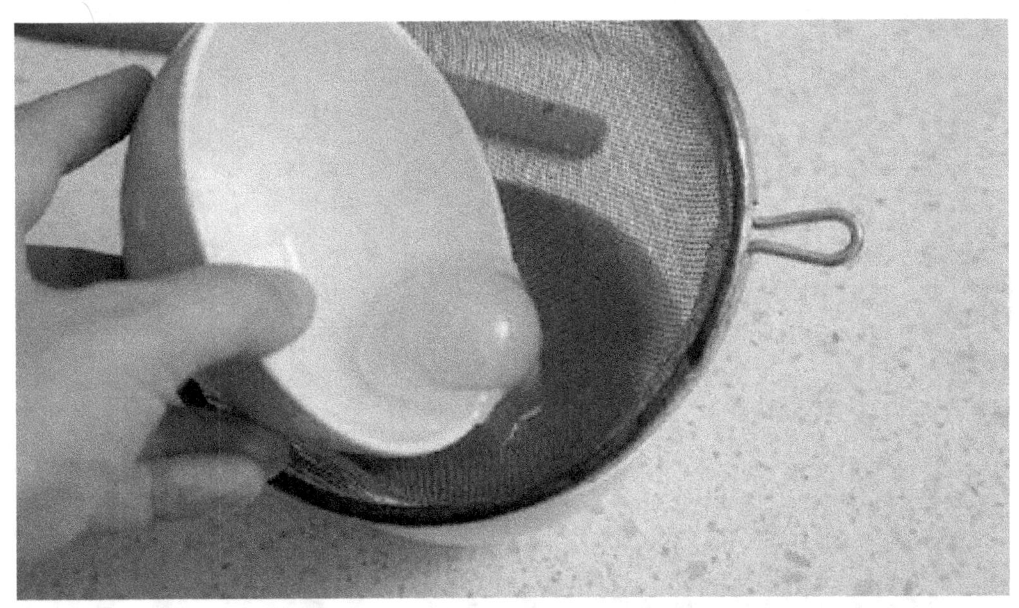

Tenderly fill a fine lattice sifter.

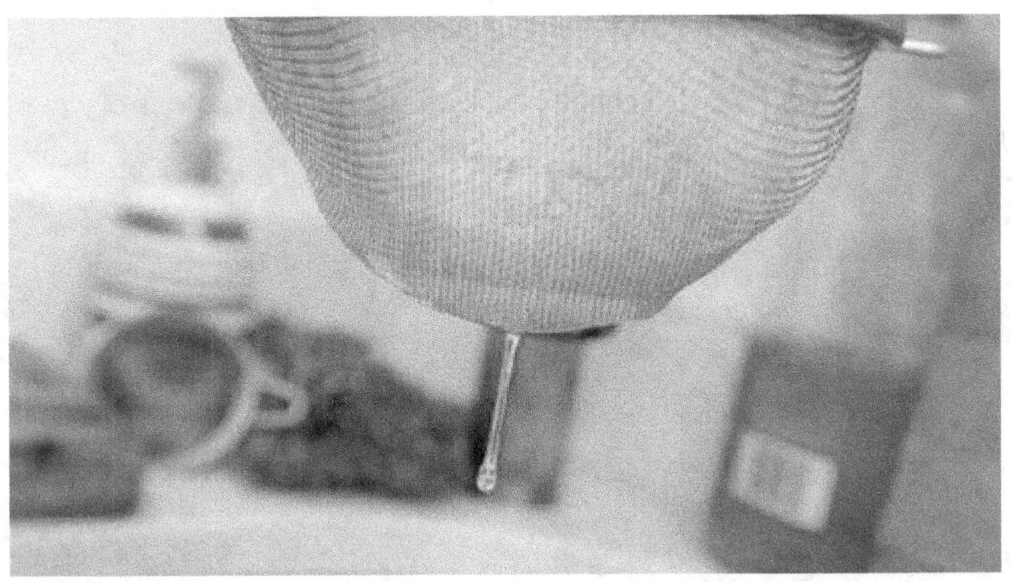

Set free whites trickle through.

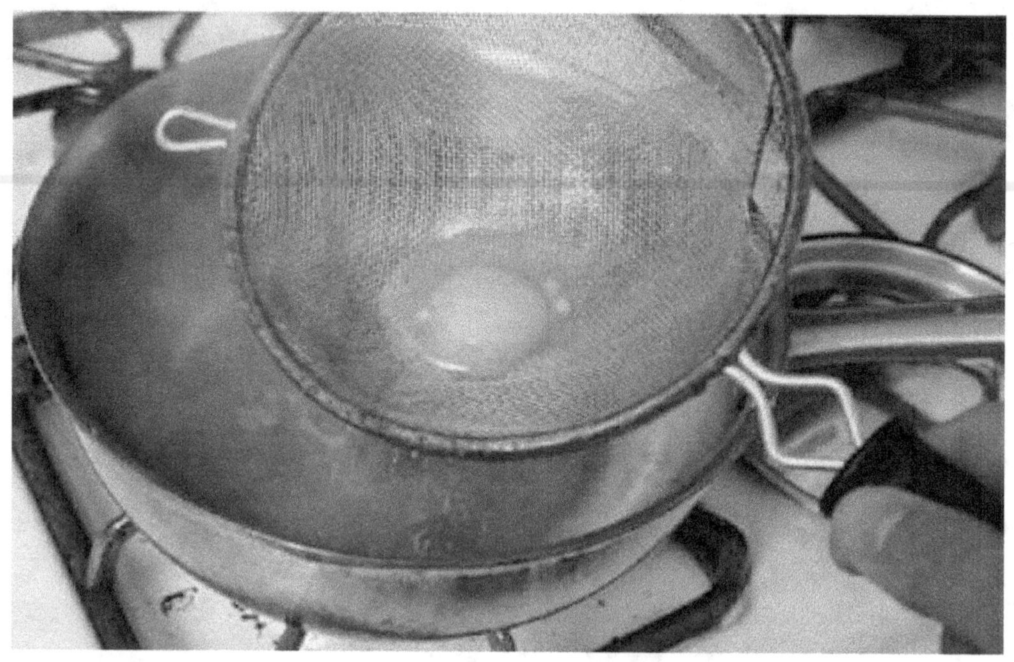

Cautiously lower into the subsimmering water.

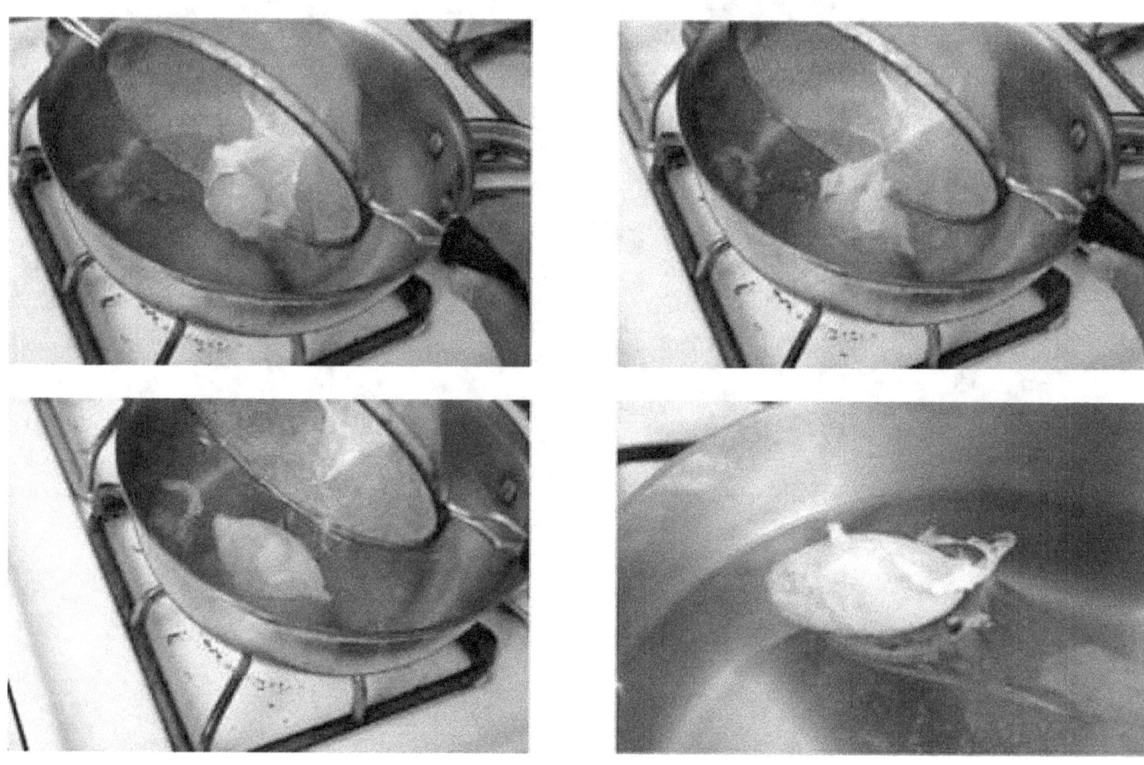

Carry the egg out, and keep it moving delicately with a wooden spoon.

COMMON POACHED EGG QUESTIONS

Q: I've read that adding vinegar to the water will help my eggs keep their shape better. Is this true?

Yes, ... sort of. Eggs set up when their proteins denature and coagulate. Egg proteins can be denatured by heat, but they can also be denatured by acid. Adding vinegar to your water indeed causes them to set faster, but the effect is not quick. Rather than causing them to set faster in the short term, which is what you care about, vinegar just causes them to overset as they cook, becoming dry and tough. What's more, vinegar can make your eggs taste, well, vinegary.

Q: Does salting make my eggs cook any better?

Nope. But there's a good reason to salt your water: *it makes your eggs tastier*. Just like pasta or potatoes, eggs absorb salt from the water as they cook, leading to a more evenly seasoned finished product.

Q: Why are poached eggs so freaking delicious?

This is a question that modern science has yet to answer and may well never get around to. Some scientists remark that the lack of progress on this particular front is due to the fact that other scientists don't spend the time to make and enjoy a good breakfast.

Q: Should I agitate my eggs as they cook, or swirl the water as I add them, as some books suggest?

The strainer-to-pan technique completely eliminates the need to swirl the water before you add the eggs, a trick designed to help the eggs keep a nice, even torpedo shape. What you *do* want to do is to make sure the eggs move around after they've started to set up. If you cook your eggs with no motion at all, they will end up resembling fried eggs in shape, with flat bottoms and a pronounced dome around the yolks. You also run the risk of overcooking the bottoms and toughening them, as they are in direct contact with the hot bottom of the pan. By moving them around in the water and gently flipping them, you get more even cooking and a more even shape. I use a wooden spoon to flip them with the water currents, rather than trying to pick them up with the spoon.

Q: Diners have, what, fifty seats in them? How the heck can I serve more than a few eggs at a time?

Diners are staffed by superhuman cooking machines known as short-order cooks, who have spent years practicing how to poach eggs perfectly. You want to get that good? One solution: practice.

OK, there's another way to get there, but don't tell anyone, promise? *Just cook the darn things in advance.* Poached eggs can be taken out of the pan right after cooking and transferred to cold water to chill. They'll stay there in a state of suspended animation for as long as you'd like. (Or as long as they don't begin to rot.) You can store them for a few hours or even a few nights in the fridge. Then, 15 minutes before you're ready to serve, just plop them into a bowl of hot water to warm up. Poached eggs by their very nature are never very hot—their yolks would solidify if they were. So 140°F, the temperature of hot water straight out of my tap, is just about the perfect temperature for reheating poached eggs.

WONDERFUL POACHED EGGS

3 quarts water

2 tablespoons legitimate salt

Huge eggs (as numerous as wanted)

1. Join the water and salt in a huge pot and heat to the point of boiling over high hotness, then decrease the hotness to the least setting.

2. Cautiously break the eggs into individual little dishes or cups. Cautiously tip one egg into a fine-network sifter set over a bowl and permit the abundance white to deplete, whirling the sifter tenderly. You ought to be left with the yolk encompassed by close egg white. Tenderly lower the sifter into the water, then slant the egg out into the water. Rehash with the leftover eggs.

3. Permit the eggs to cook, whirling the water every so often to keep them moving lethargically around the dish and delicately turning them, until the whites are completely set yet the yolks are as yet runny, around 4 minutes.

4. To serve right away, get the eggs each in turn with a punctured spoon and move to a paper-towel-lined plate to deplete momentarily. Serve.

5. Or on the other hand, to save the eggs for some other time, get the eggs each in turn with a punctured spoon and move to a bowl of cold water to chill, then, at that point, store lowered in the water in the cooler for as long as 3 days. To warm, move to a bowl of high temp water and permit to remain until warm, around 15 minutes.

HOLLANDAISE SAUCE

For some, hopeful French culinary specialists, incredible hollandaise is the worst thing about their reality. Far eliminated from the gloppy, oily stuff you get at the run of the mill cafe, or more regrettable, the powdered "simply add milk" cafeteria form, a genuine hollandaise is velvety and rich, outlandishly smooth, and completely even with the kinds of eggs, spread, and a bit of lemon juice. It ought to stream gradually off a spoon so it rests a poached egg in a thick robe. Never runny, and positively never soured, hollandaise has a fragile surface that is truly difficult to get right. In any event, it used to be. I've sorted out a method for making it entirely each and every time-even with no insight.

Hollandaise sauce, very much like mayonnaise, is an egg-balanced out emulsion of fat in a water-based fluid (see "Over the top Emulsive," here). It's customarily made by cooking egg yolks with a little water, whisking them continually, until they've quite recently started to set, then leisurely sprinkling in liquefied explained spread (see "Explained Butter," here) and preparing the sauce with lemon juice. With incredible whisking, the butterfat becomes separated into minute drops that are encircled by the water from the lemon juice and the egg yolks. Both the corrosive in the lemon juice and the protein lecithin in the egg yolks keep these fat drops from mixing and separating into an oily pool. The outcome is a thick, rich, delectable sauce.

Mayonnaise is moderately straightforward: it's produced using a fluid fat (oil), and it's made and kept at room or refrigerator temperatures (for an idiot proof formula, see here). Hollandaise is more convoluted. Butterfat starts to harden underneath 95°F, so assuming that you let your hollandaise get too cool, the strong lumps of fat will break the emulsion, turning it grainy. Warm it, and it will isolate into an oily fluid (that is the reason extra hollandaise can't be put away). Then again, in the event that you let it get too hot, the egg proteins will start to coagulate. You'll wind up with an uneven, soured sauce with the surface of delicate fried eggs. So the keys to an ideal hollandaise are two: cautious development of an emulsion by leisurely consolidating butterfat into the fluid, and temperature control.

When you understand this, the answer for idiot proofing hollandaise turns out to be very straightforward. Most exemplary plans expect you to warm both the margarine and egg yolks prior to attempting to consolidate the two. In any case, imagine a scenario where you were to simply warm one of them, so when it is joined with the other, the last temperature winds up in the right reach. I figured that assuming I warmed my margarine to a sufficiently high temperature, I ought to have the option to gradually consolidate it into a combination of crude egg yolks and lemon juice, bit by bit raising its temperature, so that when everything the spread is joined, the yolks are cooked precisely the way in which they should be. Since the causticity of lemon juice can limit turning sour, there's a smidgen of room, all things considered: anyplace in the 160° to 180°F territory for the completed sauce will work.

A blender and hot spread handily take care of hollandaise.

CLARIFIED BUTTER

Strong spread might appear as though a solitary, homogeneous substance, however liquefy it in a dish, and it rapidly becomes clear that it's comprised of a couple things.

• Butterfat makes up around 80% of the heaviness of spread (up to 84 percent for some very good quality "European-style" margarines, or as low as 65% for some new beaten, ranch stand-style spreads). Since there are various fats that make up butterfat, every last one of which relax and dissolves at a particular temperature range, spread goes through numerous textural changes as you heat it, gradually mellowing and turning out to be increasingly more pliant until at last, at around 95°F, each of the fats are melted.

• Water makes up one more 15 percent (down to 11 percent for top of the line spreads, up to 30 percent for new stirred margarines). In the cool environs of the refrigerator, the water and fat in a stick of margarine blend easily. However, apply an energy to the circumstance by warming it in a skillet, and ultimately the water converts to steam, framing little air pockets of fume and making your spread froth. When the frothing has died down, you realize that all of the water has made its departure and your spread has started to move above 212°F. Since water is denser than fat, when margarine is liquefied in a huge pot, this layer of water (and a couple of broken up proteins) will sink to the base, where it will start to bubble whenever warmed sufficiently long.

• Milk proteins, fundamentally casein, make up the excess 5% (or somewhere in the vicinity) of the spread. These proteins are the smooth white rubbish that floats to the highest point of

your margarine as you soften it, and these proteins will start to brown and ultimately consume and smoke as you heat spread in a hot skillet.

In view of its water and protein content, plain spread isn't the ideal vehicle for singing food-it can't get hot enough without consuming. Therefore, numerous gourmet experts make explained spread, margarine from which the water and protein have been taken out. It's the essential cooking fat in India, where it's known as ghee. You make it by liquefying spread, cautiously skimming the white milk proteins off the top, and afterward pouring off the brilliant fluid fat, disposing of the watery layer of proteins on the base. Once explained, margarine can be warmed to a lot higher temperatures unafraid of consuming.

As I referenced before, explained margarine is utilized to make an exemplary hollandaise, the reasoning being that the water constituent in entire spread will weaken the sauce. A lot simpler method for keeping away from this water in your completed sauce is to spill the dissolved spread gradually out of the dish until all that is left is the watery layer at the base, which you can then dispose of.

To test the hypothesis, I warmed up a few sticks of spread on the burner (the microwave likewise does fine and dandy) to 200°F, then leisurely sprinkled the margarine into my egg yolks and lemon juice, which I had running in the blender (adding a touch of water to the yolk combination keeps it from adhering to the dividers of the container). A fast smidgen of salt and cayenne pepper, and there it was: ideal hollandaise without the cerebral pain. To make it considerably more secure, I attempted it again utilizing a drenching blender and its container. I put the egg yolks, lemon, and water in the container, stuck the wand of the hand blender down in there, poured in all the dissolved spread, and turned on the blender. As the vortex drew margarine down into the spinning cutting edges, a thick, stable emulsion shaped like sorcery, until everything the spread was fused and my sauce was thick, rich, and light, the manner in which an extraordinary hollandaise ought to be.

FOOLPROOF HOLLANDAISE SAUCE

NOTE: Cooled hollandaise can be painstakingly warmed over the most reduced conceivable hotness while whisking continually. Hollandaise can't be refrigerated and afterward warmed.

MAKES ABOUT 1 CUP

3 huge egg yolks

1 tablespoon lemon juice (from 1 lemon)

1 tablespoon heated water

½ pound (2 sticks) unsalted spread, cut into unpleasant tablespoon-sized lumps

Touch of cayenne pepper

Fit salt

TO MAKE HOLLANDAISE WITH AN IMMERSION BLENDER

1. Add the egg yolks, lemon juice, and boiling water to the blender cup (or a cup that will scarcely hold the top of your blender).

2. Dissolve the margarine in a little pan over medium-low hotness and keep on warming until the spread simply starts to air pocket and registers 180° to 190°F on a moment read thermometer. Move it to a fluid estimating cup, leaving the slim layer of whitish fluid behind (dispose of it).

3. Embed the head of blender into the lower part of the cup and run the blender. Gradually pour in the hot spread. You ought to see the sauce start to shape at the lower part of the cup. As the sauce structures, gradually pull the top of the blender up to fuse more dissolved margarine, until all of the spread is fused and the sauce has the consistency of weighty cream. Season with salt and the cayenne to taste. Move to a serving bowl or little pan, cover, and keep in a warm spot (not straight over heat!) until prepared to serve.

TO MAKE HOLLANDAISE IN A STANDARD BLENDER OR FOOD PROCESSOR

1. Add the egg yolks, lemon juice, and heated water to the blender or food processor and mix on medium speed until smooth, around 10 seconds.

2. Liquefy the margarine in a little pot over medium-low hotness and keep on warming until the spread simply starts to air pocket and registers 180° to 190°F on a moment read thermometer.

3. With the blender running on medium speed, gradually shower in the spread throughout the span of 1 moment, halting to scratch down the sides as the need might arise and leaving the meager layer of whitish fluid in the lower part of the container (dispose of it). The sauce ought to be

smooth, with the consistency of weighty cream. Spice it up with some cayenne and salt to taste. Move to a serving bowl or little pan, cover, and keep in a warm spot (not straight over heat!) until prepared to serve.

EGGS BENEDICT

SERVES 2 TO 4

2 tablespoons genuine salt

2 teaspoons vegetable oil

4 cuts Canadian bacon or thick-cut ham

4 enormous eggs

2 English biscuits, split, toasted, and buttered

1 formula Foolproof Hollandaise (here), kept warm

Run of cayenne pepper (discretionary)

Minced new parsley or chives (discretionary)

1. Join 3 quarts water and the salt in a huge pot and heat to the point of boiling over high hotness.

2. While the water is warming, heat the vegetable oil in a 12-inch hardened steel or cast-iron skillet over medium hotness until gleaming. Add the Canadian bacon (or ham) and cook, turning once, until sautéed on the two sides, around 5 minutes. Move to an enormous plate and tent with foil to keep warm.

3. Cautiously break the eggs into individual little dishes or cups. Switch off the hotness under the bubbling water. Cautiously tip one egg into a fine-network sifter set over a bowl and permit the abundance white to deplete. You ought to be left with the yolk encompassed by close egg white. Delicately lower the sifter into the water, then, at that point, slant the egg out into the water. Rehash with the excess eggs.

4. Permit the eggs to cook, twirling the water every so often to keep them moving languidly around the container and delicately turning them, until the whites are completely set yet the yolks are as yet runny, around 4 minutes. Eliminate the eggs with an opened spoon and move to a paper-towel-lined plate to deplete.

5. Top every English biscuit half with a cut of Canadian bacon, trailed by a poached egg. Spoon some hollandaise sauce over the eggs, sprinkle with the cayenne pepper and spices, if utilizing, and serve right away, passing the additional hollandaise in a warm bowl as an afterthought.

EGGS FLORENTINE

Try not to eat on pig? No real reason to stress. Eggs and hollandaise go similarly too with great sautéed spinach (asparagus would likewise be extraordinary here).

SERVES 2 TO 4

Legitimate salt

2 teaspoons vegetable oil

1 medium clove garlic, finely minced

1 pack (around 4 ounces) spinach, managed, washed, and dried

Newly ground dark pepper

4 enormous eggs

2 English biscuits, split, toasted, and buttered

1 formula Foolproof Hollandaise (here), kept warm

Run of cayenne pepper (discretionary)

Minced new parsley or chives (discretionary)

1. Consolidate 3 quarts water and 2 tablespoons salt in an enormous pan and heat to the point of boiling over high hotness.

2. Heat the vegetable oil in a 12-inch tempered steel or cast-iron skillet over medium-high hotness until gleaming. Add garlic and cook, mixing continually, until fragrant, around 30 seconds. Add spinach alongside 2 tablespoons water, and cook, mixing sometimes, until the spinach is withered and the water is for the most part vanished. Season to taste with salt and pepper. Put it on a plate and put away.

3. Cook the eggs as coordinated in stages 3 and 4 of the eggs benedict formula, above.

4. Top every English biscuit half with one-fourth of the spinach, trailed by a poached egg. Spoon a portion of the hollandaise sauce over the eggs, sprinkle with the cayenne pepper and spices, if utilizing, and serve right away, passing the additional hollandaise in a warm bowl as an afterthought.

FRIED EGGS

On the off chance that you're like me, dominating seared eggs was your absolute first culinary achievement.

Or on the other hand, I ought to say, singed eggs were my absolute first effort to achieve something in the kitchen, since, honestly, the eggs were never a similar two times. This isn't really something terrible. Truth be told, assuming I'd been taking notes on precisely how and why my eggs were never the same way two times, I'd call that science. I'd likewise undoubtedly have fostered a decent strategy years sooner.

Recollect that egg whites begin setting at around 155°F, while egg yolks begin firming up as low as 145°F (see "Hotness and Eggs," here). This provides us with the fairly interesting issue of attempting to cook two distinct parts of one food in similar cooking medium at totally various rates. It's anything but a simple stunt to pull off, yet it very well may be finished.

We definitely know one thing without a doubt: assuming you believe your eggs should be picture-awesome, the yolks standing tall, fit to be punctured by a fork so their brilliant fortune falls gradually across a plane of tight, clean whites, their edges showing simply an exposed touch of freshness, you need to begin with the freshest-potential eggs. Depleting the eggs in a fine-network sifter very much as you accomplished for poached eggs (see here) helps with accomplishing this outcome, however by and by, I somewhat like the effervescent, meager whites that spread around the dish and become additional fresh as they cook. Truly amazing singed eggs are for ads.

A tight, tall yolk isn't just about looking great. With new eggs, the yolks are kept raised over the hot surface of the dish, permitting them to set somewhat more leisurely than the whites. This is critical in the event that you need your whites hazy before your yolks get hard.

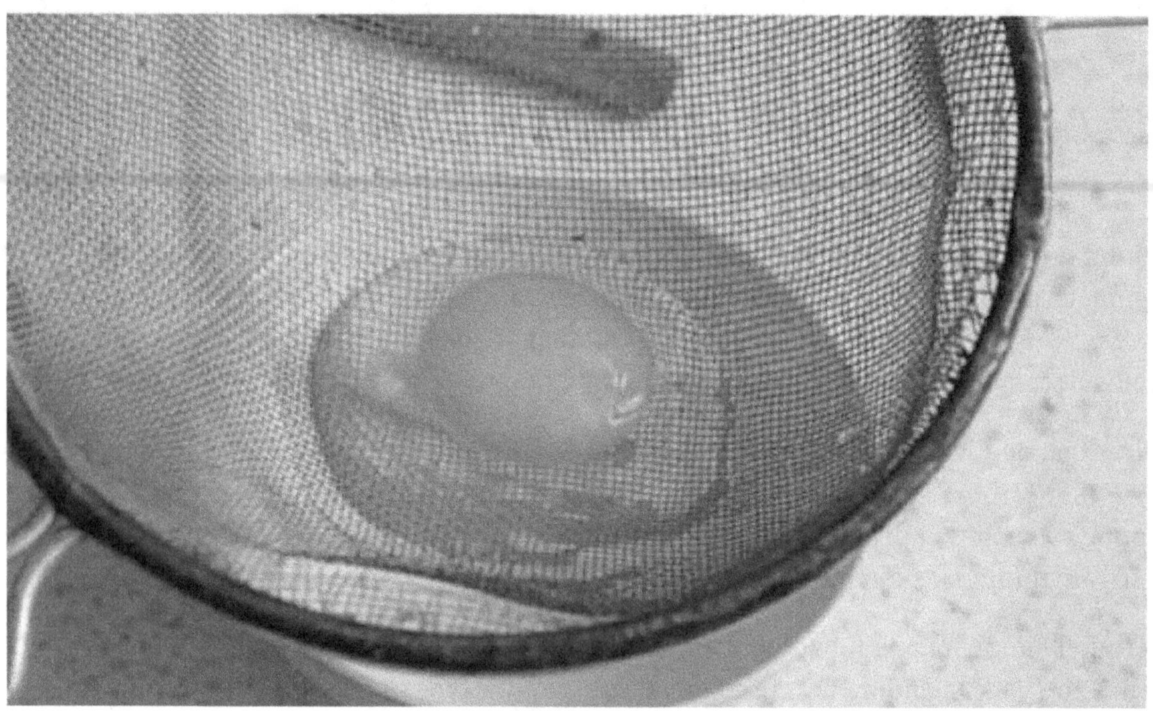

Stressing prior to fricasseeing gets you a truly amazing seared egg.

How else might you hold the yolks back from overcooking? All things considered, here's something else we know: egg yolks contain undeniably more fat than egg whites. Fortunately for us here, fat is a great protector that is, it moves energy less effectively than water does (that is the reason whales are shrouded in lard). We can utilize this reality for our potential benefit by changing the dish temperature. I cooked eggs in three distinct dish at three different hotness settings just until the whites were set.

• Over low hotness, the yolks came out totally firm and powdery at the base, with simply an exceptionally slim layer of scarcely fluid yolk at the top. The whites were incredibly rubbery and dry in everything except the thickest part around the yolk. With delicate hotness and a drawn out cooking time, the distinctions in conductivity between the egg yolks and the egg whites don't significantly affect their cooking rates-they fundamentally cook in a similar time. Furthermore, the egg whites were unadulterated white, with no crisping or sautéing by any means on the base surface. A few people prefer their egg whites as such. I think those individuals furtively simply need poached eggs.

• Over medium hotness, there was as yet a lot of fluid yolk at the highest point of the egg, while the base portion of the yolk turned out to be very firm. The whites took on a hint of carmelizing (significantly more assuming I utilized margarine rather than oil-the milk proteins in the spread brown and adhere to the eggs). This is a decent split the difference for people who like some fluid yolk yet don't maintain that their whites should show any straightforwardness whatsoever.

• Over high hotness, you can get whites that are totally set with yolks that are still totally fluid, however you run into another issue: the lower part of the eggs consumes well before the remainder of the egg is prepared to eat.

For the most straightforward singed eggs, moderate hotness is the best approach. Whether you're utilizing spread or oil has little effect in the cooking, as long as you ensure that the milk proteins in your margarine don't consume before you slip the eggs into the container; it's ideal to add them soon after the frothing dies down. (This means that the water in the spread has totally vanished and the container is some place in the 250°F territory). Spread will give you more extravagant flavor and more profound carmelizing, while oil will give you cleaner egg flavor and somewhat crisper bottoms-it's everything down to individual inclination.

For quite a while, I was content with my medium-heat eggs, forfeiting a touch of fluid yolk for the additional freshness in the whites, however at that point I saw a method in Spain that made me reevaluate the manner in which I seared eggs. There searing eggs not in a dainty layer of fat, but rather in a shallow pool of it's normal. Cooks would fill the dish with a half inch or so of olive oil and hotness it up to profound browning temperatures, then slant the container so the fat gathered on one side, drop in the eggs, and season them with the hot fat as they cooked. The eggs cooked quickly from all sides, the whites rapidly setting and changing into a gently silky, daintily frizzled shell around the still-fluid yolk. Imagine a scenario where I were to adjust part of this method to my singed eggs at home.

By warming up a couple of tablespoons of oil in a skillet (I utilize nonstick or a decent solid metal dish), I can get a comparative impact by then adding my eggs and utilizing a spoon to season the whites with the hot oil. The whites puff and fresh, setting quickly, while leaving the yolk scarcely warmed through. It's my new most loved method for eating singed eggs, particularly when I put it all on the line and utilize the extravagant jeans olive oil.

EXTRA-CRISPY SUNNY-SIDE-UP EGGS

SERVES 1

2 huge eggs

3 tablespoons olive oil (extra-virgin, assuming you like)

Legitimate salt and newly ground dark pepper

1. Break one egg into a little cup, then, at that point, move to a fine-network sifter set over a bowl and whirl delicately until any abundance white goes through. Return the egg to the cup. Rehash with the subsequent egg.

2. Heat the olive oil in a medium nonstick or cast-iron skillet over medium hotness until it registers 300°F on a moment read thermometer. Cautiously slip the eggs into the oil. Quickly slant the skillet so the oil pools on one side and utilize a spoon to spoon the hot oil over the egg whites, attempting to stay away from the yolks however much as could be expected. Keep doing this until the egg whites are totally set and fresh on the base, around 1 moment. With a spatula, move the eggs to a paper-towel-fixed plate and season with salt and pepper. Serve right away.

SCRAMBLED EGGS, TWO WAYS

There's a major separation in the realm of fried eggs . . .

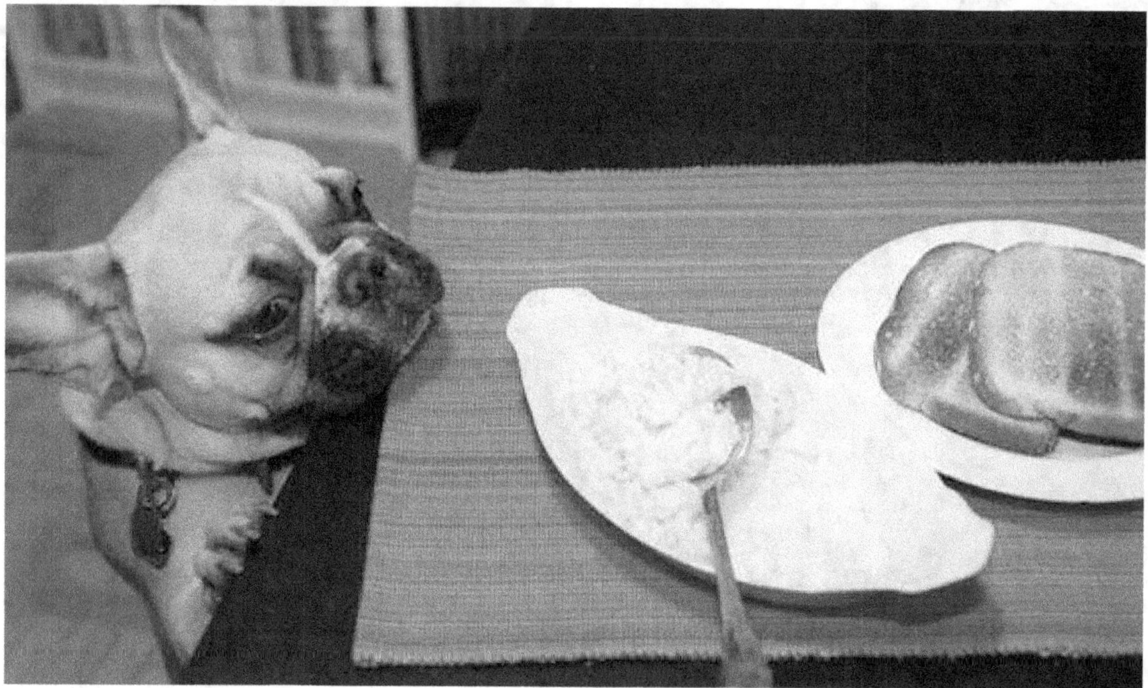

. . . between the individuals who like them rich, thick, and velvety (that is me), and the people who like them light, generally dry, and cushioned (that is my wife).* This is the sort of stuff that can truly destroy a home, so in light of a legitimate concern for keeping up with conjugal ecstasy, I concluded that it was just correct that I sorted out some way to make the two kinds of fried eggs so we could both partake in our morning meal.

Very much like with bubbled eggs, cooking fried eggs is tied in with controlling the coagulation of egg proteins, the distinction being that with fried eggs, not exclusively are the proteins in the whites and yolks combined as one, yet you likewise have the valuable chance to blend in extra fixings as well as to control the manner in which the eggs meet up by moving them as they cook. For my testing, I chose in any case downright eggs to measure the impacts of blending and other mechanical activities. The main added substance I utilized was a touch of spread in the dish to keep them from staying.

A couple of things turned out to be clear right away. The distinction between rich fried eggs and fleecy ones has generally to do with how much air they contain toward the end. As beaten eggs are warmed in a skillet, their proteins start to set. Simultaneously, the dampness inside them starts to vanish, making pockets of steam and air develop inside the eggs. Enthusiastic mixing or shaking will make these pockets of steam and air burst, making the eggs denser. Thus, for the fluffiest fried eggs, you want to limit the development of the eggs in the dish, delicately collapsing and turning them barely enough to motivate them to cook uniformly into enormous, brilliant, delicate curds.

For velvety eggs, consistent mixing is best, to eliminate abundance air and get the egg proteins to set up intimately with each other, bringing about a thick, nearly custard-like scramble.

Heat incredibly affected last surface too. Whenever cooked over extremely low hotness, even delicately collapsed eggs will not get excessively feathery. This is on the grounds that there's insufficient energy in the dish to make water fume structure or to cause air pockets to grow overwhelmingly. Thus, for feathery fried eggs, you really want to utilize somewhat high hotness (however in the event that you let the dish get excessively hot, you risk overcooking-or, more awful, carmelizing your eggs), while for velvety eggs, cooking over low hotness gives you substantially more command over their surface.

Added substances

Shouldn't something be said about normal increments to eggs-water, milk, and so forth? There are fundamentally two things they can do. To start with, they include some water, which makes for fluffier eggs (more water = more vaporization). Dairy fixings additionally add fat, which can obstruct egg proteins from connecting with one another, making a more delicate curd. This graph summarizes everything:

ADDITION	EFFECT ON TEXTURE AND FLAVOR	HOW IT WORKS
Nothing	Eggs cook fastest but are tougher	
Water	Increased fluffiness, diluted flavor	Extra water means more vaporization occurs, creating larger bubbles in the eggs and lightening them.
Milk	Increased fluffiness and tenderness	Milk is mostly water, which helps increase fluffiness, while the extra proteins and fats prevent the egg proteins from bonding too tightly, making them more tender.
Cream	Not as fluffy, but rich, with an almost cheesy flavor and texture	The high fat content of cream greatly reduces the bonding power of egg proteins.
Cold butter	Ultracreamy and dense	Cold cubes of butter not only add fat, for tenderness, but also help regulate temperature, cooling the eggs and letting them set more slowly; this leads to denser, creamier results.

With this information, my fleecy fried eggs were coming out extraordinary. I just needed to try to race in some milk alongside the eggs, to utilize moderately high hotness, to keep the blending and collapsing negligible, and to make a point to get them out of the hot dish before they were totally cooked. Indeed, even once out of the skillet, dampness will keep on vanishing from the eggs and the proteins will keep on setting more tight and more tight. Eliminating the eggs from the container when somewhat half-cooked guarantees that they show up at the table impeccably cooked.

My velvety eggs, then again, were giving me more issues. They were coming out fine when I began them with shapes of cold margarine, utilized low hotness, and mixed continually to separate curds and delivery air and fume, yet they were as yet not exactly as rich and smooth as I'd like. Salting them a long time prior to cooking (see "Salting Eggs," underneath) and allowing them to rest helped, however assuming there's one thing I got the hang of working in French cafés, it's that when all else falls flat, add more fat. My answer was to include additional egg yolks with everything else, as well as to complete the dish with a dash of weighty cream. The cream serves two capacities: it adds lavishness and smooths out the eggs' surface, and when added toward the finish of cooking, it additionally chills them off, keeping them from setting up too hard in the skillet. Furthermore, how's this for overlaying the lily?- use crème fraîche (see here) instead of weighty cream. The subsequent eggs are a definitive in extravagance: rich, delicate, nearly custard-like in surface. Eggs-ceptional! (Sorry.)

SALTING EGGS

Here is the situation: You've recently beaten a couple of eggs with a touch of salt, preparing to scramble them, when unexpectedly the canine stalls out in the latrine, your mother by marriage calls, and the UPS fellow rings the doorbell to convey your spic and span advanced thermometer. After thirty minutes, you return to those eggs and acknowledge they've totally changed shading. When radiant yellow and misty, they're presently dull orange and clear. What's happening? Also, more significant, will it influence the manner in which they cook?

Salt influences eggs by debilitating the attractive fascination that yolk proteins have for each other (indeed, egg proteins truly do think of each as other alluring). Egg yolks are contained large number of small inflatables loaded up with water, protein, and fat. These inflatables are too little to even think about seeing with the unaided eye, however they are sufficiently huge to keep light from going through them. Salt splits these circles up into much littler pieces, permitting light to go through, so the salted eggs turned clear. What's the significance here for the manner in which they cook? To find out, I cooked three clusters of eggs next to each other, taking note of their completed surface.

SALTING TIMING	RESULTS
15 minutes prior to cooking	The least watery and the most tender, with moist, soft curds
Just before cooking	Moderately tender and not watery
Toward the end of cooking	Toughest of the three, with a tendency to weep liquid onto the plate

Turns out that salt can significantly affect how eggs cook. Whenever eggs cook and coagulate, the proteins in the yolks pull increasingly tight together as they get more blazing. At the point when they get excessively close, they start to crush fluid out from the curds, bringing about eggs that sob in a most humiliating way. Adding salt to the eggs a long time prior to cooking can keep the proteins from holding too firmly by diminishing their fascination with each other, bringing about a more delicate curd and less probability of ugly sobbing. Adding salt preceding cooking helps, yet to get the full impact, the salt have the opportunity to disintegrate and turn out to be uniformly appropriated through the blend. This requires around 15 minutes-barely enough time for you to get your bacon cooked!

Eggs salted subsequent to cooking sob.

Eggs salted somewhere around 15 minutes ahead of time hold their dampness.

LIGHT AND FLUFFY SCRAMBLED EGGS

SERVES 4

8 enormous eggs

¾ teaspoon genuine salt

3 tablespoons entire milk

2 tablespoons unsalted margarine

1. Join the eggs, salt, and milk in a medium bowl and rush until homogeneous and foamy, around 1 moment. Permit to rest at room temperature for something like 15 minutes. The eggs ought to obscure in shading fundamentally.

2. Liquefy the spread in a 10-inch nonstick skillet over medium-high hotness, whirling the dish as it melts to cover equitably. Rewhisk the eggs until they are frothy, then move to the skillet and cook, gradually scratching the base and sides of the dish with a silicone spatula as the eggs cement. Then keep on cooking, scratching and collapsing continually, until the eggs have shaped strong,

damp curds and no fluid egg stays, around 2 minutes (the eggs ought to in any case show up somewhat underdone). Promptly move to a plate and serve.

CREAMY SCRAMBLED EGGS

SERVES 4

6 enormous eggs

2 enormous egg yolks

¾ teaspoon fit salt

2 tablespoon unsalted margarine, cut into ¼-inch 3D squares and chilled

2 tablespoons weighty cream or crème fraîche (see here)

1. Join the eggs, egg yolks, and salt in a medium bowl and rush until homogeneous and foamy, around 1 moment. Permit to rest at room temperature for somewhere around 15 minutes. The eggs ought to obscure in shading fundamentally.

2. Add the chilled margarine to the eggs, then, at that point, move the combination to a 10-inch nonstick skillet, place over medium-low hotness, and cook, mixing continually, until the spread totally softens and the eggs start to set. As the eggs become firmer, mix all the more quickly to separate the huge curds, and keep on cooking until no fluid egg remains.

3. Eliminate the skillet from heat, add the weighty cream, and, mix continually for 15 seconds; the eggs ought to be totally delicate with a custard-like surface that scarcely holds a shape when you heap them up. Move to a plate and serve right away.

HOMEMADE CRÈME FRAÎCHE

Crème fraîche is made by permitting weighty cream to ruin in a controlled manner. Microbes brought into the cream convert a portion of its sugar (mostly the perplexing carb lactose) into easier sugars and acidic results. This brings down the pH of the cream, making a portion of its proteins coagulate, making it thicker. Great crème fraîche has a rich, smooth surface, firm to the point of framing loosing tops, and a tart, somewhat cheddar like flavor. Locally acquired crème fraîche is extraordinary, yet it tends to be hard to find and expensive. Whenever I figured out that you can just blend buttermilk (which has live bacterial culture) into weighty cream and allow it to thicken for the time being to make a genuine crème fraîche at home, my psyche was blown. I like to share my incredible encounters, so here you go. Good for you!

I messed with the proportions of cream to buttermilk a considerable amount and in the end observed that it doesn't exactly make any difference so much. Add more buttermilk, and you'll require less time for it to thicken, yet it'll be less rich. Add less, and it takes more time, yet tastes better. One tablespoon for each cup (that is a 1:16 proportion) was about the ideal equilibrium for me.

It gets superrich and velvety at right about the 12-hour mark. You can end the interaction prior by refrigerating it to stop the bacterial activity this is valuable assuming you need a more slender Mexican-style crema agria for showering over your nachos or guacamole. For those of you stressed over cream ruining at room temp, that is the ticket: it's the great microbes from the buttermilk duplicating in there that keep the risky microorganisms from dominating.

Furthermore, let the marvelous start. Begin commencement.

SIMPLE HOMEMADE CRÈME FRAÎCHE

MAKES 2 CUPS

2 cups weighty cream

2 tablespoons buttermilk

Consolidate the weighty cream and buttermilk in a glass container or bowl. Cover and permit to rest at room temperature until thickened to the ideal surface, 6 to 12 hours. Store in the fridge in a fixed compartment for as long as about fourteen days.

OMELETS

Similarly likewise with fried eggs, there are two significant sorts of omelet:

. . . the good, large as-your-face, stuffed-to-the-overflow, fleecy, collapsed fifty-fifty, light brilliant earthy colored burger joint style omelet and its refined French cousin, the damp, delicate, light yellow assortment, tenderly moved like the world's most delectable stogie. Also, similarly likewise with fried eggs, the strategy by which the eggs are warmed and mixed is the essential variable that figures out what you end up with.

For soft, coffee shop style omelets, the key is to begin the eggs in hot margarine and move them as little as conceivable during cooking. Instead of stirring the dish and separating the huge curds, the best strategy is a move called the lift-and-slant: utilize a silicone spatula to lift up the edges of the omelet and push them toward the focal point of the skillet while shifting it, to permit the crude egg to run under. Rehashing this procedure implies virtually every one of the eggs can be set with insignificant blending. You'll in any case wind up with a smooth of crude egg across the top surface, which is not difficult to deal with: eliminate the skillet from the hotness, add anything that fixings you like (ham and cheddar are my #1), cover it with a top, and let the remaining hotness from the eggs tenderly cook the top through, then crease it fifty-fifty and serve.

A delicate, extravagant jeans omelet-the thoughtful I watched Jacques Pépin make look so natural can be made by cooking the eggs quick, however it's one of the most troublesome strategies in cooking (truly). Fortunately, however, it doesn't really need quick cooking, and whenever you've taken in the chilly spread block stunt you got with the smooth fried eggs to assist with directing the cooking temperature (see here), you can truly make a delicate French-style omelet in much a similar way, with slow cooking and steady mixing. The main troublesome aspect about this style of omelet is the rolling. Try to ensure that one side of the egg plate is thicker than the other by rapping the skillet pointedly against the oven as you get done with cooking so the eggs gather on the end inverse the handle. Then, at that point, let the base set marginally, and the omelet can be moved up, beginning at the more slender edge, prior to being turned out onto a plate.

A delicate French omelet.

DINER STYLE HAM AND CHEESE OMELET

It's essential to cook fillings without cheddar before you add them to the eggs, or they won't warm up enough while the omelet cooks. Then, at that point, throwing the cheddar with the cooked filling will assist with kicking it off dissolving, so that it's quite gooey when the omelet is done, without the need to overcook your eggs.

MAKES 1 LARGE OMELET, SERVING 2

5 huge eggs

¾ teaspoon genuine salt

¼ teaspoon newly ground dark pepper

2 tablespoons unsalted spread

4 ounces ham steak, diced

2 ounces cheddar, ground

1. Consolidate the eggs, salt, and pepper in a medium bowl and speed until homogeneous and foamy, around 1 moment. Permit to rest at room temperature for no less than 15 minutes. The eggs ought to obscure in shading fundamentally.

2. In the interim, liquefy 1 tablespoon of the margarine in a 10-inch nonstick skillet over medium hotness and cook until daintily seared. Add the ham and cook, blending habitually, until it has started to brown on the edges, around 3 minutes. Move the ham to a little bowl, add the cheddar, and throw to consolidate. Clear out the skillet with a paper towel and return it to medium hotness.

3. Add the leftover tablespoon of spread to the skillet and cook until gently carmelized. Rewhisk the eggs until frothy, then add to the skillet and cook, utilizing a silicone spatula to push the edges in toward the middle as they set and shifting the dish to spread the uncooked egg under. Keep pushing in the edges of the eggs and shifting the skillet, working generally around the dish, until the omelet is practically set, around 45 seconds. Sprinkle the ham and cheddar over portion of the omelet, eliminate from the hotness, cover, and let the omelet sit until it arrives at the ideal consistency, around 1 moment.

4. Utilizing the silicone spatula, slacken the edges of the omelet from the skillet and shake the skillet to guarantee that it's not stuck. Cautiously overlap the omelet down the middle, then slide it onto a serving plate and serve right away.

DINER STYLE MUSHROOM, PEPPER, AND ONION OMELET

1. Overlook the ham. Liquefy 1 tablespoon of the spread in a 10-inch nonstick skillet over medium-high hotness and cook until gently sautéed. Add ½ cup cut mushrooms, season with salt and pepper, and cook, mixing and throwing oftentimes, until they've delivered fluid, the fluid has vanished, and the mushrooms have begun to sizzle once more, around 3 minutes. Add ½ cup diced chime pepper and ½ cup diced onion, season with salt and pepper, and cook, blending and throwing often, until the vegetables are mellowed and delicately sautéed, around 5 minutes longer. Move to a little bowl, add the cheddar, and throw to consolidate.

2. Clear out the skillet with a paper towel, return it to medium hotness, and cook the omelet as coordinated. At the point when the omelet is practically set, sprinkle the vegetables over portion of it and continue as coordinated.

DINER STYLE ASPARAGUS, SHALLOT, AND GOAT CHEESE OMELET

1. Overlook the ham and cheddar. Liquefy 1 tablespoon of the margarine in a 10-inch nonstick skillet over medium-high hotness and cook until gently carmelized. Add 8 stalks asparagus, bottoms managed and cut into 1-inch fragments, season with salt and pepper, and cook, blending and throwing every now and again, until delicate and starting to brown, around 5 minutes. Add 1 huge shallot, daintily cut (about ½ cup) and cook until mellowed, around 3 minutes. Move the vegetables to a little bowl.

2. Clear out the skillet with a paper towel, return it to medium hotness, and cook the omelet as coordinated. Whenever the omelet is practically set, disperse the asparagus, shallots, and 2 to 3 ounces new goat cheddar, disintegrated, over portion of it and continue as coordinated.

<h1 style="text-align:center">KNIFE SKILLS:</h1>

<h2 style="text-align:center">Step by step instructions to Cut a Bell Pepper</h2>

There are two camps with regards to cutting peppers: the people who cut skin side up and the individuals who cut skin side down.

I used to be in the previous, tracking down that having the skin up was the main way I could get through it with my blade. The tissue would go about as help while the blade slice through the skin. Then, at that point, I understood that with a truly sharp blade, slicing through the skin when the pepper faces down isn't an issue, and cutting that way keeps you from packing the tissue.

To cut a ringer pepper, begin by parting it longwise in half through the stem with a sharp blade. Profoundly and dispose of. Take out the white ribs with your fingertips. For pepper strips, place each pepper half skin side down on the cutting board and cut longwise into portions of even width. For dice, hold a couple of strips all at once and cut across them.

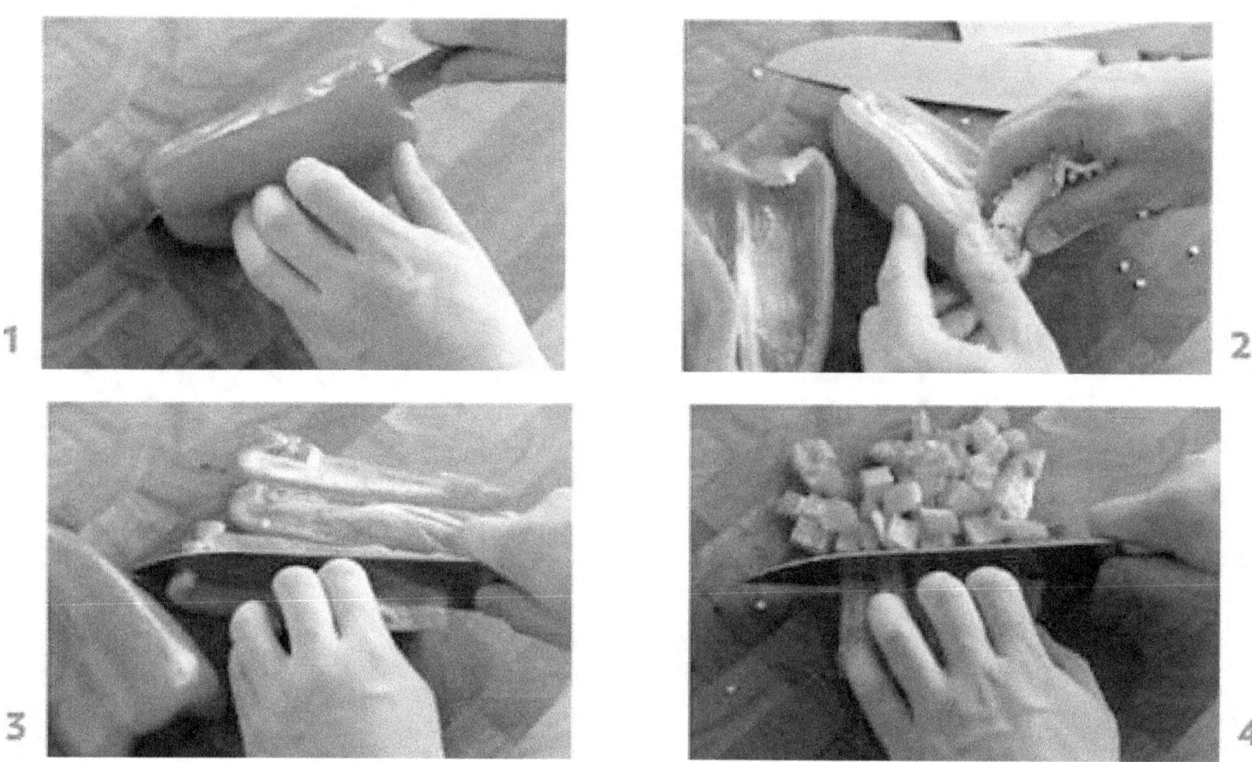

TENDER FANCY-PANTS OMELET

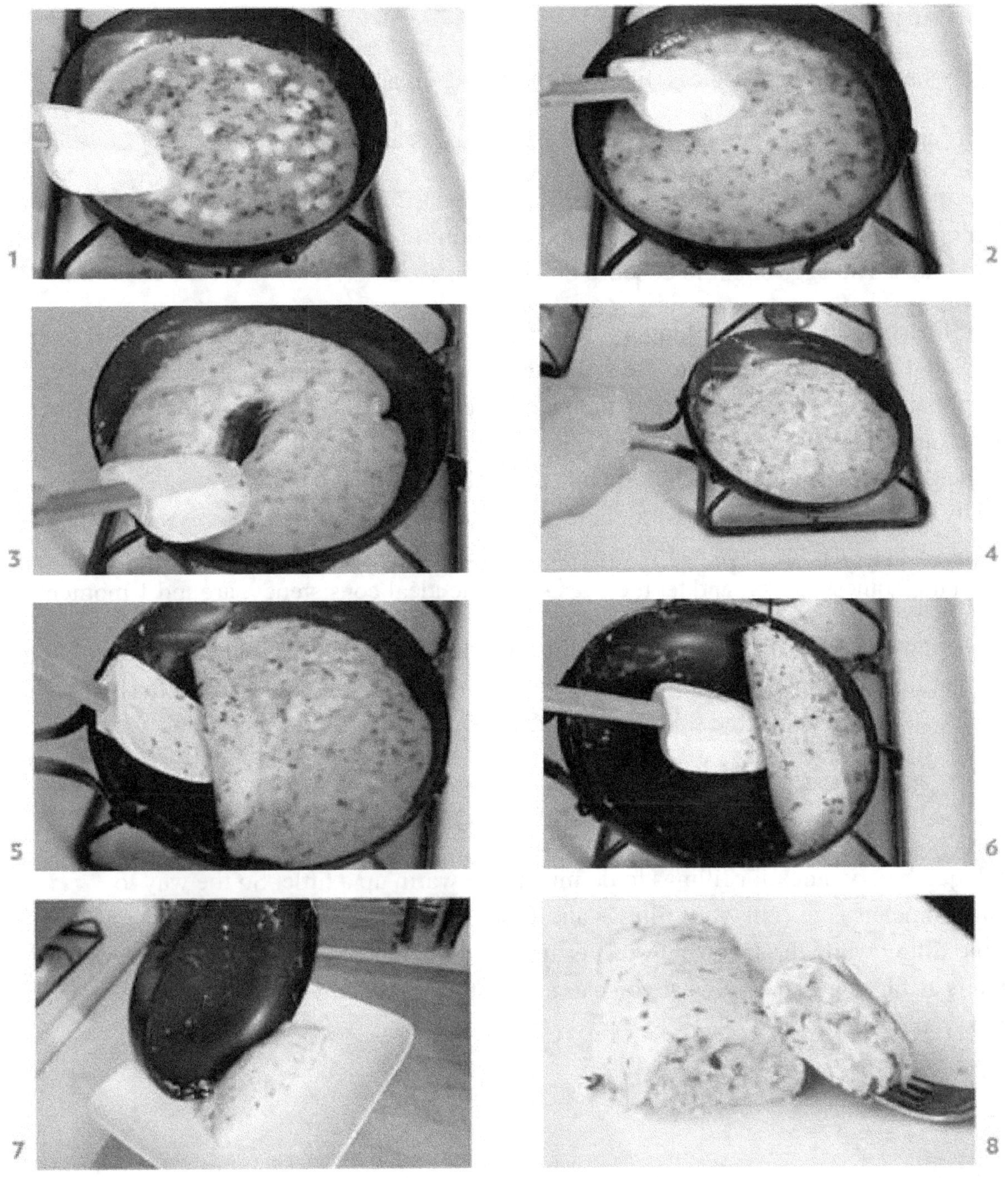

SERVES 1

3 enormous eggs

1 enormous egg yolk

½ teaspoon fit salt

¼ teaspoon newly ground dark pepper

1 tablespoon entire milk

1 tablespoon slashed blended new spices, like parsley, tarragon, and chives (discretionary)

1½ tablespoons unsalted margarine, cut into ¼-inch 3D squares and chilled

1. Consolidate the eggs, egg yolk, salt, pepper, milk, and spices, if utilizing, in a medium bowl and race until homogeneous and foamy, around 1 moment. Permit to rest at room temperature for no less than 15 minutes. The eggs ought to obscure in shading altogether.

2. Add 66% of the spread to the eggs. Liquefy the leftover spread in a 8-inch nonstick skillet over low hotness. Add the egg combination to the skillet and cook, mixing gradually and continually with a silicone spatula, scratching the eggs off the base and sides of the skillet, until the eggs have started to set, around 2 minutes. Then cook, mixing and scratching, until the eggs are sufficiently firm to hold their shape when you draw the spatula through them. Shake the dish to disseminate the eggs equally over the base and afterward, holding the handle so the container rests at a slight point, rap the skillet against the oven so the eggs are thicker on one side of the dish than the other. Eliminate from the hotness, cover, and let the eggs set to the ideal consistency, around 1 moment.

3. Eliminate the top and, utilizing the spatula, cautiously roll the omelet, beginning from the thicker side, then fold the finishes under. Cautiously turn the omelet out onto a plate (it assists with holding the plate in one hand and the skillet in the other), straighten out the shape, and serve right away.

OMELET FILLINGS

Omelets cook quick very quick for fillings to do much past warm up a little. So the way to incredible filled omelets is to cook your fillings ahead of time and have them warm and all set. Parcooking the filling while the salted eggs rest is an incredible method for getting it done. Your creative mind is as far as possible to what you can push into an omelet, yet here's a rundown of fixings to kick you off.

INGREDIENT	HOW TO PREPARE
Young cheeses of all kinds (I like cheddar, Jack, blue, feta, Gruyère, Brie, and goat cheeses)	Grate or crumble. If using in conjunction with other cooked ingredients, toss with them in a small bowl after parcooking them; the residual heat will help start the melting process.
Hard grating cheeses like Parmigiano-Reggiano, Cotija, and Pecorino Romano	Grate on a Microplane and add to the raw eggs.
Cured meats like sausage, ham, and bacon	Cut into ½-inch pieces or nuggets and parcook in butter (let bacon cook in its own fat) until crisp on the edges and well browned.
Firm vegetables like onions, shallots, bell peppers, and hot peppers	Dice and soften in butter.
Tomatoes	Dice, salt, and drain.
Tender leafy vegetables like spinach and arugula	Sauté in butter, with a bit of minced garlic if desired.
Tender squashes like zucchini and summer squash	Sauté in butter.
Asparagus	Cut into ¼-inch slices on the bias and sauté in butter.
Scallions	Thinly slice whites and sauté in butter; thinly slice greens and incorporate into the filling or reserve for garnish.
Mushrooms	Slice thin and sauté in butter until the moisture has evaporated and the mushrooms are well browned.
Herbs	Add directly to the raw eggs.

BACON

In the event that there's one certain method for ensuring a backslide in a vacillating vegan, it's to hang a segment of freshly singed bacon before him.

I in some cases imagine that the main thing keeping my marriage agreeable is the unduly huge number of make-up focuses I get each time I get my significant other bacon bed. Nowadays, I'm very great at cooking it, in the event that I in all actuality do say so myself, however this was not generally the situation. My bacon used to have a serious instance of bipolar problem: fresh and consumed in certain spots, flabby, rubbery, and half-cooked in others.

Accomplishing totally fresh, equitably cooked bacon is about tolerance. Bacon is comprised of two unmistakable components the fat (which is really a combination of fat and connective tissue) and the lean-and each cooks in an unexpected way. Fat will in general therapist rapidly when warmed, however after the underlying contracting stage, it invests in some opportunity to complete the process of cooking as the connective tissue that remains is gradually separated (half-cooked connective tissue causes rubbery bacon). The lean, then again, recoils not exactly the fat, and in view of this differential, your bacon turns and clasps (very much like the bimetal strip inside an indoor regulator). This contorting experiencing the same thing, in light of the fact that not exclusively are your fat and lean contracting at various rates, however whole segments of the strip are presently cooking at various rates, contingent upon if they are in direct contact with the container.

WET VERSUS DRY CURES

At this point, you probably seen that cocky bacon that is by all accounts attacking each rancher's market and grocery store in the country (also online sources). Is it worth its superior cost? Taking everything into account, that is just a question of individual inclination. Yet, there's an undeniably seriously convincing motivation to pick the extravagant stuff over the standard grocery store brands, and it's in the fix.

All bacon is relieved that is, treated with salt to adjust the construction of its proteins and protect it. Generally, the fix was a dry fix: salt (regularly with different flavors) was scoured onto sections of pork midsection. Throughout half a month, the salt worked its direction into the tummy at a comfortable speed, while the meat gradually lost dampness. The outcome was a thick hunk of profoundly enhanced tummy with moderately minimal leftover dampness. Some very good quality bacons are presently delivered utilizing this tedious technique.

Most store bacons, then again, are restored with a wet fix: a saltwater arrangement is infused into the meat in many spots. With this method, the salt can infiltrate the meat a lot quicker. What once required weeks is achieved surprisingly fast. Obviously, with the infusion of added water and lacking opportunity to dry, this alternate way bacon is far wetter than dry-restored bacon, with two outcomes. To begin with, it implies that you're paying more going on behind the scenes. That 1-

pound bundle contains essentially an ounce or two of added water weight. Second-and more significant it won't cook the same way.

Attempt it: fry a piece of normal grocery store bacon one next to the other with a segment of very good quality dry-relieved bacon. The store bacon will psychologist and twist significantly more than the dry-relieved bacon as its dampness vanishes. It'll likewise spit and falter undeniably more, because of the abundance water beads it's ousting as it cooks. Along these lines, setting flavor to the side, assuming you're continually maddened by bacon oil faltering onto your burner or that darned strip that simply won't lie level, you might need to consider changing to a bacon created the customary way, with a dry fix.

By cooking bacon over low hotness, the shrinkage differential can be limited, keeping your bacon compliment and permitting it to cook all the more equitably. A huge weighty skillet with even hotness appropriation is fundamental.

Need to cook bacon for a group? Do it in the stove. A stove warms considerably more uniformly than a skillet does, conveying completely fresh bacon by the trayful.

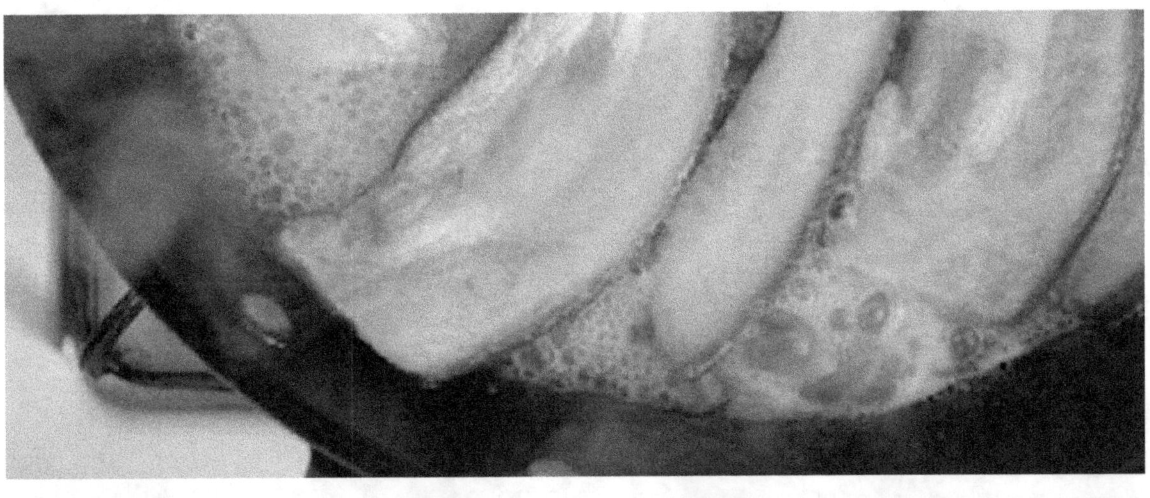

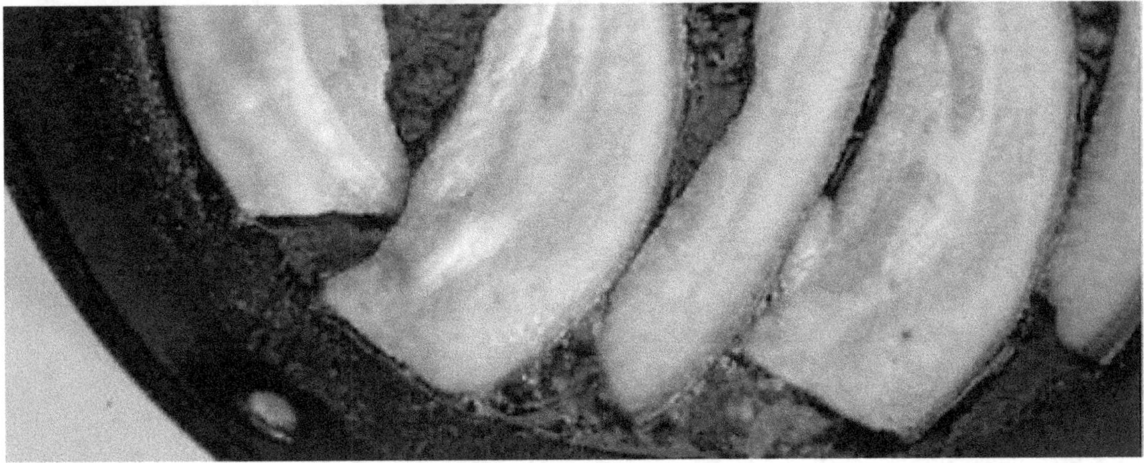

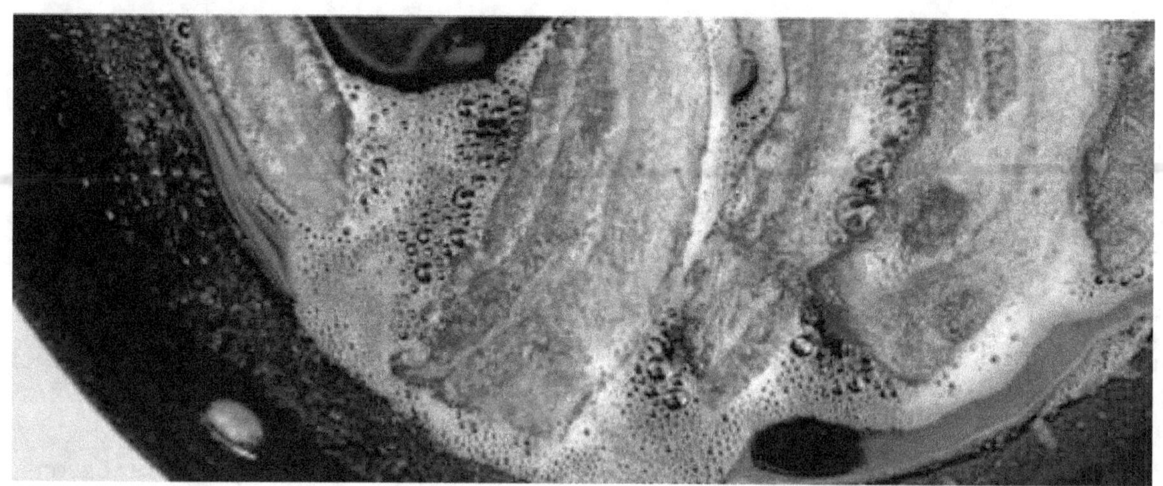

CRISPY FRIED BACON

SERVES 2 TO 4

8 cuts bacon, cut transversely down the middle

1. Place the bacon in an even layer in a 12-inch cast-iron or weighty lined nonstick skillet and cook over medium hotness until sizzling, around 4 minutes. Diminish the hotness to medium-low and keep on cooking until the fat is delivered and the bacon is fresh on the two sides, flipping and revising the cuts as needs be, around 12 minutes all out.

2. Channel the bacon on a paper-towel-lined plate and serve.

CRISPY OVEN-FRIED BACON

FOR A CROWD

SERVES 6 TO 10

24 cuts bacon (around 1 pound)

1. Change the broiler racks to the lower-and upper-center positions and preheat the stove to 425°F. Orchestrate the bacon cuts in a solitary layer on two rimmed baking sheets. Broil the bacon until it's fresh and brown, 18 to 20 minutes, turning the skillet back to front and start to finish partially through cooking.

2. Channel the bacon on a paper-towel-lined plate and serve.

CRISPY POTATO CAKE (AKA RÖSTI)

Fresh and brilliant brown outwardly, smooth and delicate in the center,

. . . with some great garlicky mayo (aioli, maybe) for plunging, the way to truly extraordinary rösti is adjusting how much starch that the completed potato cake holds. Too little starch, and it self-destructs. To an extreme, and it comes out tacky. Potato cells contain their own starch, so this truly turns into an issue of how to slice the potatoes to deliver the perfect sum. You can grind them on a case grater or in the food processor, however on the off chance that you do, you'll wind up bursting potato cells, letting a huge load of fluid and starch out of inside them. Then, at that point, you're compelled to press the shreds dry, and your rösti will come out dull and tacky, even with moderately low-starch potatoes like Yukon Golds.

Much better, however somewhat more troublesome, is to cut them on a mandoline. Assuming you have one with additional teeth or edges (which you ought to!), it'll cut the potatoes straightforwardly into $\frac{1}{16}$-inch shreds for you. On the off chance that you don't, it's adequately simple to cut the potatoes into flimsy boards and afterward utilize a blade to get the matchsticks you really want. A sharp mandoline (and a sharp blade) = less burst cells = less tacky starch discharge = better surface and more potato flavor in each chomp. A few sources prescribe flushing the slice potatoes to free them totally of their starch, then adding a deliberate measure of unadulterated potato starch to them prior to cooking, yet I find the outcomes inadmissible. Flushed potatoes don't relax as expected when cooked, and you end up with rösti with still somewhat firm pieces of crunchy potato inside.

The other key to incredible rösti is to parcook the potatoes prior to fricasseeing them. Why? Indeed, anyone who's worked the French fry station at a café realizes that potatoes start to oxidize when you cut them. Throughout fifteen minutes or thereabouts, a cut potato will go from being pale white to rosy brown, and ultimately to dark. You don't believe that your potatoes should be dark. Putting away cut potatoes in water will keep this from occurring (or possibly dial it back), however it likewise flushes away loads of starch. Too little starch is similarly all around as terrible as an excessive amount of starch in rösti, so I try not to wash or lowering my potatoes in water anytime. Parcooking the potatoes achieves the objective of keeping them from cooking and furthermore prompts a superior surface in the completed item you don't need to stress over crude potato in the focal point of the potato cake. Here the microwave is really the most ideal device to get everything done. It permits you to cook the potatoes quickly without either adding dampness or losing an over the top sum.

For a gussied-up variant, I sauté onions and mushrooms until a profound brilliant brown and flavor them with a touch of thyme to frame a focal layer in my potato cake. You could utilize whatever sautéed vegetables you need.

After you have your stuffing (if any), cooking the rösti is a straightforward matter of moderate hotness and a decent thick container that will cook it tenderly and uniformly. I utilize an all around prepared cast-iron container, yet you can utilize a decent nonstick skillet on the off chance that you don't have a solid metal one. Crisping the potatoes appropriately takes some time, which gives you a lot of chance to blend your espresso or press your mangoes, or set up whatever else it is your life partner likes presented with their early lunch.

FUNDAMENTAL CRISPY POTATO CAKE

(Otherwise known as RÖSTI)

SERVES 2 OR 3

3 medium reddish brown (baking) potatoes (around 1 pound), washed and cut into 1/16-inch matchsticks or ground on the enormous openings of a container grater

¼ cup olive oil

Legitimate salt and newly ground dark pepper

1. Spread the potatoes on a huge microwave-safe plate and microwave on high until hot the entire way through and relaxed yet at the same time marginally crunchy, around 5 minutes.

2. Heat 2 tablespoons of the oil in skillet over medium hotness until shining. Add the potatoes and press into the lower part of the skillet with an elastic spatula. Season with salt and pepper. Cook, twirling and shaking the dish at times, until the potatoes are profound brilliant brown and fresh on the primary side, around 7 minutes. Cautiously slide the rösti onto an enormous plate. Set one more plate on top of it, topsy turvy, hold the edges, and upset the entire thing so the rösti is currently concocted side.

3. Heat the leftover 2 tablespoons oil in the skillet and slide the rösti back in. Season with salt and pepper. Keep cooking, twirling and shaking the skillet incidentally, until the rösti is profound brilliant brown and fresh on the subsequent side, around 7 minutes longer. Slide onto a cutting board and serve right away, with aioli or mayonnaise, or ketchup.

CRISPY POTATO, ONION, AND MUSHROOM CAKE

(Otherwise known as RÖSTI)

SERVES 2 OR 3

3 medium chestnut (baking) potatoes (around 1 pound), flushed and cut into 1/16-inch matchsticks or ground on the enormous openings of a crate grater

5 tablespoons olive oil

1 medium onion, finely cut (around 1 cup)

4 ounces button mushrooms, finely cut

2 medium garlic cloves, minced or ground on a Microplane (around 2 teaspoons)

1 teaspoon new thyme leaves

Genuine salt and newly ground dark pepper

1. Spread the potatoes on a huge microwave-safe plate and microwave on high until hot the entire way through and mellowed yet marginally crunchy, around 5 minutes.

2. In the mean time, heat 1 tablespoon of the oil in a 10-inch cast-iron or weighty lined nonstick skillet over medium-high hotness until shining. Add the onions and mushrooms and cook, blending and throwing at times, until relaxed and beginning to brown, around 8 minutes. Add the garlic and thyme and cook, blending much of the time, until fragrant, around 30 seconds. Season to taste with salt and pepper. Move to a little bowl and crash the skillet.

3. Heat 2 tablespoons oil in the skillet over medium hotness until sparkling. Add half of the potatoes and press into the lower part of the dish with an elastic spatula. Season with salt and pepper. Spread the onion/mushroom blend equally over the potatoes and top with the excess potatoes. Push down into an even circle, utilizing the spatula. Season with salt and pepper. Cook, whirling and shaking the container sporadically, until the potatoes are profound brilliant brown and fresh on the primary side, around 7 minutes. Cautiously slide the rösti onto an enormous plate. Set one more plate on top of it, topsy turvy, hold the edges, and reverse the entire thing so the rösti is presently concocted side.

4. Heat the leftover 2 tablespoons oil in the skillet and slide the rösti back in. Season with salt and pepper. Keep cooking, twirling and shaking the container periodically, until the rösti is profound brilliant brown and fresh on the subsequent side, around 7 minutes longer. Slide the rösti into a cutting board. Serve right away, with aioli or mayonnaise, or ketchup.

POTATO HASH

Hash is the sort of breakfast that happens when I intend to go shopping for food on a Friday night. This is never really smart. Allow me to provide you with a thought of how it functions.

The Plan: I get up Friday morning new and dewy-confronted, prepared for an entire day of work, trailed by an outing to New York Mart for some produce, a speedy tram ride home, and a couple of long periods of cooking. My significant other returns home, we appreciate supper, several rounds of online Jeopardy!, get an episode of How I Met Your Mother, and hit the hay early, prepared to confront a good breakfast in the first part of the day.

The Reality: I get up Friday morning, scarcely over a cold from prior in the week, set out in toward a day at work, get found out in gatherings the entire morning before at last getting to begin my genuine work in the late evening, don't finish however much I trusted, and say, "Screw it, it's Friday, time for party time." Instead of go out on the town to shop for food, I get a blended beverage, then, comprehend that New York Mart is presently closed, perceive the grave bumble I've made in my dinner arranging, and send down one more mixed drink to stay with the first. My significant other winds up gathering me downtown for another mixed drink, trailed before supper out (that is a jug of wine and an after-supper drink), and since we've proactively made an evening of it, we should truly make an evening of it. Before I know it, it's early afternoon on Saturday, the canine should be strolled, and I have only a couple of potatoes, a few eggs, and an irregular extras in my storage room to nurture us back to great wellbeing.

Thank god for hash, isn't that so?

Hash is a definitive extra customer. All you really want is a bland root vegetable to frame the base (potatoes are the typical decision, however yams or beets are extraordinary as well), anything extras you have available cooked meat, greens, vegetables, whatever-a decent solid metal skillet, and several eggs, and you have the makings of a morning meal that will startle any headache into calm accommodation. As I notice for my rösti plans, the most effective way to get a decent soft/fresh surface out of your potatoes is to bubble them, dry them, and afterward fry them (see here). This permits the oil to enter somewhat more profound, expands the surface region by making the potatoes rankle, and makes for a far crisper completed item. Yet, who possesses energy for all that when there's a cerebral pain that requires tending to?

All things being equal, it's a lot more straightforward to cut the potatoes, put them on a plate, and microwave them for the underlying cooking venture, as I accomplish for rösti. This'll allow you to mellow them and cook them through without agonizing over them getting waterlogged or excessively wet on their outside, and what requires ten minutes in a pot requires under three minutes in the nuker. When they are parcooked, I add the potatoes to a hot skillet to start the crisping/roasting process while I generally cleave up my vegetables-for this situation, peppers and onions. In a murky daze, I've taken a stab at throwing the parcooked potatoes and different vegetables together prior to adding them to the skillet, yet that is an incredibly ill-conceived notion, bringing about consumed onions and none-too-fresh potatoes.

You want to give the potatoes an early advantage on the other vegetables, just adding the veg once a fresh hull has created.

Coincidentally, never feel like you're restricted in what the future held a decent breakfast hash. Cabbages (like bok choy or Brussels sprouts) create a wonderfully sweet nutty, flavor as they singe. Restored meats like pastrami or corned hamburger will fresh pleasantly, their fat enhancing the potatoes as they cook. Shallots and onions turn sweet and complex, while green vegetables like broccoli or asparagus get well scorched and delicate. When the potatoes are totally fresh, the peppers and onions in this one are entirely delicate and sweet, and the headache has started to discharge a weak, shrill whine of dread.

The nail in the final resting place? A sprinkle of hot sauce, which adds a hint of hotness, in any case, more significant, vinegar, to light up things up.

Every one of the amazing scents exuding from the skillet are to the point of stirring my hunger up into a close to free for all, so several eggs in the blend are an easy decision. You can sear your eggs in a different skillet, yet it's a lot simpler just to make two or three wells in the hash, break your eggs straightforwardly into the container, and polish the entire thing off in the stove until the whites are scarcely set yet the yolks still runny. Beginning to end, it requires under fifteen minutes, and that implies it's hot and on the table all before my better half is even back with the canine.

An extraordinary method for beginning your Saturday evening as early as possible.

Add your onions too early and you end up with consumed onions.

POTATO HASH

WITH PEPPERS AND ONIONS

NOTE: The potatoes can likewise be parcooked on the burner rather than in the microwave. Cover them with cold salted water in an enormous pan and heat to the point of boiling over high hotness, then lessen to a stew and cook until they are scarcely half-cooked. Channel and go on with stage 2.

SERVES 4

1½ pounds reddish brown (baking) potatoes (around 4 medium), stripped and cut into ½-inch blocks

3 tablespoons vegetable oil

1 little red ringer pepper, meagerly cut

1 little green chime pepper, daintily cut

1 little onion, meagerly cut

1 teaspoon of Frank's or other RedHot sauce, or more to taste

Genuine salt and newly ground dark pepper

4 enormous eggs (discretionary)

1. In the case of utilizing the eggs, change a broiler rack to the upper-center position and preheat the stove to 400°F. Spread the potatoes on an enormous microwave-safe plate, cover with paper towels, and microwave on high until warmed through yet somewhat half-cooked, 4 to 6 minutes.

2. Heat 2 tablespoons of the oil in a 12-inch cast-iron or nonstick skillet (or two 10-inch skillets) over high hotness until delicately smoking. Add the potatoes and cook, blending and throwing them sporadically, until all around carmelized on about a large portion of the surfaces, around 5 minutes. Lessen the hotness in the event that the dish is smoking vigorously.

3. Add the peppers and onions and cook, throwing and mixing periodically, until every one of the vegetables are carmelized and singed in spots, around 4 minutes longer. Add the hot sauce and cook, blending continually, for 30 seconds. Season to taste with salt and pepper. In the event that not utilizing eggs, serve right away.

4. In the case of utilizing eggs, make 4 wells in the potatoes and break the eggs into them. Season the eggs with salt and pepper, then, at that point, move the skillet to the stove. Cook until the whites are recently set, around 3 minutes. Serve right away.

POTATO AND CORNED BEEF HASH

Supplant the peppers and onions with 8 ounces extra corned meat, destroyed into scaled down chunks.

Instructions to Cut a Potato

Potatoes are weighty and cumbersome, with a knotty round shape that makes them difficult to hold consistent.

This is awful information assuming you need even cuts-and every one of your fingers. Try to initially cut off one side, making a steady base to lay the potato on.

To dice a potato, begin by stripping it with a Y-peeler, if stripping. Wash under cool water and utilize the eye-remover to gouge out any eyes. Hold the potato immovably on a cutting board and cut a ¼-to ½-inch-thick chunk off one side. Turn the potato cut side down and cut longwise into boards of even thickness. Working with a couple of boards all at once, stack them and cut longwise into even implement. Then, at that point, for dice, hold a couple of twirly doos at an at once across them to make dice of even width. Cut potatoes will stain, so cook right away or store in cool water.

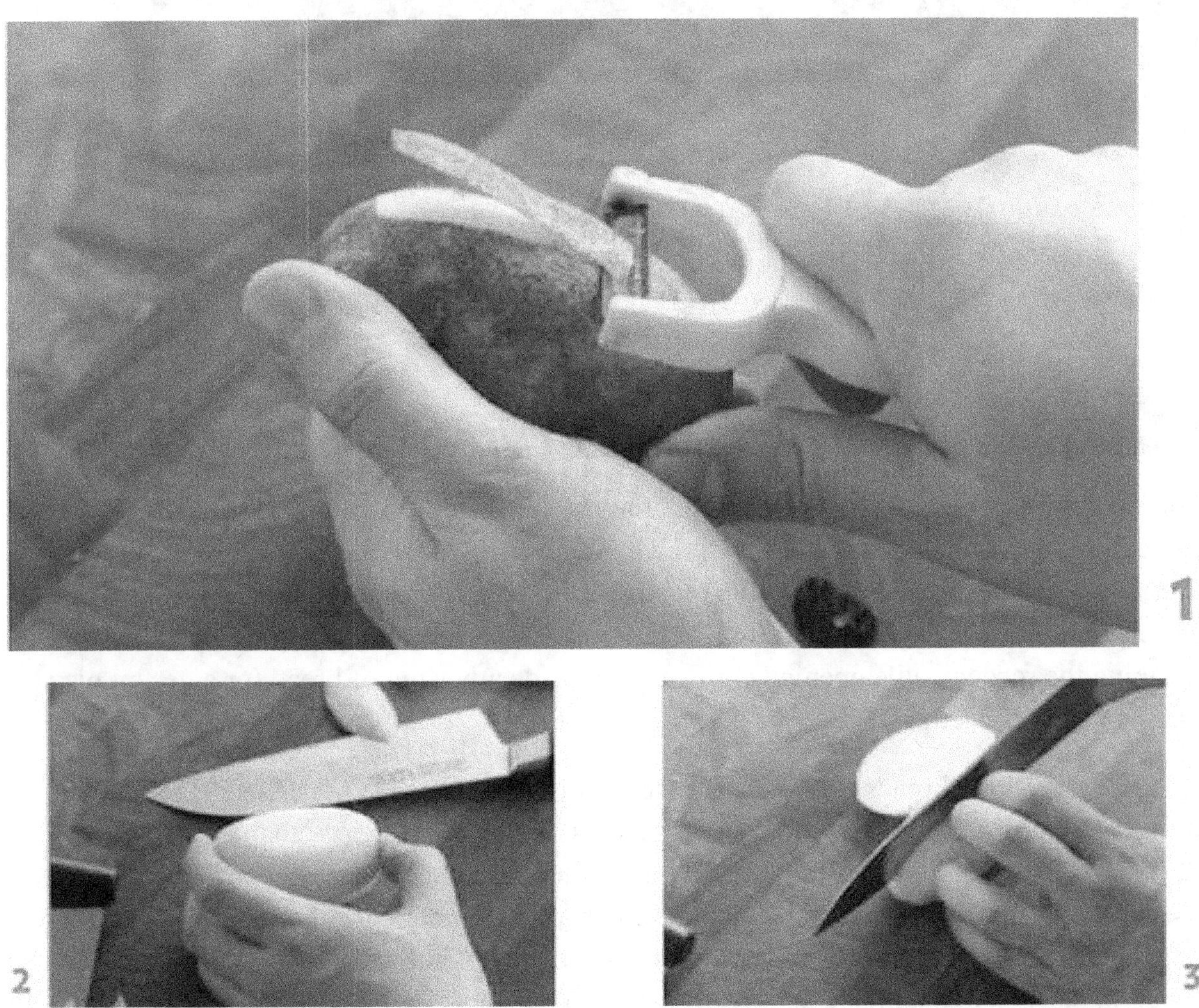

BUTTERMILK PANCAKES

They might be brilliant brown, fresh on the edges, and light and cushioned in the middle, however when you get directly down to it, exemplary American hotcakes are not too unique in relation to any raised bread.

Aside from its starch content, bread is essentially only a chunk of protein loaded up with gas (a lot of like my canine, in that respect)†. At the point when flour is blended in with fluid, two proteins normally present in wheat, glutenin and gliadin, connect together to shape the strong, stretchy protein framework known as gluten. In raised breads, air bubbles are framed in this grid and extend, making the recognizable opening construction inside a portion of bread (or a decent pizza hull, so far as that is concerned).

With customary or "slow" breads, that raising specialist is a living organism called yeast. As the yeast consumes sugars present in the flour, it discharges carbon dioxide gas, shaping a huge number of minuscule air pockets inside the batter and making it rise. When you pop that mixture into the stove, those air pockets heat up and additionally extend, and a peculiarity known as broiler spring happens. At last, as the gluten and starches get adequately hot, they set into a semisolid structure, giving design to the bread and diverting it from wet and stretchy to dry and springy.

The main issue with yeast? It takes a long, long opportunity to work. Enter baking pop. Unlimited by the extended time spans of natural creatures, it depends rather on the speedy substance response between a corrosive and a base. Baking soft drink is unadulterated sodium bicarbonate-a soluble (otherwise known as fundamental) powder. When broken up in fluid and joined with a corrosive, it quickly responds, separating into sodium, water, and carbon dioxide. Similarly as with yeasted breads, this carbon dioxide develops baking, raising the gluten protein framework. This kind of synthetically raised bread is alluded to as a speedy bread, a general class that incorporates everything from scones and rolls to banana or zucchini bread and even flapjacks.

Obviously, for baking soft drink to work, a formula needs to incorporate a critical acidic fixing. That is the reason you see such countless exemplary plans for buttermilk flapjacks and buttermilk bread rolls or cake plans that contain vinegar. The buttermilk isn't simply an enhancing specialist it furnishes the vital corrosive to respond with the baking pop and raise the bread. Around the center of the nineteenth century, somebody understood that as opposed to depending on the home cook to add an acidic fixing to respond with the baking pop, it'd be a lot more straightforward to add a powdered corrosive straightforwardly to the baking soft drink itself, and it was destined to prepare powder. Made out of baking pop, a powdered corrosive, and a starch (to retain dampness and keep the corrosive or base from responding rashly), baking powder was promoted as the across the board answer for occupied housewives. In its dry express, it's absolutely latent. Yet, when you add a fluid, the powdered corrosive and base break down and respond with one another, making air pockets of carbon dioxide, without the requirement for an outer corrosive source.

Perfect, isn't that so? Yet, hang on-there's something else.

Side Effects

The most intriguing result of involving baking soft drink in a formula is that it influences sautéing in a significant manner. The Maillard response, named after Louise Camille Maillard, who initially portrayed its cycles in the mid 20th century, is the arrangement of responses answerable for that excellent earthy colored covering on your steak and the profound shade of a decent portion of bread. Beside beauty care products, the response additionally delivers many sweet-smelling intensifies that add a supreme appetizing quality and intricacy to food varieties.

It just so happens, the response happens better in basic conditions, and that implies that whenever you've added sufficient baking soft drink to kill the corrosive in a hitter or mixture, any additional you add will attempt to increment searing. So I made five groups of hotcakes utilizing indistinguishable hitters comprising of flour, baking powder, egg, buttermilk, liquefied margarine, salt, and sugar and differing measures of baking pop, beginning with none and expanding it by ⅛-teaspoon increases up to a full ½ teaspoon for each clump. Every flapjack was cooked on a preheated iron for precisely 1½ minutes per side. The outcomes plainly exhibit the cooking impact of baking soda.

Baking soft drink influences pH, which thus influences searing.

The flapjack as far as possible on the left is unreasonably acidic, due to the unneutralized buttermilk. It concocted pale and dull. It was likewise underrisen, with a level, thick surface. The one as far as possible around on the base, with a full ½ teaspoon of baking soft drink in the player, had the contrary issue. It carmelized extremely rapidly, loaning it a bitter consumed flavor touched with the foamy substance trailing sensation of unneutralized baking pop. Strangely, this flapjack was additionally level and thick the huge measure of baking soft drink responded too savagely when blended into the hitter. The carbon dioxide bubbles expanded too quickly and, similar to an overloaded inflatable, the flapjack "popped," becoming thick and flabby as it cooked.

This searing peculiarity isn't simply restricted to hotcakes, obviously. For instance, treat plans regularly incorporate baking soft drink to help carmelizing, in any event, when there is anything but a corrosive for it to respond with.

Double Bubble

Assuming there's one significant disadvantage with artificially raised breads, it's that they should be cooked essentially following the player is blended. Not at all like a yeasted bread mixture, which is low in dampness and manipulated until an intense, versatile gluten network structures to trap the huge measures of carbon dioxide delivered, a speedy bread should be made with an incredibly soggy player baking powder basically doesn't create an adequate number of gas to actually raise a thicker batter. Hitters have somewhat little gluten development, implying that they aren't too extraordinary at catching and holding bubbles. When you blend a hitter, your baking pop or baking powder quickly starts delivering gas, and that gas very quickly being attempting to escape out of sight. While working with fast breads, the individuals who aren't into the entire quickness thing might run into hardships.

Cook your flapjacks following blending, and you get a light, tall, cushioned inside. Allow the player to sit for 30 minutes, and you get a thick, sticky inside with few air pockets. In any case, stand by a moment, there are still a few air pockets in there, correct? Where did those come from?

Indeed, essentially all baking powder is the thing is alluded to as "twofold acting." Just as the name shows, it produces gas in two unmistakable stages. The first happens when you blend it in with water; the second happens just when it is warmed (see "Test: Double-Acting Baking Powder," here). This second ascent in the skillet makes for extra-light and cushy flapjacks.

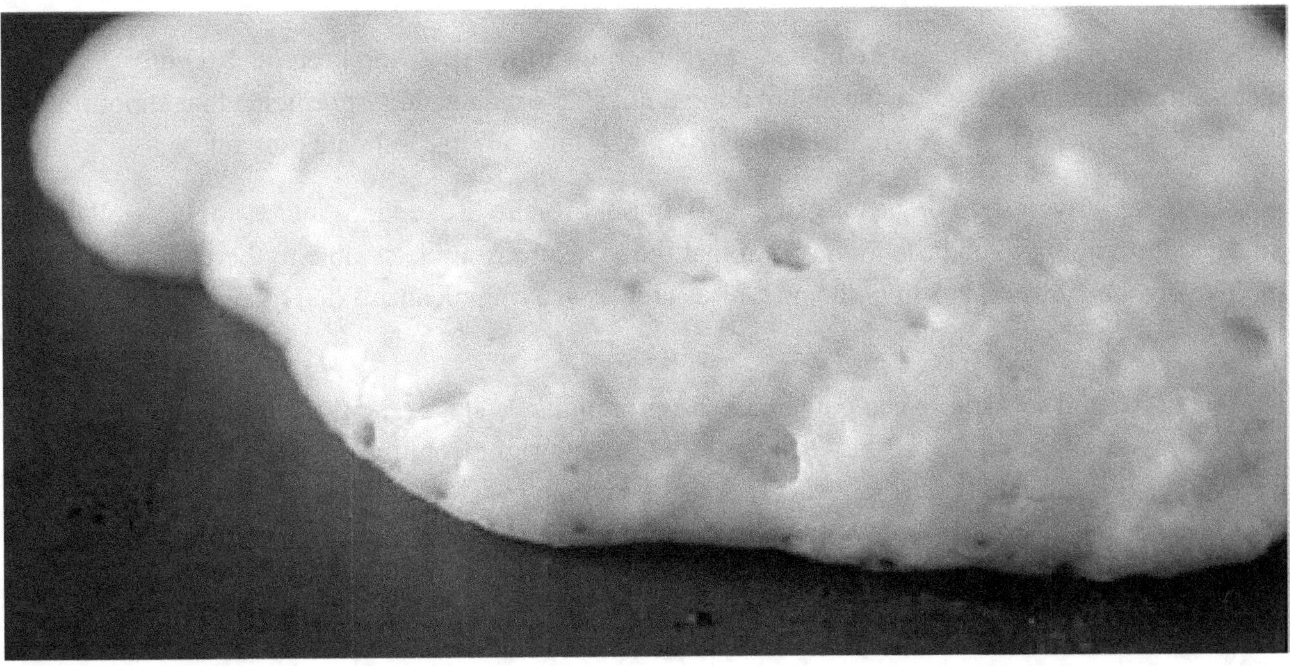

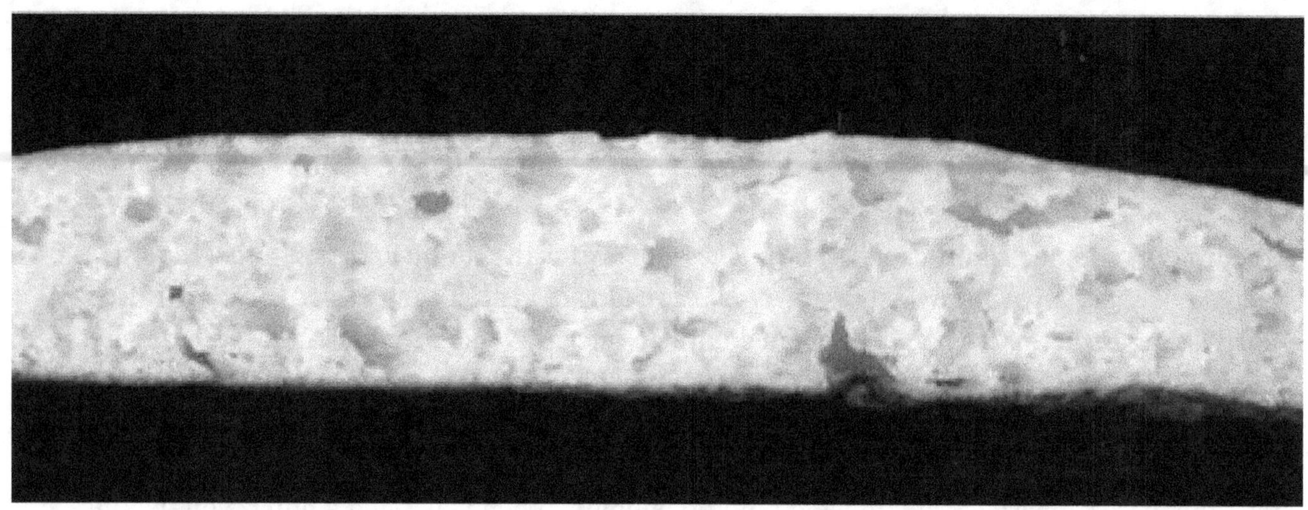

Double acting baking powder allows you a second ascent when cooked.

The Whites Are Light

So imagine a scenario in which baking soft drink simply isn't doing what's necessary for you. How would you get your flapjacks to stand significantly taller and lighter? I like to utilize a meringue-egg whites that have been whipped enthusiastically until they structure a semisolid froth. This is the carefully guarded secret:

• Froth: In the beginning stages of beating, the proteins in the egg whites-for the most part globulin and ovotransferrin-start to unfurl. Like geeks at a Star Wars show, they will more often than not assemble and bond in little gatherings. The whites begin to consolidate a couple of air pockets and look like ocean froth.

• Delicate tops: As the whites are beaten, the gatherings of fortified egg proteins become increasingly interconnected, in the end making a nonstop organization of proteins that support the dividers of the air pockets you're making. The whites start to frame delicate pinnacles.

• Solid tops: As you keep on beating, the built up bubbles are broken into increasingly small air pockets, turning out to be little to the point that they are almost undetectable to the unaided eye and in this way the whites seem smooth and white, such as shaving cream. When maneuvered into tops, they stay firm and strong.

• Breakdown and sobbing: Keep going past the firm pinnacle stage, and the proteins start to bond so firmly with one another that they extract the dampness right from the air pockets, bringing about a meringue that sobs and breaks. Acidic fixings like cream of tartar or a dash of lemon juice can forestall egg white proteins from holding too firmly, permitting you to shape a froth that stays stable regardless of how hard you beat it.

Add sugar and vanilla to the whites at the delicate pinnacle stage, whip to firm pinnacles, drop by the spoonful onto baking sheets, and heat at a low temperature, and you have yourself exemplary meringue treats. Assuming you rather shower in a cooked sugar syrup close to the furthest limit of whipping, you'll wind up with what's called an Italian meringue, a meringue that stays delicate and graceful in any event, when seared the sort of thing you'd need to finish off a lemon meringue pie with.

Here the utilization for meringue is substantially more basic: all you will do is overlay it into the hotcake player. The additional air that the egg whites have fused grows as the flapjacks cook, making them featherlight.

Whipped egg whites.

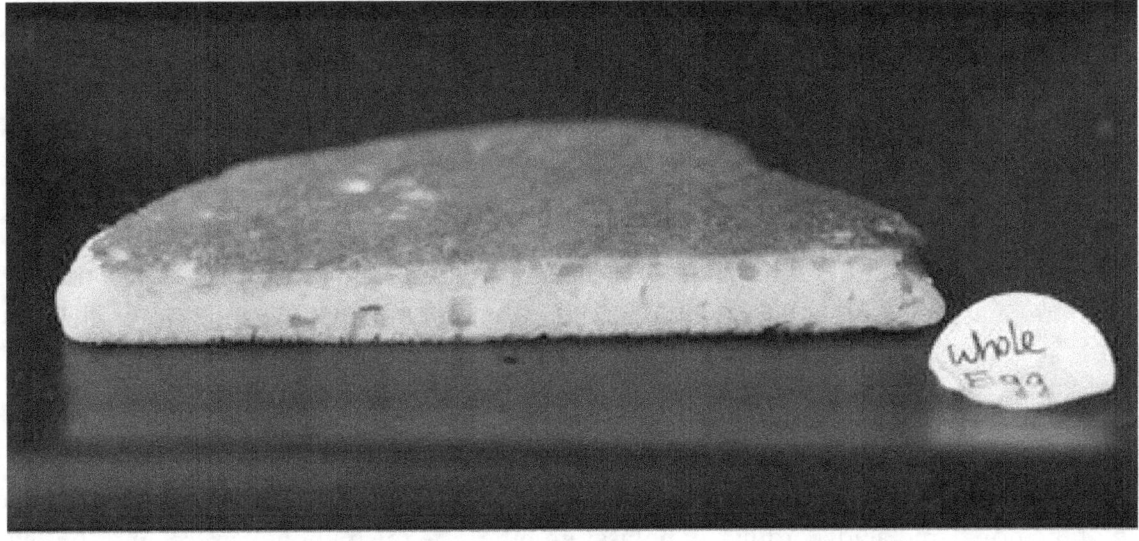

Plain eggs.

Pancake Flavor

To the extent that seasoning buttermilk hotcakes go, there are a couple of givens: Dairy fat, as liquefied spread or milk, is fundamental. In addition to the fact that it includes extravagance and flavor, yet by covering the flour and restricting gluten advancement, it additionally guarantees that your hotcakes stay delicate. Eggs assist with setting the flapjacks as they cook, as well as giving some additional lift. Buttermilk is clearly important for the situation, yet I like my flapjacks extra-tart, and straight-up buttermilk simply doesn't cut it for me. Expanding the amount doesn't stir that simply winds up tossing the fluid to-strong proportion messed up. All things being equal, I supplant part of the buttermilk with a lot of harsh cream. It's both less damp than buttermilk and more sharp, which permits me to add corrosiveness without watering down the hitter. On the off chance that you don't have acrid cream available, don't stress the hotcakes will in any case taste fine and dandy with straight-up buttermilk.

EXPERIMENT:

Double Acting Baking Powder

Twofold acting baking powder (the sort sold in any general store) is intended to create rises in two unmistakable stages: when it gets wet and afterward when it gets warmed. You can see this for yourself.

Materials

- 1 teaspoon baking powder

- 1 tablespoon water

System

1. Join the baking powder and water in a little bowl. You'll see that the baking powder promptly begins gurgling and bubbling (on the off chance that it doesn't, toss out your baking powder and purchase a new can). This is the primary response. Following 30 seconds or somewhere in the vicinity, all activity will stop, you'll wind up with a still pool of pasty looking fluid.

2. Presently microwave that fluid for around 15 seconds to bring it up to 180°F. A second, overwhelming bunch of percolating ought to happen. You may likewise see the fluid thicken marginally.

Results and Analysis

While the baking powder initially gets wet, a response happens between the sodium bicarbonate and one of the powdered acids, ordinarily potassium bitartrate (also known as cream of tartar), delivering the principal clump of air pockets. The second period of the twofold demonstration happens just at higher temperatures (around 170° to 180°F), when a second powdered corrosive (normally sodium aluminum sulfate) responds with the leftover sodium bicarbonate, delivering one more round of air pockets. The thickening activity is a symptom of the starch used to keep the baking powder dry-it retains water and gelatinizes, thickening your fluid as it warms. Presently isn't that way cooler than that baking soft drink fountain of liquid magma you worked for your 4th grade science fair?

BLENDING BATTER

It's significant not to overmix a flapjack player. Similarly likewise with the hitter on a decent onion ring or piece of singed fish (see "Examination: Gluten Development in Batter," here), the more energetically you mix a player, the more gluten creates, and the harder it becomes. The outcome is underrisen or weathered flapjacks. While blending flapjack hitter, the objective is to do it as fast as could be expected, just until it meets up, permitting a couple of pieces of dry flour to remain. Try not to stress they'll vanish as the flapjacks cook.

WHAT IS BUTTERMILK?

Genuine buttermilk is the fluid whey left after cream has been agitated to make margarine. Generally this whey was permitted to age into a somewhat thickened, acrid fluid that would keep longer than new milk. Nowadays, however, buttermilk is produced using normal milk by dosing it with Streptococcus lactis, a microbes that drinks lactose, the principle sugar in milk, and creates lactic corrosive, which adds pungency to the buttermilk, as well as influencing casein, the essential protein in milk, to turn sour, thickening, or clabbering, the milk.

In certain plans, it's feasible to substitute falsely clabbered milk-milk to which a corrosive like vineger or lemon juice has been added to thicken it-for buttermilk, yet you'll generally be left with an obvious flavor from the additional corrosive. Much better is to substitute one more soured dairy item. At the point when I have no buttermilk available, I'll utilize yogurt, sharp cream, or even crème fraîche weakened with milk.

DAIRY PRODUCT	TO SUBSTITUTE FOR 1 CUP OF BUTTERMILK
Yogurt (full-fat or skim)	⅔ cup yogurt whisked together with ⅓ cup milk
Sour Cream	½ cup sour cream whisked together with ½ cup milk
Crème Fraîche	½ cup crème fraîche whisked together with ½ cup milk

SUBSTITUTING BAKING SODA FOR BAKING POWDER

Baking soft drink is sodium bicarbonate. It responds with fluid acids quickly upon contact to create carbon dioxide. Carbon dioxide gets caught inside players and develops baking, raising your flapjacks and other speedy breads. Since baking soft drink responds right away, fast breads made with it should be heated or cooked just subsequent to blending. Furthermore, due to its alkalinity, baking soft drink can likewise hurry searing responses, adding shading (and in this way flavor) to things like hotcakes, treats, and biscuits.

Baking powder is sodium bicarbonate blended in with at least one of the powdered acids and a starch. It doesn't need one more corrosive to enact it. As referenced before, most baking powders are "twofold acting," meaning they produce carbon dioxide once after interacting with dampness and afterward again when warmed. Along these lines, baking powder-raised products are for the most part lighter and fluffier than those made with baking soft drink alone. This doesn't mean, notwithstanding, that you can allow a baking powder to player simply lounge around, anticipating that the second clump of air pockets should do all the raising the underlying response is indispensably critical to the surface of your heated merchandise, thus these hitters ought to be prepared immediately as well.

Try not to have baking powder available? It's very easy to substitute with your own hand crafted combination of baking pop, cornstarch, and cream of tartar. For each teaspoon of baking powder, use ¼ teaspoon baking pop, ½ teaspoon cream of tartar, and ¼ teaspoon cornstarch. Yet, do remember that your custom made combination won't be twofold acting, expecting you to be additional fast about getting your flapjacks onto the iron or your zucchini bread in the broiler subsequent to blending the player.

ESSENTIAL DRY PANCAKE MIX

Why purchase a locally acquired blend when custom made hotcakes are so natural thus much better? You can utilize this combine following putting it as one or, even better, do what I do: make a fourfold clump and store it in an impenetrable compartment in the storage room. Like that, at whatever point you need to prepare a clump of hotcakes, all you must do is add your wet fixings, and you're set.

NOTE: This formula can be increased to any estimate.

FOR 16 PANCAKES APPROXIMATELY, MAKES AT LEAST 2 CUPS

10 ounces (2 cups) generally useful flour

1 teaspoon baking powder

½ teaspoon baking pop

1 teaspoon legitimate salt

1 tablespoon sugar

Consolidate every one of the fixings in a medium bowl and speed until homogeneous. Move to a sealed shut compartment. The blend will remain great for a very long time.

LIGHT AND FLUFFY BUTTERMILK PANCAKES

NOTE: The sharp cream can be supplanted with more buttermilk.

MAKES 16 PANCAKES, SERVING 4 TO 6

1 formula Basic Dry Pancake Mix (above)

2 huge eggs, isolated

1½ cups buttermilk

1 cup acrid cream (see Note above)

4 tablespoons unsalted spread, dissolved

Spread or oil for cooking

Warm maple syrup and spread

1. Place the dry blend in a huge bowl.

2. In a medium clean bowl, whisk the egg whites until solid pinnacles structure. In an enormous bowl, whisk the egg yolks, buttermilk, and harsh cream until homogeneous. Gradually sprinkle in the softened spread while whisking. Cautiously crease in the egg whites with an elastic spatula until recently consolidated. Pour the blend over the dry blend and crease until recently consolidated (there ought to in any case be a lot of knots).

3. Heat a huge weighty lined nonstick skillet over medium hotness for 5 minutes (or utilize an electric frying pan). Add a modest quantity of margarine or oil to the iron and spread with a paper towel until no noticeable spread or oil remains. Utilize a ¼-cup dry measure to put 4 hotcakes in the skillet and cook until bubbles begin to show up on top and the bottoms are brilliant brown, around 2 minutes. Cautiously flip the hotcakes and cook on the second side until brilliant brown and totally set, around 2 minutes longer. Serve the hotcakes right away, or keep warm on a wire rack set on a rimmed baking sheet in a warm stove while you cook the leftover 3 groups. Present with warm maple syrup and spread.

BLUEBERRY PANCAKES

Blueberries are similar as peas in that by far most of the time, frozen are basically better for cooking with. They're picked ready and blaze frozen right away, leaving them sweet and tasty. While a new blueberry might have a really satisfying surface, with full tissue and skin that pops under your teeth, general store blueberries (especially slow time of year berries) are totally ailing in flavor. Except if you're picking blueberries yourself or approach an incredible neighborhood source, I'd propose going with frozen in many applications, especially cooked ones, where surface isn't as a lot of an issue. The one downside to know about: they filter tone, staining everything in their way purple. The stunt with hotcakes is to add them after you've spooned the hitter onto the iron. You don't need to scoop more player on top of them-they'll get wrapped up like minimal blue children in the flapjack hitter.

Sprinkle 1 to 2 tablespoons defrosted frozen blueberries on top of every flapjack when you spoon them onto the frying pan and continue as coordinated.

HOME MADE RICOTTA

News streak! Locally acquired ricotta is perpetually dreadful!

Genuine ricotta is made by adding corrosive to warmed whey, ordinarily the whey left over from the creation of Pecorino Romano, albeit different sorts of whey are now and again utilized. (Ricotta signifies "recooked," alluding to the warmed whey.) The mix of hotness and corrosive causes milk proteins (primarily casein) to tie together, catching dampness and fat and framing delicate, white curds. To make excellent ricotta, these curds are then painstakingly taken out from the whey (an excess of mechanical activity can turn them rubbery) and permitted to deplete, decreasing their water content and thinking their flavor and wealth. The outcome is mind-blowingly basic yet wanton. Or it ought to be if nothing else. Actually essentially all mass-market ricotta makers try not to invest in some opportunity to deplete their cheddar appropriately. All things being equal, they load the stuff up with gums and stabilizers expected to keep the water (and in this manner their benefits) from spilling out.

What you get is a dirty, gluey, rubbery glue. Pass. Hand crafted ricotta, however, when made right, is rich and delicate with a gentle, smooth flavor and a slight tang from the corrosive used to sour it. Truth be told, I like ricotta made at home with entire milk better compared to a customary low-fat whey-delivered ricotta. How treat you so harshly as that?

With natively constructed ricotta, the absolute most significant variable as far as both flavor and surface is the corrosive you include with everything else.

• Buttermilk has many backers, who guarantee it's the most delicious corrosive of decision. I generally disliked it. To get the milk to coagulate appropriately, I needed to add buttermilk at almost a 1:4 proportion, bringing about an end result with an extremely unmistakable harsh flavor. It wasn't awful essentially, yet the flavor unquestionably restricted its applications: I was unable to envision stuffing it into ravioli, for example. What's more, the curd structure was additionally marginally overdeveloped, giving the ricotta a tacky surface.

• Refined vinegar gives the cleanest flavor, with delicate, delicate curds. Since packaged vinegar is generally weakened to 5 percent acidic corrosive, utilizing it is likewise the most predictable strategy. However long your milk is new (more established milk is more acidic than new milk, and along these lines requires less coagulant), you'll come by indistinguishable outcomes like clockwork.

• Lemon squeeze likewise functions admirably, however I observed that at times the sum I expected to utilize shifted by around 25%, plus or minus. Undoubtedly this is because of differing pH levels from one lemon to another. Lemon juice gives the ricotta an extremely slight citrus tang that, while not quite so unmistakable as the buttermilk flavor, can be somewhat obnoxious in specific appetizing applications. Then again, it's superb for flapjacks and blintzes, or taking care of to your diligent spouse, showered with olive oil and sprinkled with ocean salt, warm off a spoon.

Primary concern? For the most adaptable ricotta, stay with vinegar. Use lemon juice when a lemon flavor is fitting, and stay away from buttermilk except if you're truly into it.

Depleting Ricotta

To deplete ricotta, place it in a fine-network sifter fixed with cheesecloth (or a great food-safe paper towel) set over a bowl. The last surface of ricotta can change extraordinarily relying upon how well it's depleted.

DRAINING TIME	TEXTURE	BEST USES
Under 5 minutes	Extremely moist and creamy, like cottage cheese, with small, tender curds	Immediate consumption, while still warm. Try it drizzled with olive oil and sprinkled with sea salt and black pepper, or, for dessert, with honey and fruit.
15 to 20 minutes	Small, tender curds with a cottage cheese–like consistency; moist and spreadable, but not runny	Moist, savory application, such as adding to a lasagna or topping a pizza, or mixing into your pancake batter
At least 2 hours, or up to overnight (refrigerated)	Large, dry, crumbly curds that can easily be molded into firm shapes	Cakes and pasta, like ricotta cheesecake or ricotta gnocchi

PASTEURIZED MILK

Unless you're buying your milk at a farm or squeezing it straight from the teats of your own herd, you're getting pasteurized milk—milk that's been heated in order to destroy bacteria and prolong its shelf life. There are three basic methods used to do this:

- **Regular pasteurized milk** has been heated to 161°F for around 20 seconds. This is the standard for most supermarket milks, which have a shelf life of a few weeks.
- **Ultra High Temperature pasteurized milk** has been heated much hotter—all the way up to 275°F—for 1 second. It is labeled UHT or "Ultra-Pasteurized" and has a shelf life of several months. Many organic milk producers use this method of pasteurization, as it allows their milks to sit in supermarket dairy cases for longer (organic milk often doesn't sell as quickly as regular milk). When packed into specially designed containers, UHT milk can actually keep, unrefrigerated, for months or even years.
- **Low-Temperature pasteurized milk** has been held at 145°F for 30 minutes. Many small farms pasteurize their milk with this method, as it doesn't produce the "cooked" flavor that UHT or regular pasteurized milk can have. The label generally doesn't indicate whether the milk is just pasteurized or if it's been low-temperature pasteurized, so unless you know the producer, chances are it's the former.

As far as their cooking qualities go, in most application, all of these types of milk will behave just about the same. For making ricotta, however, the higher the temperature the milk has been cooked to, the more breakdown you find in its proteins and sugars. For this reason, UHT milk tends to have a slightly sweeter flavor (complex carbohydrates are broken down into simpler, sweeter sugars during the pasteurization process). And UHT milks will not coagulate as well when making ricotta. I recommend standard pasteurized milk, Low-Temperature pasteurized milk, or, if you can get it, raw milk.

FRESH RICOTTA

IN 5 MINUTES OR LESS

MAKES ABOUT 1 CUP

4 cups entire milk

½ teaspoon table salt

¼ cup refined white vinegar or lemon juice (from 2 lemons)

1. Line a colander with four layers of cheesecloth or two layers of food-safe paper towels and set over a huge bowl. Join the milk, salt, and vinegar in a microwave-safe 2-quart fluid measure and microwave on high until daintily rising around the edges, 4 to 6 minutes; the milk ought to enroll around 165°F on a moment read thermometer. Eliminate from the microwave and mix tenderly for 5 seconds. The milk ought to isolate into strong white curds and clear fluid whey. In the event that not, microwave for 30 seconds longer and mix once more. On the off chance that essential rehash until completely isolated.

2. Utilizing an opened spoon or wire skimmer, move the curds to the pre-arranged colander. Cover the uncovered top with saran wrap and permit to deplete until the ideal surface is reached. Extra ricotta can be put away in a shrouded holder in the cooler for as long as 5 days.

Variety

You can make this formula on the burner rather than the microwave. Heat the milk and vinegar blend in a pot over medium-low hotness, mixing continually with a silicone spatula to forestall staying or singing until it arrives at 165°F on a moment read thermometer. Eliminate it from the hotness and permit to rest until strong white curds structure on a superficial level, around 2 minutes.

WARM RICOTTA

WITH OLIVE OIL AND LEMON ZEST

SERVES 4

1 cup Fresh Ricotta (above), recently made

2 tablespoons extra-virgin olive oil, in addition to something else for serving

2 teaspoons ground lemon zing (from 1 lemon)

Flaky ocean salt, similar to Maldon

Newly ground dark pepper

Place the ricotta in a serving bowl, shower with the olive oil, and sprinkle with the lemon zing and salt and pepper. Serve promptly with toast, passing additional olive oil.

LEMON RICOTTA PANCAKES

These are unique event flapjacks. Serve them for early lunch, despite the obvious danger you will get yourself the favorite as host for each informal breakfast from now on.

MAKES 12 PANCAKES, SERVING 3 TO 4

½ cup buttermilk

1 cup Fresh Ricotta (here), depleted for 30 minutes

2 tablespoons unsalted spread, dissolved and somewhat cooled

2 huge eggs

½ teaspoon vanilla concentrate

1 cup Basic Dry Pancake Mix (here)

2 teaspoons ground lemon zing (from 1 lemon)

Vegetable oil for cooking

Maple syrup

1. Whisk together the buttermilk, ricotta, dissolved spread, eggs, and vanilla concentrate in a medium bowl. Add the flapjack blend and lemon zing and rush until no dry flour stays (the combination ought to stay knotty be mindful so as not to overmix).

2. Heat ½ teaspoon oil in a 12-inch weighty lined nonstick skillet over medium-high hotness (or utilize an electric iron) until it shines. Decrease the hotness to medium and crash the skillet with a paper towel. Utilize a ¼-cup dry measure to scoop 4 flapjacks into the container and cook on the principal side until bubbles begin to show up on top and the bottoms are brilliant brown, 2 to 3 minutes. Flip the hotcakes and cook until the subsequent side is brilliant brown, around 2 minutes longer. Serve the flapjacks right away, or keep warm on a wire rack set on a baking sheet in a warm stove while you cook the leftover bunches. Present with maple syrup.

WAFFLES

Waffles resemble the cool cousin of hotcakes: a smidgen more convoluted, a touch seriously intriguing, and a piece crustier outwardly.

In any case, where it counts, they're practically indistinguishable. While we're talking fast American-style waffles (instead of, say, a customary sluggish rising yeasted, chewy Belgian waffle), we're talking an artificially raised hitter, very much like with flapjacks. Yet, have a go at tossing your hotcake hitter into a waffle iron, and you will run into inconvenience. With flapjacks, the steam dissipating as the hotcakes cook has a simple getaway course you can see it emerging from the highest point of the flapjacks as air pockets structure. With a waffle caught inside its metal enclosure, it's not really simple. Waffles produced using flapjack player come out sticky, with an unmistakable absence of freshness.

Yet, I needed to have the option to begin my waffles with my fundamental hotcake blend so I wouldn't need to keep two blends available in my storage space. I understood the arrangement must be twofold: I really wanted additional raising ability to assist the waffles with ascending in their compelled climate, and I really wanted a strategy to guarantee that they got fresh quicker and remained fresh.

I initially took a stab at adding a touch of additional baking powder and baking soft drink when I stirred up my player. It assisted with the surface, however with an excessive amount of substance raising, that sudsy, metallic flavor began sneaking in. I'd need to track down an actual means to raise my player all things being equal.

I was at that point adding a decent arrangement of air pockets with my whipped egg whites-imagine a scenario in which I were to add considerably more as soft drink water. It's a stunt that New Englanders have utilized for eternity: the brew in lager battered fish is similarly as much about the raising force of the air pockets all things considered about the kind of the beer. Indeed, even the Japanese use soft drink water to accomplish an additional a light tempura. Utilizing soft drink water scales back a little on the kind of the waffles, yet it's not excessively observable, and it's a trade off I'm willing to make for the sake of prevalent surface. A smidgen of vanilla (or orange alcohol, or even maple concentrate and bacon, on the off chance that you'd like) adds a lot of flavor to keep you occupied. You really should utilize super cold club pop. Cold fluids hold carbonation better, and you maintain that the player should remain as effervescent as conceivable until it begins cooking. Club soft drink is better than seltzer water for this situation, since it contains sodium, which likewise assists it with holding its air pockets.

Freshness is about lack of hydration and the setting of proteins, the two things that are achieved through hotness and time. The way to extra-fresh waffles? Simply cook them somewhat more leisurely for somewhat longer. Not in the least does this lead to prevalent surface, it additionally fortunately brings about more in any event, searing

ESSENTIAL QUICK WAFFLES

MAKES 8 SMALL ROUND WAFFLES, FOUR 4-WELL BELGIAN-STYLE WAFFLES, OR 4 LARGE SQUARE WAFFLES, SERVING 4

1 formula Basic Dry Pancake Mix (here)

2 huge eggs

1½ cups buttermilk

4 tablespoons unsalted margarine, liquefied

1 cup super cold club pop

1 teaspoon vanilla concentrate

Margarine or oil for the waffle iron

Maple syrup

1. Preheat an electric waffle iron, on the low-heat setting in the event that you have the choice, or a hotness a burner waffle iron over medium-low hotness. Place the dry blend in an enormous bowl.

2. In a medium bowl, whisk the egg whites until firm pinnacles structure. In a perfect enormous bowl, whisk the egg yolks and buttermilk until homogeneous. Gradually shower in the margarine while whisking. Cautiously overlay the egg whites into the yolk combination with an elastic spatula until recently consolidated. Overlay in the soft drink water. Pour the blend over the dry blend and overlap until recently joined (there ought to in any case be a lot of protuberances).

3. On the off chance that utilizing a 7-inch round burner waffle iron, scoop ½ cup of player into the iron and cook, flipping it infrequently, until the waffle is brilliant brown and fresh on the two sides, around 8 minutes. Assuming utilizing a Belgian waffle iron, scoop ¼ cup player into each well, close the iron, and promptly flip it, then, at that point, cook, turning sporadically, until the waffles are brilliant brown and fresh on the two sides, around 10 minutes. Assuming utilizing an electric waffle iron, preheat and cook as indicated by the maker's directions. Move to a plate, or keep warm on a rack on a baking sheet in a 200°F stove, and cook the excess groups.

ORANGE-SCENTED WAFFLES

Supplant the vanilla concentrate with 1 tablespoon orange alcohol, like Grand Marnier, and add 1 teaspoon ground orange zing to the eggs and buttermilk in sync 2.

MAPLE BACON WAFFLES

Supplant the vanilla concentrate with maple concentrate (or 2 tablespoons maple syrup) and add 6 strips fresh bacon, disintegrated, to the player toward the finish of stage 2.

BUTTERMILK BISCUITS

Assuming my better half and I at any point have indistinguishable twins, I might want to name one Stanley and the other Evil Stanley, for the motivations behind logical request.

We'll raise them precisely the equivalent, however after some time, Evil Stanley will without a doubt start to satisfy his name due to an unpretentious contrast in the manner the world treats him. There makes certain to be an awful closure or two some place in the story. In the endless discussion between nature versus sustain and their impact on the human psyche, it's continuously entrancing to me to perceive how profoundly unique the final products of apparently comparable beginning cases can be.

So it is with flapjacks and rolls. Investigate the fixings records, and they're almost indistinguishable: flour, spread, baking powder, baking pop, and fluid dairy. Yet, one winds up cushy, delicate, and generally level, and different winds up tall, flaky, and fresh. All that matters now is in the subtleties.

Most importantly, bread rolls are a mixture, not a hitter, and that implies that the proportion of flour to fluid is sufficiently high that it can arrange everything into a durable ball that is delicate however doesn't stream. Significantly more significant is the manner by which the margarine is joined. With hotcakes, the margarine is softened and raced into the hitter, bringing about a kind of uniform delicacy. For incredible flaky bread rolls, then again, the spread is added cold and hard, and it's additional before the fluid is. As you work the hard margarine into the flour, you end up with a coarse blend involved little pieces of spread covered in flour, some measure of a flour-and-spread glue, and some totally dry flour. Presently add your fluid to this blend, and what occurs? Indeed, the dry flour promptly starts to ingest water, shaping gluten. In the interim, the flour suspended in the flour-spread glue ingests no water by any means, and, obviously, you've actually got your clusters of 100% unadulterated margarine.

Manipulating the batter will make the little pockets of gluten steadily connect together into increasingly large organizations. Meanwhile, spread covered flour and unadulterated margarine are suspended inside these organizations. As you carry the batter out, everything gets straightened and prolonged. The gluten networks end up extended into flimsy layers isolated by endlessly spread covered flour.

At last, as the rolls, several things happen. To begin with, the margarine softens, greasing up the spaces between the flimsy gluten sheets. Then, dampness from both the spread and the fluid added to the batter starts to disintegrate, framing bubbles that quickly expansion in volume and blow up the interstitial spaces between the gluten layers, making them discrete. In the interim, recall there's likewise baking powder and baking soft drink included. This causes the pieces of the mixture that are comprised of flour and fluid to raise and blow up, adding delicacy and making the surface of the bread rolls lighter.

Folding

One of the keys to ultratender bread rolls isn't too not quite the same as making light hotcakes: don't overmix. You need to massage the fixings just until they meet up. Overmixing can prompt overabundance gluten development, which would make the bread rolls extreme. The other mystery is to keep everything cold. Assuming your batter heats up something over the top, the spread will start to mellow and turn out to be all the more equally conveyed in the mixture. You believe that the margarine in unmistakable pockets should assist with giving the bread rolls a shifted, fleecy surface.

There a few methods for accomplishing these objectives. First is to consolidate the spread utilizing a food processor. A food processor's quickly turning cutting edge will take care of the spread, with brief period for it to warm up and start to dissolve. The technique by which you fuse the buttermilk is additionally significant. A few people like to do it manually, others in the food processor. I observe that the very best way is with an adaptable elastic spatula, delicately collapsing the batter and compressing it onto itself in an enormous bowl. Besides the fact that the collapsing movement limits working (and along these lines gluten), it additionally makes the mixture structure many layers that will separate as they prepare, it you're after to give you the flakiness.

For an additional an increase in flakiness, I like to go above and beyond and make what's known as an overlaid cake: baked good that has been collapsed again and again itself to shape many layers. The mixtures for exemplary French overlaid cakes like puff baked good and croissants are collapsed until they structure many layers. With my bread roll batter, I'm not exactly so aggressive, however I've found that by carrying it out into a square and collapsing it into thirds in the two bearings, you make 9 unmistakable layers (3 × 3). Carry the resultant bundle out into a square again and rehash the cycle, and you have yourself an astounding 81 layers (9 × 3 × 3)! How's that for flaky?

Furthermore, think about what: an advanced flaky American scone is actually just an improved roll cut into an alternate shape. Ace one, and you've dominated the other.

1. Consolidate flour, baking powder, baking pop, and salt in a food processor, then, at that point, dissipate with spread shapes. 2. Beat until spread is broken into ¼-inch pieces. 3. Move to a huge bowl and add buttermilk. 4. Overlay with a spatula. 5. Move to a floured cutting board or work surface. 6. Ply momentarily and structure into a square shape. 7. Roll into a 12-inch square. 8. Overlap the right third over to the middle with a seat scrubber.

9. Overlap the left side over the right. 10. Overlap the top third down over the middle. 11. Overlap the base third up ridiculous. 12. Roll the more modest square out into a 12-inch square and dissipate with ground cheddar and scallions. 13. Overlay the right third over the middle. 14. Overlay the left third over the middle. 15. Overlay the top third down over the middle. 16. Overlay the base third up over the middle.

17. Re-fold the mixture into a 12-inch square. 18. Remove six rounds of the batter with a 4-inch bread roll shaper, assemble the pieces, massage delicately, re-roll, and cut out two additional rounds. Put them on a material lined baking sheet. 19. Brush the top and sides of the bread rolls with liquefied margarine. 20. Move to a preheated stove to heat. 21. Pivot the bread rolls part of the way through baking. 22. Allow the rolls to cool for 5 minutes prior to serving. 23. Make an honest effort to stand up to.

SUPER-FLAKY BUTTERMILK BISCUITS

MAKES 8 BISCUITS

½ cup buttermilk

½ cup harsh cream

10 ounces (2 cups) unbleached universally handy flour, in addition to extra for tidying

1 tablespoon baking powder

¼ teaspoon baking pop

1½ teaspoons fit salt

8 tablespoons (1 stick) cold unsalted margarine, cut into ¼-inch taps

2 tablespoons unsalted margarine, softened

1. Change a broiler rack to the center position and preheat the stove to 425°F. Whisk together the buttermilk and harsh cream in a little bowl.

2. In the bowl of a food processor, join the flour, baking powder, baking pop, and salt and interaction until mixed, around 2 seconds. Dissipate the margarine equally over the flour and heartbeat until the blend looks like coarse dinner and the biggest spread pieces are about ¼ inch at their broadest. Move to a huge bowl.

3. Add the buttermilk blend to the flour combination and crease with an elastic spatula until recently joined. Move the batter to a floured work surface and ply until it simply meets up, adding additional flour as needs be.

4. With a moving pin, fold the batter into a 12-inch square. Utilizing a seat scrubber, overlay the right third of the mixture over the middle, then crease the left third finished so you end up with a 12-by-4-inch square shape. Overlap the top third down over the middle, then, at that point, overlay the base third up so the entire thing is decreased to a 4-inch square. Press the square down and carry it out again into a 12-inch square. Rehash the collapsing system again.

5. Roll the batter again into a 12-inch square. Cut six 4-inch balances of the mixture with a floured roll shaper. Move the rounds to a material lined baking sheet, separating them around 1 inch separated. Structure the batter scraps into a ball and manipulate delicately a few times, until smooth. Carry the batter out until it's adequately enormous to remove 2 additional 4-inch adjusts, and move to the baking sheet.

6. Brush the highest point of the bread rolls with the softened margarine and prepare until brilliant brown and very much ascended, around 15 minutes, pivoting the dish partially through. Permit to cool for 5 minutes and serve.

CHEDDAR CHEESE AND SCALLION BISCUITS

In sync 4, sprinkle 6 ounces ground cheddar and ¼ cup cut scallions over the 12-inch batter square prior to collapsing it the subsequent time, and go on as coordinated.

BACON PARMESAN BISCUITS

In sync 4, sprinkle ½ cup disintegrated cooked bacon and 2 ounces ground Parmigiano-Reggiano over the 12-inch batter square prior to collapsing it the subsequent time, and go on as coordinated. Dust the rolls with more ground Parmesan prior to baking.

FLAKY SCONES

Add 2 tablespoons sugar to the dry fixings in sync 2. In sync 4, whenever wanted, disperse 1 cup frozen or cleaved new organic product or berries over the mixture prior to collapsing it the subsequent time. In sync 5, fold the batter into a 12-by-4-inch square shape, then cut the square shape into three 4-inch squares and cut each square into 2 triangles. Sprinkle the scones with 2 extra tablespoons sugar and prepare as coordinated.

CREAMY SAUSAGE GRAVY

White sauce, as exemplary French béchamel is known in the United States, is essentially just milk that has been thickened with flour. There are a couple keys to making great white sauce: the first is to ensure that the flour is cooked. Crude flour tastes, indeed, crude. You need to cook the flour in margarine until its crude fragrance disappears and it takes on an exceptionally light brilliant shading. From that point forward, it's simply an issue of gradually rushing in the milk. The more leisurely you whisk it in, the smoother your sauce will be. As your white sauce warms, starch granules in the flour-which resemble little water inflatables loaded up with starch atoms gradually retain water from the milk, puffing up and in the end exploding, delivering starch particles into the fluid. These starch particles cross-interface, thickening your sauce. White sauces should be brought to a close to bubble to thicken completely.

Velvety frankfurter sauce is essentially as basic as broiling some great breakfast wiener, (for example, the benevolent you make yourself), then making a white sauce around it. I like mine overall quite peppery. Serve right away, on top of buttermilk or other exquisite rolls.

MAKES ABOUT 3 CUPS, ENOUGH FOR 8 SERVINGS

1 tablespoon unsalted spread

1 pound Maple-Sage Breakfast Sausage (here) or great quality mass hotdog

1 little onion, finely hacked (about ⅔ cup)

2 tablespoons universally handy flour

2 cups entire milk

Legitimate salt and newly ground dark pepper

1. Heat the spread in a 10-inch weighty lined nonstick skillet over medium-high hotness until frothy. Add the hotdog and cook, utilizing a wooden spatula or spoon to separate the meat, until as of now not pink, around 6 minutes. Add the onion and cook until mellowed, around 2 minutes.

2. Add the flour and cook, mixing continually, until totally consumed, around 1 moment. Slowly add half of the milk, whisking continually, then speed in the excess milk and permit to come to a stew, whisking continually. Stew, speeding, until thickened, around 3 minutes. Season to taste with salt and a lot of dark pepper.

SIMPLE CREAM BISCUITS

Try not to need to mess with all that collapsing forming yet need delicate, rich, light, rich bread rolls or scones for the informal breakfast table? Cream bread rolls or scones are the response. Cream bread rolls are to flaky bread rolls what shortbread is to piecrust. That is, instead of getting the margarine and flour to develop into flaky, unpredictable layers that different after baking, you just add undeniably more fluid fat (as both dissolved spread and cream), enough to totally cover the flour. The outcome doesn't have the layers of a flaky bread roll, yet it has all the delicacy and an extraordinarily soft surface of its own.

The greatest aspect? Only five fixings (OK, six in the event that you add sugar to make them into scones), one bowl, and fifteen minutes beginning to end. Didn't I say these are simple?

MAKES 8 BISCUITS

10 ounces (2 cups) generally useful flour

1 tablespoon baking powder

¾ teaspoon legitimate salt

4 tablespoons unsalted spread, liquefied

1¼ cups weighty cream

1. Change a stove rack to the center position and hotness the broiler to 425°F. Place the flour, baking powder, and salt in an enormous bowl and race to join. Add 2 tablespoons of the softened margarine and the cream and mix with a wooden spoon until a delicate mixture meets up.

2. Turn the mixture out onto a floured surface and manipulate delicately until it shapes a strong ball. With a moving pin, fold it into a surmised 8-inch square, ¾ inch thick. Utilize a 3-inch round roll shaper to remove bread rolls and put on a material lined baking sheet, dividing them 1 inch separated. Get together the pieces, reroll, and cut out more rolls (you ought to wind up with 8).

3. Brush the highest point of the rolls with the excess 2 tablespoons dissolved margarine. Prepare until the bread rolls are brilliant brown and very much ascended, around 15 minutes, pivoting the dish part of the way through. Permit to cool for 5 minutes, and serve.

CREAM SCONES

Add 3 tablespoons sugar to the dry combination in sync 1. Overlap in ½ cup currants or raisins whenever wanted.

TACKY BUNS

About one time each year, at whatever point I feel that my marriage needs a counterfeit shot of undying commitment and genuine affection, I'll awaken my exquisite spouse with the indisputable aroma of gooey tacky buns baking in the stove.

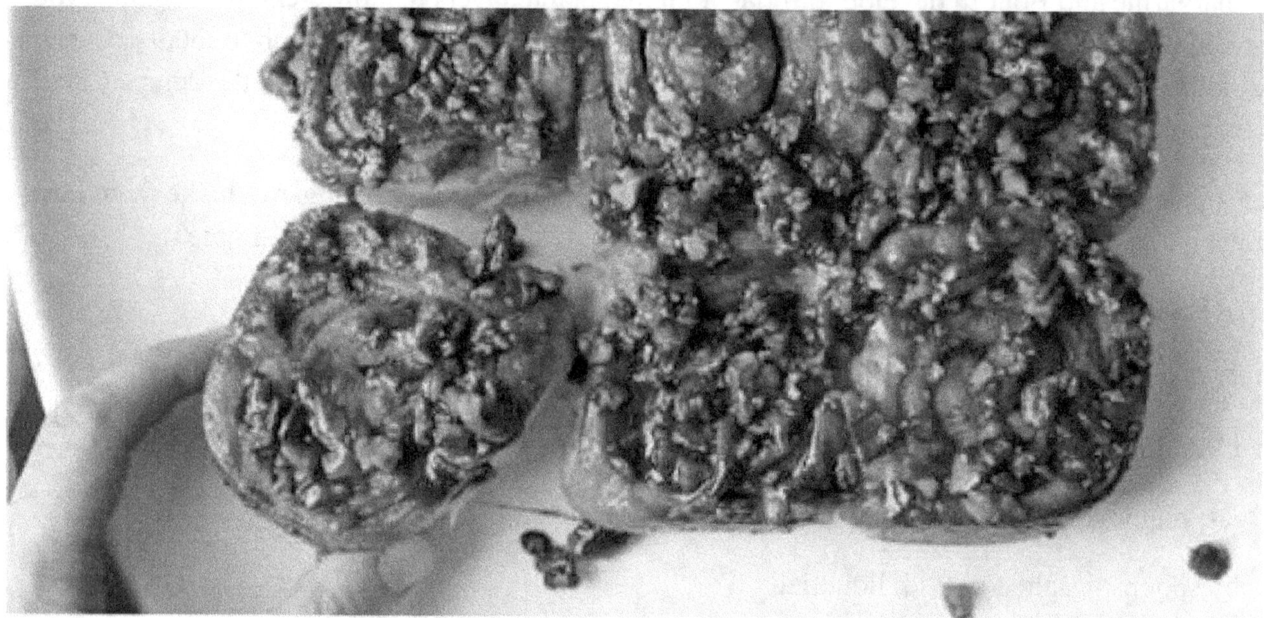

I figure this act alone is to the point of getting me free for an entire year of minor conjugal infractions-or significant ones, assuming I incorporate a ramekin of orange-cream-cheddar coat for plunging as an afterthought.

Truly, these things are wonderful. Wonderful enough that I chose to incorporate them to wrap up this section notwithstanding the way that there's not too much to the extent that "new" kitchen science goes here. Beside minor changes to consummate the formula, these tacky buns are standard. Be that as it may, in some cases a few minor changes is everything necessary to consummate a norm.

Moving in Dough

Tacky buns are made with what is called an improved mixture, actually intending that notwithstanding the flour, water-based fluid, salt, and leavener found in many batters, you've likewise got fat-for this situation, eggs and spread; fixings like milk and yogurt give both water and fat. The fat assumes a crucial part in the kind of the buns, yet additionally in their surface. In lean mixtures made without fat, gluten arrangement is incredibly amazing, on the grounds that the flour proteins are effectively ready to come into direct contact with each other, quickly framing a thick, tacky organization of gluten. Along these lines, lean mixtures will generally have bigger air bubbles caught in them (more grounded gluten implies the batter can extend longer and more slender prior to exploding), as well as a harder, chewier construction. With advanced mixtures, the fats carry on like a grease, keeping proteins from holding too firmly.

Consider flour proteins a gathering of hipster revelers shaping a dance circle during an interesting dry, bright second at Woodstock 1969. As they run into one another, they fasten each other's hands (as radicals are wont to do). Ultimately, they're totally connected together firmly. The circle can loosen up extremely far before any connection breaks. Presently we should envision similar gathering of hipsters in a similar field, however this time in the heavy storm. Whenever covered, as they are, with mud and water, fastening hands firmly turns out to be significantly more troublesome. Maybe little circles structure to a great extent, however they are no place the size and strength of the dry circle. So it is with fats: they forestall huge nonconformist circles of flour from shaping in your mixture, as it were.

Along these lines, improved batters will quite often be more sensitive than lean mixtures, with a milder surface and more modest air bubbles. Obviously, fats likewise add tone and flavor to batters. What good times could tacky buns be on the off chance that they weren't brilliant and rich?

There are plans for tacky buns that utilization substance leaveners like baking powder to initiate a fast ascent, however this strategy compromises flavor. Yeast is the best way to appropriately foster flavor and surface in a tacky bun. It couldn't be any more obvious, yeasts, as basically all living animals, want to multiply, and to do that, they should consume energy. This energy utilization comes as sugars, which they overview and let off as both carbon dioxide and liquor, alongside various other fragrant mixtures. It's the carbon dioxide getting caught in the organization of gluten shaped by the flour that demonstrations to raise yeasted prepared merchandise. The cycle takes time, nonetheless. There's just so much reproducing a yeast can do, you know? An appropriately raised tacky bun batter can require a few hours to create.

Indeed, for what reason would I be able to simply add more yeast to begin? you could inquire. The issue is that yeast has its very own kind, and it's anything but an especially charming one. Begin with a huge load of yeast, and its somewhat severe, astounding flavor will rule the mixture. The kind of appropriately risen mixture comes from the side-effects of the yeast's activities: the perplexing exhibit of fragrant synthetic compounds that are delivered as yeast gradually, gradually processes the sugars in the batter. For the best flavor, you should begin with a somewhat modest quantity of yeast and permit it a lot of opportunity to play out its wizardry. This is as valid for tacky buns for what it's worth for pizza batter or loaves.

In the event that you've never made tacky buns, you'll likely track down the interaction basically fun. You shape them by folding a huge piece of batter into a chamber, then, at that point, cutting it up to make more limited chambers with a winding example inside them. To keep these winding layers isolated from one another, a layer of margarine and cinnamon sugar is spread over the level sheet of mixture prior to moving it up.

There are actually no ifs ands or buts: tacky buns are an undertaking including different stages and a lot of time in the kitchen. (Hello, didn't I let you know I just make these about one time per year?) But assuming my as yet going-solid marriage is any sign, the outcomes are most certainly worth the work.

THE WORLD'S MOST AWESOME STICKY BUNS

NOTES: Being an evening person and a late riser, I like to set up the buns and let them rise for the time being in the refrigerator so i should simply heat them off in the first part of the day. To do as such, place the buns in the cooler following covering them in sync 5 and permit to ascend for somewhere around 6 hours, and up to 12. The following day, eliminate the buns from the cooler while the stove preheats, then continue as coordinated.

For a sans nut form, the walnuts can be overlooked from the sauce.

MAKES 12 STICKY BUNS

For the Dough

3 huge eggs

⅓ cup stuffed light earthy colored sugar

¾ cup buttermilk

2 teaspoons genuine or 1 teaspoon table salt

2 teaspoons moment yeast

6 tablespoons unsalted spread, dissolved

20 ounces (4 cups) generally useful flour, in addition to something else for tidying

For the Pecan-Caramel Sauce

4 tablespoons unsalted spread

⅔ cup stuffed light earthy colored sugar

3 tablespoons buttermilk

4 ounces (around 1 cup) toasted walnuts coarsely cleaved

Spot of fit salt

For the Filling

⅔ cup pressed light earthy colored sugar

1 tablespoon ground cinnamon

2 tablespoons unsalted margarine, softened

For the Orange-Cream Cheese Glaze (discretionary)

4 ounces cream cheddar

¼ cup buttermilk

1½ cups confectioners' sugar

1 tablespoon ground orange zing (from 1 orange)

2 tablespoons new squeezed orange

Touch of kosher salt

1. Make the batter: Whisk the eggs in a huge bowl until homogeneous. Add the earthy colored sugar, buttermilk, salt, yeast, and liquefied margarine and race until homogeneous (the combination might cluster up a piece this is OK). Add the flour and mix with a wooden spoon until a firm chunk of mixture structures.

2. Turn the mixture out onto a gently floured surface and manipulate for 2 minutes, or until totally homogeneous, smooth, and luxurious. Get back to the bowl, cover with saran wrap, and permit to increase at room temperature until generally multiplied in volume, around 2 hours.

3. Make the walnut caramel sauce: Cook the margarine and earthy colored sugar in a little pan over medium-high hotness, mixing infrequently, until the sugar is totally broken up and the combination

is rising, around 2 minutes. Add the buttermilk, walnuts, and salt and mix to consolidate, then, at that point, pour the blend equitably over the lower part of a 13-by-9-inch glass baking dish.

4. Make the filling: Combine the sugar and cinnamon in a little bowl and saved.

5. Carry out the mixture: Turn the batter out onto a floured surface and delicately flour it. Shape into an unpleasant square shape with your hands and afterward, utilizing a moving pin, roll into a square shape around 16 inches long and 12 inches wide, with a short end toward you. Brush with the dissolved margarine, leaving a 1-inch line along the top edge. Sprinkle with the cinnamon and sugar blend and spread it with your hands until the buttered segment is equitably covered. Roll the batter up jam fold style into a tight chamber, involving a seat scrubber as important to help you. Squeeze the crease shut and turn the batter so that it's crease side down. Utilize your hands to try and out its shape.

6. Utilize a sharp blade to cut the roll into 12 even cuts: The least demanding method for doing this is to slice it down the middle, cut down the middle fifty-fifty, and afterward cut each segment into thirds. Settle the 12 rolls with the whirl design looking up in the pre-arranged baking dish, ensuring the cuts from the finishes of the log go cut side down. Cover with cling wrap and permit to ascend until generally multiplied in volume, around 2 hours (for short-term directions, see Note above). The rolls ought to be very much puffed and squeezed firmly against one another.

7. While the batter is rising, change a broiler rack to the center position and preheat the stove to 350°F. Move the baking dish to the broiler and prepare until the buns are brilliant brown and very much puffed, around 30 minutes, turning the dish once. Permit to rest for 5 minutes, then transform the buns onto a serving platter; scratch out any abundance goo from the dish and spoon over the buns.

8. Make the (discretionary) coat: Combine the cream cheddar, buttermilk, confectioners' sugar, orange zing, squeezed orange, and salt in a little pot and cook over medium hotness, whisking continually, until stewing and homogeneous. Spoon a large portion of the coating over the tacky buns, holding the rest in a bowl to pass tableside. Serve right away.

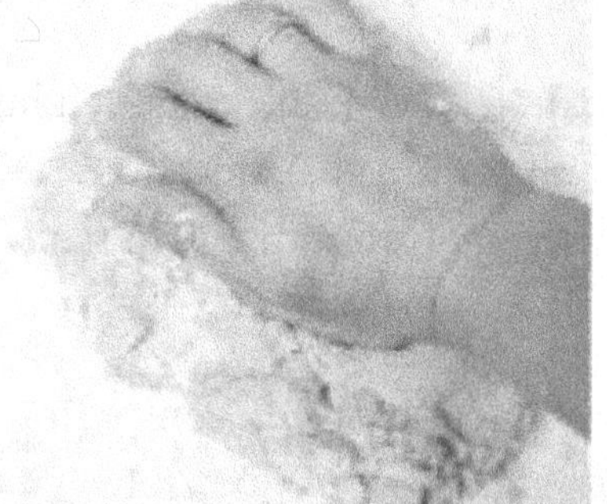

HOT CHOCOLATE MIX

As a child, I adored hot cocoa blend. I'd eat it directly from the parcel, licking it covetously off my finger. I've never, nonetheless, loved it as it is intended to be served: blended in with heated water or milk. Flimsy and watery, excessively sweet or not sweet enough, with minimal chocolate flavor.

While genuine custom made hot cocoa isn't too difficult to make (break up cocoa in spread, add chocolate and sugar, perhaps some vanilla or potentially whiskey, add milk, and speed while warming), you can't prevent the accommodation from getting essentially blending a couple of tablespoons of powder into some hot milk. So I chose to concoct a natively constructed formula that would match the accommodation of a powder and beat it regarding flavor and cost.

To begin, I attempted essentially crushing chocolate to a powder in the food processor (freezing it first makes this simple). While that made respectable cups, when I'd added sufficient chocolate to the milk to get the flavor I needed, the wealth of the cocoa margarine began to overwhelm, making drinking a full mug troublesome.

I selected rather for a blend of 100 percent cacao (unsweetened) chocolate, sugar, and Dutch-process cocoa. With these changes, my chocolate was tasting very great, yet a couple of issues remained: It covered in the capacity holder short-term, making it difficult to disintegrate the following day. It broke when added to the milk, scattering a fine layer of fat air pockets over the outer layer of the beverage. Also, the outcome just wasn't rich, thick, and sufficiently smooth.

Numerous business blends contain soy lecithin or dried milk proteins, the two of which are planned to expand richness and assist with keeping the milk fat, cocoa spread, and fluid pleasantly smooth and emulsified. I took a stab at adding soy lecithin to my blend and it worked, however I ruled against (it's accessible in wellbeing food stores, yet scarcely a typical fixing). Milk powder additionally assisted with surface, yet it left the chocolate with an unmistakable cooked-milk flavor-not right.

Eventually, the least difficult arrangement was to add a cornstarch to my blend. Besides the fact that it forestalled solidifying, it additionally thickened the milk, giving it a decent, smooth, velvety wealth without antagonistically influencing flavor.

HOMEMADE HOT CHOCOLATE MIX

MAKES ENOUGH FOR ABOUT 18 TO 36 SERVINGS

Two 4-ounce bars 100 percent cacao baking chocolate

1 cup Dutch-process cocoa powder

1 cup sugar

2 tablespoons cornstarch

½ teaspoon genuine salt

1. Freeze the chocolate bars until totally frozen, around 10 minutes. Eliminate from the cooler, break into harsh pieces, and spot in the food processor, alongside the cocoa powder, sugar, cornstarch, and salt. Process until totally powdered, around 1 moment. Move to a hermetically sealed compartment and store in cool, dull spot for as long as 90 days.

2. To make hot cocoa, add 1 to 2 tablespoons of the combination, or more whenever wanted, to 1 cup bubbling milk and mix or speed until consolidated. To thicken it further, return the container to the hotness and stew for 30 seconds, until thick and smooth.

Only the purest of heart can make a wonderful soup.

She treats the heavenly fragrances of sizzling burgers and cooking chickens like foe soldiers, utilizing guerilla strategies to conceal containers of blend in places I won't ever look-among the Russian writing, maybe, or decisively camouflaged as one of the excursion trinket odds and ends over her work area. When I start a task in the kitchen, I stand by the recognizable swisssssh-clop of the window in the lounge sliding open and the snap hum of the fan turning on, in her frantic endeavors to prudently ventilate.

That is the reason stormy days are my number one. You can't open the windows during a tempest, which guarantees that the amazing smell floating from my goliath pot of bean stew gradually stewing away on the burner soaks the drapes and covers. Also, it's there to welcome you each time you enter the condo for at minimum half a month. It lives on in the bedsheets, prepared to hush you to rest like a warm glass of milk. It waits on the shower shade, welcoming you each day with its substantial, oniony fragrance when you clean your teeth. My significant other says I'm latent forceful. I tell her she's distrustful as I grin and hotness up one more bowl of bean stew.

This part is about those great, loft soaking, sweet-smelling stews, soups, and braises-the sort of food so great that you check the meteorological forecast simply expecting a typhoon cautioning. Also, everything begins with stock.

{ **STOCK** }

100 years prior, when French culinary specialist Auguste Escoffier (maybe the most august of gourmet experts) arranged traditional French food, cooking depended on the creation and utilization of stock-the rich, exquisite fluid delivered by stewing creature matter, bones, and vegetables in water for quite a while. Meats were braised in it, vegetables were coated with it, soups and stews were based on it, and it was diminished into rich sauces. Stock was produced using chicken, duck, turkey, hamburger, veal, pork, sheep, and so on. Assuming it had four legs or quills, great bet its bones and scraps would ultimately observe their direction into a stewing pot.

Nowadays, stock isn't exactly as fundamental. Cooking is lighter, and numerous eateries get by with simply chicken stock. At home, I utilize chicken stock solely, and my significant other presently can't seem to whine that my food simply isn't adequately french. For some, plans, even a decent canned stock will in all actuality do fine and dandy, however you need to ensure that it's low sodium so you have some control over the salt level yourself. Most ordinary canned stocks or stocks are too pungent to even consider lessening into a sauce.

There's as yet one spot where an extraordinary stock is basically fundamental: soup. Like show canines and kids, soup must be essentially as great as the stock it's produced using.

Tragically, as any individual who's always worked in an eatery can see you, making stock is a sluggish business. It can take more time to remove flavor and separate the connective tissue from a pot of chicken bones and scraps. This isn't an issue when you're in the kitchen all day at any rate: simply watch out for the tremendous stockpot as a second thought stewing away for six hours. In any case, for a home cook? Disregard it. Several Sundays a year I'll surrender and put together a truly customary duck or veal stock, yet for the other 363 days, I needed to sort out a quicker, better way.

What's a Chicken?

To the surprise of no one, I began with the essentials, and for this situation, the nuts and bolts are a chicken. Whenever you've stripped away the plumes and the cackle, a chicken is really an astoundingly basic monster in culinary terms. Its matter can be separated into about four unique parts:

• Muscle is our thought process of as the meat on the chicken. The beefy stuff jerks and makes the bird go, and it tends to be additionally separated into two classifications: slow jerk and quick jerk.

• Slow-jerk muscles are intended for supported development i.e., the legs and thighs that keep the chicken standing, strolling, and twisting down or up. Since slow-jerk muscles are high-impact (they expect oxygen to work), they are ordinarily thick with vessels conveying oxygen-rich red platelets. That is the reason they have all the earmarks of being hazier.

• Quick jerk muscles are utilized for short eruptions of serious energy-they're the muscles that are found in chicken bosoms, used to drive the wings when a terrified chicken necessities to escape from a perilous circumstance. Since their action is anaerobic (they don't expect oxygen to jerk), they will quite often be less thick with vessels, giving them their trademark pale tone.

As it turns out, a similar differentiation among quick and slow-jerk muscles happens in basically all creatures, even people. At any point can't help thinking about why a fish is dark red while a cod is pale white? Fishes are made for the most part of all-strong sluggish jerk muscles, which permit the fish to quickly destroy their direction through the water for extensive stretches of time. A cod maneuvers just while he's eating or scared.

- Fat gives protection and energy stockpiling to chickens. For people, chicken fat simply tastes flavorful (if it's cooked right). Fat is predominantly found in enormous stores around the legs and back of the bird, as well as in the skin. In opposition to prevalent thinking, the skin of a chicken isn't all fat as a matter of fact, it's principally comprised of . . .

- Connective tissue. Made out of collagen, among different tissues, connective tissue keeps muscles joined to endlessly bones appended to one another. In its regular state, it looks like a piece of yarn made of three separate strands that are firmly twisted together, giving it heaps of solidarity. Heat it up, and those strands disentangle into gelatin, which can then shape a free lattice, giving stocks and sauces body and surface. Collagen is found all over the place, yet it is especially gathered in the legs, wings, back, and skin of the bird. The more seasoned the creature, the more collagen there will be.

- Bone loans construction to the bird. Without bones, chickens would be little puddles of Jell-O, and not too appealing. Many cooks accept that bones give stock flavor; I'm doubtful (read on).

Contingent upon the piece of the chicken you use, these parts are available in various proportions. To summarize, chicken legs are high in sluggish jerk muscle, have a lot of fat, and contain a lot of connective tissue and bones. Bosoms are totally quick jerk muscle. Backs and corpses have little meat of one or the other kind however a lot of bone, connective tissue, and fat. Wings have the most elevated grouping of connective tissue of all, with a high extent of fat and some bone.

To sort out the very thing every one of these different tissues brings to the pot, I cooked a couple of clusters of stock one next to the other: one made with simply white meat, one made with dull meat, one made with bones, and one made with chicken remains, which have a lot of bones and connective tissue however generally little meat.

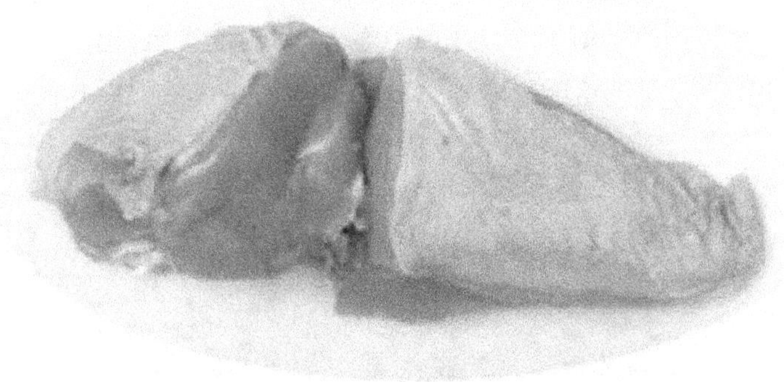

Bosoms.

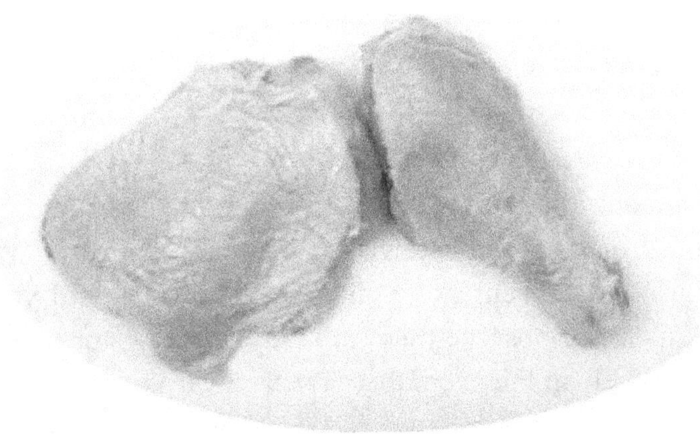

Legs.

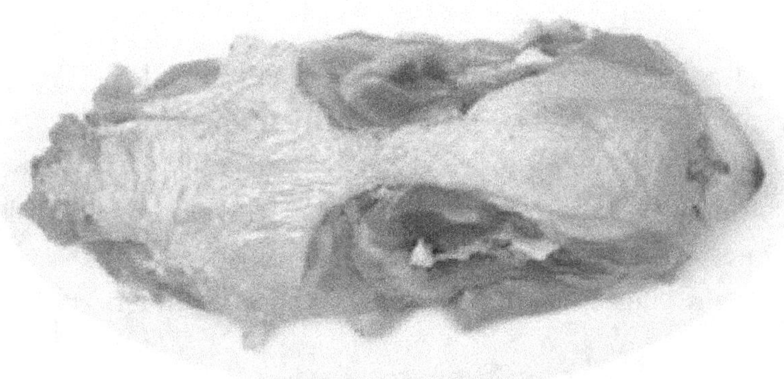

Backs.

Following 4 hours of stewing, the meat-based stocks were delightful (the one made with leg meat somewhat more so than the bosom) yet had no body-in any event, when chilled to fridge temperature, these stocks stayed a fluid, a sign that there was generally little gelatin disintegrated in the stock. The bones-just stock, as I thought, was almost flavorless, however it had a moderate measure of body. The stock made with remains was both tasty and rich. This stock turned into a strong, elastic like mass when chilled, because of the great measure of gelatin separated in stewing. When tasted as a hot stock, it covered the mouth wonderfully, leaving the meager, tacky film on the lips normal for a decent, rich stock.

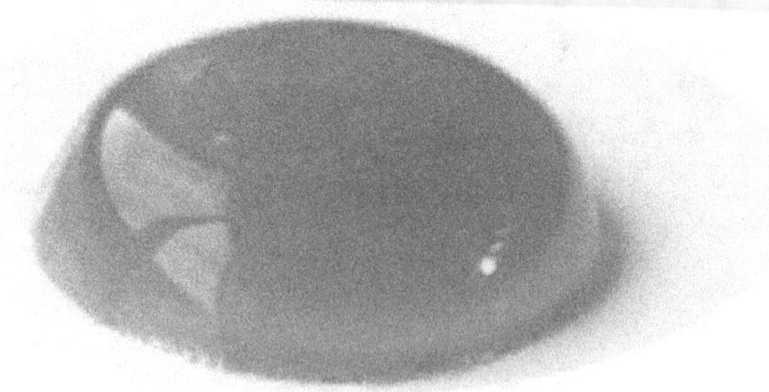

A very much made stock ought to gel strong.

So bodies are the best approach for the best harmony among flavor and body. In an intriguing instance of opposite financial matters, this likewise is the least expensive way: you can aggregate remains by separating your own chickens (keep them in the cooler until you have to the point of making a huge cluster of stock), or observe them in many grocery stores at a deal rate. However, wings will truly do fine and dandy in the event that you can't get your hands on cadavers.

So we presently know that for the ideal stock, we really want two things: extraction of delightful mixtures from inside muscle strands (as demonstrated by the stocks delivered from chicken meat) and the extraction of gelatin from connective tissue to give body. The inquiry is, is there a method for speeding things up a little?

All things considered, I realize that chicken muscles resemble long, slim cylinders, and that separating flavor from them is about leisurely cooking them to extricate their substance, similar as crushing a toothpaste tube. How much those cylinders are pressed is subject to the temperature to which the chicken is brought, yet the rate at which those flavors come out is additionally reliant upon the distance they need to go from the inside of the muscles to the stock. Things being what they are, I pondered, could shortening the length of those cylinders rush the flavor extraction process?

I cooked three stocks next to each other utilizing chicken remains cleaved to various degrees and found that without a doubt it has an effect. Cleaved bodies surrendered their flavor far quicker than entire corpses, and tossing generally slashed chicken pieces into the food processor and finely crushing them worked significantly quicker, creating a full-seasoned stock in pretty much 45 minutes. It ain't pretty, yet hello, it works!

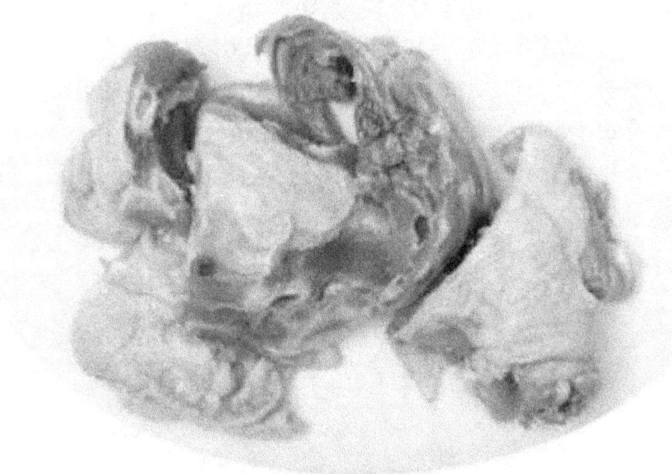

Roughly chopped.

Finely chopped.

Pulverized.

In any case, here's something intriguing: despite the fact that slashing the bones into pieces expanded the pace of flavor extraction, it didn't muchly affect body advancement. Flavor extraction is a quick interaction everything revolves around getting stuff out from inside the meat and broke up in the water. Getting the gelatin out, then again, requires not only extraction of the collagen; a compound cycle takes time, regardless of how finely that collagen is hacked.

TIME TO EXTRACT MAXIMUM FLAVOR AND BODY VERSUS DEGREE OF CHOPPING

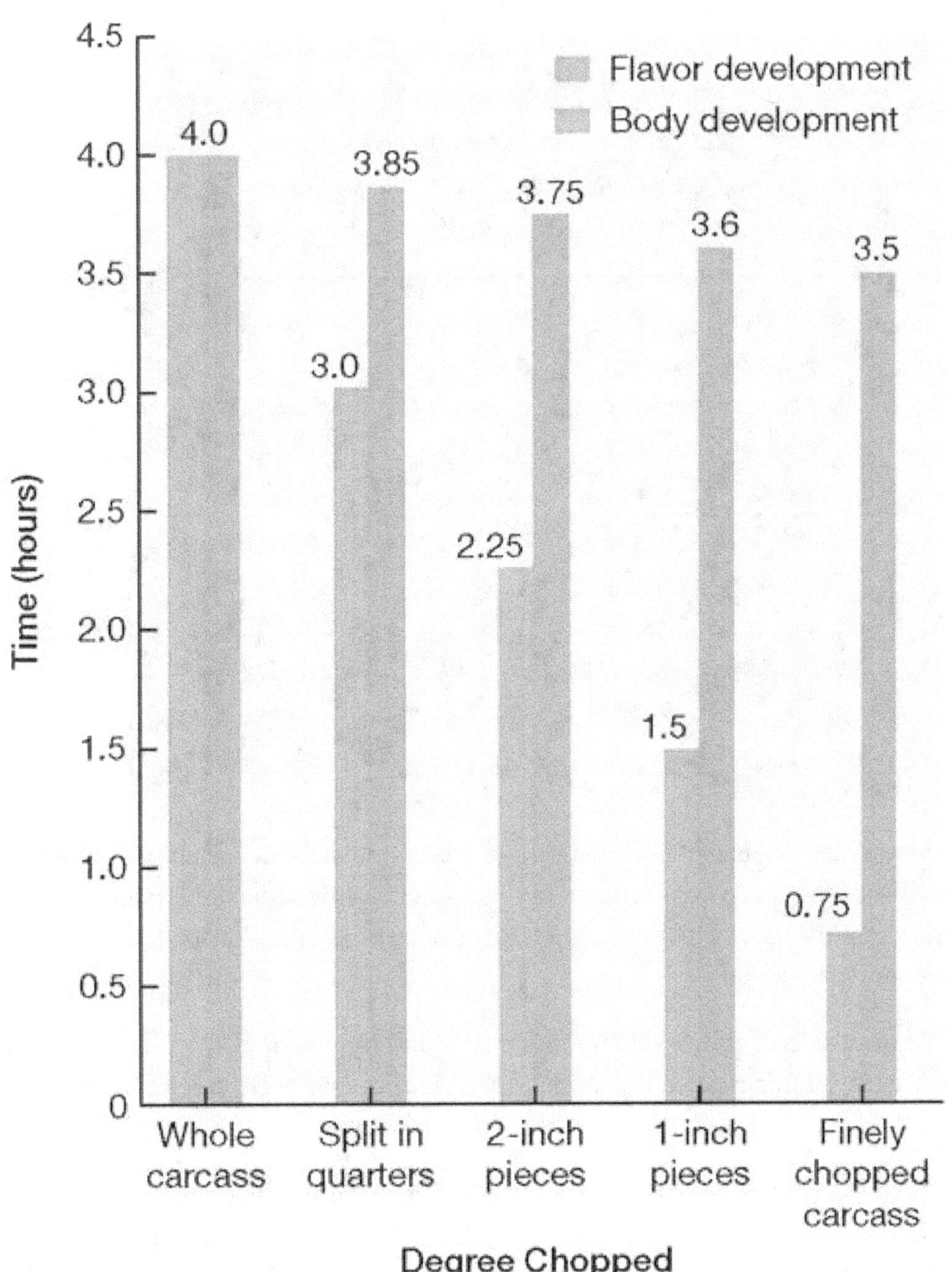

Recollect how collagen resembles a contorted piece of yarn? Have you at any point had a go at isolating the different strands in a piece of yarn? It's conceivable however tedious, and that is by and large the thing's happening in a pot of stewing connective tissue. At a 190° to 200°F stew, it requires around 3 hours for 90% of the connective tissue to change over to gelatin, and afterward about an hour something else for every last bit of it to change over. Keep cooking beyond that point, in any case, and the actual gelatin begins separating, losing its thickening power. So the ideal chicken stock ought to be stewed for around 4 hours.

Fortunately, chicken collagen isn't the main spot where you can track down gelatin. It's sitting in that general area in the grocery store, truth be told:

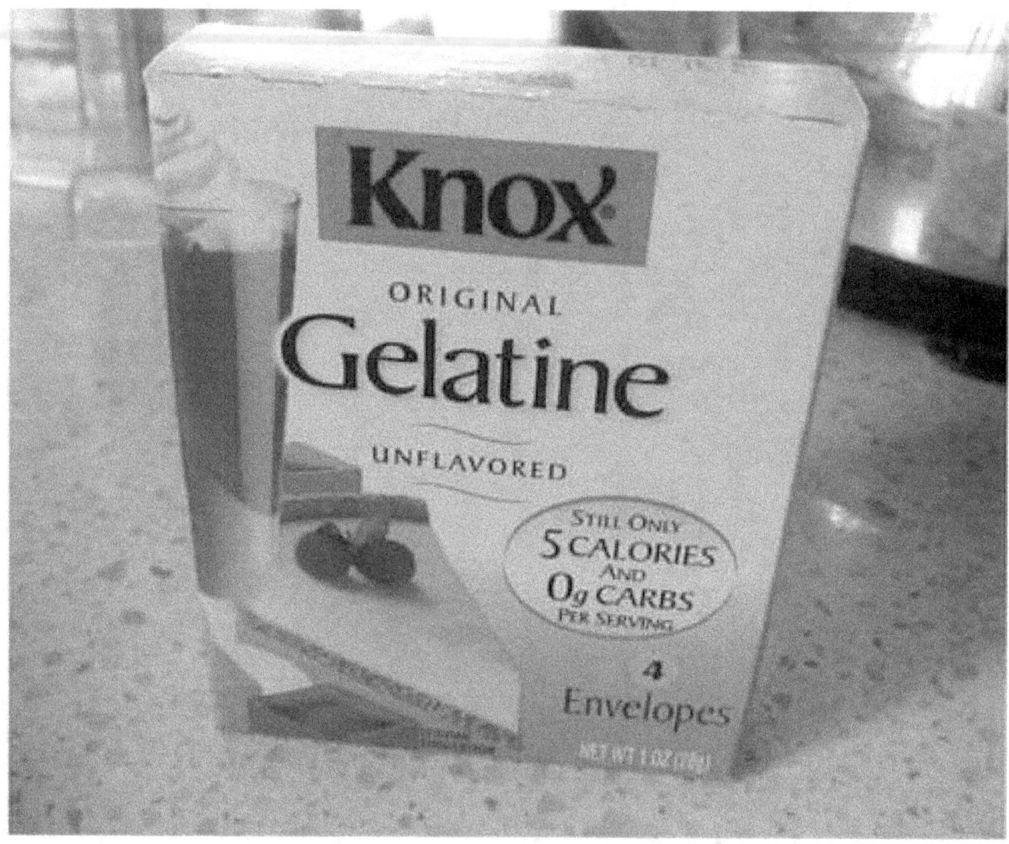

Bundled gelatin (the very stuff that makes Jell-O jiggly) is monetarily accessible in powdered or sheet structure. So all I needed to do was require my 45-minute-stewed hacked cadaver stock and add business gelatin to it to create a stock that was not just tasty as one that had been stewed for quite a long time, yet similarly as rich!

So that is all there is to it, correct? Stock shortly? Indeed, stand by consider the possibility that we could make our stock taste far superior to a customarily made French-style stock. Unrealistic, you say? I'll demonstrate it.

In a conventional French stock, clearness is esteemed regardless of anything else it's fat and broken up minerals and proteins (which we'll by and large call by their logical name, "gunk") that make stock shady. Assuming you keep a stock at an exposed stew, the fat ascents to the surface in particular air pockets that can be painstakingly skimmed off as it cooks, and the proteins coagulate into moderately huge agglomerations that can be stressed out.

However, let your stock stew enthusiastically, or-mon dieu, non!- really reach boiling point, and that gunk gets scattered into a large number of minuscule drops that can't be totally taken out from the stock. It can mean catastrophe in an extravagant eatery, where sauces and soups should be entirely gleaming and perfectly clear, however do we truly think often about that at home? I most definitely, will take flavor over appearance anytime, and fat is flavor.

A reward to crushing the chicken bones and scraps prior to making stock is that all the ground-up bits structure a kind of drifting pontoon that will gather stray proteins, minerals, and other gunk-the very same way that a French consommé is made. This takes care of part of the clearness issue. Its remainder, we can live with. Lesson of the story: let your stock stew away.

>
>
> It's not intuitive, but most of the flavorful compounds that give various types of meat its distinct flavor are not in the meat itself but in the fat that surrounds and runs through it. Don't believe me? Just think of this: why is most lean meat described as "tasting like chicken"? It's because without fat, meat has a very generic flavor. It **does** taste like a lean chicken breast. If you've got a food processor or meat grinder at home, you can even prove this to yourself with this experiment.
>
> **Materials**
> - 12 ounces boneless lean beef (a cut like eye of round or well-trimmed sirloin will do well), cut into 1-inch cubes
> - 1 ounce beef fat, trimmed from a steak (or just ask a butcher for some beef fat), cut into small pieces
> - 1 ounce lamb fat trimmed from a lamb chop (or just ask the butcher for some lamb fat)
> - 1 ounce bacon, cut into small pieces
>
> **Procedure**
> 1. Divide the beef into 3 portions and toss each portion with a different fat.
> 2. Using a food processor or meat grinder, grind the meat into hamburger (for more specific instructions on meat grinding, see here).
> 3. Form each portion into a patty and cook in a hot skillet or on the grill.
> 4. Taste the cooked patties.
>
> **Results**
> How did the cooked patties taste? Most likely you found that the first patty tasted like a regular burger, while the second patty tasted like a lamb burger. The bacon-laced patty, well, you get the gist. Still unconvinced? Try the same thing replacing the lean beef with lean lamb. The patty with beef fat will *still* taste very much like a regular all-beef burger.

DEFATTING A STOCK

As a rule, outside of extravagant cafés and style shows, some additional fat isn't really something awful go to any Japanese ramen house, for instance, and they'll truly add fat to individual dishes of noodles for additional flavor-however there's a major distinction between barely enough and to an extreme. A touch of fat emulsified into a stock and a couple of stray air pockets drifting on a superficial level add lavishness and profundity. A weighty smooth adds only an oily flavor and mouth-covering slickness. Along these lines, it's ideal to eliminate the smooth of fat that structures on top of your stock as it cooks. In any case, what's the most ideal way?

Assuming you've worked in a café, you've most likely been educated to be hyperaware of what your stock is doing consistently, cautiously skimming any filth or fat that ascents to the surface at ordinary stretches to keep the stock as clear as could really be expected. However, once more, that is a café procedure, for eatery cooking. At the point when I make stock at home, I try not to skim it until it's done. I strain the stock through a fine-network sifter into a new pot and allowed it to rest for around 15 minutes, in length enough to permit the vast majority of the fat and rubbish to ascend to the surface so it can without much of a stretch scooped off.

Much more straightforward is to prepare and refrigerate the stock for the time being; the fat will solidify into a simple to-eliminate layer that can be scratched off with a spoon, uncovering the impeccably crystallized stock under.

STOCK, BROTH, GLACE, AND JUS

Stringently talking, stock and stock are two unmistakable arrangements. Stock is made by stewing bones, connective tissue, meat scraps, and vegetables in water. Lessening a stock by tenderly warming it to vanish its water content concentrates the two its delightful mixtures and its gelatin. Lessen it adequately far, and it'll become gooey enough to frame an intelligible covering on food. At this stage, it's known as a glace, and it's extremely scrumptious. Similarly as Eskimos have many words for snow, the French have various words for diminished stock-glace, glace de viande, and demi-glace-as per how far the stock has been decreased.

Stock is made with meat and vegetables-no bones or connective tissue. It tends to be tasty, however without collagen from connective tissue, it's comparably meager as water. However while a traditionally prepared gourmet expert might have to know this differentiation, as a home cook, you don't need to stress over it. In this book, I utilize "stock" essentially only, on the grounds that my Quick Chicken Stock formula contains the two bones and added gelatin. For by far most of home-cooked plans, the two can be utilized reciprocally. The USDA sees no difference in their marking regulations about what can be classified "stock" or "stock." They express that the expressions "might be utilized conversely as the subsequent fluid from stewing meat and additionally bones in water with flavors." While certain brands will decide to utilize some phrasing on their bundling, there is as a matter of fact no genuine distinction by they way they're fabricated.

Jus alludes to the normal juices radiated by a piece of meat that is being simmered. Frequently the jus will choose the lower part of a simmering skillet and dissipate while the meat cooks, leaving a covering of what is called affectionate the scrumptious carmelized bits that structure the foundation of container sauces and flavors.

FREEZING STOCK

There's no denying it-even a fast stock is somewhat of an errand, and one that I would rather not go through each time I make a bowl of soup or need a speedy container sauce. Luckily, stock freezes strikingly well. I keep my stock frozen in two unique ways:

• In ice block plate. Empty the stock into an ice block plate, let it freeze totally, and afterward move the solid shapes to a zipper-lock cooler sack. You can pull out so a lot or as need might arise, and the solid shapes dissolve quite quick. This is great for container sauces where you don't require an excess of stock at a time.

• In quart-sized Cryovac or cooler sacks or plastic compartments. Assuming you have a vacuum-sealer (like a FoodSaver), a quart-sized sack is the best method for putting away stock. It freezes level, so it occupies almost no room in the cooler, and, even better, thaws out under hot faucet water in simply an issue of minutes. On the off chance that you don't have a vacuum-sealer, you can freeze stock in zipper-lock cooler sacks. Try to crush out however much air as could reasonably be expected prior to fixing them, then lay them level to freeze. Or then again, simply utilize standard plastic store compartments.

The other stunt to proficient and economical stock creation is to save all your chicken parts. Each time I separate a chicken, I throw the backs and wing tips into a gallon zipper-secure sack that I keep in the cooler. Whenever the sack is full, I'm prepared to make a bunch of stock.

FAST CHICKEN STOCK

NOTE: This formula likewise delivers cooked chicken leg meat, which can be utilized in different plans or put something aside for sometime in the future. On the other hand, supplant the chicken legs with more backs and wingtips.

MAKES 2 QUARTS

1 ounce (4 bundles; around 3 tablespoons) unflavored gelatin

2 pounds skin-on chicken backs and wing tips, ideally from youthful chickens

2 pounds chicken legs

1 enormous onion, generally slashed

1 enormous carrot, stripped and generally slashed

2 stems celery, generally cleaved

2 straight leaves

2 teaspoons entire dark peppercorns

1 teaspoon fennel seeds

1 teaspoon coriander seeds

6 branches new parsley

1. Empty 4 cups water into a medium bowl and sprinkle with the gelatin. Put away until the gelatin is hydrated, around 10 minutes.

2. In the mean time, slash the chicken backs and wing tips with a knife into unpleasant 2-inch pieces, or cut up with poultry shears. Working in a few groups, move the chicken to a food processor and heartbeat until the surface generally approximates ground chicken, halting in the event that an especially hard bone stalls out on the cutting edge.

3. Move the ground chicken, chicken legs, onion, carrot, celery, cove leaves, peppercorns, fennel, coriander, and parsley to an enormous Dutch stove or stockpot and add cold water to simply cover the fixings, around 2 quarts. Add the hydrated gelatin and water and heat to the point of boiling over high hotness. Change the hotness to keep an energetic stew, then skim off any froth and filth from the surface and dispose of. Cook for 45 minutes, adding water as important to keep the fixings lowered. Eliminate from the hotness and permit to cool for a couple of moments.

4. Utilizing a couple of utensils, move the chicken legs to a bowl and put away to cool. Eliminate and dispose of any huge bits of bone and vegetables from the stock. Strain the stock through a fine-

network sifter into an enormous bowl and dispose of the solids. Return the stock to the pot, bring to a moving stew, and decrease to 2 quarts, around 10 minutes.

5. In the mean time, take the meat out the chicken legs and hold for another utilization (like Chicken Vegetable Soup or Chicken and Dumplings; see here or here). Dispose of the bones and skin.

6. Whenever the stock has completed the process of decreasing, permit it to rest until the overabundance fat and filth structure a particular layer on a superficial level, around 15 minutes, then, at that point, skim off with a spoon dispose of the fat or save it for another utilization. On the other hand, you can refrigerate the stock for the time being and eliminate the strong fat from the top. The stock will keep in a water/air proof holder in the cooler for as long as 5 days, or it very well may be frozen for somewhere around 90 days.

FUNDAMENTAL VEGETABLE STOCK

MAKES 2 QUARTS

1 ounce (4 bundles; around 3 tablespoons) unflavored gelatin

2 enormous onions, generally slashed

2 enormous carrots, stripped and generally slashed

4 stems celery, generally slashed

1 enormous leek, managed

8 ounces mushroom stems and scraps and additionally entire mushrooms

2 Granny Smith apples, quartered

2 cove leaves

2 teaspoons entire dark peppercorns

1 teaspoon fennel seeds

1 teaspoon coriander seeds

6 branches new parsley

1. Empty 4 cups of water into a medium bowl and sprinkle with the gelatin. Put away until the gelatin is hydrated, around 10 minutes.

2. In the mean time, put the onions, carrots, celery, leek, mushrooms, apples, cove leaves, peppercorns, fennel, coriander, and parsley in a huge Dutch broiler or stockpot and add cold water to simply cover the fixings. Add the hydrated gelatin and water and bring to a stew over medium hotness. Change the hotness to keep a sluggish, consistent stew and cook for 60 minutes, adding high temp water as important to keep the fixings lowered.

3. Strain the stock through a fine-network sifter fixed with cheesecloth into an enormous bowl and dispose of the solids. Return the stock to the pot, bring to a stew, and diminish to 2 quarts, around 20 minutes. Eliminate from the hotness. The stock will keep in an impermeable compartment in the fridge for as long as 5 days, or it tends to be frozen for as long as 90 days.

CHICKEN SOUP WITH RICE (OR NOODLES)

As a no-nonsense Colombian from the mountains of Bogotá, my significant other cases that she could live on soup alone. My normally curious psyche is tormented by the compelling impulse to thoroughly test this case, however every time I choose to drive her to set out on the principal day of the remainder of her fluid eating regimen based life, the piece of me that adores her mediates and advises me that life just wouldn't be as fun without her, soup or no. She, coming from a rice-eating nation, favors rice in her soup, while I, coming from New York, lean toward the unrivaled egg noodle. I have ages of Jewish grandmas on my side, however she has the secret weapon of Maurice Sendak-however I really do get a kick out of the chance to bring up that had there been more words in the English language that rhyme with noodle, Sendak might well have composed an alternate arrangement of sonnets altogether. For what it's worth, "In January, while I doodle/swirly designs on my poodle" doesn't have the an incredible same ring to it as the first.

All things considered, we truly do eat a ton of soup around here, and whenever you have an extraordinary chicken stock to work with, you've won close to 100% of the fight for The Ultimate Vegetable Chicken Soup with Rice (or Noodles). The rest is basically as basic as adding the vegetables and rice or noodles. I like to begin with a base of carrots, onions, and celery, then, at that point, stir it up. Anything that's in season, anything that looks best-hell, anything that you can get your hands on and want to add is the best procedure here. The memorable way is that various vegetables should be prepared and cooked in various ways to augment their soupworthiness.

SOUP VEGETABLES: BEST STRATEGIES

Simplifying any, stock based vegetable soup is simple the length of you know how to set up the different vegetables and when to add them. This outline depicts how to manage the most widely recognized soup vegetables.

VEGETABLE	PREP	COOKING TIME
Carrot	Peel and cut into ½-inch chunks	20 minutes
Cauliflower	Separate into florets, slice stems ¼ inch thick	20 minutes
Celery	Peel and cut into ½-inch chunks	20 minutes
Celery Root (celeriac)	Peel and cut into ½-inch chunks	20 minutes
Jicama	Peel and cut into ½-inch chunks	20 minutes
Kohlrabi	Peel and cut into ½-inch chunks	20 minutes
Leek	Thinly slice or dice	20 minutes
Onion	Thinly slice or dice	20 minutes
Parsnip	Peel and cut into ½-inch chunks	20 minutes
Potato	Peel and cut into ½-inch chunks	20 minutes
Radish	Cut into ½-inch chunks	20 minutes
Rutabaga	Peel and cut into ½-inch chunks	20 minutes
Sweet Potato	Peel and cut into ½-inch chunks	20 minutes
Asparagus	Cut into 1-inch lengths	10 minutes
Bell Pepper	Cut into ½-inch chunks	10 minutes
Broccoli	Separate into florets, slice stems ¼ inch thick	10 minutes
Butternut Squash	Peel and cut into ½-inch chunks	10 minutes
Cabbage	Slice ⅛ inch thick	10 minutes
Collard Greens	Roughly chop leaves, cut stems into 1-inch segments	10 minutes
Green Beans	Trim and cut into 1-inch pieces	10 minutes

Kale	Roughly chop leaves, cut stems into 1-inch segments	10 minutes
Summer Squash	Cut into ½-inch chunks	10 minutes
Zucchini	Cut into ½-inch chunks	10 minutes
Arugula	Remove tough stems	5 minutes
Brussels Sprouts	Pull off leaves	5 minutes
Chard	Roughly chop leaves, cut stems into 1-inch lengths	5 minutes
Corn Kernels	Cut off cobs (separate into individual kernels if necessary)	5 minutes
Lima Beans, frozen	None	5 minutes
Peas, frozen	None	5 minutes
Baby Spinach	None	5 minutes
Curly Spinach	Roughly chop	5 minutes
Watercress	Roughly chop	5 minutes

THE ULTIMATE CHICKEN VEGETABLE SOUP

WITH RICE (OR NOODLES)

NOTES: Instead of utilizing the stock, you can stew 4 chicken legs in 2 quarts low-sodium canned chicken stock for 30 minutes. Eliminate the legs, skim the fat from the stock, and add sufficient water to make 2 quarts. At the point when the legs are sufficiently cool to deal with, take out the meat, disposing of the bones and skin, and save.

The carrots, celery, and onion are simply ideas go ahead and utilize anything that vegetables you'd like (see the diagram here-here), focusing on around 2½ cups all out prepared vegetables.

SERVES 4 TO 6

1 formula Quick Chicken Stock (here), including the picked leg meat (see Note above)

2 medium carrots, stripped and cut into medium dice (around 1 cup)

1 medium stem celery, cut into medium dice (about ½ cup)

1 little onion, daintily cut (around 1 cup)

½ cup of long-grain white rice or 2 cups of medium egg noodles

¼ cup hacked new parsley

2 cups kale attacked 1-inch pieces (around 6 leaves)

Legitimate salt and newly ground dark pepper

1. Consolidate the chicken stock (save the meat for some other time), carrots, celery, onion, and rice, if utilizing (not the noodles), in a Dutch broiler and heat to the point of boiling over high hotness. Decrease to a stew and cook until the vegetables are practically delicate, around 15 minutes.

2. Add the greens and noodles, if utilizing, and cook until every one of the vegetables and the rice (or noodles) are delicate, around 5 minutes longer. Mix in the parsley and chicken meat and warm through. Add some pepper and salt seasoning to taste.

MEAT AND BARLEY STEW

Whenever you grind as much meat as I do, you frequently end up with an additional a pound or two of short ribs lying around. You could braise them in red wine and be all French, or you could cook them for a couple of days sous-vide like a cutting edge eatery, and both are extraordinary strategies. Here and there, however, I'm in the mind-set for something more straightforward.

Short rib and grain stew is awesome in light of the fact that it:

• is imbecilic simple to do,

• is made with storage room and ice chest staples (beside the short ribs),

• goes on for quite a long time and gets better with time,

• calms the spirit or warms the cockles of your heart, or then again, in the event that you're truly fortunate, both simultaneously, and

• tastes super great.

The technique is really clear: burn the meat to add a touch of flavor, sauté the vegetables, and afterward stew the entire thing down with a touch of Marmite, soy sauce, and tomato glue added for that umami kick.

All through the cold weather months, there are generally a couple of leaves of kale kicking around my refrigerator, since they make such an incredible plate of mixed greens (simply marinate in olive oil and vinegar for a few hours-it stays fresh for a really long time even subsequent to dressing! See here), and they go quite far in making this stew considerably more delectable and heartier. On the off chance that you lean toward hamburger and grain soup to stew, simply add a more stock toward the finish to thin it to the ideal consistency.

MEAT AND BARLEY STEW

SERVES 4 TO 6

2 pounds boneless meat short ribs, cut into 1-inch pieces

Genuine salt and newly ground dark pepper

2 tablespoons canola oil

2 medium carrots, stripped, split in half longwise, and cut into ½-inch pieces (around 1 cup)

2 medium stems celery, split in half the long way, and cut into ½-inch pieces (around 1 cup)

1 enormous onion, finely diced (around 1½ cups)

½ teaspoon Marmite

1 teaspoon soy sauce

2 medium cloves garlic, minced or ground on a Microplane (around 2 teaspoons)

1 tablespoon tomato glue

4 cups custom made or low-sodium canned chicken stock

One 14½-ounce can entire tomatoes, depleted and generally cleaved

1 cup pearl grain

2 straight leaves

4 cups inexactly stuffed generally torn kale leaves

1. Throw the short ribs in an enormous bowl with salt and pepper to cover. Heat the oil in a Dutch broiler over high hotness until smoking. Add the hamburger and cook, without moving it, until all around seared on first side, around 5 minutes. Mix the meat and cook, mixing at times, until carmelized everywhere, around 10 minutes absolute; lessen the hotness on the off chance that the lower part of the pot starts to sear. Return the meat to the bowl and put away.

2. Return the pot to medium-high hotness and add the carrots, celery, and onion. Cook, blending regularly, until the vegetables start to brown, around 4 minutes. Add the Marmite, soy sauce, garlic, and tomato glue and cook, blending, until fragrant, around 30 seconds.

3. Add the stock and scrape up the carmelized bits from the lower part of the pot with a wooden spoon. Add the tomatoes, grain, and narrows leaves, then return the meat to the pot, increment the hotness to high, and heat to the point of boiling. Lessen to the most reduced conceivable hotness and cover the pot, leaving the top somewhat unlatched. Cook, mixing periodically, until the hamburger is totally delicate and the grain is cooked through, around 2 hours.

4. Mix in the kale and cook, blending continually, until shriveled, around 2 minutes. Season to taste with salt and pepper. Serve, or, for best flavor, cool and refrigerate in a fixed compartment for as long as 5 days prior to warming and serving.

WHERE'S THE BEEF (STOCK)?

You might be asking why I utilize chicken stock in my hamburger soup as opposed to meat stock, and the response is straightforward: I'm lethargic. Hamburger bones are enormous and it takes a long, long chance to extricate flavor and gelatin from them (cafés will keep them stewing on a sideline day in and day out). Chicken stock is speedy, I ordinarily have it available, and it has a decent impartial flavor that can undoubtedly get different flavors without overpowering them. A hamburger stew made with chicken stock as the base will in any case be bounty bulky whenever it's finished stewing.

Shouldn't something be said about locally acquired stock? On most store racks, you'll track down chicken, meat, and vegetable stock, for about a similar cost. Yet, that doesn't seem OK, makes it happen? On the off chance that hamburger stock requires quite a lot more exertion greater bones, longer extraction times, more costly meat-how might they sell it at a similar cost as chicken stock?

Here is the mystery: locally acquired meat stock isn't actually hamburger stock. There is almost no hamburger in canned meat stock. Very much like different people, food makers are apathetic and worried about their main concern. As opposed to going the entire day stewing veal or hamburger bones, they pick to utilize regular and counterfeit flavorings. As per the USDA's naming rules, meat or pork stock just must have a Moisture Protein Ratio (MPR) of 135.1 to 1-that is, for each ounce of water, there is just 0.007 ounce of hamburger protein present. No big surprise the stocks don't taste similar as meat!

To rapidly and efficiently support the kind of canned meat stock, most makers depend on yeast and vegetable concentrates. While yeast extricates are extraordinary for adding a flavorful lift to your stews, I'd much prefer have command over its option myself (a considerable lot of my plans call for Marmite, a yeast remove). Assuming you will go canned, go with low-sodium chicken stock.

SHOPPING FOR BROTH

Continuously purchase chicken or vegetable stock, not meat (see "Where's the Beef (Stock)?," above). Here two or three hints for what to search for in a canned stock:

• Purchase low-sodium stock. This will permit you to change the flavoring as you would prefer as opposed to being attached to the (generally extremely high) salt levels of the canned stock.

• Purchase stock in resealable Tetra-packs, not jars. In the same way as other bundled food varieties, stock will begin turning sour when you open it. A resealable Tetra-pack will assist with dragging out its lifetime, permitting you to use as nearly nothing or as the need might arise while putting away the rest in the refrigerator.

INSTRUCTIONS TO MAKE CANNED BEANS TASTE GOOD

I love beans and my significant other loves soup, which makes winter an incredible season for the two of us. Indeed, not actually. Actually my significant other loves soup and I love bourbon. It's an eventual fortunate circumstance for the two players included, taking into account how regularly the soul moves me to make soup when I'm sloshed. I inadvertently made soup once more, dear, I tell her. I say would-be, on the grounds that my significant other appears to incline toward my clearheaded soup to my alcoholic soup (despite the fact that the last option generally tastes better to me). So this year I concluded that I love beans nearly however much I love bourbon, and that I love my better half essentially more than I love either, thus I would exchange the container for the vegetable, and smashed soup for bean soup.

Obviously, with the chilly climate and absence of spirits, I was prepared to move breaking immediately. Issue is, dried beans are not by and large cheap food, requiring, best case scenario, a few hours, and to say the least, an entire day of dousing, trailed by stewing. So I did what any reasonable, sober man would do: I got them canned. There are several unmistakable benefits that canned beans have over dried. As far as one might be concerned, their surface is basically consistently spot on. Bean canners have the cycle down to a workmanship, and you'd presently be unable to open a can and observe beans that were broken, white, hard, or anything shy of entirely smooth and unblemished not generally something simple to achieve at home. For something else, canned beans accompany some pleasant, full-bodied fluid. Numerous plans advise you to flush the stuff off. That checks out assuming you're making, say, a bean salad, however the fluid is marvelous in soups, adding flavor and body to a generally slim stock.

There's just a single genuine issue with canned beans: flavor.

With dried beans, you have the choice of cooking your beans in quite a few media-water, chicken stock, pork stock, dashi, a sweet molassesy pureed tomatoes and adding whatever aromatics you like-onions, carrots, celery, inlet leaves, thyme, pork fat to get flavor incorporated directly into them. Canned beans, then again, are intended to taste nonpartisan that will function admirably in any dish however sparkle in none.

Fortunately for us, there are means to getting a touch of flavor once again into those folks.

Most basic canned bean soup plans assemble for blending the fixings, heating the soup to the point of boiling, and serving it right away. There's no issue in doing that-canned beans, all things considered, are a comfort food. Yet, imagine a scenario where I let you know that by adding a huge load of delightful fragrant fixings and a speedy (15-minute) stew, you could enhance the nature of your soup by a request for magnitude?*

Alright, no sensational drumroll there, I presume. Let's face it: these are 30-minute bean soups. They won't change your life the way, say, purchasing your dearest companion a lottery ticket that is worth huge number of dollars would, however they might well change your weeknight cooking schedule.

30-MINUTE PASTA E FAGIOLI

Pasta e fagioli is the bean and pasta soup customarily made with the extras from the Sunday sauce and was known to cause episodes of absurdity in Dean Martin. My form isn't loaded with meat like nonna's without a doubt was, however a huge load of garlic, pancetta (you can utilize bacon, guanciale, or even disintegrated wiener assuming you like), oregano, and a couple straight passes on include a lot of flavor.

SERVES 4

One 28-ounce can entire tomatoes

2 tablespoons extra-virgin olive oil, in addition to something else for serving

1 tablespoon unsalted spread

3 ounces pancetta, finely hacked (discretionary)

1 medium of onion, finely diced (just a cup)

6 medium cloves garlic, minced or ground on a Microplane (around 2 tablespoons)

½ teaspoon dried oregano

½ teaspoon red pepper chips

4 cups hand crafted or low-sodium canned chicken stock

Two 15-ounce jars red kidney beans, with their fluid

2 inlet leaves

1 cup little pasta, like shells, ditali, or elbows

Genuine salt and newly ground dark pepper

2 tablespoons cleaved new parsley

1. Empty the tomatoes into a medium bowl and just barely get every one through your fingers to split it up into little pieces (be cautious they can spurt). Put away.

2. Heat the olive oil and spread in a huge pan over medium-high hotness until the margarine is dissolved. In the case of utilizing pancetta, add it to the dish and cook, blending continually, until fragrant, around 2 minutes. Decrease the hotness to medium, add the onion, garlic, oregano, and red pepper drops, and cook, mixing, until the onion is fragrant and relaxed yet not seared, around 3 minutes. Add the tomatoes, with their juice, the chicken stock, kidney beans, and inlet leaves, heat to the point of boiling over high hotness, and afterward lessen to an exposed stew. Cook for 20 minutes, adding the pasta to the soup for the last 5 to 10 minutes (contingent upon the bundle bearings).

3. Put some seasoning of pepper and salt to the soup for taste. Dispose of the sound leaves, mix in the parsley, and serve, showering each presenting with olive oil.

<h1 style="text-align:center">30-MINUTE MINESTRONE</h1>

Minestrone is my soup of decision throughout the spring and late-spring, when vegetables from the ranchers' market are at their most brilliant and generally delightful. Some minestrone soups get cooked down for a really long time. I really lean toward my speedy adaptation, since it keeps the vegetables somewhat fresh and crisp tasting. I generally start with onion, carrot, celery, and canned tomatoes as my base, yet what's more, you can utilize the vegetables proposed here or go with anything from the table here-here. Simply make a point to keep the aggregate sum of additional vegetables at around 3 to 4 cups (not including greens, which will cook down significantly).

SERVES 6 TO 8

2 tablespoons extra-virgin olive oil, in addition to something else for serving

1 medium of finely diced onion (around 1 cup)

2 medium carrots, stripped and finely diced (around 1 cup)

2 stems celery, finely diced (around 1 cup)

4 medium cloves garlic, minced or ground on a Microplane (around 4 teaspoons)

6 cups natively constructed or low-sodium canned chicken stock

1 cup of diced tomatoes (canned), with their juice

One 15-ounce can Roman (borlotti or cranberry) cannelini, or extraordinary northern beans, with their fluid

2 narrows leaves

1 little zucchini, cut into ½-inch shapes or ½-inch half-moons (about ¾ cup)

1 little summer squash, cut into ½-inch 3D shapes or ½-inch half-moons (about ¾ cup)

1 cup green beans cut into ½-inch sections

2 cups generally slashed wavy spinach or kale

1 cup little pasta, like shells, ditali, or elbows

½ cup frozen peas

½ cup cherry tomatoes, cut down the middle

Fit salt and newly ground dark pepper

¼ cup slashed new basil

1. Heat the olive oil in an enormous pan over medium-high hotness until shining. Lessen the hotness to medium, add the onion, carrots, celery, and garlic, and cook, blending, until relaxed however not seared, around 3 minutes. Add the chicken stock, tomatoes and beans, with their fluid, and the cove leaves and heat to the point of boiling over high hotness, then lessen to an uncovered stew. Cook for 20 minutes, adding the zucchini, squash, green beans, and spinach throughout the previous 10 minutes, and the pasta for last 5 or 10 minutes (contingent upon the bundle headings).

2. Try to season the soup to have a good taste with salt and pepper. Dispose of the straight leaves, add the peas, cherry tomatoes, and basil, and mix until the peas are defrosted. Serve, showering each presenting with olive oil.

30-MINUTE DON'T-CALL-IT-TUSCAN WHITE BEAN AND PARMESAN SOUP

Given the horrid history of the utilization of the word, I'm not positive that there's really anything Tuscan about this bean soup, yet all at once it's heavenly all things considered. The key is a lot of rosemary and a hunk of skin from some great Parmigiano-Reggiano threw in while it stews. Similar as stewing chicken bones, a Parmesan skin will include both flavor and body. The thing that matters is that this requires just minutes to arrive at greatness. That, and a lot of good olive oil for sprinkling.

SERVES 4

2 tablespoons extra-virgin olive oil, in addition to something else for serving

1 medium of finely diced onion (around 1 cup)

2 medium carrots, stripped and finely diced (around 1 cup)

2 stems celery, finely diced (around 1 cup)

4 medium cloves garlic, minced or ground on a Microplane (around 4 teaspoons)

½ teaspoon red pepper drops

4 cups natively constructed or low-sodium canned chicken stock

Two 15-ounce jars cannellini or extraordinary northern beans, with their fluid

Four 6-inch branches rosemary, leaves eliminated and finely cleaved, stems saved

One 3-to 4-inch lump Parmesan skin, in addition to ground Parmigiano-Reggiano for serving

2 straight leaves

3 to 4 cups generally cleaved kale or Swiss chard leaves

Genuine salt and newly ground dark pepper

1. Heat the olive oil in an enormous pan over medium-high hotness until shining. Add the onions, carrots, and celery and cook, blending, until relaxed however not seared, around 3 minutes. Add the garlic and red pepper pieces and cook, blending, until fragrant, around 1 moment. Add the chicken stock, beans, with their fluid, the rosemary stems, Parmesan skin, and straight leaves, increment the hotness to high, and heat to the point of boiling. Diminish to an uncovered stew, add the kale, cover, and cook for 15 minutes.

2. Dispose of the cove leaves and rosemary stems. Utilize a drenching blender to generally puree a portion of the beans until the ideal consistency is reached. Then again, move 2 cups of the soup to a customary blender or food processor and interaction until smooth, beginning on low speed and progressively expanding to high, then return to the soup and mix to consolidate. Try to season with pepper and salt to taste.

3. Scoop into bowls, sprinkle with the slashed rosemary, shower with olive oil, and sprinkle with a grinding of Parmigiano-Reggiano. Present with toasted dry bread.

30-MINUTE BLACK BEAN SOUP

Dark bean soup was a #1 of mine when I was a child, it actually is. Cumin, garlic, and hot pepper drops, alongside onions and peppers, structure the flavor base. The kicker is the canned chipotle pepper, which is wherever nowadays, however no less scrumptious for it.

SERVES 4

1 tablespoon vegetable oil

2 green chime peppers, finely diced

1 huge onion, finely diced

2 medium cloves garlic, minced or ground on a Microplane (around 2 teaspoons)

1 jalapeño or serrano pepper, cultivated and finely cleaved

1 teaspoon ground cumin

½ teaspoon red pepper pieces

1 chipotle chile stuffed in adobo, finely cleaved, in addition to 1 tablespoon of the adobo sauce

4 cups hand crafted or low-sodium canned chicken stock

Two 15-ounce jars dark beans, with their fluid

2 sound leaves

Legitimate salt

For Serving (discretionary)

Generally hacked new cilantro

Crema (Mexican-style sharp cream)

Diced avocado

Diced red onion

1. Heat the oil in a huge pan over medium-high hotness until gleaming. Add the chime peppers and onions and cook, blending much of the time, until relaxed yet not seared, around 3 minutes. Add the garlic, jalapeño, cumin, and red pepper chips and cook, blending, until fragrant, around 1 moment. Add the chipotle and adobo sauce and mix to consolidate. Add the chicken stock, beans, with their fluid, and the sound leaves, increment the hotness to high, and heat to the point of boiling. Decrease to an uncovered stew, cover, and cook for 15 minutes.

2. Dispose of the sound leaves. Utilize an inundation blender to generally puree a portion of the beans until the ideal consistency is reached. On the other hand, move 2 cups of the soup to a blender or food processor and cycle until smooth, beginning on low speed and steadily expanding to high, then return to the soup and mix to join. Season to taste with salt.

3. Scoop the soup into serving bowls and serve, with cilantro leaves, acrid cream, diced avocado, or potentially diced red onion whenever wanted.

STEP BY STEP INSTRUCTIONS TO MAKE CREAMY VEGETABLE SOUPS WITHOUT A RECIPE

Whenever I was an absolutely green cook with my first genuine café work, working under Chef Jason Bond at what's currently a milestone Boston eatery, No. 9 Park, there were numerous minutes when I took in another procedure or consummated an old one and told myself, "Blessed poo, I just made this?"

Yet, the absolute originally was when Chef Bond showed me how to make a smooth chanterelle soup (read: Campbell's cream of mushroom soup on delectable, delicious break), perspiring aromatics, sautéing mushrooms, adding a decent stock, and pureeing everything while at the same time emulsifying the combination with new margarine.

Like any extraordinary vegetable soup, the outcome was something that possessed a flavor like a condensed, cleansed, increased variant of itself-this soup tasted more like chanterelles than real chanterelles. The enchanted lies in the manner that fragrant fixings can bring out different flavors, as well as the manner by which fluids coat your mouth, giving more straightforward contact as you would prefer buds and olfactory sensors, and making for simpler arrival of unpredictable mixtures.

Nowadays, there aren't an excessive number of vegetables on the planet that I haven't made into a smooth, rich soup, and there are significantly less that I've not loved,† yet my experience has shown me something: that first course of making a chanterelle soup wasn't simply a formula for chanterelle soup. It was an outline for making any smooth vegetable soup. You simply need to separate it into its singular advances and sort out some way to universalize them.

Suppose, for example, that I've never made a smooth carrot soup enhanced with ginger and harissa, yet I truly like the thought. This is how i am going about it.

Stage 1: Prepare Your Main Ingredient

The least complex soups can be made by simply adding your fundamental fixings crude and stewing them in fluid later on. While setting up this kind of soup, all you must do is prepare your fundamental fixing by stripping it (if vital) and cutting it into reasonably little pieces. The more modest you cut, the speedier your soup will cook down the line.

There are times when you might need to support the kind of a principle fixing by, say, simmering or sautéing it. This is a particularly viable method for sweet, thick vegetables like yams and squashes, or brassicas like broccoli or cauliflower, all of which heighten in pleasantness with some carmelizing. To cook them, cut them into enormous pieces, throw them with some olive oil, salt, and pepper, set them in a baking sheet fixed with aluminum foil or material paper, and dish in a 375°F broiler until delicate, with their edges touched brown.

This works in two ways. In the first place, the course of caramelization separates enormous sugars into more modest, better ones. Second, enzymatic responses that make basic sugars are sped up with heat.

Stage 2: Choose Your Aromatics

Alliums-onions, leeks, shallots, garlic, and so forth resemble the Best Supporting Actor of the soup pot. They're not there to get everyone's attention, but rather without them, your soup would exhaust. Essentially every soup I make begins with either onions or leeks, alongside some garlic or shallot (and here and there each of the four!) cooked down in olive oil or spread.

Other firm vegetables, for example, diced carrots, ringer peppers, celery, meagerly cut fennel, or ginger can function admirably in specific circumstances, however they will generally strongerly affect the completed kind of the dish, so ensure that you truly need them there. Make a carrot soup with just onions and it'll pose a flavor like carrot soup. Make a carrot soup with fennel or ginger, and it will possess a flavor like carrot-and-fennel soup or carrot-and-ginger soup.

Stage 3: Sweat or Brown Your Aromatics

Next central issue: to perspire or to brown?

• Perspiring is the course of gradually cooking hacked vegetables in a fat. You do it over moderate hotness, and the objective is to dispose of a portion of the abundance dampness inside those vegetables, and to separate their cell structure with the goal that their flavor is delivered. With the instance of alliums, there's another cycle going on: onion fragrance is made when certain antecedent particles that exist inside independent compartments in onion cells break out and join with one another. Perspiring an onion will separate cell dividers, permitting this cycle to occur. Similar remains constant for garlic, shallots, and leeks.

• Carmelizing begins like perspiring, however for the most part happens over higher hotness. When overabundance fluid from vegetables has dissipated, the vegetables can start to brown and caramelize, making rich flavors, all the more sweet notes, and greater intricacy. You could feel that more flavor is generally better, and accordingly you ought to generally brown your vegetables, yet as a rule, this searing can be overwhelming, making soups excessively sweet or contending a lot with the subtler kinds of your primary vegetable.

Stage 4: Add Second-Level Aromatics Like Spices and Pastes

After your aromatics have perspired or carmelized, the following stage is your auxiliary aromatics, and a discretionary stage's frequently precluded. Assuming you like extremely perfect, unadulterated tasting soups, get out ahead. In the event that you like playing with flavors and flavors, you'll mess around with this progression.

These are things like ground flavors (say, curry powder, ground cumin, or bean stew powder) and wet glues (like tomato glue, harissa, or cleaved chipotle peppers in adobo sauce). These kinds of fixings benefit from a concise toasting or browning in hot oil, which modifies a portion of their constituents into more complicated, more fragrant items, as well as extricating fat-solvent flavors with the goal that they scatter all the more equally into the soup.

Since ground flavors have such a high proportion of surface region to volume and most glues have previously been cooked, the interaction takes a couple of seconds - just until the flavors begin smelling fragrant.

Stage 5: Add Your Liquid

Your decision of fluid can hugely affect the completed dish.

• Chicken stock is a simple contingency plan and a decent decision 100% of the time. It has a nonpartisan, gentle flavor that adds substantiality and appetizing quality to a dish without overpowering any flavors. In like manner vegetable stock can bring comparable intricacy, however purchaser be careful: not normal for locally acquired chicken stock, most locally acquired vegetable stocks are detestable. Making your own is your own ideal situation.

• Vegetable juice is what you need in the event that you esteem power of vegetable flavor over balance. Carrots cooked and pureed in carrot juice will taste madly carroty. You can purchase numerous vegetable juices at the general store nowadays, or juice your own with a home juicer. Blending and coordinating a principle fixing with an alternate vegetable juice (like in my formula for Roasted Squash and Raw Carrot Soup) can prompt extraordinary outcome.

• Dairy, for example, milk or buttermilk is a decent method for getting yourself a heartier, creamier dish, however dairy fat tends to dull splendid flavors. This isn't really something terrible: dairy is the ideal foil for the serious kind of broccoli in a velvety broccoli soup, or tomatoes in a cream of tomato soup, for example.

• Water is a totally fine decision in the event that different choices aren't accessible.

Anything fluid you pick, don't utilize excessively. Utilize barely to the point of covering your fixings by an inch or something like that. You can generally thin a thick soup out subsequent to mixing, however lessening a pureed soup that is too flimsy is a considerably more troublesome thing to do (if you would rather not risk consuming it to the lower part of the pot).

In the wake of adding your fluid and principle fixing, carry the soup to a stew and let it cook until the vegetables are simply cooked through; you maintain that them should be sufficiently delicate to puncture with a blade with no obstruction. For things like carrots, parsnips, and other root vegetables, you have a touch of slack. Overcooking won't be the apocalypse. However, for dazzling green vegetables like broccoli, asparagus, peas, string beans, or salad greens, you need to make a point to quit cooking them before they begin turning a dreary green tone assuming a splendidly hued soup is something you care about, that is.

Stage 6: Puree and Emulsify

Here is the tomfoolery part: pureeing. The perfection of your last soup will rely upon the apparatus you use.

• A blender will give you the smoothest result, because of its fast and vortex activity. While mixing hot fluids, consistently hold the top down with a kitchen towel, begin the blender on low speed, and gradually bring it up to high. Except if you appreciate wearing hot soup.

• An inundation blender can give you an appropriately smooth outcome, contingent upon the force of your blender. It's by a wide margin the most advantageous method for making soup, and it's a decent decision assuming that you're fine with a provincial, sort of thick surface.

• A food processor ought to be your last decision. In view of its wide base and generally low turning rate, a food processor accomplishes more hacking than pureeing.

Anything the pureeing strategy, I like to emulsify my soup with some fat during this stage-either margarine or olive oil. This adds a rich surface to the soup.

A few plans (counting large numbers of mine) will advise you to gradually sprinkle in fat or add spread a handle at a time while the blender is running, which is a reliable method for getting your fat to emulsify appropriately, yet entirely here's confidential: insofar as you don't have the world's most awful blender (and someone who might be listening does!), there's no genuine need to shower in the fat gradually. The vortex activity of a blender is bounty adequately strong to emulsify the fat regardless of whether you simply dump everything in simultaneously.

Assuming a definitive in perfection is your objective, polish off your pureed soup by utilizing the lower part of a scoop to squeeze it through a chinois or a super fine-network sifter. The outcome ought to be smoother than John Travolta swaggering with a two layer pizza cut.

Stage 7: Finish with Acid and Season

Preparing is the last advance not long prior to plating and serving in any formula. You can prepare as you go, however who knows whether your soup has the right degree of salt until you taste it in its last structure. This is the ideal opportunity.

Similarly critical to draw out the best flavor in a formula is corrosive. Since acidic fixings rapidly dull in flavor when cooked, it's ideal to add new corrosive right toward the end, not long prior to serving. For most vegetable-based dishes, lemon squeeze or lime juice is an incredible choice, as their smell supplements vegetal flavors. Other great choices would be a smidgen of juice vinegar, wine vinegar, or my #1, sherry vinegar. The last option goes especially well with soups made with a lot of extra-virgin olive oil.

Stage 8: Garnish and Serve

Your soup is basically done at this stage, yet a little enhancement never harmed anyone. Here are a few choices:

• Tasty oils, similar to pecan, pistachio, squash seed, or argan.

• Slashed new spices or delicate alliums, similar to parsley, tarragon, chives, or cut scallions.

• Sautéed vegetables, similar to mushrooms, leeks, or garlic.

• Nuts, similar to almonds, hazelnuts, or pine nuts, toasted in olive oil or spread.

• Basic gremolata-style combinations, similar to a mix of parsley, lemon zing, and ground garlic.

• Meagerly cut chilies.

• A sprinkle of seared spread.

• Dairy items, similar to harsh cream, crème fraîche, or weighty cream; plain or seasoned with flavors or glues. Utilizing a smidgen of a similar zest you utilized before in sync 4 can be a decent method for helping flavor.

I consider the topping a last advance to layer flavor or potentially surface into the bowl.

Stage 9: Rinse and Repeat

Whenever you have these eight essential strides down, you have the stuff to begin making quite a few velvety soups, joining any flavors you like. I'm not promising that each and every blend of vegetables and aromatics will work out, however utilize this aide as a diagram and you're well headed to building the soup of your fantasies. We as a whole long for soup, isn't that so?

BOOM GOES THE BLENDER

Here is a situation that happened to me simply last week: I was making a cluster of tomato soup for my significant other (who can't get enough of the stuff), and I'd quite recently unloaded the hot tomato combination into the blender. As I went after the On button, a minuscule voice in my sub-conscience told me, All of this has occurred previously, and every last bit of it will repeat. Pose yourself this inquiry: "Would a simpleton do this?" If the response is "yes," then don't do this thing. Obviously, I felt free to turn on the blender in any case. The top popped off in a vicious blast, and my canine jumped behind the sofa in dread as hot tomatoes splattered across the loft with all the wrath of a VEI-7‡ volcanic emission. This sort of stuff happens on the grounds that there are a few missteps I never gain from and, more significant, due to thermodynamics and the physical science of fume development.

Obviously, there are various variables engaged with the transformation of heated water to steam. Pressure is a major one. Obviously, steam occupies considerably more room than water. Along these lines, assuming that you apply sufficient strain to a waterway, steam won't get away. At the point when a major clump of tomato soup is sitting in a blender, there is critical strain on all of the soup with the exception of the stuff at the surface. Steam escapes from the top alone, while the fluid underneath the surface stays there quietly holding up. Switch on the blender, however, and out of nowhere you make huge loads of disturbance. A vortex is framed, the surface region of that assemblage of fluid unexpectedly turns out to be a lot greater, and steam is quickly and savagely delivered. Additionally, the additional openness will likewise warm up the air in the headspace of the blender, making it extend. This quick extension makes the highest point of your blender pop off and the hot tomatoes to go flying. Blast!

Things being what they are, how would you forestall it? There are two different ways: First off, set aside certain that there's space for extension in the blender. The hot steam needs a departure valve. The most straightforward thing to do is to eliminate the focal module your blender top and cover the opening with a towel. This will permit extending gases to get away however keep fluids from flying out. The second, and simpler, method for forestalling victory is to begin mixing delicately. Begin your blender at the least speed and gradually move gradually up to the most noteworthy. Extension will happen all the more leisurely, permitting the gases a lot of opportunity to get away, and empowering your kitchen and your canine to move away safe.

Straining

If "smooth" and "knot free" are terms that you might want to have the option to use to portray your soups and sauces, a fine-network sifter is your apparatus of decision. However, have you at any point emptied a group of soup into a sifter set over a pot or bowl and hung tight for it to all go through? Chances are, you wound up holding up a long, long time. As the soup goes through, the openings in the sifter get obstructed.

There are two answers for this. The first is The Rap: Holding the soup-filled sifter over your compartment with one hand, rap a long weighty device more than once against the edge of the sifter with your other hand (I utilize a weighty spatula or a sharpening steel). Soup ought to stream out of the base with each rap. For extra-thick or stout soups, I utilize a subsequent technique, The Spoon Press: Holding the soup-filled sifter over your compartment with one hand, mix the substance utilizing an enormous metal serving spoon, a scoop, or an elastic spatula, scratching the edge of the utensil against the cross section. This ought to drive seeds, protuberances, and other obstruct initiating material far removed so your soup can stream openly.

FAST TOMATO SOUP WITH GRILLED CHEESE

Is there any blustery day passage more exemplary than tomato soup and barbecued cheddar?

It's fast, it's simple, it's filling, and it returns you to feeling like a child again (assuming you at any point left that stage in any case).

Obviously, there's the exemplary Campbell's tomato-soup-in-a-can, which, similar to a little dog that won't quit licking your face, is cloyingly charming and pleasant to a certain degree, yet now and then what you need is the grown-up adaptation. Fortunately, making it is nearly as basic. This adaptation utilizes entire canned tomatoes pureed with a combination of sautéed onions, oregano, and red pepper chips, which gives it a perfectly measured proportion of flavor and hotness to carry equilibrium to the dish. Likewise with stew, adding a sprinkle of alcohol to the soup not long prior to serving assists its smell with jumping out of the bowl and into your nose, where it should be, however it'll in all actuality do fine without it. A shower of excellent olive oil and a sprinkling of new spices change this youth exemplary into a tremendously exquisite lunch. Ensure you put on a tie and coat prior to consuming.

A plain barbecued cheddar is extraordinary, yet . . .

. . . including some extra ground Parmesan the outside . . .

. . . gets you the cheesiest of barbecued cheeses.

Concerning the barbecued cheddar? Everybody knows how to make barbecued cheddar, correct? The key is a lot of margarine and low-and-slow cooking. Cook it excessively quick, and your toast consumes some time before the cheddar has gotten an opportunity to settle the score somewhat gooey. That is the manner by which I'd been cooking my barbecued cheeses for a really long time until my companion Adam Kuban showed me a superior way. His stunt: toast two cuts of bread in spread, then add the cheddar to the toasted side of one cut prior to shutting the sandwich and continuing as expected. The hot toasted bread not just adds rich extravagance and extra-hot flavor to the inside, it likewise kicks the cheddar off on its way toward sublime gooeyness.

The cheddar you use is truly dependent upon you, however I truly do concede that very much like in my cheeseburgers, I like my barbecued cheddar with the meltiness of American. A decent trade off is to involve one cut of American for the goo factor and an additional a cut of a more delightful sharp cheddar or Swiss (or then again, if you need to be truly extravagant, Gruyère).

At long last, to go full cheddar on this one, I like to add a layer of Microplaned Parmigiano-Reggiano to the outside of my sandwich. It crisps up like an Italian frico in the skillet, providing you with an additional a layer of messy crunch.

15-MINUTE PANTRY TOMATO SOUP

NOTE: I like to utilize great canned tomatoes like Muir Glen in this soup.

SERVES 4

3 tablespoons unsalted spread

1 huge onion, finely diced (around 1 ½ cups)

Touch of red pepper chips

½ teaspoon dried oregano

1 tablespoon generally useful flour

Two 28-ounce jars entire tomatoes, with their juice

½ cup entire milk or weighty cream

Legitimate salt and newly ground dark pepper

2 tablespoons bourbon, vodka, or cognac (discretionary)

2 tablespoons extra-virgin olive oil

2 tablespoons hacked new spices, like parsley, basil, or chives (discretionary)

Extra-Cheesy Grilled Cheese Sandwiches (formula follows)

1. Soften the spread in a medium pot over medium-high hotness. Add the onions and cook, blending often, until mellowed yet not sautéed, 6 to 8 minutes. Add the pepper drops and oregano and cook, mixing, until fragrant, around 30 seconds. Add the flour and cook, blending, for 30 seconds. Add the tomatoes, with their juice, and mix, scratching the flour up off the lower part of the skillet. Add the milk or cream and cook, mixing sporadically and separating the tomatoes with the spoon, until the entire thing reaches boiling point. Diminish to a stew and cook for 3 minutes.

2. Eliminate the soup from the hotness and puree utilizing an inundation blender. Or on the other hand move to a standing blender, in clusters if fundamental, and puree, beginning on low speed and continuously expanding to high, then, at that point, return to the dish. Try to season the soup with pepper and salt to taste. Mix in the bourbon, if utilizing, and bring to a stew. Serve right away, finishing off each presenting with a liberal shower of olive oil, a sprinkle of spices, and in the event that you like, a break or two of newly ground pepper, with the sandwiches close by.

Extra-Cheesy Grilled Cheese Sandwiches

I as a rule utilize a cut every one of American and cheddar, swearing off a classification B cheddar. Serve a large portion of a sandwich for each individual with the soup, or twofold this formula and make the sandwiches in two skillets. (Assuming you have just a single skillet, make the sandwiches in bunches and keep the primary cluster warm in a low stove, on a rack on a baking sheet.)

NOTE: Category A cheeses are great softening cheeses like American, cheddar, Jack, Fontina, youthful Swiss, Gruyère, Muenster, youthful provolone, and youthful Gouda, among others. Classification B cheeses are emphatically enhanced grinding cheeses like Parmigiano-Reggiano, Asiago, Pecorino, matured Manchego, and matured Gouda.

MAKES 2 SANDWICHES

2 tablespoons unsalted margarine

4 cuts great white, entire wheat, or rye sandwich bread

4 ounces cut Category A cheddar

Fit salt

½ ounce classification B cheddar, ground (discretionary; see Note above)

Earthy colored mustard

1. Soften ½ tablespoon of the spread in a 12-inch tempered steel or cast-iron skillet over medium hotness. Add 2 bread cuts and twirl them around the skillet with your hands until everything the margarine is ingested. Cook, whirling the bread once in a while, until softly seared, around 1 moment. Eliminate to a cutting board, toasted side up, and quickly top with the cut A cheddar. Liquefy another ½ tablespoon spread in the skillet and toast the leftover 2 bread cuts until daintily cooked, then, at that point, promptly press them toasted side down onto the cheddar bested cuts to frame sandwiches.

2. Soften another ½ tablespoon margarine in the skillet and sprinkle with a touch of salt. Lessen the hotness to medium-low and spot the sandwiches in the skillet. Whirl them around with your hands until everything the margarine is ingested. Cook the sandwiches, twirling them with your hands and pushing down on them tenderly with a wide solid spatula every so often, until the bottoms are a profound, even brilliant brown, around 4 minutes. Eliminate the sandwiches to your cutting board with the spatula. Liquefy the leftover ½ tablespoon margarine in the skillet, sprinkle with a touch of salt, and rehash the toasting strategy with the subsequent side, until the sandwiches are brilliant brown on the two sides and the cheddar is completely softened, around 4 minutes longer. Move the sandwiches to the cutting board.

3. Whenever wanted, spread the ground cheddar equitably over a huge plate. Press the sandwiches into the ground cheddar, turning once and going ahead them until you get an in any event, covering of cheddar on the two sides. Return the sandwiches to the skillet and cook until the ground cheddar has dissolved and shaped a brilliant earthy colored outside, around 1 moment. Cautiously flip the sandwiches and rehash with the subsequent side. Move to the cutting board.

4. Cut the sandwiches in half on the corner to corner, and serve right away, with mustard and the tomato soup.

CORN CHOWDER

My mom's corn chowder formula included a jar of creamed corn, an equivalent measure of creamer, and a teaspoon of chicken bouillon. I cherished that variant growing up (it's as yet a foundation of my younger sibling's formula collection), yet similar to a semi-New Englander, chowder is a semisacred thing in my book, with a couple of firm guidelines: All chowders contain dairy (don't give me absolutely no part of that Manhattan shellfish chowder poo), most contain potatoes, and some contain pork-all conventional and modest New England items. I used to make my corn chowder with bacon, the most promptly accessible restored pork item at the grocery store, however I was never excessively content with its overwhelming smoky flavor, so I exchanged over to unsmoked salt pork, which adds the trademark porkiness without overwhelming the sweet corn. Also, every so often, while I'm attempting to feel extra valorous or have basically allowed my cooler to run unfilled, I'll renounce the pork through and through.

Most chowder plans call for perspiring a few onions in margarine, adding your corn parts, potatoes, and dairy, and allowing it to cook down. As it cooks, the potatoes discharge some starch, thickening up the stock. Absolutely no part of this annoys me. What annoys me goes into the waste: the stripped corncobs.

Any other individual out there go for a few rounds on their fresh corn just to suck at the small amounts of sweet milk left in the cob after you've eaten the portions? Like the firm fat around a rib bone, that is the most delectable part. How could you need to discard it? All things being equal, I utilize the corn-draining strategy here: scratching out the smooth fluid from the cobs with the rear of a blade. By then injecting your base stock with both the scratched milk and void corncobs (alongside a couple aromatics like coriander and fennel seed), you can unfathomably build the feebleness of the completed soup. (I intend that positively.)

It doesn't take more time to implant the stock-all of 10 minutes, which is just about sufficient opportunity to perspire off your onions and corn parts. Whenever you have your corn-milk stock made, the rest is straightforward: stew the onion-margarine stock-potato blend until the potatoes are delicate, add some milk (I incline toward it to cream, as the greasiness of cream can veil a portion of that sweet corn flavor), and afterward puree barely enough of it to give the soup a few body and assist with keeping the butterfat appropriately emulsified in with the general mish-mash.

The incredible thing about this stock-it is that implanting technique's absolutely versatile. Once in a while I want to make a smooth and sweet corn velouté, which I'll make like my chowder, yet overlooking the potatoes and cream and mixing until totally smooth. What's more, assuming you really do like the kind of bacon in your chowder, take the plunge nothing's halting you, with the exception of maybe your cholesterol and your companion.

I, luckily, have a life partner who can be handled with corn soup when I truly need to get everything I might want. Might I propose you attempt something similar?

Step by step instructions to Buy Corn

Need to know the key to extraordinary chowder or old fashioned corn? Extraordinary corn. That's all there is to it. The stunt is getting the corn. From that point forward, it's a cake walk.

Whenever I first tasted truly extraordinary corn-one of those early food recollections that caused me to acknowledge food was something beyond fuel-was on a 2nd grade field outing to an Upstate New York ranch: me and the rancher on a work vehicle, the rancher getting an ear of corn as he drove by the field, shucking it, and giving it to me to taste. In my mind I was thinking, "Heavenly Skeletor! I'd exchange my Battle-Armor He-Man for a greater amount of this!" which generally means my present jargon as, "Heavenly f*&k, this preferences astounding!" (My persuasiveness has decreased essentially as the years progressed.) Incredibly sweet, splendid, and tasty, it turned into the embodiment of good corn to me, the corn that all corn since has attempted to satisfy something that happens just once in a blue moon.

In view of the aftereffect of a cheerful change a few hundred years prior, sweet corn has a far higher grouping of sugar in its portions than customary field corn (that is the stuff they feed creatures with). However, here's the hitch: when the ear leaves the tail, that sugar starts changing over to starch. Inside a solitary day of collect, an ear of corn will lose up to 50 percent of its sugar when left at room temperature-and, surprisingly, more, up to 90 percent, while it's hanging out in the blistering sun at the ranchers' market.

Lesson of the story. Purchase your corn as new as possible conceivable (from the rancher on the off chance that you would be able!), refrigerate it in a hurry, and cook it the day you get it.

KNIFE SKILLS:

Step by step instructions to Prepare Corn

While choosing corn, search for ears that are firmly closed, with dazzling green leaves that give no indications of shrinking.

Press the ears, especially around their tips, to guarantee that the parts inside are full and delicious. A decent ear of corn ought to have almost no give and feel weighty for its weight.

Keep away from ears of corn that have been preshucked or come bundled in cling wrap. Any additional dealing with or bundling implies that those ears are that a lot farther away from their unique season of reap.

Keep away from ears of corn that have been preshucked or come bundled in cling wrap. Any additional dealing with or bundling implies that those ears are that a lot farther away from their unique season of reap.

The most ideal way to store corn isn't at all-don't get it until the day you anticipate eating it. On the off chance that you should store it, keep it in its husks in the fridge's crisper cabinet, yet don't store it for over a day, or you'll have boring, flavorless corn on your hands. All things being equal, for longer-term capacity, eliminate the pieces and afterward whiten them in bubbling water for 1 moment, trailed by an unclog into an ice water shower to chill them. Spread the whitened bits out on a rimmed baking sheet and spot in the cooler until completely frozen. Put the frozen pieces in a zipper-lock cooler pack and store them in the cooler for as long as 90 days.

To eliminate the portions from an ear of corn, first strip off the husk and silk and dispose of. Hold the cob in one hand and lay the end on the lower part of a huge bowl. Hold your blade against the highest point of the ear, then, at that point, cut descending, cutting the parts as near the cob as could be expected. They ought to fall flawlessly into the bowl. Rehash with the excess pieces, pivoting the cob as you go. Save the cobs to remove their milk and make stock.

THE BEST CORN CHOWDER

NOTE: Buy without a doubt the freshest corn you can find, and use it the day you bring it home.

SERVES 6

6 ears corn, husks and silks eliminated

6 cups natively constructed or low-sodium canned chicken stock

1 cove leaf

1 teaspoon fennel seeds

1 teaspoon coriander seeds

1 teaspoon entire dark peppercorns

4 ounces salt pork or section bacon, cut into ½-inch 3D shapes (discretionary)

3 tablespoons unsalted spread

1 medium of finely diced onion (around 1 cup)

2 medium cloves garlic, minced or ground on a Microplane (around 2 teaspoons)

1 to 2 chestnut (baking) potatoes, stripped and cut into ½-inch dice (around 1½ cups)

Genuine salt

2 cups entire milk or cream

Newly ground dark pepper

Sugar (if vital)

3 scallions, finely cut

1. With a sharp blade, cut the bits off the corn cobs. Hold the cobs. Utilize the rear of the blade to scratch the "corn milk" from the corncobs into an enormous pan. Break the cobs into equal parts and add to the skillet. Add the stock, straight leaf, fennel seeds, coriander seeds, and peppercorns and mix to join. Heat to the point of boiling over high hotness, then, at that point, lessen to simply under a stew and let steep for 10 minutes. Strain the stock through a fine-network sifter into a bowl; dispose of the cobs and flavors.

2. While the stock imbues, heat the pork, if utilizing, and spread in a 3-quart pan over medium-high hotness until the margarine softens. Add the onions, garlic, and corn parts and cook, blending often, until the pork has delivered its fat and the onions are mellowed, around 7 minutes. Lessen the hotness in the event that spread starts to brown.

3. Add the corn stock, potatoes, and 1 teaspoon salt, bring to an endlessly stew, mixing periodically, until the potatoes are delicate, around 10 minutes. Add the milk and mix to join. The chowder will look broken, with softened spread drifting on top. Utilize a submersion blender to mix the soup until the ideal consistency is reached. Then again, move half of the soup to an ordinary blender and mix, beginning on low speed and slowly expanding to high, until smooth, around 1 moment, then return to the excess soup and mix well. Season to taste with salt, pepper, and sugar (with extremely new corn, sugar ought not be essential). Serve right away, sprinkled with the cut scallions.

SMOOTH BROCCOLI-PARMESAN SOUP

This velvety soup depends on the thickening and emulsifying force of a roux-cooked flour and spread to give it a rich consistency without the requirement for weighty cream, which can dull flavors. For quite a long time, dreary armed force green vegetables got negative criticism, yet I'm attempting to take attractive back to completely cooked broccoli (and green beans). There are most certainly extraordinary things to be said about smart, radiant green stalks, however the flavor that creates when broccoli is cooked to all around good is unparalleled by that of its still somewhat firm partner. A touch unpleasant, a sprinkle of sulfur (positively), and a rich, green profundity all arise as the stalks mellow.

The main drawback here is that trusting that broccoli will relax this much can be a monotonous cycle that takes more time to an hour or more. In any case, there's an old stunt that the English use to make their customary fish 'n' chips side of soft peas: add a baking soft drink to the water. Baking soft drink raises the pH of the fluid, causing the gelatin that keeps the cells of the broccoli intact to mellow. Simply a small squeeze is to the point of chopping stewing time somewhere near 66%.

To add a profundity to the soup, I throw in a modest bunch of anchovies (you can skip them for a vegan form), as well as a lot of ground Parmesan, whose nutty tang plays pleasantly off the profound kind of the broccoli. A modest bunch of speedy rich bread garnishes adds both surface and flavor.

SERVES 6

5 tablespoons unsalted margarine

1 medium of finely diced onion (around 1 cup)

4 medium stems celery, finely diced (around 1 cup)

2 medium cloves garlic, minced or ground on a Microplane (around 2 teaspoons)

4 anchovy filets, finely cleaved (discretionary)

3 tablespoons universally handy flour

2 cups milk

2 cups natively constructed or low-sodium canned chicken stock or vegetable stock, in addition to more if fundamental

¼ teaspoon baking pop

12 cups broccoli florets, stems, and stalks cut into 1-inch pieces (around 1 huge head)

3 ounces Parmigiano-Reggiano, ground

2 tablespoons lemon juice (from 1 lemon)

Fit salt and newly ground dark pepper

4 cuts generous white sandwich bread, coverings eliminated and cut into ½-inch dice

INCORPORATING STARCHES

Have you ever tried adding flour or cornstarch directly to a hot soup in an attempt to thicken it, only to find that the starch clumps up into frustratingly impossible-to-destroy little balls? Here's the problem, and it has to do with the nature of the interaction between starch—a complex carbohydrate found in all sorts of plant matter, including flour—and water. Remember those little dinosaur-shaped sponges you'd get as a kid, which you'd drop into water, then wait for them to grow? That's exactly what starch molecules are like. When dry, they are tiny and shriveled. They can flow freely past each other. But expose them to water, and they start growing, getting bigger and bigger, until they eventually rub up against each other and bind, creating a water-resistant barrier. Are you starting to get the picture?

When a spoonful of flour or cornstarch lands on the surface of a pot of water or milk, the first parts to get wet are the starches on the outside of the granules, which rapidly expand, forming a waterproof seal. As you stir and submerge the clumps, a seal ends up forming around the entire clump, keeping the interior from getting wet.

So, how do you solve this problem? Two ways.

With a starch that doesn't need to be cooked before it is incorporated (such as cornstarch or potato starch), just dissolve the starch in a small amount of liquid to start. Starting with a smaller amount of liquid makes the mechanical stirring action of your spoon, fork, or whisk much more effective. Smaller amounts of liquid also get viscous more easily, making it simpler to bash up those pockets of dry starch. I use an equal volume of starch to liquid to start and stir it until homogeneous before adding the remaining liquid, or adding it to the rest of the liquid.

For starches that need to have their raw flavor cooked out of them, such as flour, start them in fat. Starch does not swell in fat, so by first combining flour with a fat like butter or oil and mixing it until homogeneous, you end up coating the individual starch granules, preventing them from swelling and sticking together when you first add the liquid. After you add it, the fat eventually melts away, so the starch is exposed and can be incorporated smoothly. This is the premise behind using a roux to thicken a soup or sauce.

Finally, remember that for starches to thicken properly, they must be brought to a complete boil to reach their optimal swelling size. You'll notice a soup thicken dramatically as it goes from just plain hot to actually boiling.

HOW TO BUY BROCCOLI AND CAULIFLOWER

Shopping for broccoli and cauliflower is pretty much the same and, luckily, finding good specimens is not too difficult. These hearty members of the brassica family have a good shelf life and are firm enough that they don't bruise or break easily during storage and shipping. A head of broccoli should have tight florets that are an even dark green with greenish to purple buds. Cauliflower should be an even pale white; yellow or brown spots should be avoided, though if they are minor, you can simply trim them off. Look to the leaves as well, which should be tight around the base and appear bright pale green.

Once you get the broccoli or cauliflower home, keep it loosely wrapped in plastic or in a vegetable bag inside the crisper. It should stay good for at least a week. Once you've cut it into florets, it's best to use it as quickly as possible to prevent excess moisture loss, though florets can be stored in an airtight container or zipper-lock plastic bag with a damp paper towel placed in it for up to 5 days.

KNIFE SKILLS:

Step by step instructions to Cut Broccoli and Cauliflower

• For Broccoli: Trim the woody closures of the stalks and dispose of. Utilize the tip of your blade to remove bigger branches, then cut the florets off the stalks and trim to the ideal shape and size. Remove any stubs the stalks and dispose of. Strip the stalks, quarter them the long way, and cut into 1-to 2-inch lengths to cook alongside the florets.

• For Cauliflower: Split the head in half through the middle. Utilize the tip of a sharp blade to eliminate the hard focal center as well as any green leaves around the base and dispose of. Break the cauliflower into huge pieces with your hands, then, at that point, utilize the tip of your blade to cut into florets of the ideal size and shape.

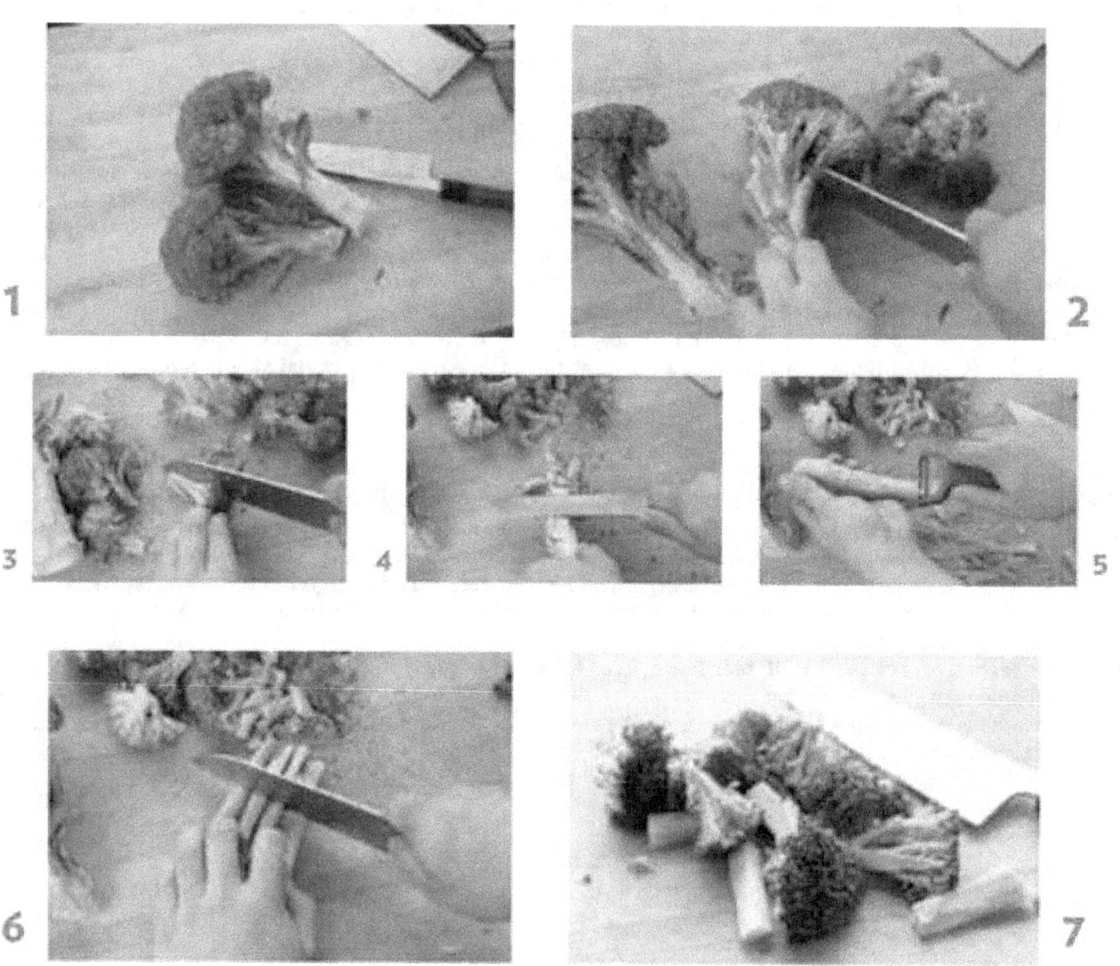

CREAMY MUSHROOM SOUP

The way to extraordinary mushroom soup is to cook the mushrooms in margarine adequately long to drive off overabundance dampness and permit them to begin to brown, extending their flavor.

NOTE: You can utilize plain button mushrooms, however for the best flavor, utilize a blend of mushrooms, for example, buttom, portobello, shiitake, or potentially other scavenged or developed mushrooms.

SERVES 6

2 pounds mushrooms (see Note above), cleaned and cut ¼ inch thick (around 3 quarts)

4 tablespoons unsalted spread

1 huge leek, white and light green parts in particular, split down the middle and cut into ¼-inch-thick half-moons (around 1 cup)

1 medium onion, finely cut (around 1 cup)

2 teaspoons new thyme leaves

3 tablespoons universally handy flour

1 cup milk

4 cups natively constructed or low-sodium canned chicken stock, in addition to more if essential

2 narrows leaves

Fit salt and newly ground dark pepper

1. Put away 1 cup of the mushrooms. Soften 3 tablespoons of the margarine in a huge Dutch broiler or soup pot over medium-high hotness. Add the excess mushrooms and cook, blending sometimes, until they have radiated their fluid and are starting to brown, around 10 minutes. Add the leeks, onions, and a big part of the thyme and cook, mixing habitually, until the vegetables are relaxed, around 5 minutes.

2. Add the flour and cook, mixing continually, until everything the flour is consumed, around 30 seconds. Blending continually, gradually pour in the milk, trailed by the stock. Add the cove leaves and heat to the point of boiling, then decrease the hotness to keep a stew, cover, and cook, mixing sporadically, until the fluid is thickened and gently diminished, around 10 minutes. Dispose of the narrows leaves.

3. Working in clumps, move the combination to a blender and mix, beginning on low speed and steadily expanding to high, until a harsh puree structures, around 1 moment; add extra stock or water if important to thin to the ideal consistency (I like mine thick). Go through a fine-network sifter into a spotless pot and season to taste with salt and pepper. (On the other hand, utilize an inundation blender to mix the soup straightforwardly in the first pot.) Keep hot.

4. Dissolve the excess tablespoon of spread in a huge nonstick skillet over medium-high hotness. While the frothing dies down, add the held 1 cup mushrooms and cook, blending and throwing every now and again, until profound brown, around 8 minutes. Add the leftover thyme and season to taste with salt and pepper.

5. Serve the soup embellished with the sautéed mushrooms.

WORKING WITH MUSHROOMS

While looking for mushrooms of any kind, search for ones that have no delicate or stained spots on their covers, which can demonstrate rot. For mushrooms with gills, (for example, portobellos and shiitakes), inspect the gills under the cap also, as they'll regularly begin to turn before the remainder of the 'shroom. It's OK on the off chance that the lower part of the stem is somewhat stained, however it ought not be excessively dry, soft, or beginning to shred separated. With respect to soil, it is no sign regardless. Mushrooms fill in soil, so it's inescapable you'll discover some connected to them. Clearly, cleaner mushrooms are more straightforward to work with, however a little soil on the cap or grouped close to the stem is no issue.

When you get the mushrooms home, store them in a plastic sack with the upper left open or in a punctured plastic holder in the vegetable cabinet of your cooler. New mushrooms ought to save for 3 to 5 days under ideal circumstances.

Will I Wash My 'Shrooms?

You've presumably had people let you know things like, "Mushrooms are fundamentally living wipes. Try not to get them wet, or they'll get spongy and you won't ever cook them right." Those equivalent individuals will suggest that you clean mushrooms by brushing them with an exceptional mushroom brush (c'mon), or perhaps with a sodden paper towel. No big surprise individuals could do without mushrooms-they're an undeniable irritation to clean!

In any case, is this degree of dread truly important? I tried out this hypothesis by cooking a couple of bunches of mushrooms one next to the other. One I cleaned fastidiously with a sodden paper towel. One more I cleaned under the tap and shook dry in a sifter. The last I cleaned under the tap and turned dry in a serving of mixed greens spinner. I gauged every one of the clusters prior to cooking and found that-hello, you don't claim to know everything?- the washed-then-depleted mushrooms acquired something like 2% of their weight in water, while the washed-then-turned mushrooms acquired around 1%. That is around 1½ teaspoons of water per pound, which thus means an additional a 15 to 30 seconds of cooking time.

What's the significance here? It implies that the majority of the water you add by washing mushrooms sticks just to the surface. Inasmuch as you dry your mushrooms cautiously prior to cooking, you can flush them however much you'd like. Cooking the twist dried mushrooms one next to the other with the paper-dried mushrooms affirmed this: the two of them cooked at the very same rate.

KNIFE SKILLS:

Cutting Mushrooms

Button and Cremini Mushrooms

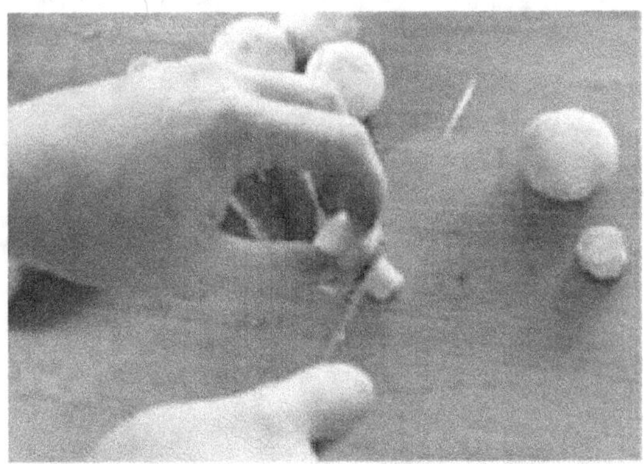 

White button and cremini mushrooms can be arranged the same way. Begin by managing off the bottoms of the stems, which can be woody or intense, and dispose of. Then, at that point, hold each mushroom level against the cutting board, with the stem side down, and cut into quarters for simmering or cut into dainty strips for sautéing.

Portobello Mushrooms

 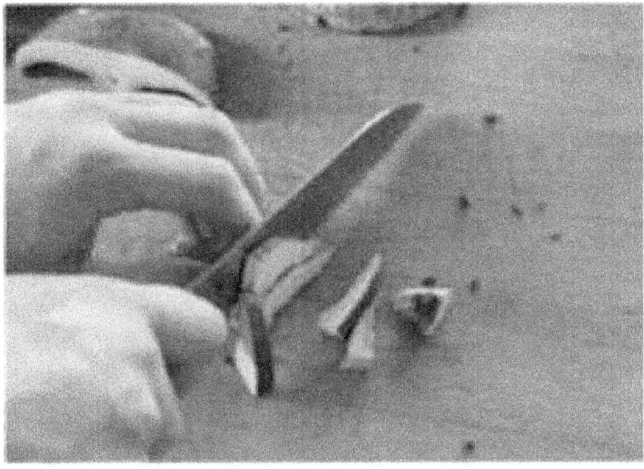

Portobello mushrooms are experienced cremini. Begin by managing off the woody bottoms of the stems. Then, at that point, supporting each mushroom in your grasp, utilize a spoon to eliminate the dim gills, which can stain a dish and turn it sloppy. The mushrooms can now be scored for simmering or barbecuing entire, or split down the middle and cut into meager cuts for sautéing.

Shiitake Mushrooms

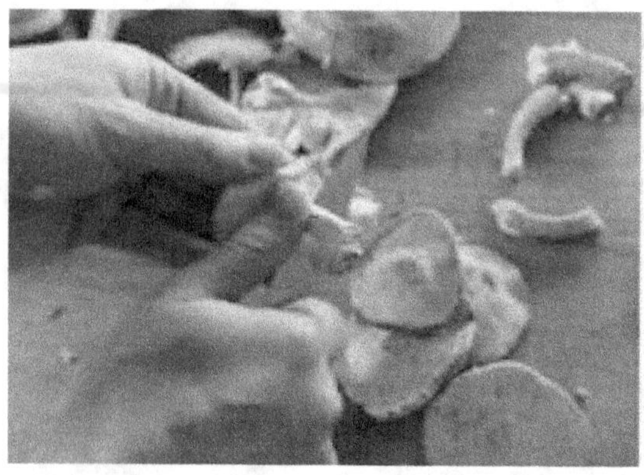 

Shiitakes have exceptionally rubbery stems which ought to be disposed of. Utilize a paring blade to manage them off (eliminating them by hand can wind up tearing the covers). Cut the covers into meager strips.

PUMPKIN SOUP

In some cases vegetables are so bland on their own that no extra thickener or emulsifying specialist is expected to make a rich, ultrasmooth pureed soup. Sweet sugar pumpkin and squash are ideal competitors.

You could make a pumpkin soup very much like the smooth broccoli soup here by stewing the cubed pumpkins in stock and pureeing the parcel, yet a whole lot more delectable is to broil the pumpkin first. There's more going on behind the scenes to the method involved with simmering bland vegetables like pumpkin (or, say, yam)- it's not just about mellowing.

Most importantly, broiling drives off some dampness, concentrating flavor. Second, there are chemicals normally present in pumpkins, different squashes, and yams that will support the transformation of starches to sugars, strengthening their pleasantness. While this cycle will happen normally after some time, slow-simmering hurries these responses.

At last, as the pumpkin broils, fluid breaks from within it, advancing toward the surface and carrying along a few broke up sugars with it. As the fluid dissipates, the sugars are left on the uncovered surfaces of the pumpkin, where they start to caramelize. The course of caramelization not just makes better sugars, it likewise creates many shifting flavor intensifies that add profundity to the completed soup.

I like to utilize a blend of pumpkins and squashes, dividing them, throwing them in olive oil, and afterward simmering them as delayed as I have the persistence for prior to scooping out their innards and pureeing them with stock and different flavorings.

ROASTED PUMPKIN SOUP

SERVES 6 TO 8

4 pounds entire pumpkins and winter squash, ideally a blend, like sugar, kabocha, delicata, and oak seed (around 2 to 3 medium or little or 1 huge)

2 tablespoons olive oil

Genuine salt and newly ground pepper

2 tablespoons unsalted spread

1 medium onion, finely cut (around 1 cup)

¼ teaspoon ground cinnamon (discretionary)

¼ teaspoon ground nutmeg (discretionary)

4 cups custom made or low-sodium canned chicken stock in addition to more if essential

2 tablespoons maple syrup

1. Change a stove rack to the lower-center position and preheat the broiler to 350°F. Divide the pumpkins and additionally squash in half through the stem and utilize a huge spoon to scoop out and dispose of the seeds. Move to a foil-lined rimmed baking sheet, cut side up. Rub done with the olive oil and season with salt and pepper. Cook until the tissue is totally delicate and shows no obstruction when a sharp blade or cake analyzer is embedded into it, around 60 minutes. Eliminate from the stove and permit to cool.

2. While the pumpkin is cooling, dissolve the margarine in a huge Dutch stove or soup pot over medium-high hotness. Add the onion and cook, mixing regularly, until mellowed yet not carmelized, around 4 minutes. Add the cinnamon and nutmeg, if utilizing, and mix until fragrant, around 30 seconds. Add the chicken stock.

3. Utilizing a huge spoon, cautiously scoop out the broiled pumpkin tissue and move it to the pot. Add sufficient water to scarcely cover the pumpkin and bring to a stew.

4. Working in bunches, move the combination to a blender and mix, beginning on low speed and bit by bit expanding to high, until totally smooth, around 1 moment, adding extra stock or water if important to thin to the ideal consistency (I like mine thick). Go through a fine-network sifter into a perfect pot and warm tenderly. Mix in the maple syrup, and season to taste with salt and pepper. Serve.

TWO PATHS TO

FRENCH ONION SOUP

What's French onion soup doing in a book of American food, you could inquire? Here is the response: I want to wean you off of those little bundles of powdered earthy colored stuff to show you that with science next to you, making truly caramelized onions, and French onion soup, isn't so tedious or troublesome as you suspect!

There is positively no deficiency of plans for French onion soup out there, and the overall strategy starts with a similar fundamental method: cook down finely cut onions over low, low hotness so their regular sugars gradually and equally caramelize. When the onions are totally separated to a profound brown, jam-like consistency, simply add stock, a sprinkle of sherry, and a few aromatics, stew it down, season with a touch of salt and pepper, and present with messy bread garnishes.

It's a straightforward cycle, and the outcomes are endlessly better compared to any business adaptation, however it's a significant agony in the cul. All that sluggish caramelizing takes a decent 3 to 4 hours of steady pot looking after children. Release it somewhat excessively lengthy or step away for 5 minutes, and you've consumed your onions, making the end result too harsh to even consider utilizing.

Similarly as with exercise and marriage, I regularly ponder how extraordinary it'd be assuming there were a strategy that could convey precisely the same (or better!) results without the monstrous time responsibility. The terrible news? Following a while (OK, long stretches) of testing, and in excess of fifty pounds of onions later, I've found that there isn't exactly an ideal substitute for customary caramelizing. The uplifting news? You can get 90% of the way there in around 10% of the time. That is a really good conversion scale.

Here are the essentials.

Looking for Sweetness

In the first place, it's essential to see the very thing's going on when an onion earthy colors.

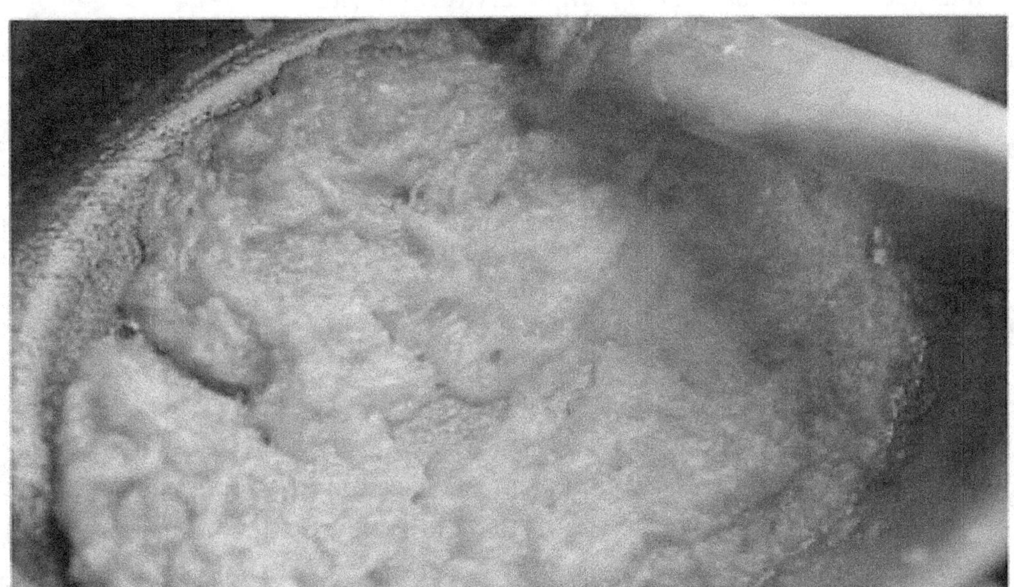

Onions go from firm to delicate to dissolving and brilliant brown as they cook.

• Perspiring is the principal phase of sautéing onions or different vegetables. As they gradually heat up, dampness from their inside (onions are around 75% water by weight, a few different vegetables are significantly more watery) starts to dissipate, compelling right out of the cells and making them burst all the while. This breakdown of the cells makes vegetables relax.

• Enzymatic responses occur as the substance of the vegetable cells-a mind boggling blend of sugars, proteins, and sweet-smelling compounds (on account of onions, mercaptans, disulfides, trisulfides, thiopenes, and other such lengthy, not a great explanation to-retain synthetics)- are poured out and start to blend in with one another.

- Caramelization starts to happen once the vast majority of the fluid has vanished and the temperature of the onions fires crawling up into the 230°F-and-above zone. This response includes the oxidation of sugar, what separates and structures many new mixtures, adding shading and profundity of flavor to the onions.

- Improving of the onions additionally happens. The huge sugar atom sucrose (otherwise known as white sugar) separates into the more modest monosaccharides glucose and fructose (the very two sugars that corn syrup is made of). Since one glucose particle in addition to one fructose atom is better than a solitary sucrose atom, the kind of the caramelized sugars is really better than the sugar they began as.

- The Maillard response, otherwise known as the carmelizing response, likewise happens at these temperatures. This is the very response that causes carmelizing on your toast or your steak when you cook it (see here). The Maillard response is undeniably more intricate than caramelization, including collaborations among sugars, proteins, and chemicals. The results of the response number in the hundreds, and are as yet not completely recognized.

In an optimal world, as the onions keep on cooking, three things will occur simultaneously: (1) the total mellowing of the onions' cell structures, (2) greatest caramelization (i.e., as brown as you can get before severe items start to create), and (3) most extreme Maillard searing (with a similar proviso as caramelization).

By upgrading these outcomes, I ought to have the option to accelerate my general cycle.

Mission 1: Increase the Effects of Caramelization

The clearest method for accelerating caramelization is to add more crude fixings, specifically, sugar. The sugars in onions, as referenced above, are glucose, fructose, and sucrose (a blend of one glucose and one fructose atom)- precisely equivalent to the caramelization results of granulated sugar. So I had a go at cooking a dash of sugar in a dry skillet until it arrived at a profound brilliant brown, then adding the onions and throwing them to cover them in the hot caramel. It had exactly the intended effect, shaving a decent 4 to 5 minutes off my absolute cooking time and giving me better, more profoundly caramelized outcome, without influencing the general flavor profile of the completed item.

Mission 2: Increase the Maillard Reaction

There are various things that influence the Maillard response, however the superseding factors are temperature and pH. Now, I had no protected method for expanding the temperature-very much like with a steak, in the event that you cook the onions too hot, the edges and exterior of each piece start to consume before the insides get an opportunity to deliver their synthetic compounds. The best way is the low and slow way to go.

Then again, I had a touch of command over the pH. As a rule, the higher the pH (i.e., the more essential or basic), the quicker the Maillard response happens. The key is control. While a lot of baking soft drink drastically expanded the carmelizing rate (by north of 50%!), any more than ¼ teaspoon per pound of cleaved onions ended up being an excessive amount of the metallic kind of the baking soft drink dominated.

I likewise saw that the baking-powdered onions were a lot milder not a bothersome quality for a soup. This is on the grounds that gelatin, the compound magic that binds vegetable cells, debilitates at higher pH levels. Quicker breakdown implies quicker arrival of synthetic compounds, and that implies quicker in general cooking.

Mission 3: Increase the Heat

Back to the hotness. As I referenced, the issue with expanding the hotness an excess of higher than medium-low is that the onions start to cook unevenly. A few pieces and edges will begin to darken some time before different pieces reach even the brilliant earthy colored stage. Furthermore, the sugars and proteins that stall out to the lower part of the pot as the onions cook quickly become a brilliant shade of brown, in view of their immediate contact.

Anyway, the inquiry is, assuming you're cooking with high hotness, how might you all the while even out the cooking the whole way across the onions, eliminate the tacky carmelized gunk from the lower part of the dish, and control the general temperature so that nothing consumes? Assuming you've made a container sauce, the response is so blindingly straightforward that I'm astounded it's not a totally considered normal practice: simply add water.

From the get go, adding water might appear to be counterproductive-it chills off the onions and the pot, constraining you to use important energy warming it up and vanishing it. In any case, here's the way things are looking: both the sautéed patina on the lower part of the pot and the cooked pieces on the edges of the onions are comprised of water-solvent sugar-based intensifies that end up being gathered in a solitary region. Adding only a modest quantity of fluid to the pot at customary spans implies these mixtures get broken up and reallocated equally all through the onions and the pot. Indeed, even dissemination prompts in any event, cooking, which prompts no single part consuming before the rest is cooked.

So how might this affect your onions? It implies that you can cook them over a lot higher fire (medium-high functions admirably even most extreme hotness is plausible, however it requires somewhat more consideration), and each time they take steps to begin consuming, simply two or three tablespoons of water and you're going great indeed.

As I said, the flavor isn't exactly just about as profound and sweet as generally sluggish cooked onions (at times there are essentially no easy routes to quality), yet it's universes better than anything you'll at any point escape a can, box, or parcel and it can go beginning to end and come to the table in less than 30 minutes. That is some truly quick onion soup!

QUICK FRENCH ONION SOUP

SERVES 4

1 tablespoon sugar

5 pounds yellow onions (around 5 huge), finely cut (around 7½ cups)

2 tablespoons unsalted spread

¼ teaspoon baking powder

Legitimate salt

¼ cup dry sherry

6 cups hand crafted or low-sodium canned chicken stock

2 inlet leaves

6 to 8 twigs new thyme

Newly ground dark pepper

1 loaf, cut ½ inch thick and toasted

8 ounces Gruyère or Swiss cheddar, ground

1. Empty the sugar into a huge Dutch broiler and cook over high hotness, twirling the pot tenderly as the sugar liquefies, until it is totally fluid and a brilliant earthy colored caramel. Add the onions and cook, blending with a wooden spoon and throwing continually until they are equally covered in the caramel, around 30 seconds. Add the spread, baking powder, and 2 teaspoons salt and cook, mixing sporadically, until the onions are light brilliant brown and an earthy colored covering has begun to develop on the lower part of the pot, around 10 minutes.

2. Add 2 tablespoons water and scratch the cooked covering from the lower part of the pot. Shake the pot to convey the onions equally over the base and cook, shaking at times, until the fluid dissipates and the carmelized covering begins to develop once more, around 5 minutes. Add 2 additional tablespoons water and rehash, permitting the covering to develop and scratching it off, then recurrent two additional times. By this point, the onions ought to be a profound brown. On the off chance that not, proceed with the deglazing and mixing process until the ideal tone is reached.

3. Add the sherry, chicken stock, inlet leaves, and thyme, heat to the point of boiling, and lessen to a stew. Stew, uncovered, until the fluid is profoundly enhanced and somewhat decreased, around 15 minutes. Season to taste with salt and pepper. The thyme and cove leaves should be disposed.

4. To serve, heat the grill. Spoon the soup into four broilerproof bowls. Float the bread garnishes on top and cover with the ground cheddar. Sear until the cheddar is dissolved, effervescent, and brilliant brown in spots. Serve right away.

ABOUT ONIONS

In the temperament for some stew? You will require three cups of onions, medium dice. Making chicken stock? Two onions, huge pieces, please. What's more, what might be said about onion soup? Indeed, in all honesty, you'll require onions for that as well.

Regardless of how you cut them, onions are utilized in a decent 30 to 40 percent of any cook's flavorful dish collection, while perhaps not more. They are the primary thing you ought to figure out how to cut when you get a blade, and, basically for me, still perhaps the most pleasurable food to take a sharp edge to.

What shading onion would it be advisable for me to utilize?

There are four fundamental onion assortments accessible in many grocery stores: yellow, white, sweet (Vidalia or Walla), and red. You may likewise at times see Spanish onions, which are bigger, milder family members of yellow onions. Albeit sweet onions have around 25% more sugar than standard onions, their flavor contrast when crude has more to do with how much tear-initiating lachrymators they contain (see beneath). Yellow and white onions have a greater amount of these sharp mixtures, yet subsequent to cooking, they everything except vanish.

Generally, onions can be utilized conversely without disastrous outcomes (except if you believe red onions on a slider to be a disaster). However, a few onions are more qualified for specific errands than others.

- Yellow onions are the kitchen workhorse. They gloat a decent equilibrium between pleasantness and appetizing quality, however they can be very sharp, and are best for cooked applications. On the off chance that there is one onion you ought to never be without, this is all there is to it.

- White onions are very gentle in flavor and have an unmistakable pleasantness. When caramelized, they have a level, one-layered flavor that can seem to be cloying. They are best utilized crude or in soups.

- Sweet onions (Vidalia, Walla, Maui, and so on) cook much the same way to yellow onions, yet their gentle sharpness and pleasantness are better appreciated crude in arrangements like hacked servings of mixed greens or new salsas, or cut for sandwiches.

• Red onions are seldom utilized for cooking, as their shade can turn an unappetizing blue with delayed cooking, losing the shade of your completed dish. Somewhat more impactful than white or sweet onions, red onions are best utilized crude or in basic, fast cooking applications, as on the barbecue or under the grill.

• Shallots are the humble cousins of onions. They have a particularly sweet and sharp flavor and are extraordinary both crude in salad dressing or cooked with different vegetables. Consider them more onion preparing than genuine onions, with the capacity to give onion flavor without overpowering a dish.

Q: Does estimate matter?

Ahh, the everlasting inquiry. The size of an onion has minimal bearing on flavor, however I incline toward bigger onions since I need to strip less of them to get a similar volume of prepared onions.

Q: How would I tell the great onions from the awful?

Regardless of what kind of onions you pick, ensure that they are firm to the touch when you get them. Assuming they give even a tad especially at the root or stem end-there's a decent opportunity a portion of the inside layers might have started to decay.

Q: Where's the best spot to store them?

Store onions in a cool, dry, dull spot, never in a fixed holder, which can trap dampness, prompting mold and decay. I keep mine in a Chinese bamboo liner.

Half-utilized onions can be put in a plastic pack in the cooler. Simply use them inside a couple of days.

Q: that's what i've seen, similar to grandmas and cinemas, a few onions smell more than others. Is there a method for knowing before I purchase?

How much an onion smells is to a great extent reliant upon how long it's been put away. The more drawn out onions have been away (now and again, up to months), the more sharp they'll be. Tragically, it's not generally simple to tell, as they don't accompany a date on the name. For the most part, more established onions have thicker, harder skins, while more up to date onions will have more slender papery skins. However, dislike you have a decision at any rate showcases don't offer "old onions" and "new onions."

The appalling response is that with onions, you must play the hand you're managed. Yet, we have a couple of stunts for managing them in our stockpile. Peruse on.

Q: What is it that makes onions smell, in any case?

My number one Calvin and Hobbes strip is the one where Calvin strolls into the kitchen and sees his mother crying while at the same time cutting an onion. In any case, there's an undeniable explanation we cry when onions are cut into: safeguard.

Onions take up sulfur from the dirt as they develop, putting away it inside bigger atoms in their cells. Independently, they store a protein that catalyzes a response that separates these bigger particles into sharp, bothering sulfurous mixtures. Solely after the onion's phones are harmed by cleaving or squashing do the antecedents and chemical blend, delivering what are called lachrymators, the mixtures that assault nerves in our eyes and nose, making us destroy and sniffle. Nature at its generally protective!

That is the reason a whole onion will have almost no fragrance, however when you cut it, the smell starts to saturate the room.

Q: Those lachrymators truly get my tears streaming. Anything I can do to help it?

There's no deficiency of home cures that are professed to stifle or limit destroying: Light a fire (evidently catalyzes some response that keeps lachrymators from shaping it doesn't work except if you are cutting your onion straight finished or under the fire). Flush the onion as you go (works OK, however wet hands and sharp blades don't blend). Put a slice of bread on the cutting board (does literally nothing). Suck on an ice solid shape or bite a toothpick (I couldn't actually start to understand the reasoning). Cool the onions in ice water for 10 minutes first (this functions admirably the virus dials back enzymatic responses). In any case, of the relative multitude of fixes, there's one in particular that is truly successful: simply block your eyes. Assuming you're a contact focal point wearer, you've presumably currently seen that onions don't actually annoy you. For most of you, ski goggles or swimming goggles are the best approach. Furthermore, they make you look truly cool. Believe me.

Q: Is there a method for disposing of that onion scent?

Suppose you end up having a few extra-impactful onions (it works out this way sometimes unfortunately)- is there a method for restraining them? I evaluated a couple techniques, from lowering them in cool water for times going from 10 minutes to 2 hours to chilling them to allowing them to ventilate on the counter.

Absorbing the cut onions a compartment of cold water just prompted onion-scented fluid in the holder, without a very remarkable diminishing in the smell in the actual onions. Maybe assuming that I'd involved an absurdly limited quantity of onion in a nonsensically enormous holder, the water would have weakened it all the more effectively. Air-drying prompted a milder smell yet additionally to dried-out onions and a papery surface.

The best strategy ended up being the quickest and most straightforward: simply flush away that multitude of extra-impactful mixtures under pursuing water you cut the onions-and in addition to that, however warm water. The velocities of synthetic and actual responses increment with temperature. Utilizing warm water makes onions discharge their unstable mixtures quicker around 45 seconds is to the point of freeing evening the most impactful onions of their kick.

Be that as it may, doesn't boiling water turn the surface of an onion limp? No. Regardless of whether you utilize exceptionally hot regular water, it by and large emerges at around 140° to 150°F or thereabouts, while gelatin, the principle starch "stick" that keeps plant cells intact, doesn't separate until around 183°F. There are different pieces of the onion that, given sufficient opportunity, will start to mellow at hot-faucet water temperatures, however it takes far longer than the 45-second wash needed. Worry not, the whole onions are all safe.

KNIFE SKILLS:

Cutting and Dicing Onions

The principle question with regards to cuts is one of course.

In the event that you call the stem and root finishes of an onion its north and south poles, then, at that point, an orbital cut resembles this:

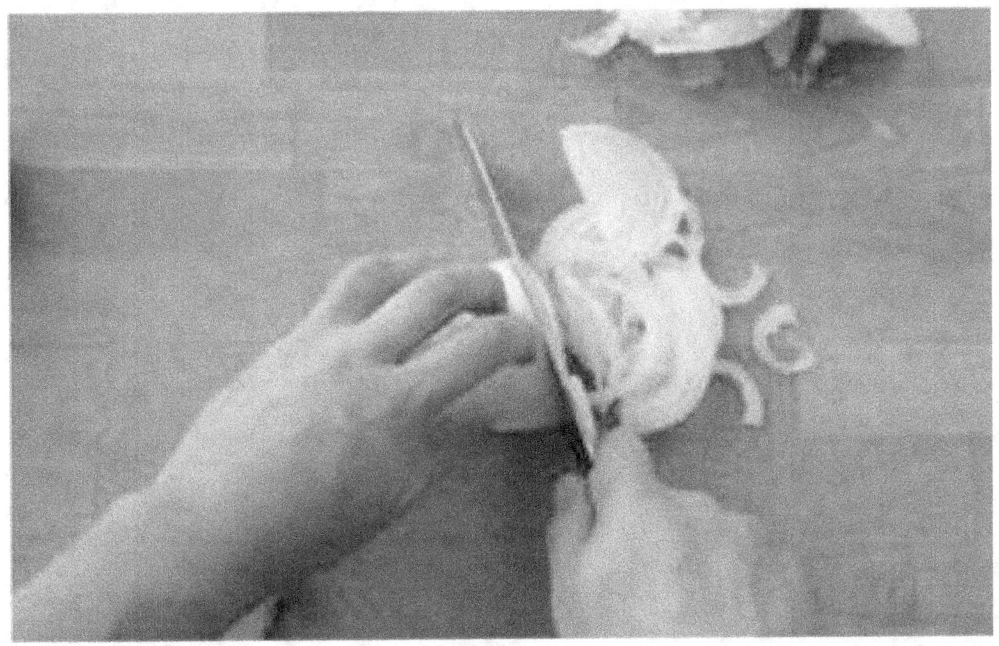

. . . while a post to-shaft cut resembles this:

From the beginning, you might think, what's the enormous contrast?

Allow me to address your inquiry with my very own issue: do you think often about the kind of what you put in your mouth? On the off chance that the response is no, by all means cut your onions whichever way. Be that as it may, assuming the response is indeed, think about this: onion cells are not entirely even they're longer in the post to-shaft heading than in the orbital direct. Subsequently the heading you cut your onions will influence the quantity of cells you crack and in this way how much lachrymators that are shaped. We realize that a few measure of this stuff is attractive: it makes your onions taste more oniony, your stews taste more substantial, your French onion soup better. However, an excess of can overpower.

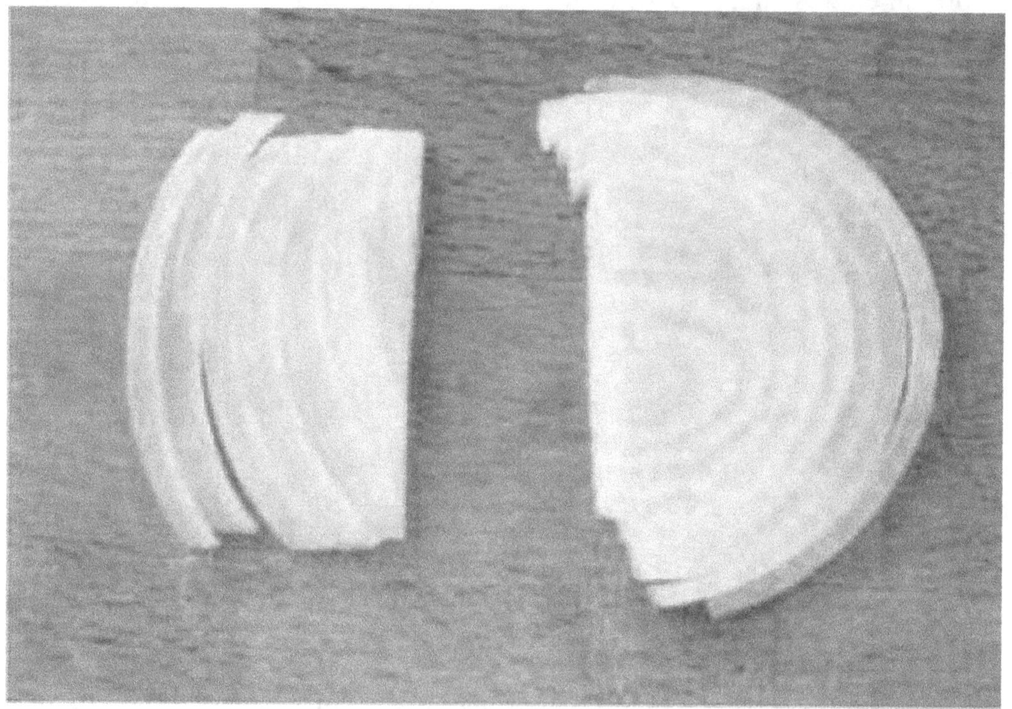

To see what improvement it made, I split an onion into equal parts, cutting every one of the two parts in various ways, then, at that point, set the onion cuts in indistinguishable covered holders and allow them to sit for 10 minutes on the counter prior to opening them and taking a whiff. There was no question that the orbitally cut onion was more grounded, emitting the strong smell of White Castle dumpsters and awful dates.

When cooked into a formula like a sauce or a soup, orbitally cut onions likewise have a sub-par surface they come out harder and diseased. With intriguing exemption, I use post to-shaft cut onions for all applications.

Dicing an onion is an errand you will do many, many, commonly, so you would do well to become accustomed to it.

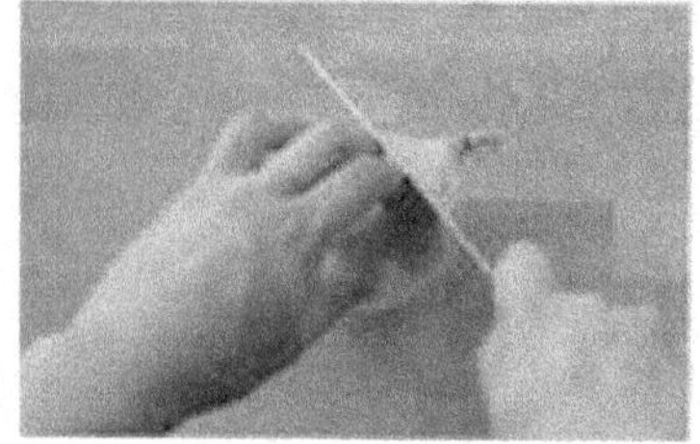

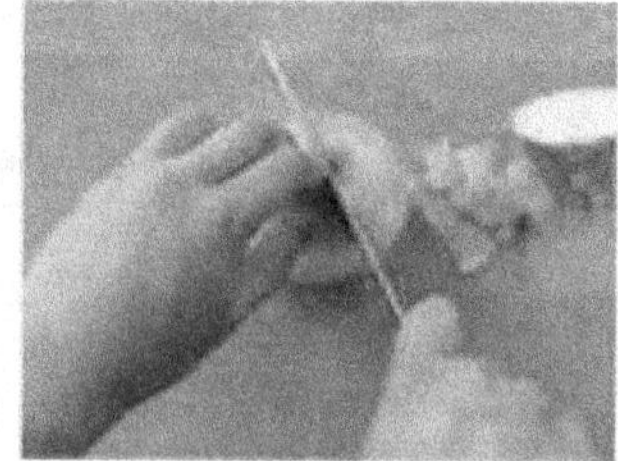

• THE BASIC PROCESS generally begins something very similar: Place the onion on your removing board and cut the stem end (1), then put it on the face you recently cut and split the onion down the middle (2). Strip the onion (3), and afterward from that point . . .

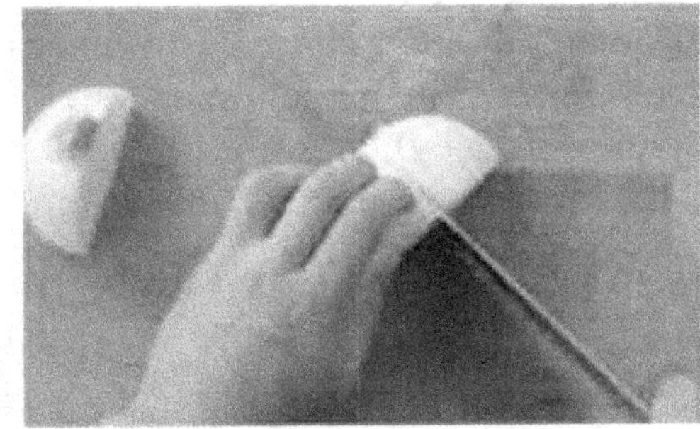
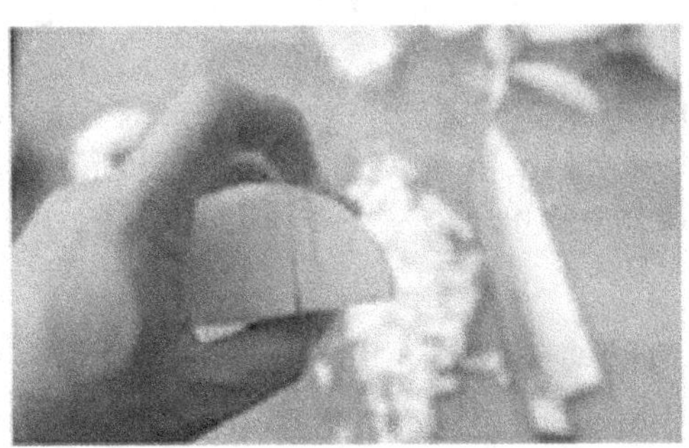

• FOR MEDIUM OR LARGE DICE: Make 2 to 6 cuts in the onion half, running from one post to another (4), leaving the root end in salvageable shape to keep the onion intact (5). Then make 2 to 6 opposite slices to frame enormous dice.

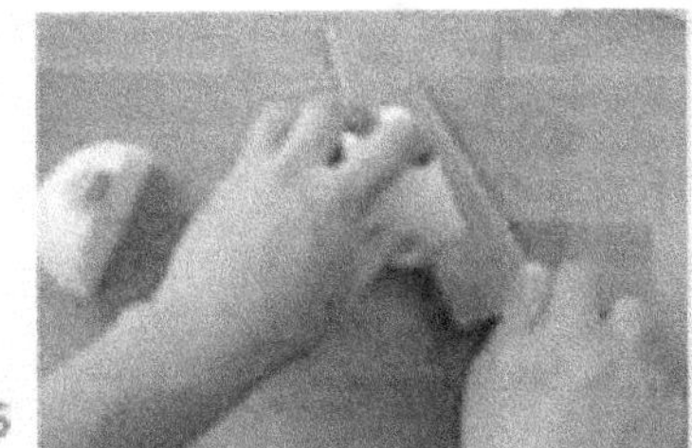
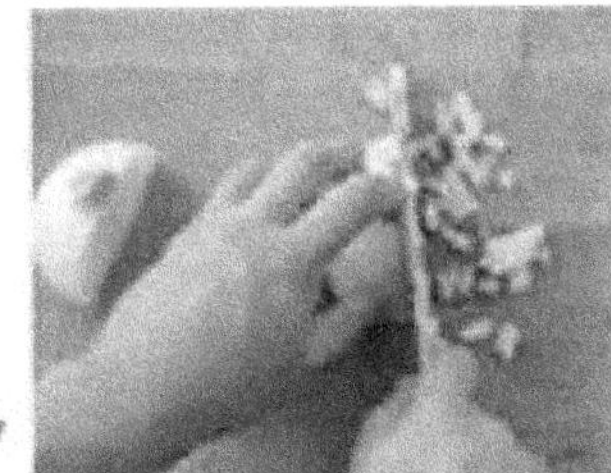
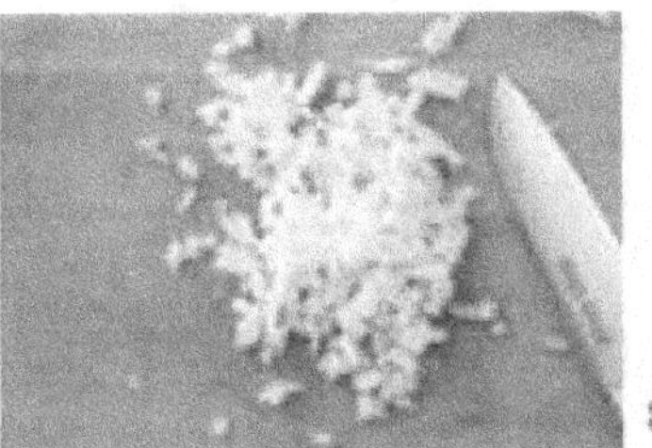

• FOR SMALL DICE: Make equal slices running post to shaft at ¼-inch stretches, leaving the root end in one piece. Then, at that point, hold your blade evenly and make a solitary cut about ¼ inch up from the base (6). Cut across the equal cuts, involving your bended knuckles as an aide for the blade (7). The onion ought to isolate into fine dice (8). Dispose of the root end.

Speedy TIP: If you're working with an enormous volume of onions, to boost effectiveness, make each onion through each stride prior to continuing to the subsequent stage. All in all, strip every one of the onions before you begin cutting any of them. Also, make every one of your level cuts prior to making your upward cuts. It will keep your work area more coordinated, require less outings to the trash bin (or fertilizer can), and make you resemble a professional.

CLASSIC FRENCH ONION SOUP

What might be said about those languid Sundays when you wouldn't fret staying nearby the kitchen for the few hours it takes to caramelize onions appropriately what's the best strategy then?

Most plans have you play the sitter, cooking the onions gradually on the burner, mixing at regular intervals. There are truly two separate cycles happening here. The onions are mellowing, delivering water and different broke down sugars and other substance compounds from inside their phones. At the same time, there's caramelization as those sugars are warmed. In a perfect world, both of these things wind up completing at around a similar time.

Yet, this is the thing I pondered: would I be able to partition the interaction into two unmistakable advances, first allowing the onions completely to relax and deliver their juices, then diminishing those juices and carmelizing them? Provided that this is true, I ought to have the option to save myself a touch of minding by restricting my blending to the last phase of cooking. To get it done, I returned to a strategy I'd gained from Chef Jason Bond for making a sweet white onion puree back when I was a line cook at No. 9 Park: you should simply to cook onions meagerly cut post to-shaft (they'll have a superior surface when cooked) in margarine in a weighty plated cast-iron or treated steel Dutch stove. When they get rolling, toss on the cover, turn the hotness down as low as could be expected, and let them stay there. As the onions heat, they radiate fluid, some of which goes to steam, re-gathers on the top of the pot, and afterward falls down, keeping the onions damp as they relax.

A few hours (with only a couple of mixes in the center), the onions will be totally relaxed and have given all the fluid and broke down flavor intensifies they will surrender. At this stage, it's a basic matter of decreasing that sweet fluid over moderate hotness until it's profoundly caramelized and brown, utilizing the searing and-deglazing process I use for my speedy caramelized onions.

The resultant soup is sweet, rich, and profoundly complicated.

TRADITIONAL FRENCH ONION SOUP

NOTE: If your pot doesn't have a weighty tight-fitting cover, place a layer of aluminum foil over the pot, creasing the edges to seal firmly, then, at that point, add the top.

SERVES 4

4 tablespoons unsalted spread

5 pounds yellow onions (around 5 huge), finely cut (around 7½ cups)

Legitimate salt

¼ cup dry sherry

6 cups custom made or low-sodium canned chicken stock

2 straight leaves

6 to 8 twigs new thyme

Newly ground dark pepper

1 loaf, cut ½ inch thick and toasted

8 ounces Gruyère or Swiss cheddar, ground

1. Liquefy the spread in a huge Dutch broiler over medium hotness. Add the onions and 1 teaspoon salt and cook, mixing oftentimes with a wooden spoon, until the onions have started to mellow and subsided into the lower part of the pot, around 5 minutes. Cover the pot with a tight-fitting top (see Note above), diminish the hotness to the most reduced setting, and cook, mixing at regular intervals, until the onions are totally delicate, around 2 hours.

2. Eliminate the top and increment the hotness to medium-high. Cook, blending often, until the fluid has vanished and an earthy colored patina has begun to shape on the lower part of the pot, around 15 minutes. Add 2 tablespoons water and scratch the seared covering from the lower part of the pot. Shake the pot to appropriate the onions equitably over the base and cook, shaking sporadically, until the fluid vanishes and the sautéed covering begins to develop once more, around 5 minutes longer. Add 2 additional tablespoons water and rehash, permitting the covering to develop and scratching it off, then, at that point, rehash two additional times. By this point, the onions ought to be a profound brown. On the off chance that not, proceed with the deglazing and blending process until the ideal tone is reached.

3. Add the sherry, chicken stock, straight leaves, and thyme, heat to the point of boiling, and decrease to a stew. Stew, revealed, until the fluid is profoundly seasoned and marginally decreased, around 15 minutes. Season to taste with salt and pepper. Dispose of the straight leaves and thyme.

4. To serve, heat the oven. Spoon the soup into four broilerproof bowls. Float the bread garnishes on top and cover with the ground cheddar. Sear until the cheddar is dissolved, effervescent, and brilliant brown in spots. Serve right away.

CHICKEN AND DUMPLINGS

It will be extreme not to stick a kid about my late puppy Dumpling in here some place, yet I'll make an honest effort.

When you understand that chicken and dumplings is just chicken stock joined with roll batter, adding this dish to your collection is a simple task. Here, you figured out how to make a great chicken stock in record time, and we investigated the study of bread rolls in our morning meal section (see here), so the main inquiry is: does a roll formula require any change to cook appropriately in the clammy climate of a soup pot?

The response, sadly, is yes. However, not much. Normal bread roll mixture will in general be extremely high in fat-an entire 4 ounces of margarine for each 10 ounces of flour. The flour can't frame extreme gluten sheets as promptly as it in any case would, in light of the fact that its proteins are greased up by spread. In a broiler, this is no issue. All you must do is get your bread rolls on a baking sheet, and from that point, don't contact them until they're prepared and set. In the unique climate of a pot of soup, notwithstanding, with bubbles stewing all over, buildup dribbling from the roof, and bits of chicken jarring it all over, the fragile roll batter doesn't have a potential for success: it's nearly ensured to crumble, turning the stock sludgy and oily.

The initial step to adjusting roll batter for dumplings is to lessen the fat. I tracked down that 6 tablespoons, down from 8, was a decent split the difference, actually leaving a lot of flavor yet expanding steadiness. However, this presented another issue: with less fat, the dumplings were coming out somewhat dry and thick, harder than they ought to have been. I took a stab at expanding how much baking powder and baking pop, yet neither one of the ones worked-the dumplings wound up with a solid compound delayed flavor impression. The simple arrangement? An egg.

Every one of the two pieces of an egg further develops a dumpling batter in its own particular manner. The greasy, protein-rich yolk replaces a portion of the fat that was lost when I cut back on the spread. However, not at all like butterfat, what starts liquefying and spilling out of the dumplings at around 90°F, an egg yolk does the inverse, becoming firmer as it is warmed. Emulsifying specialists found in the yolk, similar to lecithin, likewise assist with guaranteeing that the fat waits inside the dumplings. The egg white for this situation goes about as a leavener. As the dumplings cook, their free protein framework starts to cement, catching air pockets of water, sodden air, and carbon dioxide made by the baking powder and the baking pop/buttermilk response. As the dumplings keep on cooking, this damp air grows, bringing about gentility and delicacy.

CHICKEN AND DUMPLINGS

NOTE: Instead of utilizing the chicken stock, you can stew 4 chicken legs in 2 quarts low-sodium canned chicken stock for 30 minutes. Eliminate the legs, skim the fat from stock, and add sufficient water to make 2 quarts. Whenever the legs are sufficiently cool to deal with, take out the meat, disposing of the bones and skin, and save.

SERVES 4 TO 6

1 formula Quick Chicken Stock (here), including the picked leg meat (see Note above)

2 medium carrots, stripped and cut into medium dice (around 1 cup)

1 medium stem celery, cut into medium dice (about ½ cup)

1 little onion, finely cut (around 1 cup)

For the Biscuit Dough

¾ cup buttermilk

1 huge egg

10 ounces (around 2 cups) unbleached generally useful flour

1 teaspoon baking powder

¼ teaspoon baking pop

1½ teaspoons fit salt, in addition to something else for preparing

4 tablespoons cold unsalted margarine, cut into ¼-inch taps

¼ cup slashed new parsley

Newly ground dark pepper

1. Join the chicken stock (not the meat), carrots, celery, and onion in an enormous Dutch broiler and heat to the point of boiling over high hotness. Lessen to a stew and cook until the vegetables are delicate, around 20 minutes.

2. In the mean time, make the bread rolls: Whisk together the buttermilk and egg in a medium bowl.

3. In the bowl of a food processor, consolidate the flour, baking powder, baking pop, and salt and interaction until blended, around 2 seconds. Dissipate the margarine uniformly over the outer layer of the flour and heartbeat until the combination looks like coarse dinner and the biggest spread pieces are about ¼ inch at their most stretched out aspect. Move to an enormous bowl, add the buttermilk combination, and overlay with an elastic spatula until recently consolidated. The batter will be somewhat shaggy and really tacky.

4. Mix the parsley and chicken meat into the stock. Season to taste with salt and pepper and bring to a stew. Utilizing a lubed tablespoon measure, drop dumplings onto its surface, leaving a little space between them. Cover the pot, lessen the hotness to low, and cook until the dumplings have multiplied in volume and are cooked through (you can cut one open with a blade to look, or addition a cake analyzer or toothpick-it ought to tell the truth). Serve right away.

POT ROAST

Give me a decent American-style pot cook, in the entirety of its dribbling, exquisite, untidy, meaty greatness, over a French boeuf bourguignon anytime.

I love the way the meat shreds under the smallest strain from your fork. I love the rich onion-scented sauce, studded with bits of hamburger flotsam and jetsam. I love the delicate carrots and potatoes, weighty with meat juices. For soul-fulfilling chilly climate charge, it's comparably great as it gets.

Pot broil is basically an enormous piece of braised meat. Braising is the demonstration of gradually cooking a piece of meat in a sodden climate. The dampness can emerge out of lowering it in fluid (in which case, it's in fact called stewing) or by cooking it in a covered or to some degree covered vessel intended to trap sodden air around the food. As the meat cooks at a low temperature in a wet climate, similarly as while making stock, the connective tissue, principally comprised of the protein collagen, gradually changes over into gelatin. This is fundamental, since cooking additionally changes meat in another significant manner: it drives out dampness regardless of whether you cook it in a totally clammy climate. For sure, on the grounds that water is a particularly incredible guide of hotness, meat bubbled in 212°F water will really get more smoking and lose dampness quicker than hamburger broiled in 212°F broiler! In any case, there are different motivations to keep fluid in your pot. To begin with, it directs the temperature, so that there's no possibility of anything truly getting more sultry than the limit of water. Second, it works with the exchange of flavors among various pieces of the meat and the vegetables. At long last, what great's a pot cook without sauce?

Generally great meat plans start with the right cut. For pot broil, quite a few cuts high in connective tissue will do, however I lean toward the toss eye. It's thick and has a lot of gelatin-rich connective tissue to keep it clammy (see "Stewing Beef," here). Subsequent to searing the meal in a Dutch stove, I further support the flavor by adding a mirepoix of carrots, celery, and onion, cooking them in a similar pot (the dampness radiating from the vegetables will help deglaze the affectionate left behind by the sautéed meat). Time for the umami bombs: anchovies, Marmite, and soy advance into basically every braised dish I make, for their appetizing glutamates.

While French-style braises may fall back on rich decreased veal stocks to thicken the sauce, flour is the thickener of decision stateside. Following up, a jug of wine. It's not particularly customary in an American pot broil, but rather, very much like anchovies, Marmite, and soy sauce, wine is wealthy in appetizing glutamates, adding substantiality to the stock, as well as mind boggling smell and clue of causticity. A few chicken stock, a couple of peppercorns, and a few twigs of thyme and sound leaves balance my flavor profile.

Subsequent to building my braising fluid, I set the hamburger back, set up a top on the pot and set it in a 275°F stove to cook until delicate, trying to leave the cover marginally broke. Why, you might inquire? Temperature guideline. With a totally fixed cover, the water inside the pot quickly arrives at the edge of boiling over a temperature at which, given time, north of 50% of the dampness in a piece of hamburger will be constrained out. By keeping the top partially open, you can keep the substance of the pot at around 185°F, even in a 275°F stove! (For a more complete clarification, see "Investigation: Boiling Water Under Cover," here, and "Burner Versus Oven," here). This lower temperature permits the collagen to gradually separate while as yet keeping a decent degree of dampness inside the meat.

Cutting a pot cook subsequent to chilling for the time being gives you uniform, wear out free cuts.

Steady Heat Versus Constant Temperature

You might ask why many braised plans call for cooking in the broiler as opposed to stewing on the burner. Here's the way things are looking: a burner keeps a consistent hotness yield, while a broiler keeps a steady temperature. This really intends that on the burner, a similar measure of hotness energy is being moved to the pot regardless of how much stuff is inside it, and regardless of how hot that stuff as of now is. A pot of stew that is scarcely stewing toward the beginning of cooking over medium-low hotness may be at a fast bubble around the finish of cooking, when a portion of the fluid has dissipated and the volume of the stew has lessened. In a stove, regardless of how much or how little food there is in the pot, the temperature of the food continues as before. Additionally, a broiler warms delicately from all sides, while a burner zeros in the hotness on the lower part of the pot. Move all your braises to the stove, and you'll obtain better outcomes ensured.

Whenever I made the pot cook, after around 3 hours the meat was at simply the point I needed it- delicate enough that a blade or cake analyzer could sneak all through it effectively, yet not so delicate that it had lost its design. (The stock, incidentally, smelled wonderful.) The issues emerged when I attempted to cut the meat. While hot, it was delicate to the point that it was almost a unimaginable assignment it destroyed and self-destructed even with the most keen blade and the gentlest touch. The most effective way to cut braised meat is to permit it to initially cool totally.

Initially I believed it'd be ideal to permit the meat to chill off in the demeanor of the kitchen rather than in the hot fluid inside the pot. Be that as it may, I tried indistinguishable parts of a similar dish cooled in the air versus in the fluid and this is the thing I found:

RETAINED WEIGHT VERSUS COOLING METHOD

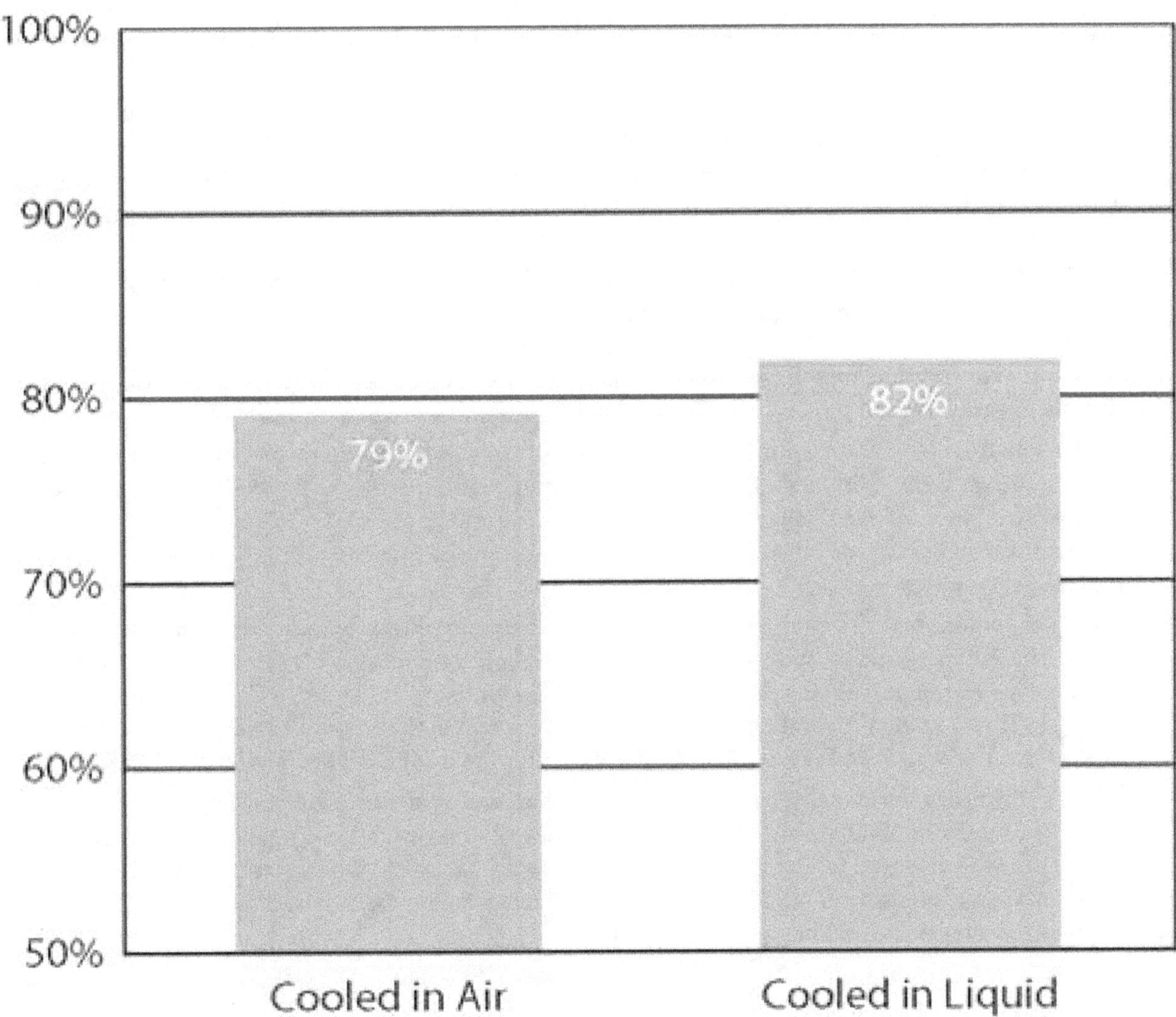

As may be obvious, the meat cooled in the fluid wound up with a decent 3 percent more dampness than the one cooled in the air. This is on the grounds that cooler meat can hold dampness more effectively than hot meat. Along these lines, as the meat cools in the fluid, a portion of the fluid is reabsorbed. I additionally observed that then, at that point, permitting the pot meal to rest in the cooler for as long as 5 days really worked on both flavor and surface, and that intends that for the ideal pot broil insight, you should cook the thing a few days before you intend to eat it.

The best cuts of beef for stewing or braising have plenty of robust beefy flavor and lots of connective tissue to break down into rich gelatin. Here are a few of my favorites:

- **Chuck** comes from the shoulder of the steer and is intensely beefy, with a good deal of fat. The best chuck cuts for braising are the 7-bone and the chuck roll. I prefer the latter, which is a boneless cut that makes for easier slicing. Look for well-marbled pieces with a nice cylindrical shape for even cooking.
- **Brisket** comes from the steer's chest. A whole brisket contains two parts: the flat (also called "thin cut" or "lean") and the point (also called "deck" or "moist"). The flat is more commonly available in supermarkets, but if you can find the point, it's worth buying for its larger amount of connective tissue, fat, and flavor. Brisket is not quite as rich as chuck and has a distinctive metallic, grassy aroma.
- **Flap meat,** also known as sirloin tip, is generally sold as an inexpensive steak, but it's great stewed, which makes it one of the most versatile steaks around. A whole flap steak is a rectangular block of meat about 1½ inches thick, weighing about 2 to 3 pounds, with a very strong grain and plenty of fat. It has a deep, beefy flavor and a robust, ropy texture that holds up well to long cooking.
- **Round** comes from the rear leg and is available as many different cuts. Bottom round, with a flavor similar to chuck, is the best for braising, though its odd shape makes it a bit harder to handle. Eye of round is by far the leanest of all of the braising cuts and so has a tendency to dry out a bit. If you keep a careful eye on the temperature and make sure to remove it from the oven as soon as it is tender, it does make a decent lower-fat option (but where's the fun in that?).
- **Short ribs** are technically part of the chuck but are sold separately. They come in three forms: as hunks of meat on top of 6-inch sections of rib bones (called English-cut short ribs); as pieces of meat attached to three- to four-rib-bone cross-sections (flanken cut); and boneless. All three make great stew meat. Their abundant fat and connective tissue ensure that they'll be meltingly tender and rich when properly cooked.

Does leaving the lid on or off really make much of a difference when cooking in an oven that's supposed to be maintaining a constant low temperature? Try this quick experiment to see for yourself.

Materials

* Two identical pots filled halfway with water
* One lid
* An instant-read thermometer

Procedure

Preheat the oven to 275°F. Place both pots in it, one with the lid on and the other with the lid off. Let the water heat for 1 hour, then open the oven and immediately take the temperature of each pot of water.

Results

The water in the lidded pot should be at around 210°F, while the water in the uncovered pot is probably closer to 185° to 190°F. Because of the cooling effect of evaporation (it takes a significant amount of energy for those water molecules to jump from the surface of the liquid—energy that they steal from the liquid itself, cooling it down), an open pot of stew in a 275°F oven will max out at around 185°F. Good news for you, because that's right in the optimal subsimmer stewing temperature zone.

Pop the lid on, and you cut down on the amount of evaporation. Less evaporation means a higher max temperature. In my simple test, putting the lid on increased the temperature in the pot by almost 25 degrees!

ALL-AMERICAN POT ROAST

WITH GRAVY

SERVES 6 TO 8

1 boneless throw broil (around 5 pounds), pulled separated at the crease into 2 huge pieces, abundance fat and cartilage managed

Legitimate salt and newly ground dark pepper

2 tablespoons vegetable oil

4 anchovy filets

2 medium cloves garlic, finely minced or ground on a Microplane (around 2 teaspoons)

1 teaspoon Marmite

1 tablespoon soy sauce

2 tablespoons tomato glue

2 enormous carrots, stripped and slice into 1-to 2-inch pieces

2 stems celery, cut into 1-inch lumps

2 enormous onions, finely cut (around 4 cups)

2 tablespoons generally useful flour

1 container (750-ml) dry red wine

4 cups custom made or low-sodium canned chicken stock

¼-ounce (1 bundle) unflavored gelatin

2 sound leaves

4 twigs new thyme

1 pound reddish brown baking potatoes (around 2 huge), stripped and slice into 1-to 2-inch lumps

1. Change a stove rack to the lower-center position and preheat the broiler to 225°F. Pat the throw cook dry and season it with salt and pepper. Tie kitchen twine firmly around each piece at 1-inch stretches to assist it with holding its shape.

2. Heat the oil in a huge Dutch stove over high hotness until softly smoking. Add the hurl and cook, turning infrequently, until very much carmelized on all sides, around 8 to 10 minutes. Move the hamburger to a huge bowl.

3. In the mean time, consolidate the anchovy filets, garlic, Marmite, soy sauce, and tomato glue in a little bowl and squash with the rear of a fork until a smooth, homogeneous glue is framed.

4. Return the pot to medium-high hotness, add the carrots and celery, and cook, blending as often as possible, until the vegetables start to brown around the edges, around 5 minutes. Add the onions and cook, blending as often as possible, until extremely delicate and light brilliant brown, around 5 minutes. Add the anchovy combination and cook, mixing, until fragrant, around 1 moment. Add the flour and cook, blending, until no dry flour stays, around 1 moment. Increment the hotness to high and, whisking continually, gradually add the wine. Bring to a stew and cook until the wine is diminished considerably, around 15 minutes.

5. In the interim, empty the chicken stock into a huge fluid estimating cup or a bowl and sprinkle the gelatin on top. Permit it to hydrate for 10 minutes.

6. Add the gelatin and chicken stock, straight leaves, and thyme to the Dutch stove, return the hamburger to the pot, and carry the fluid to a stew. Cover, place in the stove, and cook until the meat is totally delicate (it ought to offer next to zero obstruction when you jab it with a cake analyzer or slight blade), around 3 hours; add the potatoes to the pot around 45 minutes before the hamburger is finished. Eliminate the pot from the stove and permit to cool for 60 minutes.

7. Move the entire pot to the cooler and let rest to some degree short-term, or as long as 5 evenings.

8. Whenever prepared to serve, cautiously eliminate the solidified layer of fat from the highest point of the cooking fluid and dispose of. Move the meat to a cutting board. Dispose of the inlet leaves and thyme branches. Heat the fluid to the point of boiling over high hotness and decrease it until coats the rear of a spoon however doesn't taste weighty. Try to season with pepper and salt to give taste.

9. In the interim, eliminate the twine from the meat and cut it contrary to what would be expected into ½-inch-thick pieces. Place the pieces in covering layers in a 12-inch skillet and add a couple of spoons of sauce to dampen them. Cover the skillet and set over medium-low hotness, shaking every so often, until the meat is warmed through, around 15 minutes.

10. Move the meat to warmed serving plates or an enormous platter and top with the cooked vegetables and more sauce. Serve right away.

GLUTAMATES, INOSINATES, AND THE UMAMI BOMBS

For a long time, food researchers accepted that our tongues were delicate to four unique fundamental preferences: pleasantness, pungency, acridity, and harshness. Turns out that there's a fifth: umami. First found in Japan, it's best interpreted as "exquisite." It's the spit initiating characteristics that, say, a decent steak or a hunk of Parmesan cheddar has in your mouth. Similarly as the vibe of pleasantness is set off by sugar, pungency by salt, harshness by corrosive, and sharpness by various somewhat toxic classes of compound, umami flavor is set off by glutamates-fundamental amino acids found in numerous protein-rich food varieties. The way to getting many dishes to taste meatier-turkey burgers, stew, stew, soups, and so on is to build their degree of glutamates.

Presently, you can do this with powdered monosodium glutamate-a characteristic salt separated from monster ocean kelp-however a few people are queasy about utilizing it (I for one keep a little container of it right close to my saltcellar). In any case, there are choices, to be specific, what I like to call the three umami bombs: Marmite, soy sauce, and anchovies.

In the event that you've at any point been to England, you've most likely seen Marmite. It's that bizarre dull earthy colored goo with a sharp, pungent, appetizing flavor that the Brits like to spread on toast toward the beginning of the day. On toast, it's a mixed bag no doubt, yet there's a ton of possible stowing away in that little container. Produced using a result of liquor creation, it's basically focused yeast proteins, wealthy in both salt and glutamates. Soy sauce is produced using aged soybeans and gets elevated degrees of glutamates from both the amino-corrosive rich soybeans themselves and the yeast and microorganisms used to age them into the appetizing sauce. Anchovies and numerous other little sleek fish are normally wealthy in glutamates, and salting and maturing them expands their focus. Indeed, even numerous conventional plans for rich meat-based stews will require a couple of anchovies to assist with supporting the dish's appetizing characteristics.

There are numerous different fixings that have elevated degrees of glutamates-Worcestershire sauce, Parmigiano-Reggiano, powdered dashi (a Japanese stock made with ocean kelp and bonito), to give some examples however they all have pretty solid flavor profiles. My three umami bombs are the only ones I am aware of that can increment substantiality while mixing out of spotlight, making the regular kinds of meat more grounded without forcing their own will on the dish.

Yet, which one to utilize? I made a few clumps of turkey burgers fusing the fixings straightforwardly into the drudgery. Turns out that adding each of the three together is dramatically more strong in setting off our substantiality locators than utilizing any one all alone. For what reason shows improvement over only one? Indeed, glutamates are the rulers of substantiality, yet there's a subsequent synthetic, disodium inosinate, that has been found to work in cooperative energy with glutamic corrosive to expand the exquisiteness of food. Truth be told, in the August 2006 issue of the Journal of Food Science, analyst Shizuko Yamaguchi observed that the synergistic impact of the two mixtures is as a matter of fact quantifiable!

Along these lines, join the two, and you get a synergistic impact, making every more remarkable than if utilized all alone. Consider inosinates as the Robin to glutamate's Batman-they aren't required for the gig, however they sure assistance a dreadful lot.§ By relieving pork and fish, say, into prosciutto and Thai fish sauce, you can make a superconcentrated wellsprings of inosinates. Anchovies really have very elevated degrees of inosinate-an excess to adjust their own degrees of glutamate-while Marmite and soy don't have much by any means. Joining the inosinate in the anchovies with the glutamate in the soy and Marmite makes for a definitive blend.

GLUTAMATE CONTENT IN COMMON INGREDIENTS

Numerous food sources that we cook with consistently are high in glutamates. Here is a graph of their overall glutamate content.

Kombu (giant sea kelp)	22,000 mg/100g
Parmigiano-Reggiano	12,000
Bonito	2,850
Sardines/Anchovies	2,800
Tomato Juice	2,600
Tomatoes	1,400
Pork	1,220
Beef	1,070
Chicken	760
Mushrooms	670
Soybeans	660
Carrots	330

SKILLET-BRAISED CHICKEN

Many different things might be basically as flavorful as braised chicken legs, yet couple of things braise quicker or simpler, along these lines, generally when I'm in the state of mind for delicate, sodden, stewed meat, chicken it is.

I seldom braise chicken utilizing same formula two times, yet there are a few normal subjects in every one of them. The way to truly extraordinary braised chicken is in the cooking. You must brown the skin in the skillet until it's profoundly brilliant brown and exceptionally fresh, then, at that point, ensure that the skin stays over the level of the fluid the whole time it's cooking so the freshness remains. What you end up with is tumble off-the-bone-delicate meat profoundly seasoned with sauce and the fresh skin of an impeccably simmered chicken.

You most certainly need to involve dim meat for this. It has more connective tissue, which gradually separates into gelatin as the chicken braises, greasing up the meat and adding a pleasant wealth to the sauce. White meat will simply dry out.

One of my number one plans utilizes a sprinkle of white wine, a container of tomatoes, a modest bunch of cleaved tricks and olives, and a decent sprinkle of cilantro. Assuming that I'm in the temperament, I substitute smoked paprika for the ordinary kind and sautéed peppers and onions for the tomatoes, preclude the tricks and olives, and polish it off with parsley and a sprinkle of vinegar. Similarly great is a variant with more white, a few cups of chicken stock, and a lot of parsley and pancetta. One more variety fuses mushrooms, shallots, and piece bacon. Once more, the method matters-the flavors really depend on you.

These braises are far superior flavorwise the second or third day, however you really do lose a portion of the freshness in the chicken skin.

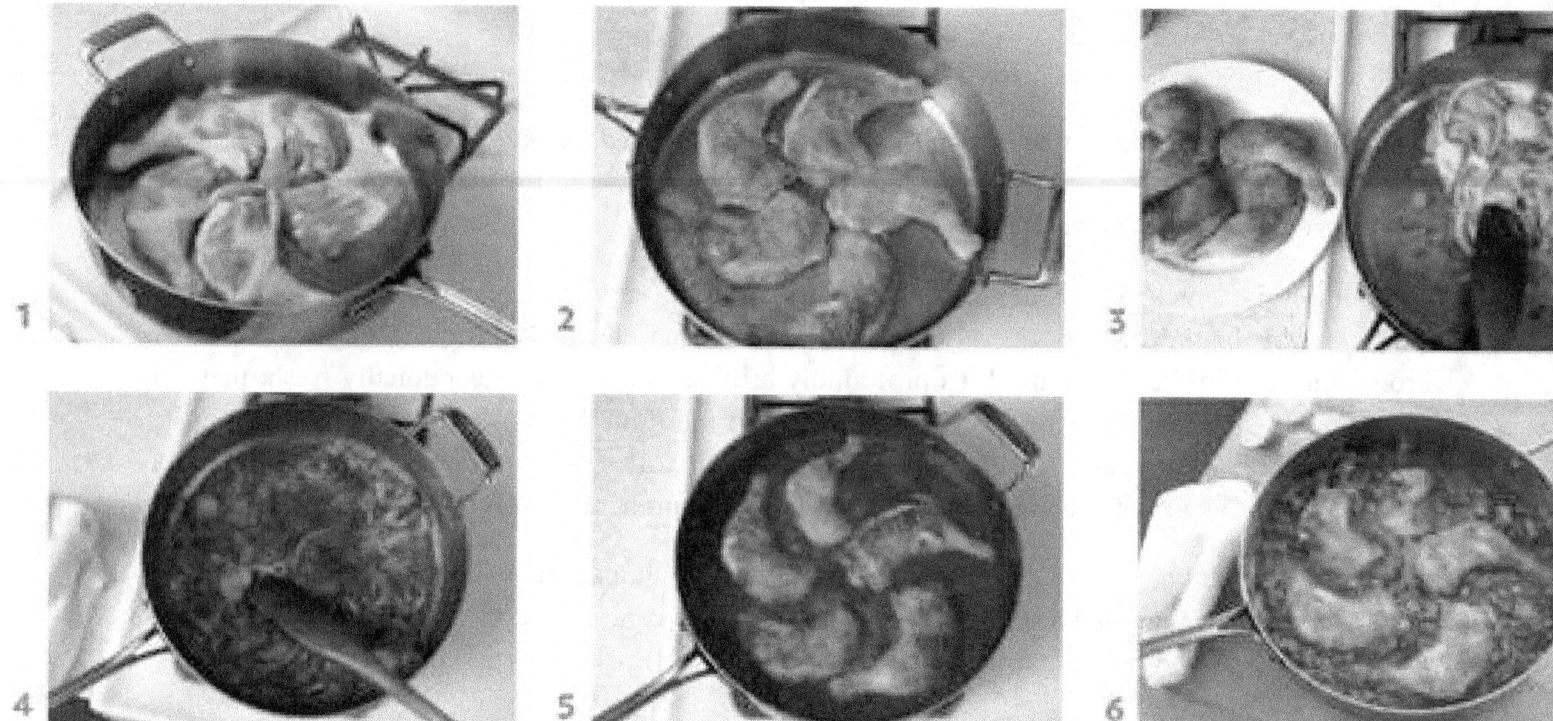

SIMPLE SKILLET-BRAISED CHICKEN

WITH TOMATOES, OLIVES, AND CAPERS

NOTE: You can make this dish completely on the burner by bringing the hotness down to the most reduced setting when you add the chicken in sync 4, covering the container, and cooking until the chicken is delicate, around 45 minutes.

SERVES 4 TO 6

4 to 6 chicken leg quarters

Genuine salt and newly ground dark pepper

1 tablespoon vegetable oil

1 enormous onion, finely cut (around 1½ cups)

2 cloves garlic, finely cut

1 tablespoon paprika

1 tablespoon ground cumin

1 cup dry white wine

One 28-ounce can entire tomatoes, depleted and squashed the hard way

½ cup natively constructed or low-sodium canned chicken stock

¼ cup escapades, washed, depleted, and generally slashed

¼ cup cleaved green or dark olives

¼ cup new cilantro leaves

¼ cup lime juice (from 3 to 4 limes)

1. Change a stove rack to the lower-center position and preheat the broiler to 350°F. Softly season the chicken legs with salt and pepper.

2. Heat the oil in a 12-inch ovenproof skillet or sauté container over high hotness until daintily smoking. Utilizing utensils, cautiously add the chicken pieces skin side down. Cover with a splatter screen or to some degree cover with a top to forestall splattering and cook, without moving it, until the chicken is profound brilliant brown and the skin is fresh, around 4 minutes. Flip the chicken pieces and cook until the subsequent side is brilliant brown, around 3 minutes longer. Move the chicken to a huge plate and put away.

3. Decrease the hotness under the container to medium-high, add the onions, and cook, utilizing a wooden spoon to scrape up the carmelized bits from the lower part of the skillet and afterward blending regularly, until totally mellowed and simply beginning to brown, around 4 minutes. Add the garlic and cook, blending, until fragrant, around 30 seconds. Add the paprika and cumin and cook, blending, until fragrant, around brief longer.

4. Add the white wine and scrape up the cooked pieces from the lower part of the skillet. Add the tomatoes, chicken stock, escapades, and olives and heat to the point of boiling. Settle the chicken pieces into the stock and vegetables with the goal that main the skin is appearing. Cover the skillet and move to the stove. Cook for 20 minutes, then, at that point, eliminate the cover and keep on cooking until the chicken is tumbling off-the-bone delicate; and the sauce is rich, around 20 minutes longer.

5. Mix the cilantro and lime juice into the sauce and season to taste with salt and pepper. Serve right away.

SIMPLE SKILLET-BRAISED CHICKEN

WITH WHITE WINE, FENNEL, AND PANCETTA

NOTE: You can make this dish completely on the burner by bringing the hotness down to the most reduced setting when you add the chicken in sync 4, covering the skillet, and cooking until the chicken is delicate, around 45 minutes.

SERVES 4 TO 6

4 to 6 chicken leg quarters

Genuine salt and newly ground dark pepper

1 tablespoon vegetable oil

3 ounces pancetta, diced

4 cloves garlic, finely cut

1 huge onion, finely cut (around 1½ cups)

1 bulb fennel, managed and finely cut (around 1½ cups)

1 huge tomato, generally hacked

1½ cups dry white wine

½ cup Pastis or Ricard

1 cup custom made or low-sodium canned chicken stock

1 straight leaf

¼ cup cleaved new parsley

2 tablespoons unsalted spread

1 tablespoon lemon juice (from 1 lemon)

1. Change a stove rack to the lower-center position and preheat the broiler to 350°F. Delicately season the chicken legs with salt and pepper.

2. Heat the oil in a 12-inch ovenproof skillet or sauté dish over high hotness until delicately smoking. Utilizing utensils, cautiously add the chicken pieces skin side down. Cover with a splatter screen or somewhat cover with a top to forestall splattering and cook, without moving it, until the chicken is profound brilliant brown and the skin is fresh, around 4 minutes. Flip the chicken pieces and cook until the subsequent side is brilliant brown, around 3 minutes longer. Move the chicken to a huge plate and put away.

3. Add the pancetta to the skillet and cook, blending every now and again, until delicately carmelized, around 3 minutes. Add the garlic and cook, mixing, until gently seared, around 1 moment. Add the onions and fennel and cook, utilizing a wooden spoon to scrape up the seared pieces from the lower part of the skillet and afterward blending habitually, until totally mellowed and simply beginning to brown, around 5 minutes.

4. Add the tomato, white wine, and Pastis, and scrape up the sautéed bits off from the lower part of the skillet. Add the chicken stock and sound leaf and heat to the point of boiling. Settle the chicken pieces into the stock and vegetables with the goal that main the skin is appearing. Cover the dish and move to the broiler. Cook for 20 minutes, then, at that point, eliminate the top and keep on cooking until the chicken is tumbling off-the-bone delicate and the sauce is rich, around 20 minutes longer. Move or transfer the chicken to a platter for serving purpose.

5. Mix the parsley, spread, and lemon juice into the sauce and season to taste with salt and pepper. Pour the sauce around the chicken and serve right away.

KNIFE SKILLS:

Step by step instructions to Cut Fennel

Fennel is a by and large troublesome vegetable.

Fresh, with an unmistakable anise flavor, it very well may be overwhelming for certain individuals. I incline toward my fennel in little dosages. Cut superthin on a mandoline and prepared with citrus supremes and a decent lemony vinaigrette, an extraordinary winter salad works out positively for frankfurters, terrines, and other charcuterie. The frilly green fronds that outgrow the top are no doubt eatable and make a lovely trimming.

With fennel, very much like the characters in an episode of ThunderCats, the heroes and the trouble makers are not difficult to recognize. Search for fennel bulbs that are light green or white with no staining. The principal thing you'll see when fennel is over the hill is sautéing at the edges of the layers, so really take a look at there first. The layers ought to be firmly stuffed, and the fronds ought to be dazzling green and energetic (1).

In its entire structure, fennel will keep going for about seven days in an approximately shut plastic pack in the vegetable crisper in the fridge, yet when you cut it, it can brown quickly, so slash it not long prior to utilizing.

To cut fennel, begin by removing the thick stalks (they can be held for stock) (2). Standing the bulb on its base, split it fifty-fifty (3). Utilize the tip of your blade to remove the center of every half (4)- it ought to come out effectively in a three-sided formed wedge (5). Meagerly cut the fennel from one post to another (6).

For diced fennel, split and eliminate the center concerning cut fennel. Cut the fennel into thicker boards (7), then, at that point, cut across them into dice (8).

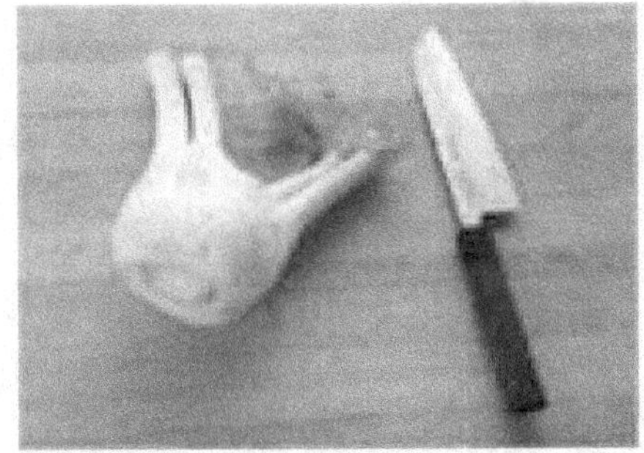
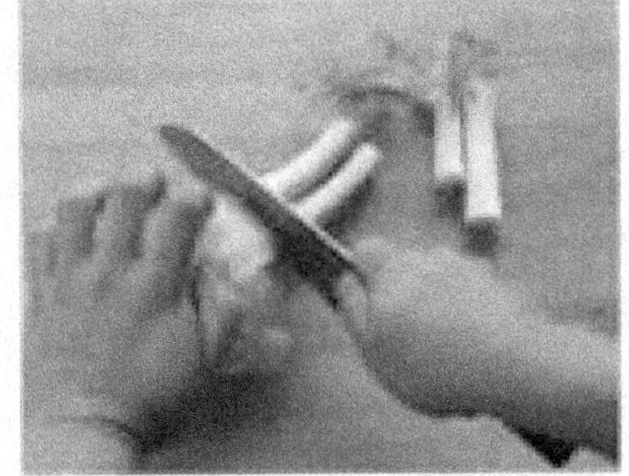
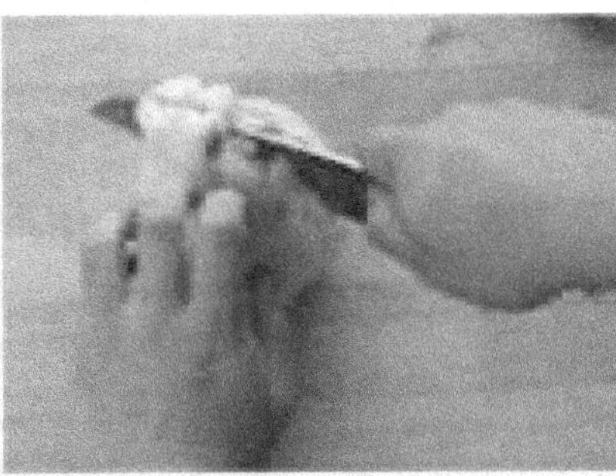

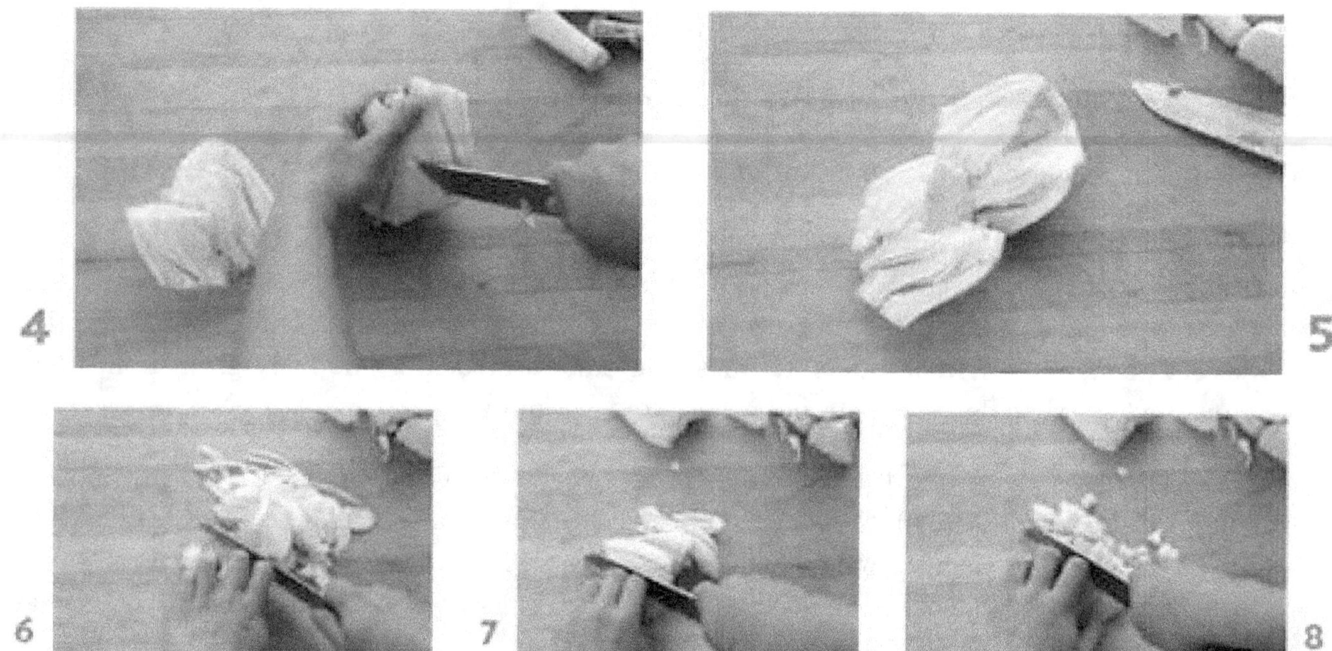

4

5

6

7

8

SIMPLE SKILLET-BRAISED CHICKEN

WITH PEPPERS AND ONIONS

Serve this with egg noodles, spätzle, rice, or bubbled potatoes.

NOTE: You can make this dish totally on the burner by bringing the hotness down to the least conceivable setting when you add the chicken in sync 4, covering the container, and cooking until the chicken is delicate, around 45 minutes.

SERVES 4 TO 6

4 to 6 chicken leg quarters

Legitimate salt and newly ground dark pepper

1 tablespoon vegetable oil

1 huge onion, finely cut (around 1½ cups)

1 green chime pepper, finely cut (around 1 cup)

1 red chime pepper, finely cut (around 1 cup)

2 cloves garlic, finely cut

1 tablespoon sweet Spanish smoked paprika (or normal paprika)

1 teaspoon dried marjoram (exquisite or oregano will likewise turn out great)

1 tablespoon generally useful flour

1 cup dry white wine

3 cups natively constructed or low-sodium canned chicken stock

1 enormous tomato, stripped, cultivated, and cut into ½-inch pieces

1. Change a stove rack to the lower-center position and preheat the broiler to 350°F. Softly season the chicken legs with salt and pepper.

2. Heat the oil in a 12-inch skillet ovenproof or sauté container over high hotness until daintily smoking. Utilizing utensils, cautiously add the chicken pieces skin side down. Cover with a splatter screen or somewhat cover with a top to forestall splattering and cook, without moving it, until the chicken is profound brilliant brown and the skin is fresh, around 4 minutes. Flip the chicken pieces and cook until the subsequent side is brilliant brown, around 3 minutes longer. Move the chicken to an enormous plate and put away.

3. Add the onions and peppers to the skillet and cook, utilizing a wooden spoon to scrape up the seared pieces from the lower part of the skillet and afterward mixing often, until totally relaxed and simply beginning to brown, around 4 minutes. Add the garlic and cook, blending, until fragrant, around 30 seconds. Add the paprika, marjoram, and flour and cook, blending, until fragrant, around 1 moment.

4. Add the white wine and scrape up the carmelized bits from the lower part of the skillet. Add the chicken stock and tomato and heat to the point of boiling. Settle the chicken pieces into the stock and vegetables so just the skin is appearing. Cover the skillet and move to the broiler. Cook for 20 minutes, then, at that point, eliminate the top and keep on cooking until the chicken is tumbling off-the-bone delicate and the sauce is rich, around 20 minutes longer. Season the sauce to taste with salt and pepper and serve.

SIMPLE SKILLET-BRAISED CHICKEN

WITH MUSHROOMS AND BACON

NOTE: You can make this dish altogether on the burner by bringing the hotness down to the least setting when you add the chicken in sync 4, covering the container, and cooking until the chicken is delicate, around 45 minutes.

SERVES 4 TO 6

4 to 6 chicken leg quarters

Fit salt and newly ground dark pepper

1 tablespoon vegetable oil

3 ounces piece bacon, diced

5 ounces button mushrooms, cleaned and cut (around 2 cups)

1 huge shallot, finely cut (about ½ cup)

2 cloves garlic, finely cut

2 teaspoons new thyme leaves

1 tablespoon unsalted spread

1 tablespoon generally useful flour

1 cup dry white wine

3 cups hand crafted or low-sodium canned chicken stock

½ cup weighty cream

2 tablespoons new parsley leaves

1. Change a stove rack to the lower-center position and preheat the broiler to 350°F. Gently season the chicken legs with salt and pepper.

2. Heat the oil in a 12-inch ovenproof skillet or sauté container over high hotness until softly smoking. Utilizing utensils, cautiously add the chicken pieces skin side down. Cover with a splatter screen or to some degree cover with a top to forestall splattering and cook, without moving it, until the chicken is profound brilliant brown and the skin is fresh, around 4 minutes. Flip the chicken pieces and cook until the subsequent side is brilliant brown, around 3 minutes longer. Move the chicken to a huge plate and put away.

3. Add the bacon to the skillet and cook, mixing often, until daintily carmelized, around 3 minutes. Move to a plate. Add the mushrooms and cook, utilizing a wooden spoon to scrape up the sautéed bits from the lower part of the skillet and afterward mixing often, until the mushrooms surrender the entirety of their fluid and begin to sizzle, around 8 minutes. Add the shallots and garlic and cook, mixing, until fragrant, around 1 moment. Add the thyme and spread and cook until the margarine is dissolved. Add the flour and cook, mixing continually, for 30 seconds.

4. Add the white wine and scrape up the sautéed bits from the lower part of the skillet. Add the chicken stock and heat to the point of boiling. Settle the chicken pieces into the stock and vegetables so just the skin is appearing. Cover the skillet and move to the stove. Cook for 20 minutes, then eliminate the cover and keep on cooking until chicken is tumbling off-the-bone delicate and the sauce is rich, around 20 minutes longer. Try to move or put the chicken to a platter for serving purpose.

5. Add the weighty cream to the sauce and cook, mixing, over high hotness until thickened somewhat, around 1 minutes. Season the sauce to taste with salt and pepper, mix in the parsley, and pour around the chicken. Serve.

IN SEARCH OF

THE ULTIMATE CHILI

In spite of its Mexican starting points, the present bean stew is a positively American dish. All things being equal, similar to a religion, the universe of stew darlings is parted into various groups, large numbers of whom are ready to battle to the passing over what can and can't be utilized in "genuine" bean stew. Would it be advisable for it to be made with ground hamburger or lumps? Are tomatoes permitted? Would it be a good idea for us to try and make reference to beans? Since nobody will settle on these variables, we will manage not one, yet two minor departure from meat stew one a conventional Texas-style made with only hamburger and chiles and the other the sort a large portion of us experienced childhood with, with beans and tomatoes, including both a form made with short ribs and one made with ground hamburger.

Regardless, there are various things we can all settle on about a decent bean stew:

• It ought to have a rich, complex flavor that consolidates sweet, harsh, hot, new, and fruity components in balance.

• It ought to have a hearty, substantial, thick flavor.

- In the event that it contains beans, the beans ought to be delicate, rich, and flawless.

- It ought to be bound together by a thick dark red sauce.

To accomplish these objectives, I chose to separate stew into its unmistakable components the chiles, the meat, the beans, and the flavorings-and ideal every one preceding assembling them across the board large cheerful pot.

The Chiles

I have awful recollections of my stew eating school days-when bean stew was made by adding a jar of beans and a container of tomatoes to ground hamburger, then, at that point, including one of each zest the rack (and an excessive amount of cumin) and stewing it. The completed item unavoidably had a completely unequal flavor with a fine, dirty mouthfeel from every one of the dried flavors.

Packaged stew powder is fine after all other options have been exhausted, however to get a definitive stew, my first game plan was to dump the powdered flavors and premixed bean stew powders and go directly to the source: genuine dried chiles. Dried either in the sun, over a smoky fire (on account of smoked chiles like chipotles), or-all the more normally these days-in moistness and wind-controlled rooms, dried chiles have strikingly complex flavors. Very much like meat that is matured, as a chile dries, it loses dampness, focusing its delightful mixtures inside every cell. These mixtures draw into nearer contact with one another, permitting them to respond and deliver new flavors that were absent in the new pepper.

Dried chiles are accessible in a confusing cluster, so to make my determination more straightforward, I chose to taste each assortment of entire chile I could find, observing the two its zest level and its flavor profile. I saw that the greater part of them could be categorized as one of four particular classifications: sweet and new, hot, rich and fruity, or smoky (see "Dried Chiles," here).

For my taste, a blend of chiles from the initial three classes created the most adjusted blend (the smoky chiles will more often than not overwhelm different flavors). Despite the fact that chiles are dried, their flavor can disperse with time, so getting new dried chiles' significant. They ought to have a rugged quality despite everything be adaptable. On the off chance that a chile parts or breaks when you twist it, move along to an alternate one. Dried chiles ought to be put away in a fixed compartment away from the light (I keep mine in zipper-secure packs in the storage space and utilized inside around a half year of procurement.

Toasting chiles creates flavor.

Similarly as with dried flavors, the kind of the chiles can be upgraded by toasting them dry (see "Entire Versus Ground Spices," here). This achieves two objectives: First, the hotness catalyzes responses among individual mixtures inside the stew, making new flavors. Second, the Maillard cooking response happens, bringing about many exceptionally delightful new mixtures.

Subsequent to toasting, I could go the conventional course and just join the chiles and crush them into a powder, however I'm not one to bow to custom. All things considered, I tracked down that by cooking them down in chicken stock and pureeing the soggy chiles, I could make a totally coarseness free glue for a concentrated flavor base for my bean stew. The greatest aspect? In the event that I made a twofold or triple clump, I could freeze the puree in ice 3D square plate for long haul stockpiling, providing me with the comfort of bumped bean stew powder yet tremendously better surface and flavor.

I utilize a chile puree rather than powder for better flavor and surface.

The Meat

Beside beans, the meat is the greatest wellspring of conflict among stew darlings. Some (like my beautiful spouse) demand ground meat, while others (like me) incline toward bigger stew-like pieces. As a general rule, I hesitantly let my significant other have her direction, which is the reason this time not entirely settled to battle for my own privileges or, at any rate, make her undermine her bean stew convictions.

Subsequent to attempting store-ground hamburger, home-ground meat, meat cut into 1-inch lumps, and hamburger generally slashed manually or in a food processor into a finished blend of ⅛-to ½-inch pieces, it was obvious that the last one was the champ. It gave small amounts of almost ground meat that additional body and aided keep the stew (and my marriage) very much bound while as yet giving an adequate number of huge, chunkier parts of give textural interest.

There are a lot of meat cuts that are incredible for stewing (see "Stewing Beef," here), however for my bean stew, I chose to go with powerful, burly short rib.

As anybody who's always cooked ground meat knows, it's almost difficult to brown an enormous pot of it appropriately. It's a basic matter of surface-region to-volume proportion. Ground hamburger has huge loads of surface region fluid and fat can escape from. When you begin cooking it, fluid starts pooling in the lower part of the pot, lowering the meat and passing on it to sputter and stew in its own dim earthy colored juices, which self-direct its temperature to 212°F, unreasonably low for delightful carmelizing to occur. Solely after its juices have totally dissipated can any sautéing activity happen. The miserable truth? With ground (or, for our situation, finely slashed) hamburger, you need to agree to one or the other dry, coarse meat or no sautéed flavor.

Attempting to brown ground meat is a waste of time.

However at that point I had an idea: for what reason would i say i was trying attempting to brown the meat after I hacked it? On the off chance that cooked flavor in the stew was the thing I was pursuing, did it much matter when I seared the meat as long as it wound up getting sautéed? I got one more cluster of short ribs, this time burning them in a hot dish prior to eliminating the meat from the bone and hacking it to measure.

The outcome? Stew with cleaved meat surface yet profoundly carmelized flavor. Yahoo ki-yippee.

Entire cuts brown quickly.

Slashing entire cuts in the wake of cooking gives you carmelized flavor and unrivaled surface.

The Beans

Assuming that you are from Texas, you should jump right to here. In any case, on the off chance that you're like me and accept beans are as basic to an extraordinary bowl of stew as the hamburger, while possibly not all the more along these lines, read on. Frankly, involving canned beans in stew checks out. They are consistently cooked, hold their shape well, and here the general absence of flavor contrasted with cooked dried beans isn't an issue. There are an adequate number of different flavors proceeding to redress. However, at times the inclination to break a few culinary skulls and the longing for some food-science legend busting is solid to such an extent that I can't help it. In this way, a fast redirection into the place that is known for dried beans.

Assuming you have worked for a gourmet expert or have a grandma from Tuscany or a mother by marriage from South America, you might have at one point been told never to add salt to your beans until they were totally cooked, in case you keep their hard skins from mellowing completely. As a matter of fact, in certain cafés I worked in, it was felt that overcooked beans could really be saved by salting them subsequent to cooking. To think!

In any case, how frequently have you really cooked two clusters of beans one next to the other, one splashed and cooked in salted water and the other doused and cooked in plain water? Chances are, never. Also, presently you won't ever need to. I present to you the aftereffects of simply such a test:

Salting beans can assist with softening their skins, forestalling victories.

The two clumps of beans were cooked just until they were completely relaxed, with none of the papery strength of half-cooked skins (around 2 hours for the two groups, after a short-term douse). As may be obvious, the unsalted beans (left) wound up retaining an excess of water and extinguishing well before their skins had appropriately mellowed, while the salted beans remained completely in one piece.

The issue? Magnesium and calcium, two particles found in bean skins that act similar to braces, supporting the skins' cell construction and keeping them firm. Assuming you absorb beans salted water for the time being, however, a portion of the sodium particles wind up playing a game of seat juggling with the calcium and magnesium, leaving you with skins that relax at similar rate as the beans' insides.

What influences the cooking pace of beans is the pH level. Acidic conditions will generally make beans seize up-which is the reason, for instance, Boston prepared beans, cooked in acidic molasses and tomato, can take as long as short-term to appropriately mellow. Tenderizing the beans in saltwater mitigates this impact somewhat, yet the best way to be certain that your beans will cook appropriately in acidic stews (like, say, stew) is to relax them independently and add them to the pot later on.

Anyway, where does the old enemy of salting legend come from? Likely similar spot most culinary fantasies come from: grandmas, aunties, and cooks. Never trusted them, won't ever will.

The Flavorings

The bean stew standard team of cumin and coriander was guaranteed, just like several cloves. Their therapeutic, mouth-desensitizing quality is an ideal equilibrium for the hot hotness of the chiles, much as desensitizing Sichuan peppers can play off chiles in the Chinese flavor blend known as mama la (numb-hot).

I likewise chose to check star anise out, in a gesture to British cook Heston Blumenthal and his treatment of Bolognese sauce. That's what he observed, with some restraint, star emerge can help the kind of carmelized meats without spreading the word. He was right, as I immediately found. For greatest flavor, make a point to toast your flavors entire prior to crushing them (see "Entire Versus Ground Spices," here).

All I wanted now was the conventional combo of onion, garlic, and oregano, alongside a few new chiles (for added hotness and newness) and tomatoes. I stewed everything together, added my cooked beans, stewed once more, prepared, and tasted.

So how'd it taste? Amazing. In any case, not exactly deserving of its "Ideal" title yet. It might in any case do with some more substantiality. The time had come to venture into my Bat tool belt of culinary stunts for the one weapon that still can't seem to bomb me, my umami bombs: Marmite, soy sauce, and anchovies.

These can expand the substantiality of almost any dish including ground meat or of stews (see "Glutamates, Inosinates, and the Umami Bombs," here). Adding a spot of each to my chile puree helped my all around husky short ribs to the farthest reaches of substantiality, a domain where burned skinless cows gallivant across slopes of ground hamburger, shooting all through fields of skirt steak, halting just to take tastes of waterways spilling over with thick glace de viand.

I woke up from my dream with one thing at the forefront of my thoughts: alcohol. Liquor has a lower edge of boiling over than water and, much more significant, it can really make water vanish at a lower temperature. Water atoms are held freely together like little magnets. At the point when water and liquor are blended, every individual water particle turns out to be farther away from the other water atoms, making it a lot simpler for it to get away and disintegrate. Since water-and-liquor solvent fragrant particles must be identified by your nose assuming they escape high up, it makes sense that the more vanishing happened, the more sweet-smelling my stew would be.

ENTIRE VERSUS GROUND SPICES

You regularly hear culinary specialists and formula essayists saying to utilize entire flavors rather than ground and to toast your flavors prior to utilizing them, yet you don't frequently find out about why. To sort out the response, I made five clusters of my Easy Weeknight Ground Beef Chili (here), utilizing flavors and chiles treated the accompanying ways:

1. Preground, directly from the container

2. Preground, toasted prior to adding

3. Entire flavors and dried chiles, ground and utilized without toasting

4. Entire flavors and dried chiles, ground and afterward toasted

5. Entire flavors, toasted and afterward ground

Each bunch of stew made with entire flavors and chiles-including those that weren't toasted-was better in flavor than those made with preground flavors. Of the two made with preground flavors, the toasted rendition was somewhat more complicated, and of the three made with entire flavors, the one with flavors that were toasted prior to crushing was extraordinarily better than the one that pre-owned ground and afterward toasted flavors. For what reason was this?

All things considered, toasting entire flavors achieves two objectives: First, it powers fragrant compound-loaded oils from profound inside individual cells to the outer layer of the zest and the interstitial spaces between the cells. This makes it a lot simpler to separate flavor when the zest is accordingly ground and consolidated into your food. Second, toasting likewise catalyzes an entire course of synthetic responses that produce hundreds tasty side-effects, extraordinarily expanding the intricacy of the flavor.

While toasting preground flavors, this last response will happen, yet you've likewise got an issue: vaporization. The tasty mixtures inside flavors are by and large very unpredictable they frantically need to escape out of sight and fly away. With entire flavors, they remain generally secured: they can't escape effectively from their cell detainment facilities. With ground flavors, then again, there's nothing keeping them down. They'll quickly fly out of sight. You might have seen that preground flavors become undeniably more sweet-smelling as you toast them. Recall this-assuming you smell it while you're cooking, it won't be in your food when you serve it.

There are uncommon special cases for the toast-before-crushing guideline. Indian and Thai curries, for instance, begin with ground or pureed aromatics sautéed in fat. Since the greater part of the fragrant mixtures in flavors are fat-solvent, they end up disintegrated in the fat, enhancing the remainder of the dish equitably and effectively when different fixings are added. In any case, for by far most of utilizations, and any time you will toast your flavors dry, try to do it prior to crushing them.

DRIED CHILES

Dried chiles come in scope of flavors and hotness levels. To assist with making choice simpler, I've separated them into a couple of classes. The ideal stew ought to join components from a few of them.

• Sweet and new: Distinct fragrances suggestive of red ringer peppers and new tomatoes. These peppers incorporate costeño, New Mexico (also known as dried Anaheim, California, or Colorado), and choricero.

• Hot: Overwhelming hotness. The best, similar to cascabels, additionally have some intricacy, while others, as pequin or árbol, are about heat and not much else.

• Rich and fruity: Distinct fragrances of sun-dried tomatoes, raisins, chocolate, and espresso. Probably the most popular Mexican chiles, as ancho, mulatto, and pasilla, are in this classification.

• Smoky: Some chiles, similar to chipotles (smoked dried jalapeños), are smoky due to how they are dried. Others, as nora or guajillo, have a characteristic smelly, scorched wood smokiness.

CHILE PASTE

NOTE: Chile glue can be utilized instead of stew powder in any formula. Utilize 2 tablespoons glue for each tablespoon powder.

MAKES 2 TO 2½ CUPS

6 ancho, pasilla, or mulato chiles (about ½ ounce), cultivated and attacked harsh 1-inch pieces

3 New Mexico red, California, costeño, or choricero chiles (about ⅛ ounce), cultivated and attacked harsh 1-inch pieces

2 cascabel, árbol, or pequin chiles, cultivated and torn into equal parts

2 cups custom made or low-sodium canned chicken stock

1. Toast the dried chiles in a Dutch broiler over medium-high hotness, mixing regularly, until marginally obscured, with an extraordinary cooked fragrance, 2 to 5 minutes; turn down the hotness on the off chance that they start to smoke. Add the chicken stock and stew until the chiles have relaxed, 5 to 8 minutes.

2. Move the chiles and fluid to a blender and mix, beginning on low speed and step by step speeding up to high and scratching down the sides as the need should arise, until a totally smooth puree whenever shaped, around 2 minutes; add water if fundamental in the event that the combination is too thick to even consider mixing. Let cool.

3. Freeze the chile glue in ice shape plate, placing 2 tablespoons into each well. When the blocks are frozen, move to a zipper-lock cooler pack and store in the cooler for as long as 1 year.

THE BEST SHORT-RIB CHILI

WITH BEANS

Serve the stew with ground cheddar, acrid cream, hacked onions, scallions, cut jalapeños, diced avocado, as well as slashed cilantro, alongside corn chips or warmed tortillas.

NOTE: Canned beans can be utilized instead of dried. Utilize three 15-ounce jars red kidney beans, depleted, and add them toward the start of stage 5. Or then again exclude the beans altogether.

SERVES 8 TO 12

5 pounds bone-in hamburger short ribs (or 3 pounds boneless short ribs or hurl), managed of silverskin and overabundance fat

Fit salt and newly ground dark pepper

2 tablespoons vegetable oil

1 enormous yellow onion, finely diced (around 1½ cups)

1 jalapeño or 2 serrano chiles, finely slashed

4 medium cloves garlic, minced or ground on a Microplane (around 4 teaspoons)

1 tablespoon dried oregano

1 cup Chile Paste (here) or ½ cup stew powder

4 cups custom made or low-sodium canned chicken stock

4 anchovy filets, squashed into a glue with the rear of a fork

1 teaspoon Marmite

1 tablespoon soy sauce

2 tablespoons tomato glue

2 tablespoons cumin seeds, toasted and ground

2 teaspoons coriander seeds, toasted and ground

1 tablespoon unsweetened cocoa powder

2 to 3 tablespoons moment cornmeal (like Maseca)

2 straight leaves

1 pound dried red kidney beans, absorbed salted water at room temperature for something like 8 hours, ideally short-term, and depleted

One 28-ounce can squashed tomatoes

¼ cup juice vinegar, or more to taste

¼ cup bourbon, vodka, or cognac (discretionary)

2 tablespoons Frank's RedHot or other hot sauce

2 tablespoons dull earthy colored sugar

Trims as wanted (see the headnote)

SIMPLE WEEKNIGHT GROUND BEEF CHILI

Now and again even awesome of us don't want to go full scale. Here is a much speedier weeknight stew that utilizes a couple of the stunts gained from my Best Short-Rib Chili (here) and the 30-minute bean soup plans (here-here). I use ground meat here, which blocks genuine searing as a choice, however two or three smoky chipotle chiles included along with the remaining blend loan a comparative kind of profound intricacy. Serve the stew with ground cheddar, harsh cream, hacked onions, scallions, cut jalapeños, diced avocado, and additionally cleaved cilantro, alongside corn chips or warmed tortillas.

SERVES 4 TO 6

4 tablespoons unsalted spread

2 medium onions, ground on the huge openings of a container grater (around 1½ cups)

2 huge cloves garlic, minced or ground on a Microplane (around 4 teaspoons)

1 teaspoon dried oregano

Legitimate salt

2 chipotle chiles stuffed in adobo, finely hacked

2 anchovy filets, squashed to a glue with the rear of a fork

½ cup Chile Paste (here) or ¼ cup stew powder

1 tablespoon ground cumin

½ cup tomato glue

2 pounds boneless ground hurl

One 28-ounce can entire tomatoes, depleted and cleaved into ½-inch pieces

One 15-ounce can red kidney beans, depleted

1 cup custom made or low-sodium canned chicken stock, or water

2 to 3 tablespoons moment cornmeal (like Maseca)

2 tablespoons bourbon, vodka, or cognac (discretionary)

Newly ground dark pepper

Trims as wanted (see the headnote)

1. Liquefy the spread in an enormous Dutch stove over medium-high hotness. Add the onions, garlic, oregano, and a touch of salt and cook, mixing as often as possible until the onions are light brilliant brown, around 5 minutes. Add the chipotles, anchovies, chile glue, and cumin and cook, blending, until fragrant, around 1 moment. Add the tomato glue and cook, blending until homogeneous, around 1 moment.

2. Add the ground hamburger and cook, utilizing a wooden spoon to separate the meat into pieces and mixing oftentimes, until at this point not pink (don't attempt to brown the meat), around 5 minutes. Add the tomatoes, beans, stock, and cornmeal and mix to consolidate. Heat to the point of boiling, decrease to a stew, and cook, blending periodically, until the flavors have created and the bean stew is thickened, around 30 minutes.

3. Mix in the bourbon, if utilizing. Present with some or the recommended trims in general, alongside corn chips or tortillas.

VEGGIE LOVER CHILI

For what reason does vegan bean stew get such a bum rap?

When it's all said and done, there's the self-evident: stew is a troublesome issue, particularly among the individuals who love bean stew. Be that as it may, hello, prepare to be blown away. Beans can taste great in stew. Tomatoes can taste great in stew. Hell, even pork and tomatillos can taste great in stew. So is there any valid reason why we shouldn't have the option to make a totally meatless form that preferences extraordinary also?

I've seen a couple of nice veggie lover bean stews in the course of my life, yet for reasons unknown, they all appear to fall into the "30 minutes or less" camp. That all by itself is anything but something awful veggie lover stew when in doubt shouldn't be cooked the length of meat-based stews since vegetables, particularly canned beans, soften quicker than meat-yet lengthy, slow cooking nets you benefits in the flavor improvement. Quick bean stew plans are definitely not exactly as rich and complicated as you'd like them to be. My objective was to make a 100% veggie lover (really, it's vegetarian) stew that has the entirety of the profound flavor, textural difference, and rib-staying lavishness that the best bean stew ought to have.

Priorities straight: artificial meat isn't in the image. I believe that my vegan stew should commend vegetables and vegetables, not to attempt to impersonate a substantial stew. With that far removed, we'll continue on to the subsequent thing: incredible bean stew needs to begin with extraordinary chiles. That is what's really going on with it. I've seen plans calling for a few tablespoons of prefab stew powder for a whole pot of beans and tomatoes. The best way to accomplish extraordinary flavor is to mix up the chiles yourself, beginning with entire dried chiles. Also, we've previously got an incredible formula for a complicated chile glue conceived for the meat stew, so why not use it here too?

Following up, the beans. For my purposes, an incredible stew needs to show a few person and variety. You don't need totally uniform beans in each nibble, you need a scope of surfaces. Here's the place where you must go with a few innovative decisions.

Numerous veggie lover chiles take the kitchen-sink, enormous vehicle remuneration approach: Hey, we can't utilize meat, is the clear perspective, so we should toss in every damn sort of bean and vegetable under the sun. That strategy most certainly gets you textural as well as flavor assortment, yet it can turn into altogether too confused. Better to settle on several even decisions and spotlight on idealizing them.

Kidney beans are an absolute necessity in my stews; I grew up with kidney beans in my stew, and I will keep on appreciating them in my stew. You, then again, are allowed to substitute anything sort of bean you need. There is something particularly valuable about dried beans, and I truly do once in a while select to salt water dried beans for the time being to make stew 100% without any preparation, however canned beans are a slam dunk. They're rarely finished or half-cooked, they're rarely swollen or busted. They are deficient in the flavor office, yet with a decent stew in an extremely delightful fluid, you can without much of a stretch make up for this (see "How to Make Canned Beans Taste Good," here). Furthermore, interestingly, the fluid base for stew is normally low in pH (both the chiles and the tomatoes are acidic), and beans and vegetables relax gradually in acidic fluid. This implies you can stew your canned beans for a huge timeframe in your stew before they truly begin to separate.

Yet, what might be said about more surface? I had a go at utilizing a combination of kidney beans and other more modest beans and grains (chickpeas, flageolets, grain), however the genuine key ended up being utilizing the food processor. By two or three jars of chickpeas in the food processor, I had the option to hack them into a combination of huge lumps and little pieces generally. Adding this to my bean stew gave it extraordinary body and a huge load of textural contrast.

Amping Up Flavor

The way to rich flavor in vegetable stew is twofold: initial, a long stew during which water is driven off so that flavors are concentrated and different unstable mixtures separate and afterward recombine to add intricacy, and second, a decent wellspring of glutamic corrosive, the synthetic liable for the flavor we perceive as exquisite, once in a while called umami. In this way, time to go after the umami bombs once more (see here). Anchovies are good and gone for clear reasons, yet a hint of Marmite and soy sauce adds a huge load of extravagance to the bean stew. Other than that, the flavor base is really clear: onions perspired in a little vegetable oil, garlic, oregano (the dried stuff is fine for long-cooking applications like this), and two or three canned chipotle chiles in adobo sauce to add a dash of smokiness and hotness, remunerating pleasantly for the absence of sautéed hamburger.

THE BEST VEGETARIAN BEAN CHILI

Present with ground cheddar, acrid cream, slashed onions, scallions, cut jalapeños, diced avocado, as well as cleaved cilantro, alongside corn chips or warmed tortillas.

SERVES 6 TO 8

Two 14-ounce jars chickpeas (with their fluid)

One 28-ounce can entire tomatoes

1 cup Chile Paste (here) made with water rather than chicken stock

2 chipotle chiles in adobo sauce, finely cleaved, in addition to 2 tablespoons of the sauce

2 tablespoons vegetable oil

1 huge onion, finely diced (around 1½ cups)

3 medium cloves garlic, minced or ground on a Microplane (around 1 tablespoon)

tablespoons ground cumin

2 teaspoons dried oregano

1 tablespoon soy sauce

1 teaspoon Marmite

Two 14-ounce jars red kidney beans, depleted and fluid held

2 tablespoons vodka, whiskey, tequila, or Cognac

Fit salt

2 to 3 tablespoons moment cornmeal (like Maseca)

Trims as wanted (see the headnote)

1. Channel the chickpeas, saving the fluid in a medium bowl. Move the chickpeas to a food processor and heartbeat until just generally hacked, around three 1-second heartbeats. Put away.

2. Add the tomatoes, with their juice, to the chickpea fluid and utilize your hands to split the tomatoes up into unpleasant pieces, about ½ inch each. Add the chile glue and chipotles, alongside their sauce, and mix to join.

3. Heat the oil in a Dutch broiler over medium-high hotness until sparkling. Add the onion and cook, mixing regularly, until mellowed however not seared, around 4 minutes. Add the garlic, cumin, and oregano and cook, stirringly, until fragrant, around 30 seconds. Add the soy sauce and Marmite and cook, stirringly, until fragrant, around 30 seconds. Add the tomato blend and mix to join.

4. Mix in the chickpeas and kidney beans. If important, add some of saved bean fluid so the beans are scarcely lowered. Heat to the point of boiling over high hotness, decrease to an uncovered stew, and cook, mixing periodically, until thick and rich, around 1½ hours; add more bean fluid as needs be on the off chance that the stew turns out to be excessively thick or adheres to the lower part of the pot.

5. Add the vodka and mix to consolidate. Season to taste with salt and speed in the cornmeal in a sluggish, constant flow until the ideal thickness is reached. Serve, or, for best outcomes, permit the stew to cool and refrigerate for the time being, or as long as seven days, then warm to serve.

6. Present with some or the recommended trims in general, alongside corn chips or tortillas.

Alright, people, this is all there is to it.

The genuine article. For every one of you Texans who turned your noses up or feigned exacerbation at my bean-filled stew formula, I will make it dependent upon you. This formula is genuine article bean stew con carne, old-school Texas-style. What's the significance here? Above all else, positively no beans. Also, no tomatoes. For sure, there's tiny that goes into the pot other than meat and chiles (and a lot of both!). That doesn't mean there are certainly not a couple of things to talk about, notwithstanding. We should get to it.

The Meat

The first stew was made with dried hamburger beat along with suet and dried chiles into a kind of pemmican-like dry blend expected to keep going quite a while and be fast and nutritious for cowpokes to rehydrate and stew up out on the reach. Nowadays, we have fridges and new meat. So we use them. What we're searching for here is a meat that is great for stewing-that is, wealthy in connective tissue and fat and high in flavor.

By and large, meat falls across a range of delicacy, with the somewhat boring yet delicate cuts toward one side and the exceptionally tasty yet intense cuts on the other. These cuts by and large compare with the muscles that the cows utilize least to most during their life: So, on the extreme left side would be moderately unworked muscles like tenderloin or midsection cuts (strip steak, porterhouse, and so forth)- exceptionally delicate however generally flavorless. On the opposite finish of the range are dedicated muscles like short ribs, shin, oxtail, and throw (shoulder). Hurl is the ideal stew cut, with extraordinary flavor, a lot of fat, and a lot of connective tissue in one even bundle. As the meat gradually cooks down in delightful fluid, all of that connective tissue-generally made out of the protein collagen-separates into rich gelatin, which gives great stewed hamburger its sumptuous surface.

Cut and Sear

The stew of my childhood was made with ground hamburger, which is vital if you would rather not invest the energy to stew your meat appropriately. Crushing hamburger abbreviates its filaments, making it undeniably more delicate, and ground meat bean stew can be prepared to eat in less than 60 minutes. Yet, that is not the thing we're pursuing here. Genuine Texas bean stew is made with huge lumps of meat and requires long, slow stewing. I messed with one or two sizes and chose 2-inch pieces (they psychologist to about an inch and a half subsequent to cooking). I like destroying a huge block of hamburger separated with my spoon prior to eating it, if by some stroke of good luck to remind myself how totally delicate the meat has become.

With respect to burning, as we probably are aware, there's generally a compromise. Singing creates decent carmelized flavors through the Maillard response, however it additionally brings about harder, drier meat. At the high temperatures expected for carmelizing, meat muscle filaments contract significantly and oust such a lot of fluid that even after a long stew in the pot, the edges of the meat solid shapes are moderately dry. I immensely lean toward the milder surface of unseared meat.

The arrangement? You could burn enormous pieces of meat as I accomplished for the Short-Rib Chili with Beans (here), yet here's another arrangement: brown just a large portion of the meat. You foster a lot of carmelized flavor yet hold great surface in the remainder of the meat. Stressed that the flavor will be gathered distinctly in the meat that you singe? Try not to perspire it. The vast majority of those delightful mixtures are water-solvent, intending that there's a lot of time for them to disintegrate and convey themselves all through the stew as it cooks.

We definitely know how to take full advantage of chiles, so I won't hit your head into it once more. Alright, perhaps one final time:

1. Utilize new dried chiles, not bean stew powder.

2. Toast the chiles, then stew them in fluid and, at long last, mix them to forestall any lumpiness in the end result.

Furthermore, . . . that's the long and short of it. Hamburger, chiles, and time are everything necessary. I sporadically add an onion and maybe a couple of cloves of garlic that I sauté in the pot in the wake of braising the meat. Assuming that I'm feeling fiery, I may likewise add a couple of flavors from the rack: cumin, cinnamon, allspice, a touch of dried oregano-all are great in little amounts, however absolutely discretionary (Texans, kindly don't kill me!).

The main inquiry left is the way to stew the meat. In a perfect world, you need to cook the meat at as low a temperature as could be expected (to try not to cause unjustifiable muscle fiber withdrawal) while as yet relaxing its connective tissues. The least demanding approach to this is to utilize an exceptionally huge, weighty pot with a lot of surface region for dissipation (this helps limit the bean stew's most extreme temperature) and to use as low a fire as conceivable on the burner or, even better, put the pot into a low-temperature (200° to 250°F is great) stove, which will warm more delicately and equitably than a burner.

Leaving the top marginally partially open decreases fume strain on the outer layer of the stew, which can likewise restrict its upper temperature. With a weighty top, stew temperatures can push up to 212°F. Leave that equivalent top somewhat broken, and your stew will remain nearer to 190° or even 180°F-much better. Indeed, even sluggish cooked meat can be overcooked, so you need to painstakingly screen your stew and pull it off the hotness exactly when the meat becomes delicate. This generally takes more time to 3 hours.

Then you can leave the stew with no guarantees, however I like to thicken mine with a touch of cornmeal.

Like any great marriage, the marriage among meat and stew improves and more private with time. Allow the stew to sit for the time being in the refrigerator and it'll taste stunningly better the following day. I guarantee, it merits the pause. Substantial? Check. Hot, rich, complex bean stew flavor? Check. Furthermore, that is actually all Texas bean stew needs. A sprinkle of cilantro, cut scallions, and maybe some ground cheddar (I like cotija, yet Jack, Colby, and cheddar will all turn out great) make for good backups. As do warm tortillas or corn chips. As ends up being beneficial lager or whisky. What's more, fine, on the off chance that you'd like, you can feel free to add a container of beans. Simply don't tell anybody I told you to.

Toss is an adaptable and modest muscle, but on the other hand it has a ton of large areas of fat and connective tissue. Whenever ground for burgers, this isn't something awful, however no one needs to nibble into a major piece of delicate fat in their bean stew, so it's vital to manage it off.

- TO TRIM A WHOLE CHUCK ROAST, begin by partitioning it fifty-fifty. This will make it less awkward to move on your cutting board.

• Pivot THE ROAST until you track down its significant crease (contingent upon precisely which part of the toss you get, it might have mutiple). The meat ought to pull separated effectively at this crease; if fundamental, utilize the tip of a sharp butcher's or alternately culinary expert's blade to scratch any difficult connective tissue.

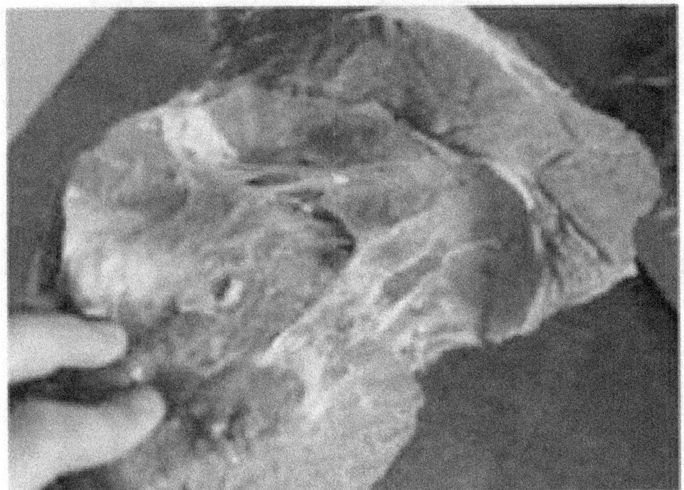

• Whenever YOU'VE SEPARATED the throw into single huge muscle gatherings, all of the fat and connective tissue ought to be uncovered. Utilize your sharp blade to manage them, then dispose of and cut the throw into pieces as wanted.

GENUINE TEXAS CHILI CON CARNE

Present with ground cheddar, harsh cream, cleaved onions, hacked scallions, cut jalapeños, diced avocado, as well as slashed cilantro, alongside corn chips or warmed tortillas.

SERVES 6 TO 8

4 pounds boneless meat throw, managed of cartilage and overabundance fat and cut into 2-inch pieces

Fit salt and newly ground dark pepper

2 tablespoons vegetable oil

1 enormous onion, finely diced

4 medium cloves garlic, minced or ground on a Microplane (around 4 teaspoons)

1 tablespoon ground cumin

½ teaspoon ground cinnamon (discretionary)

¼ teaspoon ground allspice (discretionary)

2 teaspoons dried oregano

1 cup Chile Paste

2 quarts natively constructed or low-sodium canned chicken stock

2 to 3 tablespoons moment cornmeal (like Maseca)

Trims as wanted (see the headnote)

1. Season half of the meat with salt and pepper. Heat the oil in an enormous Dutch broiler over high hotness until smoking. Add the carefully prepared meat and cook, without moving it, until very much carmelized on base, around 6 minutes. Move the meat to an enormous bowl, add the uncooked meat, and put away.

2. Return the Dutch broiler to medium-high hotness, add the onion, and cook, blending regularly, until mellowed however not seared, around 6 minutes. Add the garlic, cumin, cinnamon and allspice, if utilizing, and oregano and cook, mixing, until fragrant, around 1 moment.

3. Add the meat, alongside the chile glue and chicken stock, and mix to consolidate. Heat to the point of boiling over high hotness, then lessen to a stew, cover, leaving the top scarcely slightly open, and cook, mixing sporadically, until the meat is totally delicate, 2½ to 3 hours. (Then again, the bean stew can be cooked in a 200° to 250°F broiler with the cover of the Dutch stove marginally partially open.)

4. Season the fluid to taste with salt and pepper. Race in the cornmeal in a sluggish, constant flow until the ideal thickness is reached. Serve, or, for best outcomes, permit the stew to cool for the time being, then, at that point, warm the following day to serve. Present with some or the proposed trims in general, alongside corn chips or tortillas.

CHILE VERDE

We as a whole realize that bean stew is thick, rich, hot, substantial, complex, and red, correct?

In any case, what might be said about green stew, that similarly perplexing, fresher, porkier cousin normal to numerous Southwestern states? The most essential and no-nonsense adaptation of New Mexico chile verde is made by stewing rich cuts of pork in a thick stew of broiled Hatch chiles, onions, garlic, salt, and little else. As the meat is braised until delicate, the stock gets the kind of the softened pork fat alongside the particularly sweet and severe taste of the chiles, made smoky from broiling until almost darkened.

Filled in the town of Hatch (populace: ~2,000) in southern New Mexico, these chiles give a complicated spine that couple of other single fixings would be able. I don't invest a lot of energy in New Mexico-I have a thing about hotness and dream catchers-and new Hatch chilies seldom advance toward the Northeast, which leaves me with canned or frozen chiles. In any case, neither of these two dish especially well, and that smoky burn is the most amazing aspect of green stew. Fortunately, I likewise don't put a lot of belief in validness. I'll make due with heavenly. I live far enough away from New Mexico that, ideally, I'll have the option to see the residue trail awakened up by the viciously disposed green stew aficionados drawing closer and beat a rushed retreat.

The Peppers

It's positively conceivable to get a type of Hatch chile to your entryway, regardless of where you reside. The web is overflowing with Hatch chile wholesalers, promising to send you legitimate canned or frozen peppers directly from the source. The issue with these isn't exactly a surface or flavor issue it's that canned or recently frozen chiles are absolutely difficult to roast appropriately prior to stewing them. They're basically excessively wet. Furthermore, preroasted canned or frozen chiles don't have the profound kind of home-simmered chilies, which left me with one choice: discover a few appropriate substitutes.

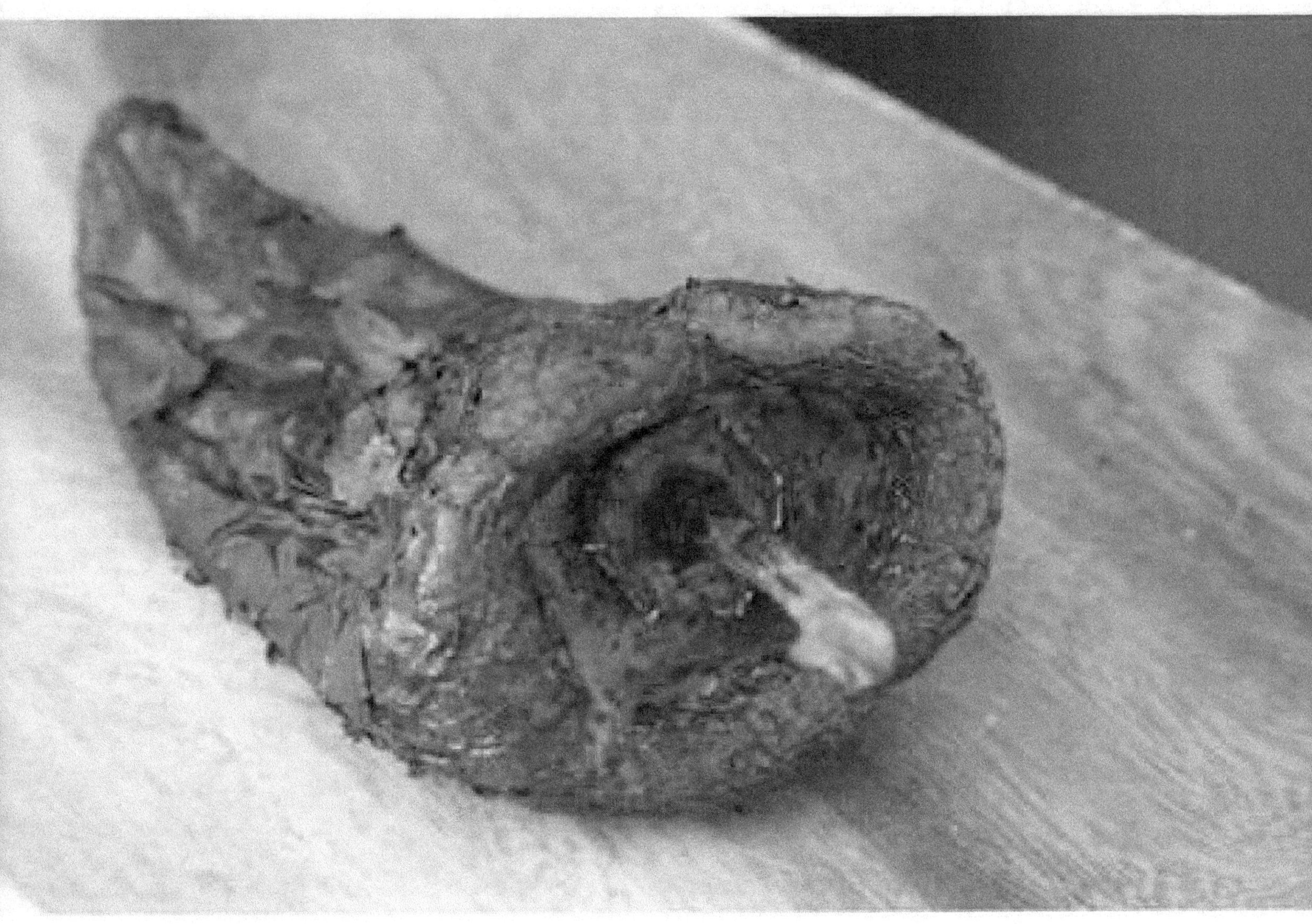

Poblano peppers were a conspicuous spot to begin. They're promptly accessible, and they have a profound, hearty flavor. To add a touch of splendor and a portion of those trademark harsh notes to the blend, I likewise added a couple cubanelle peppers. Several jalapeños, with their hotness and greenness, balanced things. To go for all out smoke, you can get a fire going in an outside barbecue and meal your chiles over the gleaming ashes until totally darkened everywhere. For us loft inhabitants, cooking them over an open gas fire or under an oven works comparably well. The objective here is absolute carbonization of the outside. As it warms, the fluid simply underneath converts to steam, compelling the skin outward and away from the tissue. This little area of air and water fume simply under the skin protects the tissue under, keeping it from consuming. After the peppers are totally darkened, the slackened skin slips right off, leaving the tissue clean and uncharred yet injected with profound smoky flavor from the roasted skin.

The Tomatillos

Indeed, even among the less passionate chiliheads out there, tomatillos are a disputed matter. Despite the fact that tomatillos are an individual from similar family as tomatoes (however totally not the same as unripe green tomatoes), it's most firmly connected with gooseberries. The kinds of the two-overwhelmed by a citrus-like poignancy with an unmistakable, exquisite completion are amazingly comparative too, however gooseberries will quite often be better. An incredible aspect concerning tomatillos is that they are likewise very high in gelatin, the sugar-based solidifying specialist that is the essential thickener in many jams. Assuming you incorporate tomatillos, you truly need no other thickener in your stew (numerous exemplary tomatillo-less plans call for flour or another starch), and the poignancy it brings to the party is a welcome flavor expansion also. I singe mine under the grill to amplify that smoky smell.

It's in plans like these when the significance of everything about comes out: Charring each surface of the chiles to expand smokiness. Cautiously observing your simmering tomatillos with the goal that they singe and relax while as yet holding a portion of their new acridity. Here and there the course of gradually, purposely constructing flavors is similarly just about as remunerating as the completed dish.

The Pork

Red bean stew is about meat, yet with green bean stew, pork is best. I attempted perhaps one or two cuts, including sirloin, paunch, country-style ribs, and shoulder. The shoulder and sirloin fared the best, keeping up with dampness and favor all through the cooking. The paunch was just excessively greasy, and keeping in mind that pieces of the ribs were incredible, different segments slice closer to the lean flank of the pig were excessively dry. Pork shoulder requires a smidgen more work than sirloin to prepare for stewing (boning, cutting back away overabundance excess), yet it's essentially less expensive, which gives it an edge in my book.

In my past stew tests, I'd observed that sautéing little bits of meat is an exceptionally wasteful strategy, and that it's greatly improved to brown entire cuts and cut them up thereafter. With shoulder, that is somewhat more troublesome you essentially need to appropriately destroy the entire thing to spotless and bone it. My answer? Utilize a similar strategy I use for the Texas stew con carne: as opposed to sautéing the entirety of the pork, brown just 50% of it, however permit the pot to foster a rich, profound brown affectionate prior to adding the onions and the remainder of the pork. The shading developed by the primary group of pork is above and beyond to give the completed dish a rich, substantial flavor. What's more, the delicate surface of the unbrowned pork is far better than that of the sautéed stuff.

Burner Versus Oven

The main inquiry remaining was the means by which to cook the dish. Intermittently, for short-stewed sauces, I'll do them straightforwardly on the burner, simply watching out for them as they cook to keep them from consuming. In any case, for braised dishes that should be cooked for vertically of 3 or 4 hours, the stove shows two or three particular benefits.

On the burner, the stew cooks just from the base, which can prompt food consuming on the lower part of the pot if you don't watch out. A broiler mitigates this by warming from all sides simultaneously. Additionally, a gas or electric fire set at a specific hotness level is a steady energy-yield framework, intending that at some random time, it is adding energy to the pot above it at a set rate. A stove, then again, is a steady temperature framework. That is, it has an indoor regulator that controls the temperature of the air inside, adding energy simply on a case by case basis to keep the temperature in a similar fundamental reach. That implies that whether you are cooking a goliath pot of stew or the Derek Zoolander Stew for Ants, it'll cook at a similar rate from start to finish. Therefore, it's smarter to involve the broiler for a really long time, thick braises. (For additional on this, see "Pot Roast," here.)

Here is one more inquiry we addressed before (see here): cover on or top off? Assuming that you accept the old style shrewdness, you need your cover on as firmly as could be expected, to safeguard dampness. Furthermore, more dampness in the pot implies more dampness in the meat, isn't that so? Tragically, that is not actually the way in which braising works. Fundamentally, when you are braising, there are two neutralizing powers that you want to adjust.

Collagen breakdown-the change of extreme connective tissue into delicate gelatin-starts gradually at around 140°F and increments at a remarkable rate as the temperature goes up. Pork shoulder cooked at 140°F could require 2 days to completely mellow, while at 180°F, the time is chopped down to a couple of hours. Then again, muscle filaments fix and press out dampness as they are warmed, starting at around 130°F and deteriorating as the temperature increases. Dissimilar to collagen breakdown, which takes both time and hotness to occur, the muscle pressing happens promptly meat that has been warmed to 180°F for even one second will be wrung dry.

Like a relentless power meeting an ardent item, it's almost difficult to accomplish collagen breakdown without at the same time crushing muscle filaments. The uplifting news: the gelatin made by collagen breakdown goes far to moderating the drying impacts of fixing muscle strands. However, the genuine key to an all around cooked braise is to cook it at a low temperature so the meat doesn't enter the so-close even-gelatin-can't-save-it range.

Presently we as a whole realize that water bubbles at 212°F, correct? Be that as it may, strangely, even in a 250°F broiler, you can extraordinarily influence the temperature of the water inside a pot by permitting vanishing or not. This is on the grounds that vanishing, the demonstration of changing over water into steam, takes such a lot of energy-it takes more time than 500 fold the amount of energy to change over one gram of water into steam as it does to raise that equivalent gram of water's temperature by one degree!

Look at this chart showing the braising temperature of a pot with the cover fixed versus that with the top left somewhat slightly open:

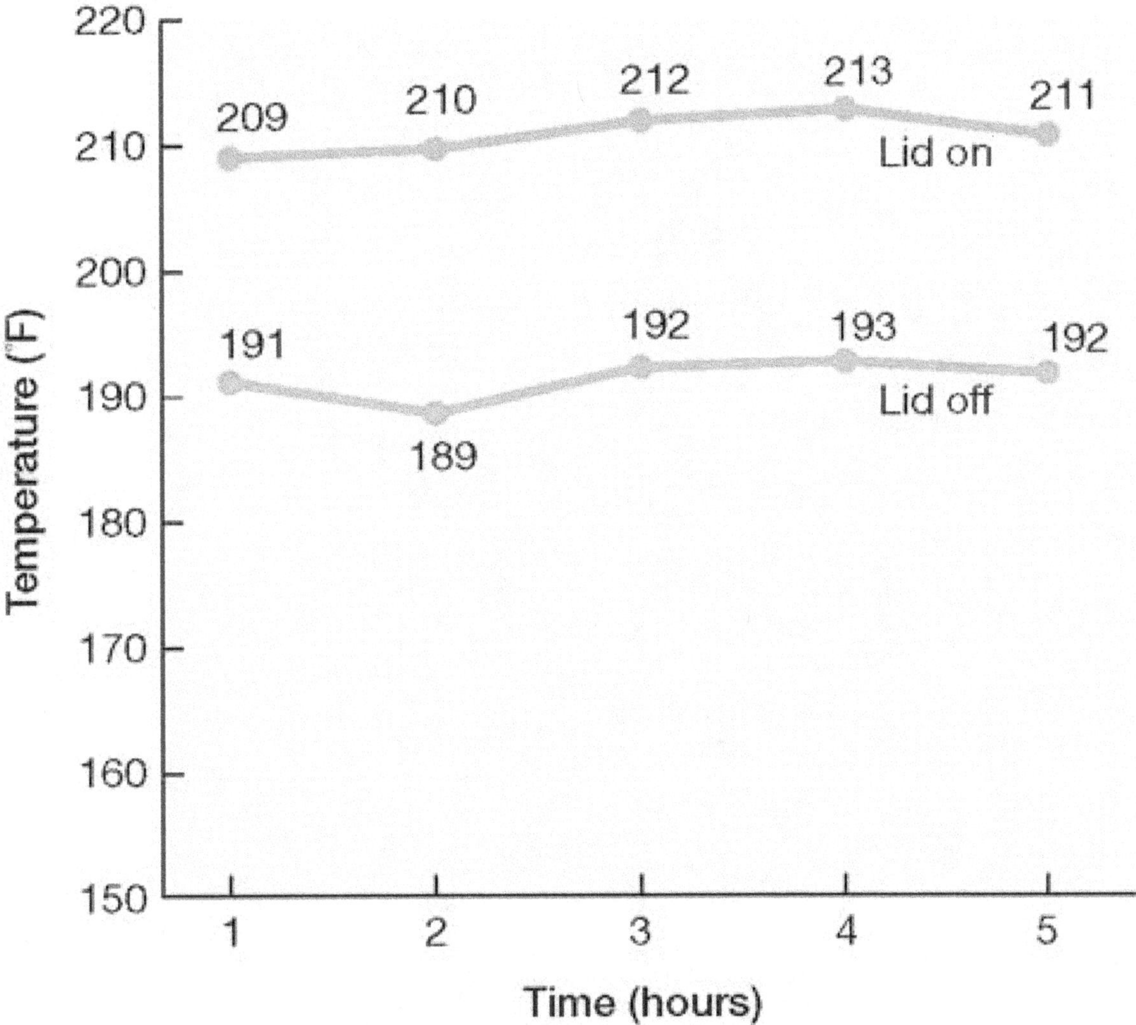

With the cover shut, the fluid inside the pot floats around bubbling temperature, at times in any event, transcending it (the tension from the firmly fixed weighty top permits the fluid to go over its ordinary limit, similarly as in a strain cooker). So the meat winds up overcooking, and when it is delicate, it's additionally moderately dry and wiry. The uncovered pot, then again, stays a decent

20 degrees lower, keeping the meat inside at a temperature far nearer to the ideal. The meat gets delicate and holds dampness as it cooks, giving us a far juicer, more delicate final product.

Don't you simply can't stand that? You attempt your hardest to be cool and simply expound on the delights of slow-cooking pork, then, at that point, a chart needs to proceed to slip its direction into the works. Charts are continuously doing that to me. My statements of regret. (It is The Food Lab, all things considered.) Anyhow, presently you see precisely why your pork chile verde is so profoundly enhanced, delicious, and complex.